BANK RESTRUCTURING

Lessons from the 1980s

Edited by Andrew Sheng

THE WORLD BANK

WASHINGTON, D.C.

The findings, interpretations, and conclusions expressed in this publication are those of the authors and do not necessarily represent the views and policies of the World Bank or its Board of Executive Directors or the countries they represent.

The material in this publication is copyrighted. Requests for permission to reproduce portions of it should be sent to the Office of the Publisher at the address shown in the copyright notice above. The World Bank encourages dissemination of its work and will normally give permission promptly and, when the reproduction is for noncommercial purposes, without asking a fee. Permission to copy portions for classroom use is granted through the Copyright Clearance Center, Inc., Suite 910, 222 Rosewood Drive, Danvers, Massachusetts 01923, U.S.A.

The complete backlist of publications from the World Bank is shown in the annual *Index of Publications*, which contains an alphabetical title list (with full ordering information) and indexes of subjects, authors, and countries and regions. The latest edition is available free of charge from Distribution Unit, Office of the Publisher, The World Bank, 1818 H Street, N.W., Washington, D.C. 20433, U.S.A., or from Publications, The World Bank, 66, avenue d'Iéna, 75116 Paris, France.

Andrew Sheng is Deputy Chief Executive (Monetary) of the Hong Kong Monetary Authority.

Library of Congress Cataloging-in-Publication Data

Bank restructuring : lessons from the 1980s / edited by Andrew Sheng.
    p. cm.
  Includes bibliographical references.
  ISBN 0-8213-3519-7
  1. Bank management. 2. Bank failures—Case studies. 3. Banks and banking—United States—Case studies. 4. Banks and banking—Spain— Case studies. 5. Banks and banking—Developing countries—Case studies. I. Sheng, Andrew.
  HG1615.B3515   1996
  332.1—dc20   95-49776
                                                        CIP

Contents

About the authors

Andrew Sheng is Deputy Chief Executive (Monetary) of the Hong Kong Monetary Authority.

Fernando Montes-Negret is Principal Financial Economist, Financial Sector Development Department, at the World Bank.

Archibald A. Tannor is Director, Banking Supervision, Bank of Ghana.

Luis A. Giorgio is Deputy Director, Center for Latin American Monetary Studies.

Silvia Sagari is Chief, Industry and Energy Division, Western Africa Department, at the World Bank.

iv

Foreword

The decade of the 1980s saw major stresses and strains in the developing world. Fiscal adjustment, trade liberalization, financial deregulation, and privatization were major policy reforms that sought to deal with the problems of high debt overhang, balance of payments problems, and slow growth in many developing countries. The financial sector in many countries witnessed tumultuous change as bank balance sheets reflected the devastating effects of external and internal shocks as well as major policy responses to such adjustments. Major initiatives were undertaken in financial sector reform: the building of new legal and regulatory frameworks, strengthening of banking and financial institutions, removal of interest rate and exchange rate restrictions, liberalization of market entry into the financial sector, commercialization and privatization of state-owned financial institutions, and opening of financial markets to greater domestic and foreign competition.

During this period banking systems in industrial and developing countries alike underwent fundamental change. Many banks were devastated by the burden of nonperforming loans, brought on by a variety of causes. A centerpiece of financial policy reform was bank restructuring, as policymakers sought to improve the process of financial intermediation that would fund and foster stronger growth.

This book is part of a series of research studies stemming from *World Development Report 1989: Financial Systems and Development.* Two books, *Financial Reform: Theory and Experience,* edited by

Gerard Caprio, Jr., Izak Atiyas, and James Hanson, and *Banking Institutions in Developing Markets,* by Diana McNaughton, are companion publications to this book. The first deals with the policy reform agenda in financial sector policy, the second with institutional reforms in individual banking institutions. This book surveys experience with systemwide bank restructuring, focusing on the policy and process of the legal, institutional, financial, and managerial restructuring demanded by systemic bank problems.

Bank restructuring is a process, not an event. The causes of bank failure are often country specific, and the solutions to bank failure may require special consideration of country conditions. However, lessons from international experience suggest that there are common techniques and approaches that can help clarify the issues, reduce their complexity, and identify possible solutions.

Given the magnitude of bank losses in many industrial and developing countries today, we hope that *Bank Restructuring: Lessons from the 1980s* will be a useful guide for policymakers, bank supervisors, and bankers for dealing with these pressing problems of the 1990s and beyond.

Gary Perlin
Director
Financial Sector Development Department
The World Bank

Acknowledgments

Having moved from the World Bank's development advisory function to the core central bank function of regulating and promoting financial markets in Hong Kong, one of the freest of market economies, I have had the opportunity to reflect on what went right, what went wrong, and what should have been done during the banking crises in developing countries in the 1980s. Extrapolating lessons from the past runs the danger of boiling down essential truths to such bland cliches that the advice becomes tautological. To say that macroeconomic stability was critical to recovery merely states the obvious—if there had been macroeconomic stability in the first place, banking systems wouldn't have gotten into the mess they did.

This volume had its genesis in the pioneering work of Millard Long, who directed the World Bank's *World Development Report 1989: Financial Systems and Development.* I was brought on board as the author for the paper on the Malaysian case, and was delighted that a group of people, led by Manuel Hinds and Aristobulo de Juan (then at the World Bank), was exploring banking problems in developing countries. This volume forms part of three massive works that emanated from these forays: Gerard Caprio's *Financial Reform: Theory and Experience,* Diana McNaughton's *Banking Institutions in Developing Markets,* and this attempt at understanding the techniques used in bank restructuring in the 1980s.

This volume therefore owes its intellectual debt to the above persons, but also to Alan Gelb, Vince Polizatto, Silvia Sagari, and Dimitri Vittas, colleagues in the former Financial Policy and Systems Division of the Bank, who helped identify, conceptualize, and research the intricacies of financial sector market failure. Much of the research in this volume was undertaken by Susan Hart, who helped extensively in the study on the United States and sharpened many of the arguments. Izabela Rutkowska continued where Susan left off, and Bo Wang created many of the tables and figures.

Gerard Caprio, Yoon Je Cho, Samuel Talley, Melanie Johnson, and Ross Levine read chapters and offered valuable insights, comments, and suggestions. Helpful comments were also provided by several anonymous referees.

Maria Raggambi, Wilai Pitayatonakarn, and Karin Waelti, at the World Bank, and Helen Moy at the Hong Kong Monetary Authority, were able to make out my unintelligible scrawls and assemble the drafts with great cheerfulness and accuracy. The chapters were edited by Meta de Coquereaumont and Paul Holtz and laid out by Christian Perez, of American Writing Corporation.

Finally, encouragement and support came from Nancy Birdsall, Johannes Linn, and Jean-François Rischard of the Bank, the more so for sparing me the valuable time to complete this task. Since moving to Hong Kong, I have learned considerably about the impact of the marketplace and free competition on banking systems from my colleagues, David Carse and Joseph Yam. To all the above, credit is due. All debits, errors, and omissions are mine.

Last but not least, my wife Suan Poh deserves thanks for putting up patiently with the trials and tribulations of my writing.

Introduction

Not since the Great Depression had as many banks failed as during the 1980s. To the casual observer most bank failures are the result of abuses of power and trust by bank owners and managers—and in many cases this diagnosis is correct. But large-scale bank failures are symptoms of a broader malaise. Accordingly, bank restructuring—defined as the package of macroeconomic, microeconomic, institutional, and regulatory measures taken to restore problem banking systems to financial solvency and health—must address the causes and effects of widespread bank distress.

Banks are important because they are the main channels of savings and the allocators of credit in an economy. Banks offer instruments that are money substitutes, and they operate the payments system. Their efficiency affects the entire economy, and banking system failure erodes public wealth and confidence in the economy. The failure of 10,000 banks in the United States between 1930 and 1933 made the Great Depression much deeper and long-lasting than it might otherwise have been (LaWare 1994). That trauma led to the extensive U.S. deposit insurance scheme and its associated regulatory framework. Policymakers everywhere protect or regulate the banking system on efficiency, welfare, and public policy grounds. As this volume shows, these regulations sometimes build perverse incentives in the banks—such as moral hazard through deposit insurance—that themselves give rise to problems.

Identifying Problems

Banking problems have many roots, ranging from distorted management incentives to institutional failure to misguided macroeconomic policies. No study of such a complex subject can cover all these issues; thus readers of this volume should bear in mind two caveats. First, this volume addresses the resolution of systemic bank problems, not the restructuring of individual banks. As a guide to best practice on the techniques and tools used by different countries to resolve large-scale bank distress, its intended audience is policymakers—whether bank supervisors, central bankers, treasury officials, or informed bankers.

A strictly market-based approach to failed banks would call for their liquidation. Indeed, this is the best solution for isolated, small bank failures: clean surgery is often less messy than slow medicine. But where large banks suffer from a lack of public confidence and large segments of the banking system are insolvent, liquidation only masks the problem. If banking fragility is a symptom of economywide problems, liquidation alone is neither practical nor useful. The resolution of systemic bank problems therefore must be part of an overall strategy to restructure and reform fundamental inefficiencies in the economy.

Second, this volume does not attempt to draw quantitative empirical conclusions, mainly because of the lack of comparable cross-country data. Accounting standards in banking vary, particularly in loan classification and income accrual on nonperforming loans, making comparisons of bank losses extremely difficult. In addition, countries are reluctant to publish data on bank losses because of the potential impact on confidence in the banking system. Such empirical work will not be possible until there is greater transparency in international accounting and regulatory standards, as well as better data on the size of fiscal and quasi-fiscal deficits.

Despite these limitations, important lessons can be drawn from the eight case studies in this volume:

Spain and the United States in the industrial country group and Argentina, Chile, Colombia, Ghana, Malaysia, and Yugoslavia in the developing country group. These studies indicate that banking problems in the 1980s were essentially an outcome of bad policies, poor management, and weak institutional frameworks.

Both external and internal factors contributed to systemic bank failures. Dramatic changes in the international economy created fragility and volatility in the macroeconomic environment. Globalization of trade and finance, liberalization and deregulation of real and financial markets, and changes in technology all increased competition and risks for banking, while also eroding the franchise value of protected bank markets. The willingness of governments and enterprises to incur large debts in the inflationary 1970s and the ensuing debt crisis and adjustment in the 1980s created enormous strains on the banking community.

Nevertheless, as a number of the case studies show, bank failures can occur because of perverse incentives even where growth is stable. Excessive concentration of bank resources, connected ownership of banks and enterprises, inadequate supervision, and deposit insurance coverage (even if only implicit) can result in extensive losses.

Recognizing Causes—and Solutions

Given the variations in initial country conditions—legal framework, banking practices, industrial and ownership structure, resources, and policies—what is successful in one restructuring could easily be disastrous in another. There are many parallels between the resolution of domestic banking crises and the resolution of the international debt crisis of the 1980s. A case-by-case approach was applied for many countries affected by the debt crisis, designing custom solutions for each case. As recent experience with bank problems in Eastern Europe and the former Soviet Union has shown, there are common problems but no common solutions.

Still, a number of lessons emerge from the experience of the 1980s. These lessons can help guide the bank restructuring efforts that are under way in a number of countries:

1. *Financial stability rests on the government's ability to maintain a stable currency.* Fiscal and financial discipline are the anchors of a stable financial system; without them reliable credit decisions cannot be made. High-inflation economies are more prone to

bank fragility than low-inflation economies. Inflation disguises the extent of damage to the banking system, which a period of deflation quickly exposes. In the cases studied, bank restructuring was part of price stabilization or occurred during a period of deflation, as bank assets became compressed and eroded available bank capital. Governments' ability to transfer real sector inefficiencies to savers through the inflation tax became severely weakened as financial markets globalized. Savers simply escaped the inflation tax through capital outflows, putting grave pressure on the exchange rate. Deregulation of financial markets and liberalization of trade and capital flows open up the possibility of large portfolio shifts from domestic financial assets (disintermediation) as wealthholders perceive potential losses from bad policies, bad management, or bad institutional frameworks. The restoration of financial discipline begins with the restoration of fiscal and monetary discipline.

2. *Banks fail because of losses in the real sector, compounded by poor risk management and fraud.* Deregulation, technological advances, and globalization—in both the real and financial sectors—have increased the volatility and risks to which banks are exposed. The move toward flexible exchange rates in the 1970s and subsequent interest rate deregulation opened banks up to much higher credit and market risks relative to their capital base. Competition from nonbanks in the deposit and credit markets has largely eroded the franchise value of banking, particularly for U.S. banks. At the same time, changes in relative prices in real markets have brought about large losses in the enterprise sector. The bursting of asset (real estate and stock market) bubbles—created as a result of low interest rates, excessive tax incentives, and information asymmetry—further eroded bank capital, as in Japan and Scandinavia. Bank losses in a number of countries were compounded by an overconcentration of assets—geographically, sectorally, or in terms of ownership (as in Latin America)—which encouraged connected lending and credit abuses. At both the microeconomic and macroeconomic levels, bank managers and policymakers have not managed these risks very well.

3. *Liberalization programs often fail to take into account the wealth effects of relative price changes, and inadequate supervision creates further losses.* Rapid trade liberalization may create losses for previously protected enterprises, leading to large bank losses. If these enterprises belong to groups that also own banks, in a situation without adequate bank super-

vision, these banks are likely to finance distress borrowing at unrealistically high real interest rates. These high rates quickly become a systemic problem, calling for a public bailout. Strong bank supervision and enforcement, together with laws that encourage debt discipline and avoid bank owner-borrower conflicts, are important components of bank restructuring programs. This is perhaps the major lesson of financial sector liberalization in the Southern Cone economies (Argentina, Chile, and Uruguay).

4. *Bank losses ultimately become quasi-fiscal deficits.* Large-scale bank failures are simply not acceptable in most economies. In none of the cases studied did governments dare to pass widespread bank losses on to depositors. Most bank losses are absorbed by the budget or by the central bank through explicit or implicit deposit protection schemes. Such schemes place enormous burdens on the budget. During financial crises governments are made to assume considerable debt: all external debt (public or private), internal debt (including debt of public enterprises), and losses in the banking system (public or private). In almost all the cases studied financial stability was restored only when governments were able to maintain a sustainable fiscal balance without monetary creation. Banking failures in the 1980s were largely market failures, caused in large part by moral hazard induced through implicit or explicit deposit insurance. Deposit insurance demands sound preventive bank supervision.

5. *Failure recognition is important because a banking crisis is a solvency problem, not a liquidity issue.* The resolution of banking problems is often delayed because officials are unwilling or unable to determine the magnitude of the problems. In many cases banks that may not appear to be insolvent in accounting terms are in fact insolvent when assets and liabilities are priced at current market values. Any banking system with nonperforming loans (net of provisions) exceeding 15 percent of total loans is probably reaching a crisis stage. Insolvent banks can hide such losses with bad accounting, but failing to deal with hidden losses can create perverse incentives in the banking system, leading to inefficient resource allocation and adding to macroeconomic instability.

6. *Stopping the flow of future losses is critical.* Stemming future losses involves changing the incentives within the real and financial sectors. Where lossmakers are public enterprises and banks, changing the incentives structure requires changing ownership, particularly through privatization and foreign capital and expertise. Enforcing hard budget constraints may

require liquidating some institutions. At the microeconomic level, changing management is vital. Managers who are part of the problem cannot be part of the solution.

7. *The method of loss allocation determines the success of the restructuring program.* Bank losses ultimately are borne somewhere in the economy. Since no one is willing to accept such losses voluntarily, loss allocation is a major political issue. The wealthy may attempt to escape such losses through capital flight. The poor cannot escape an inflation tax. Since there is no formula for the democratic distribution of losses, losses have to be allocated by accepted law or by arbitrary policy. The ability to allocate losses depends on a country's political and institutional framework. The technique adopted, either a flow or a stock solution, depends on the degree of distress. As mentioned, when banks are in severe distress governments tend to absorb bad debts and to exchange—"carve out"—government or central bank bonds for bad debts to recapitalize banks. Insolvent institutions, however, cannot be rescued by another insolvent institution. As shown in Argentina and Yugoslavia, overreliance on seigniorage to finance bank debts ultimately explodes into hyperinflation. Loss allocation that maintains macroeconomic stability requires a budget that is able to generate a primary surplus to service its debts (including debts incurred by the carve out) without excessive monetary creation. Losses are allocated either to depositors through an inflation tax or to taxpayers. In the most extreme cases, when the budget is unable to bear the huge internal and external debt without creating hyperinflation, the government may have to undertake a deposits-to-bonds conversion, as occurred in Argentina and Brazil in 1990. Such forced losses—borne by the depositors—gave the government breathing space for other reform measures to work, particularly in fiscal reform, trade, and privatization of state-owned enterprises.

8. *Success depends on sufficient real sector resources to pay off losses, adequate financial sector reforms to intermediate resources efficiently and safely, and the budget's ability to tax "winners" and wind down "losers" without disturbing monetary stability.* Because bank losses are rooted in real sector financial imbalances—enterprise losses or large fiscal deficits—bank restructuring is inextricably linked to fiscal and enterprise reforms. Recapitalizing banks without addressing the underlying enterprise losses or inefficiencies runs the risk of repeating banking problems in the future. The Yugoslav experiment with worker ownership of enterprises and banks in the 1980s showed how the inability to change ownership

and to separate ownership between borrowers and lenders can create large amounts of distressed borrowing that ultimately culminates in inflation.

9. *Rebuilding a safe and profitable banking system requires good policies, reliable management, and a strong institutional framework.* At the policy level, governments must maintain credible macroeconomic policies that encourage stability, competition, and growth. At the management level, incentives have to be right and the ownership and governance of banks must be addressed. Good managers should be rewarded for prudent risk management and punished for speculative and fraudulent behavior. Bank laws and regulations should be enforced. The accounting framework should encourage the measurement and disclosure of economic performance using internationally accepted accounting standards. The payments system must work efficiently and robustly. New financial markets should be created to help mobilize risk and long-term capital and permit better monetary management using indirect tools.

10. *Time and timing are of the essence.* Policies can change overnight, but it takes much more time to get management incentives right and to restructure the institutional framework—law, accounting, regulation, and infrastructure. Bank losses develop over time and should not be expected to disappear quickly. But the sooner the problem is recognized and dealt with, the lower the costs to the economy and the banking system.

From these lessons it is easy to assume that banking crises arise from recession alone. But countries with strong growth and good fundamentals also had banking problems, the obvious example being Japan in the 1980s. Banking weaknesses can develop because of excessive risk-taking during periods of growth, particularly if insufficient supervisory attention is paid to such excesses. Without growth in real output or extensive reserves, it is difficult for a country with banking losses to pay for them—but someone has to pay. Although each country must find its own solutions, international experience offers an array of techniques to draw on.

Implementing Change

The pace and model of reform are determined by a country's political and institutional framework.

Successful reforms call for, among other things:

- Political will and strong leadership, with a dedicated, unified economic team.
- A carefully sequenced, coherent, and comprehensive implementation plan.
- The ability to sell the plan to every level of society (Rhodes 1992).

Bank restructuring techniques are simply a set of tools. How these tools are used depends on how well policymakers understand the nature of the problem and what combination of tools is best suited to deal with the problem. The most successful bank restructurings have been those that are simple yet committed. Political will and the ability to execute changes simply and transparently worked, for example, in Chile, Malaysia, and Spain. But as with any policy, the design of bank restructuring programs involves tradeoffs between risk and return. And the choice ultimately depends on how each country values social welfare relative to efficiency.

Prevention is better than a cure. But can a fail-proof banking system be designed? U.S. Federal Reserve Chairman Alan Greenspan has said that "the optimal degree of bank failure is not zero, and in all likelihood, [is] not even close to zero." Even if banks held nothing but low-risk government obligations, there is no guarantee that the government itself would never default on its debt.

The process of bank restructuring continues in many countries. For the post–centrally planned economies in transition to market-based economies, bank restructuring will be a challenge that continues well into the 1990s. For the post-liberalization economies, that is, economies that have opened their capital accounts, the challenge now is how to manage the banking system risks in a volatile world of global capital flows (chapter 12). It is hoped that this volume will help these countries better understand the techniques and processes involved in the difficult road ahead.

References

LaWare, John P. 1994. "Bank Failures in a Sound Economy." In Frederick C. Schadrack and Leon Korobow, eds., *The Basic Elements of Bank Supervision.* New York: Federal Reserve Bank of New York.

Rhodes, William. 1992. "Third World Debt: The Disaster that Didn't Happen." *The Economist,* September 12.

CHAPTER 1

Banking Fragility in the 1980s: An Overview

Andrew Sheng

The 1980s may well be remembered as the decade of debt, inflation, and adjustment. The decade began with the deepest international recession since the 1930s, saw the eruption of the debt crisis, and ended with the fragmentation of the socialist economic bloc and its integration with the global economy. Despite the increasing globalization of financial markets and unprecedented financial innovation and liberalization, bank crises and restructuring were common in both industrial and developing countries. By the end of the decade the Scandinavian countries (except Denmark), Spain, and the United States had all experienced severe banking problems. Financial fragility (defined as the deterioration of bank solvency due to poor asset quality and declining profitability) was evident in the banking systems of Taiwan (China) and Japan and a number of other member countries of the OECD.

In selected OECD countries provisions against nonperforming loans rose toward the end of the decade (table 1.1). In the developing world the World Bank provided financial sector adjustment loans to twenty-two countries in the 1980s, and in almost all of these countries financial distress—in which large parts of the financial system had negative capital—was present to some degree. In the formerly socialist economies in transition to market economies, a new group of problem banks has emerged in the nascent financial systems. These banks are struggling with inherited portfolios of dubious quality while trying to transform themselves into market-oriented institutions.

Important lessons can be drawn from this decade of bank distress and adjustment. In the United States more than 1,300 banks and 1,400 thrift institutions failed or were merged and consolidated during 1980–91, compared with only 210 closures during

Table 1.1 Provisions against nonperforming loans in OECD countries, 1981–90

(as a percentage of net income)

Country	1981	1982	1983	1984	1985	1986	1987	1988	1989	1990
Denmark										
Commercial and savings banks	57.0	56.8	21.7	89.2	20.7	—	66.5	53.1	75.9	129.0
Finland										
Savings banks	76.8	80.6	74.0	70.4	71.8	69.9	70.0	54.9	43.7	77.4
Japan										
Commercial banks	3.2	10.8	6.7	7.1	4.0	6.8	5.4	7.6	8.7	7.2
Norway										
Commercial banks	46.5	54.4	42.7	48.0	54.2	59.1	138.4	125.8	90.3	209.8
Spain										
Commercial banks	50.2	60.8	63.3	63.9	54.8	49.3	47.7	37.0	27.9	27.9
United Kingdom										
Commercial banks	—	—	—	43.7	33.7	31.5	89.5	17.9	94.0	60.7
United States										
Large commercial banks	23.5	34.8	39.9	44.9	42.0	46.8	99.7	31.5	65.4	65.6
Mutual savings banks	−1.8	−3.2	41.5	19.8	9.8	8.8	12.2	24.4	89.7	196.9
Savings and loan associations	−4.8	−16.5	29.1	52.1	40.3	72.3	175.8	480.3	—	—

— Not available.
Source: Schuijer 1992.

1945–79. At the end of 1991 the U.S. Federal Deposit Insurance Corporation (FDIC) estimated that there were 1,069 problem banks, or 8.6 percent of the banks in the United States, with assets totaling $611 billion, or 18 percent of total bank assets. The number of bank failures has declined since the late 1980s, but the assets of failed banks have been increasing. In 1991 the total assets of failed banks reached $66.2 billion, the highest figure since the 1930s. Of the U.S. banks that failed in 1991, eleven had assets of more than $1 billion. Resolution of the thrift crisis cost at least $180 billion, or 3 percent of gross domestic product (IMF 1993).

In Japan estimates of bank exposure to bad debt from real estate and other problem loans were as high as ¥ 40 trillion ($160 billion), or 10.4 percent of total loans outstanding, at the end of 1992 (Huh and Kim 1994). Banks' exposure to real estate debt was caused by their exposure to nonbank financial institutions, where 41 percent of total loans were made for property (IMF 1993). The Japanese government recently announced several packages of measures to stimulate the economy and aid the banking industry. In Scandinavia loan losses incurred by banks in Finland, Norway, and Sweden during 1991–92 amounted to 4.2 to 6.7 percent of gross domestic product (GDP). The overnight failure of the U.K.'s Barings Bank in February 1995 due to speculative activities in East Asia demonstrated the vulnerability of banks to weaknesses in internal controls.

In the developing countries problem loans of 15 to 30 percent of total loans were not uncommon during the 1980s, while recent estimates of bank bad debt in the transition economies run as high as 55 to 60 percent of total loans (Sheng 1992). (See annex 1.1 for a summary of major banking problems around the world in the 1980s.)

A number of studies have examined the causes and economic effects of financial crises (Hinds 1988, Davis 1989, Sundararajan and Baliño 1991). This book focuses on the macroeconomic, microeconomic, institutional, and regulatory measures taken to restore problem banking systems to financial solvency and health. It draws on the lessons of bank restructuring in eight countries based on a number of background papers prepared for *World Development Report 1989* (World Bank 1989). Specifically, it analyzes various bank restructuring techniques and their applicability under different conditions of bank distress.

Table 1.2 Growth and inflation, 1965–80 and 1980–90
(percent)

Country group	1965–80		1980–90	
	GDP	Inflation	GDP	Inflation
Low and middle income	5.9	16.7	3.2	61.8
Developing Europe	—	13.9	2.1	38.8
East Asia and the Pacific	7.3	9.3	7.8	6.0
Latin America and the Caribbean	6.0	31.4	1.6	192.1
Middle East and North Africa	6.7	13.6	0.5	7.5
South Asia	3.6	8.3	5.2	8.0
Sub-Saharan Africa	4.2	11.4	2.1	20.0
Severely indebted	6.3	27.4	1.7	173.5
OECD	3.7	7.6	3.1	4.2
World average	4.0	9.2	3.2	14.7

Source: World Bank 1992.

Background to Financial Fragility

The 1980s were a decade of slow growth, large financial imbalances, and high inflation. Average annual growth rates in the low- and middle-income developing countries dropped to almost half their late 1960s and 1970s levels, while inflation rates more than tripled (table 1.2).

After enjoying strong terms-of-trade gains averaging 8 percent a year in the 1970s, the developing countries' terms of trade deteriorated, on average, by 1.8 percent a year in the 1980s. Export growth in developing countries slowed to 2.6 percent a year, reducing their share of world exports from one-third in 1980 to one-quarter by 1990. As a result of these downturns, the overall balance of payments of developing countries deteriorated considerably—from a surplus of $145 billion in the 1970s to a deficit of $245 billion in the 1980s. By any measure, the debt burden of the developing countries roughly tripled between the 1970s and 1980s (table 1.3).

Table 1.3 External debt indicators for developing economies, 1970–75 and 1983–89
(percent)

Country group	External debt/GNP		Interest payments/ exports	
	1970–75	1983–89	1970–75	1983–89
Low income	10.2	28.5	2.9	9.8
Low income (excluding China and India)	20.5	60.7	2.9	11.8
Middle income	18.6	54.9	5.1	15.4

Source: World Bank 1991.

Despite efforts to roll back state intervention through privatization and tighter fiscal discipline, the state's role in the economy continued to grow in both developing and industrial countries. In the OECD countries general government spending as a share of gross national product (GNP) reached 42 percent in 1989, compared with 33 percent in 1970. Central government deficits almost doubled in the decade, while in Latin American countries fiscal deficits almost tripled.

Financial trends

In contrast to the disappointing macroeconomic environment of the 1980s, world financial markets today are characterized by globalization, liberalization, innovation, and re-regulation.

Globalization of financial markets. The roots of bank distress in the 1980s can be traced to the emergence of global financial markets and flexible exchange rates in the 1970s. During that decade the Eurocurrency markets expanded rapidly as banks began to internationalize their operations, seeking higher profits offshore in order to escape the interest rate ceilings imposed on domestic markets. Gross new issues of Eurobonds rose from $27 billion in 1981 to $319 billion in 1991. During 1972–82 international banking assets grew two-and-a-half times faster than the GDP growth of OECD countries and an average of 10 percent a year faster than world trade (Bryant 1984). By the early 1980s developing countries had become highly leveraged and were not prepared for the sharp increase in interest rates when the U.S. Federal Reserve tightened in 1981. By the time the Mexican debt crisis erupted in 1982, the developing countries had accumulated an external debt of $720 billion, or roughly one-third of the assets of the Eurocurrency market. Global interdependence had reached the point where the solvency not only of debtor countries but also of the lender banks was at stake.

By 1990 total foreign liabilities of the global banking system had grown to $7 trillion, more than twice the level of annual world exports. Much of the growth in the international banking system was in the industrial world, whose share of international bank liabilities grew from 71.1 percent of the total in 1976 to 76.6 percent in 1990. At the end of 1991 crossborder interbank claims within the area of the Bank for International Settlement (BIS) alone were $4 trillion. Global trading in financial instruments had reached such a level that in a single day the value of payments through twenty-one countries studied by the BIS in 1989 totaled $3 trillion. The annual transactions turnover of the eleven BIS countries (Group of Ten plus Switzerland) was more than fifty times annual GNP in 1989 (BIS 1990). BIS estimates in April 1992 indicate that foreign exchange market turnover was about $880 billion a day.

Volatile relative prices. The trend toward global interdependence coincided with the emergence of higher volatility in relative prices, beginning with the abandonment of fixed exchange rates in the early 1970s and the rise of global inflation. The world commodity price index rose by 269 percent between 1970 and its peak in 1980, before falling 27 percent to its trough in 1986. Inflation in the low- and middle-income developing countries rose to an annual average of 62 percent in the 1980s, compared with 17 percent in the 1970s. As inflation rose, real interest rates reached record levels. In the United States real lending rates averaged 6.2 percent in the 1980s, compared with 0.5 percent between 1974 and 1979. Real lending rates for countries that underwent financial crisis varied from more than 40 percent a year in Chile (1981–83) to over 200 percent in Argentina (1984–85). Nominal exchange rates plunged as inflation rose. The U.S. dollar, in which more than half the foreign currency assets of the BIS reporting banks are denominated, depreciated by 30 percent in real terms during the 1980s, compared with a variation of less than 10 percent during 1976–80.

The world banking system, which had experienced relatively stable interest rates during the 1950s, 1960s, and most of the 1970s, suddenly had to cope with rapidly changing interest and exchange rates and large capital flows as funds moved rapidly both domestically and internationally in search of higher yields at lower risks.

Innovation and competition. At the same time, rapid improvements in international transport, telecommunications, and computer technology transformed the business of finance. The emergence of credit cards and electronic funds transfer technology made severe inroads into the traditional payments system business of the banking sector. New nonbank competitors—especially money market funds, travel companies, retailers, insurance companies, mortgage specialists, and pension funds—began to offer higher-yielding deposit substitutes that eroded the low-cost "captive" deposit base of the banking system.

On the asset side, innovations in financial engineering pioneered by investment banks created financial instruments that offered lower costs and higher liquidity to borrowers—eating into the previously bank-dominated loan market. Highly leveraged transactions (junk bonds) evolved to assist the mergers and acquisitions and management buyouts in the United States. These high-risk, high-yield bonds attracted many investors, including banks, thrifts, and pension and insurance funds.

Moreover, the rise of international banking brought competition from foreign banks, which began to rapidly penetrate domestic markets, especially if they had lower costs of capital and were not subject to domestic deposit constraints. Technology made the cost of intermediation cheaper and the transmission of credit information faster. In short, the traditional "franchise" of banking, which was protected by legal and market barriers, came under severe attack from changing market conditions, competition, and technology.

Banks in the industrial countries responded to the changing environment in three ways: innovation, credit expansion, and deregulation. First, they engaged in financial innovation—such as asset securitization and use of derivatives—that "saved" on capital requirements by placing assets and risks off the balance sheet. By the end of 1990 more than one-third of U.S. mortgages were securitized and sold in the secondary market. Credit card and consumer debt were also being packaged and sold. One of the most spectacular growth areas in financial innovation is trading in derivative instruments (swaps and options). Trading in financial futures and options has grown phenomenally because of lower transaction costs, high liquidity, and lower capital costs. Total outstanding derivatives (mainly interest rate futures and options and currency and interest rate swaps) amounted to $7.5 trillion at the end of 1991, a fivefold increase since the end of 1986.

Second, the threats of new competition and innovation induced banks to lobby policymakers to deregulate their range of activities to allow them to engage in businesses previously barred to them, such as stock-market trading and funds management. By the early 1980s most OECD countries had embarked on both interest rate liberalization and removal of exchange controls. The United Kingdom began its "big bang" liberalization by removing exchange controls in 1979 and thereafter allowing commercial banks to enter into securities market trading. This was followed by major liberalization efforts in Australia (1983) and New Zealand (1984). The liberalization of Japan's financial market after the 1985 Plaza Accord had a profound impact on capital flows around the world, particularly in the Asia-Pacific region.

By the late 1980s deregulation of the financial sector had swept most of the OECD countries and many developing economies. The trend was toward complete freeing of the capital account, liberalization of interest rate controls, freeing of competition between banks and nonbanks, and allowing banks to enter new fields, such as securities trading and even (under certain conditions) insurance. Change was coming not only to banks, but also to bank regulators, who had to adjust to more complex supervision in a more volatile market environment.

The banking sector also responded to new competition by lending more aggressively in traditional but higher-risk markets such as real estate. In the United States the threat of large losses from banks' exposure to developing countries' sovereign debt swung banks toward domestic lending, particularly consumer lending and commercial real estate. The real estate boom in the United States was partly stimulated by tax incentives and by the ready availability of credit, which arose from competition to lend among the distressed thrifts, the commercial banks, and insurance and pension funds—all in search of higher yields.

Real estate exposure was particularly evident in a number of countries that exhibited the "Dutch disease," with overvaluation of the exchange rate stimulating domestic spending on nontradables. This was most noticeable in Malaysia, Norway, Sweden, and the United States. Banks in Japan and the United Kingdom also faced high exposure in the real estate and housing sectors.

Domestic policy distortions. Most of the banking systems and financial markets in developing countries were unprepared for these structural changes. Many of these financial systems were underdeveloped because of severe financial repression—governments controlled interest rates, directed the allocation of credit, and used highly negative real interest rates to finance fiscal deficits and inefficient state-owned enterprises. The shortfall between domestic savings and investment was financed mainly by external borrowing. Financial markets were highly segmented, with little or no competition among markets. Banks were highly protected, and nonfinancial institutions were prohibited from innovation and competition. Legal and accounting structures became obsolete in an era of changing market prices and new financial instruments and market practices.

Thus, when external shocks came in the form of the severe international recession of 1980–81 and the cutoff of external resources as a result of the international debt crisis, many developing countries were totally unprepared for the severity of the impact of relative price changes on their financial sector balance sheets.

By the mid-1980s the combined effect of high levels of bank lending and deterioration of asset quality (in particular, the developing countries' debt burden on OECD banks) had eroded banks' capital base to a historic low of 5 to 6 percent, compared with 7 to 8 percent in the 1960s and 1970s. The international regulatory response to the market changes was to stem the capital erosion by harmonizing risk-based capital adequacy standards and improving overall supervision. In 1988 the Basle Committee on Bank Supervision agreed to enforce a minimum risk-weighted capital-asset ratio of 8 percent by the end of 1992. In a number of countries, however, the damage had already been done.

Structural weaknesses

In a world of more volatile relative prices, changing technology, and intense competition, the global banking system was caught in a double bind. On the liabilities side of the balance sheet, which comprised mostly deposits, disintermediation from banks occurred wherever banks faced deposit rate ceilings or high inflation or where nonbanks with lower reserve or intermediation costs offered more competitive rates. On the assets side, increasing competition and improved capital and money markets lured away low-risk customers, forcing banks to take higher credit risks. Interest rate and exchange rate risks rose with higher inflation as policymakers sought to engage more actively in macroeconomic stabilization measures, particularly in countries caught in the debt crisis. As real interest rates rose and exchange rates depreciated, the asset side of bank balance sheets deteriorated, while banks in countries with net foreign exchange liabilities were hit with large revaluation losses.

By 1980 the developing countries' banks had a net foreign liability exposure of $81 billion, which subjected them to large revaluation losses when their currencies depreciated in the wake of structural adjustment programs (table 1.4). The largest exposures were in Eastern Europe (Hungary, Romania, Turkey, and Yugoslavia) and Latin America, with net foreign liabilities exceeding $40 billion. By 1990 African and Latin American banks were still facing large net foreign liabilities, while Asian banks had moved to a large net foreign asset position.

Deposit insurance

There was, however, a fundamental asymmetry in the financial sectors' risk profile. Although formal deposit insurance exists in a limited number of countries, the unwillingness of governments to allow banks to fail for fear of systemic failure (bank capital is negative systemwide) has meant that implicit and explicit government guarantees exist for almost all banking liabilities. Despite the limited stated coverage of most formal deposit insurance schemes, actual coverage has been almost 100 percent because bank failure would create social and economic upheaval. Consequently, a central problem in the global banking system is that, irrespective of public or private ownership of banks, commercial bank losses in excess of capital have become de facto quasi-fiscal deficits (for a survey of quasi-fiscal deficits, see Blejer and Cheasty 1991).

The blanket state guarantee on bank deposits, coupled with weak bank supervision and enforcement, created massive problems of moral hazard in almost every country. Bank management could and did take risks far beyond prudential levels because losses were ultimately borne by the state. Under perverse incentives and poor supervision, even good bank managers became bad managers, engaging in speculation, excessive spending, and ultimately fraud (de Juan 1987). Recent studies in the United States blame moral hazard for major losses in the savings and loan crisis.

Table 1.4 Net foreign liabilities of domestic banks
(billions of U.S. dollars)

Region	1976	1980	1990
World	42.9	64.9	330.2
Industrial countries	4.6	–16.0	315.1
Developing countries	38.3	81.0	15.2
Africa	2.0	4.0	8.9
Asia	0.7	8.4	–29.9
Europe	—	42.1	19.4
Middle East	–4.3	–15.9	–52.5
Western hemisphere	21.3	42.5	69.3

Source: IMF, various years.

Inadequate capital base

The capital base of many banks around the world is probably inadequate relative to the risks in a world of volatile relative prices and their impact on asset values. Despite efforts to raise the level of capital in industrial countries, total capital-asset ratios have fallen from around 50 percent in the nineteenth century, to around 15 to 20 percent during the 1930s, to less than 10 percent today.

The Basle Committee on Bank Supervision agreed to impose minimum risk-weighted capital-asset ratios of 8 percent for the end of 1992. Capital-asset ratios of banks in the *Euromoney* Top 500 banks display an average ranging from 4.6 percent in OECD countries to 20.1 percent in Latin America (annex 1.2). International comparisons of capital adequacy are deceptive, however, because of different standards of loan provisioning.

The impact of declining market yields (price volatility) on the market valuation of bank assets is also deceptive (figure 1.1). Because banks have increasingly extended loans of longer maturity, particularly to the real estate and industrial sectors, and because of the practice of short-term loan rollovers, the average maturity of a bank loan today is much longer than reported in the books. According to de Juan (1987), who draws on his experience in the Spanish banking crisis, the worst loans are those that are reported "current," because banks roll over bad debts and continue to make loans to borrowers who are "too big to fail" through the process of "evergreening" (the extension or rollover of bad loans to loss-making borrowers to cover up the extent of damage from nonperforming loans).

The economic maturity of a bank loan is not its contracted maturity, but depends on the borrower's ability to service his or her debts. Theoretically, the maturity of a debt in which the borrower is able to service only interest but not principal is infinity. During a recession many borrowers fall into this category, while at the same time the maturity profile of the bank's deposit base shortens as depositors try to reduce their exposure to the risks of bank default. At the height of the Argentine bank crisis in 1989, the bulk of the deposit base had only seven days' maturity.

Assuming that the maturity of the loans of a banking system is roughly seven years, figure 1.1 illustrates the discount in asset value if all the assets are marked to market like a seven-year bond. A 15

Figure 1.1 Capital deterioration as a function of nonperforming loans

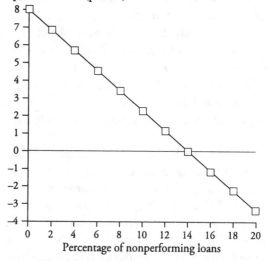

Capital/asset ratio (percent)

Percentage of nonperforming loans

Note: Assumes the loan portfolio has a maturity of seven years and yields 10 percent a year. Nonperforming loans would reduce yield proportionally.

percent decline in loan yield due to a corresponding increase in nonperforming loans would totally decapitalize a bank with an 8 percent capital-asset ratio.

As a rule of thumb, therefore, financial distress is likely to become systemic when nonperforming loans, net of provisions, reach roughly 15 percent of total loans. An alternative way of confirming this is to assume that the average ratio of loan loss provisions against nonperforming loans is 50 percent. When nonperforming loans exceed 15 percent of total assets, the capital base of 8 percent would be totally eroded by loan loss provisions.

Inadequate loan loss provisioning

The 15 percent threshold is confirmed when we examine time-series data on nonperforming loans in a number of countries (table 1.5). International comparisons of nonperforming loans are not totally valid because of varying definitions of nonperformance. Until recently, for example, loans in one South Asian country that were not serviced for more than three years were still treated as performing. The U.S. norm for a nonperforming loan is one that has not been serviced for more than ninety days, although general international practice varies between 90 and 180 days. Some countries treat all loans to state-owned enterprises as performing, since these are state guaranteed, even though many of these loans have not been serviced.

Table 1.5 Ratio of nonperforming loans to total loans, selected countries, 1980–90
(percent)

Country	1980	1981	1982	1983	1984	1985	1986	1987	1988	1989	1990
Argentina	—	—	—	16.9	29.1	30.3	24.6	25.1	27.1	—	—
Colombia	7.2	8.7	14.6	16.2	25.3	25.1	22.6	18.5	11.7	—	—
Ecuador	9.9	13.5	16.2	17.4	13.9	11.9	10.8	—	13.4	—	—
Malaysia	—	—	—	—	—	10.3	20.8	26.8	32.6	24.5	20.8
Philippines	11.5	13.2	13.0	8.9	12.7	16.7	19.3	—	—	—	—
Uruguay	8.9	14.6	30.4	24.7	22.3	36.2	45.9	25.2	—	—	—
Venezuela	7.6	8.3	9.3	15.6	15.3	13.3	9.8	7.0	10.8	—	—
United States	—	—	3.3	3.5	3.3	3.2	3.3	4.1	3.6	3.7	—

— Not available.
Source: Morris 1990; Montes-Negret 1990; Yusof and others 1994; U.S. Bureau of the Census 1991.

Whatever the variation in definitions, banking systems with problem loans of more than 15 percent inevitably have encountered crises and failure of some institutions. Bad debts do not occur overnight, but they can quickly build up over two to three years, and once they exceed 10 percent of total loans, the likelihood of bank failure escalates rapidly unless the banking system is completely state owned. In contrast, even though the ratio of nonperforming loans to total loans has never exceeded 4 to 5 percent in the United States (because of early detection through good accounting standards and fairly strict supervision and enforcement), many banks still failed because of their exposure to geographical or sectoral concentration of risks. For example, four of the five largest banks in Texas failed and were merged or sold because of large exposure to property, commercial, and energy loans during the downturn of energy prices in 1985–87.

In Malaysia, where nonperforming loans were defined as those that were not serviced for more than 365 days (reduced to 180 days in 1990), the sharp increase in provisions from 51 percent of total nonperforming loans in 1986 to 66 percent by 1990 brought the net exposure to nonperforming loans to only 7.1 percent of total loans by 1990 (Yusof and others 1994). The banking system was also required to increase capital and provisions through rigorous supervision and, where necessary, injection of capital by the central bank (chapter 7). Once the economy began to recover in 1987–89, the proportion of nonperforming loans began to decline rapidly.

Who is to blame?

Controversy still persists over whether bank failures have been due to bad bankers or the bad economic environment. Bankers are likely to blame bad government policies, banking system supervisors are apt to blame bad bankers, and depositors are quick to blame inadequate supervision. The evidence from the eight case studies suggests that no single cause, but rather a combination of causes, may be nearer the truth.

In all eight cases banking crises or problems were associated with declines in real economic growth either before or during the crisis period (table 1.6). The sharper the decline in growth, the more severe the economic "losses" to the private sector. The real wealth losses to the private sector in Chile in 1982 were estimated at 28 percent of GDP (based on a proxy that included the decline in dollar terms of the fall in the capitalization of the stock market and the real value in money and quasi-money; table 1.7). In 1989 holders of Argentine broad money lost the equivalent of 27 percent of GDP in real terms, but borrowers gained from the inflation tax (erosion in the value of real debt) to the extent of 16 percent of GDP.

Though the twin macroeconomic imbalances of fiscal and current account deficits existed in all eight countries, there was no clear relationship between the size of fiscal or balance of payments deficits and nonperforming loans, partly because of major problems in standardizing the measurement of fiscal deficits and nonperforming loans. In the United States data on nonperforming loans are stringently applied, and industry averages for nonperforming loans, at 1 to 5 percent of total loans, are very low by international standards. Nevertheless, more U.S. banks failed, partly because of the large number of banks in the United States (29,000) and partly because the system is designed to merge or liquidate problem banks much faster than in other countries, as a deliberate exit policy. Thus, despite the well-known problems of the thrift industry and concern in certain pockets of the industry about the fragility of the banking system, the safety and soundness of the U.S. banking industry as a whole is not in question.

Table 1.6 Banking problems in selected countries
(percent unless otherwise specified)

Indicator	Argentina	Chile	Colombia	Ghana	Malaysia	Spain	United States	Yugoslavia
Period of banking problems	1980–90	1974–87	1982–88	1983–89	1985–88	1977–85	1981–91	1983–90
Peak decline in GDP	–9.8	–14.1	0.9	–4.5	–1.0	–0.2	–2.5	–7.6
Peak current account deficit/GDP	–8.5	–14.5	–7.5[a]	–4.3	–6.0	–2.6	–3.6	–5.4
Peak fiscal deficit/GDP	–15.9	–3.0	–4.8	–2.7	–11.2	–6.9	–6.0	–0.1
Peak inflation rate (annual)	4,923.6	30.7	24.1	122.9	5.8[b]	24.5	13.5	1,239.9
Peak decline in terms of trade	–7.9	–29.3	–29.6	–18.5	–18.2	–14.9	–34.4	–7.2
Peak real interest rate (lending)	44.8[c]	56.9[c]	16.1	9.8	12.0	5.0	18.9[d]	1,539.9
Peak nonperforming loans as a percentage of total loans	30.3	18.7[e]	25.3	39.5[f]	32.6	n.a.	3.7, 27.6[g]	–40.0
Real estate losses	Yes	Yes	Yes	Yes	Yes	Yes	Yes	No
Foreign exchange losses	Yes	Yes	Yes	Yes	No	No	No	Yes
Connected lending	Yes	Yes	Yes	Yes	Yes	Yes	Yes	Yes
Excessive government borrowing	Yes	No	No	Yes	No	No	No	No
State-owned enterprises	Yes	No	No	Yes	No	No	No	No
Number of banks involved	168 financial institutions	13 banks and 6 *financieras*	7	9	4 banks, 4 finance companies, and 32 deposit-taking cooperatives	52	2,203	69
Restructuring method	Forced deposit conversion	Swap for central bank bonds	Guarantee fund	Swap for central bank bonds	Central bank capital injection	Swap for guarantee fund bonds	Deposit insurance liquidation and merger	Across-the-board and case-by-case

Note: Reported peaks are during period of banking problems.
a. Current account deficit/GNP.
b. 1982, before the crisis. Inflation was below 1 percent during most of the crisis period.
c. Yearly average.
d. Prime lending rate, not adjusted for inflation.
e. Commercial bank loan defaults as a percentage of total loan portfolio.
f. Provisions only.
g. FDIC-insured commercial banks in 1990 and FSLIC-insured thrifts in 1988 (no data available for subsequent years, which were worse).
Source: Morris 1990; Velasco 1991; chapters 4–11.

The size of the published fiscal deficit can also be misinterpreted. Although Yugoslavia's central government fiscal deficit in the 1980s was almost negligible, the quasi-fiscal deficit in the books of the National Bank reached 11.8 percent of gross social product in 1986 (Gaspari 1989). The fiscal deficits of Argentina and Chile would similarly have increased had they included the quasi-fiscal deficits of the central bank in absorbing the foreign exchange losses of the private and public sectors, as well as losses incurred in bank interventions. By the end of 1986 the Central Bank of Chile had "carved out" bad loans from banks equivalent to 20 percent of GDP (chapter 10).

External shocks probably triggered banking problems in Chile, Colombia, Malaysia, and Yugoslavia. Chile suffered significantly from a decline in its terms of trade, mainly because of its heavy reliance on copper exports. Colombia suffered a decline in terms of trade that exacerbated its banking problems during 1982–88, which were triggered in part by the cutoff of external resources caused by the Mexican debt crisis of 1982. Malaysia also suffered an across-the-board decline in terms of trade in 1983–86, when the prices of its major commodities—tin, rubber, oil, and palm oil—declined simultaneously. Yugoslavia was hit hard by oil price shocks.

Table 1.7 Banking crises and private sector "wealth"
(change in U.S. dollars as a percentage of GDP)

Country	Crisis peak year	Private "loss"	Decline in M3	Decline in bank credit to the private sector
Argentina	1981	6.2	13.8	9.1
	1989	7.3	26.7	15.8
Colombia	1985	4.0	5.1	2.3
Chile	1982	28.3	14.3	31.2
Ghana	1983	20.3	22.6	2.3
Malaysia	1985	13.9	5.0	6.0
Spain	1982	6.4	9.0	7.0
United States	1981	5.7	4.0	4.0
Yugoslavia	1988	0.6	7.2	6.6

Note: Because changes in inflation and exchange rates make measuring the decline in "real" wealth difficult, money stock and private sector credit have been converted into U.S. dollars at the prevailing rate. Private losses are estimated as the decline in the value of stock market capitalization, plus the decline in real value of the money stock, less the decline in real value of bank credit to the private sector.
Source: Chapters 4–11.

In the United States terms-of-trade changes affected different regions. The savings and loan crisis was sparked by high interest rates in 1980–81, which, because of the institutions' fundamental interest rate and maturity mismatch, caused their economic insolvency. In the early 1980s the farm belt was hurt by declining exports brought on by the high value of the U.S. dollar. In the mid-1980s the energy-producing states, particularly Texas, were hurt by the decline in energy prices. By the second half of the 1980s excessive investment in real estate, stimulated by tax incentives and by consumer hedging against inflation, caused large bank losses in the Northeast.

One phenomenon common to all eight countries was the close association between high real interest rates and banking problems. In the United States annual real interest rates in the 1980s were 3 to 6 percent, significantly higher than in the 1960s and 1970s. In Argentina and Chile high annual real interest rates of 30 to 50 percent were the norm rather than the exception during the debt crisis. At such high real interest rates, borrowers quickly became decapitalized. The result was "to transfer the ownership of real enterprise wealth from debtors to creditors, a mechanism doomed to failure when no more shareholders' wealth was left" (Diaz-Alejandro 1985, p. 16). When the central bank itself had to pay such high real interest rates in attempts to maintain monetary stability, the result was unsustainable growth of internal debt, as occurred in Argentina and Chile. In Malaysia the

capping of bank spreads and tough action by the central bank in preventing further lending to nonperforming borrowers curbed interest rate growth.

Another common feature was losses in lending to real estate. Caprio, Atiyas, and Hanson (1994) have suggested that banks tended to expand their real estate lending immediately after financial sector liberalization or relaxation of lending guidelines. Information asymmetry or bank myopia may be involved in lending to real estate. First, banks assume that collateral value alone, particularly real property, is sufficient to demonstrate good credit, instead of assessing the underlying cash flow capacity of real estate developers to service their debt. Because developers assume that debt can always be serviced out of rentals or property sales, they forget that the "lumpiness" of real property and the thinness of markets can create situations where property cannot be sold except at massive losses.

Second, there is a fallacy of composition problem in real estate lending. Each developer assumes that his or her project is good at the margin, but forgets (as does the banker) that if all developers were to make the same assumption, there would be such an oversupply of property that prices would fall sharply. Information on cumulative property construction and its oversupply generally is not available to the market until the economy turns downward, by which time it is too late.

Third, both bankers and real estate borrowers have frequently been deluded by the initial high returns on property. Bankers forget that property "booms" are sometimes fueled by the increase in bank credit provided and that the oversupply can result in large loan losses. However, because property price cycles are long, the next generation of bank credit managers may repeat the same mistake.

Fourth, speculative "bubbles" in real assets have been closely associated with financial liberalization, particularly deregulation in bank lending, interest rate decontrol, and the opening of the capital account (Park and Park 1992). In the absence of high returns in tradables, new funds seek shelter in nontradables, such as land. Before deregulation, cartelized banks earned protected profits. After liberalization, banks lost their market share to capital markets and, faced with such downsizing, increased their risk appetite, "a strategy that was also encouraged by the existence of a net of explicit and implicit government guarantees that both protected depositors and made 'failure' a less credible deterrent to excessive risk taking" (IMF 1993).

In almost all countries connected lending between banks and their shareholder-managers was found to be a problem. In Argentina, Chile, and Spain the presence of economic *grupos* that owned banks was a major factor. Yugoslavia's banking problems were inextricably linked to the nation's experimentation with socialized ownership of banks and enterprises, in which worker councils owned groups of enterprises, including the banks that served as treasuries for such groups. Consequently, socialized banks were unable to exercise financial discipline (the hard budget constraint) on their borrower-owners, leading to considerable distress borrowing. In Malaysia and the United States, where regulations limited the amount of connected lending, the damage was felt only in areas where supervision was weak, as in the case of Malaysian deposit-taking cooperatives and in U.S. savings and loan institutions.

Institutional and structural issues also led to bank problems. In the United States legal and structural issues of geographical and sectoral segmentation prevented banks and thrifts from diversifying their risks adequately. Competition among more than 29,000 banks and thrifts and such newcomers as money market funds, corporate bond markets, and foreign banks led depository institutions to take risks in real estate, highly leveraged securities, and developing country debt without adequately pricing such risks. In Japan financial liberalization allowed banks and nonbank financial institutions to finance the asset bubble. Fortunately, the economy was strong enough to withstand the large asset losses that came with deflation of the bubble.

In Chile and Spain the entry of new financial institutions without adequate separation of ties between owners of banks and enterprises created overgearing of the private sector, which required a "shakeout" when the economies went into a recession. Large fiscal deficits were clearly the source of problems in Argentina, Chile, and Malaysia. In Argentina and Chile the central banks' absorption of private external debt complicated the conduct of monetary policy. Chile's and Malaysia's ability to reverse their fiscal deficits generated enough resources to stabilize their economies and turn around the banking problems. Ghana's banking problems were the legacy of years of financial repression and economic decline. As in other socialist economies, banks were state owned and controlled, lending mainly to finance the budget or state-owned enterprises (chapter 8).

In almost all cases there was clear agreement on the need for better supervision and more transparent legal and accounting frameworks. Yet the evidence from this survey of bank failures is that, so far, even the strongest supervision available in the OECD countries has failed to prevent bank failures. Clearly, improved supervision and banking laws are necessary but are not sufficient to prevent bank failure.

Evidence suggests that while fraud and bank mismanagement were responsible for many individual bank failures and losses, macroeconomic factors such as external shocks, policy mistakes, and inadequate risk management at all levels—institutional, sectoral, and national—created the conditions of financial imbalance that led to widespread bank distress. No unique set of factors, macroeconomic or microeconomic, created the distress, nor did bank failures happen overnight. Many policymakers failed to correct key structural defects, particularly legal impediments to geographical or sectoral distribution of risks or inherent interest rate risks, before liberalizing the banking system. In Argentina, Chile, and Uruguay, with de facto state guarantee of the deposit base, it was widespread moral hazard behavior by banks, worsened by the presence of connected lending to economic *grupos* that controlled banks, that generated large losses in the banking system. Moreover, the severe imbalances in these economies, such as the large fiscal deficits financed by excessive external debt, were entwined with the political economy and so were beyond the powers of bank supervisors to control.

Trade liberalization, price reforms, and industrial policy changes also generated large losses to banks, which had lent heavily to support inefficient state-owned enterprises or domestic private sector firms that borrowed heavily to finance investments behind high tariff barriers. In Africa and Eastern Europe rapid trade liberalization exposed the large inefficiencies of state-owned enterprises, and their losses were quickly passed on to their creditor banks. In Ghana, for example, trade and price reforms made state-owned enterprises uncompetitive, and they were unable to repay their debts to the bank.

In sum, banking problems in the 1980s resulted from a combination of bad policies, bad management, and a bad institutional framework.

Banks as intermediators of economic loss

Although banks are seen primarily as intermediators of savings and investments, it is useful in the context of financial crises to treat banks as the allocators of loss in an economy. The coincidence of widespread bank losses throughout the world cannot be attributed solely to incidental speculative or fraudulent behavior by bank management. Fraud and mismanagement occur when conditions of incentives are distorted; that is, when speculative risks are privately rewarded and socially absorbed, and enforcement against fraud and criminal misappropriation is lax. Sound supervision and tough enforcement can prevent cases of individual fraud and mismanagement at the margin but may not be able to prevent systemic or economywide losses from being absorbed by the banking system.

Wealth losses for the private sector in peak crises years can be very large. For the eight countries studied here they varied from 0.6 percent of GDP for Yugoslavia in 1988 to 28.3 percent of GDP for Chile in 1982 (see table 1.7). Even these broad numbers can be deceptive, because the household sector in Yugoslavia lost the equivalent of 7.2 percent of GDP in the real value of money holdings through hyperinflation and devaluation, while the socialized enterprise sector gained from the depreciation of the real value of its debt. The Chilean case was the most severe because of the massive decline in GDP (14.1 percent) and the sharp jump in the real value of private sector debt (31.2 percent of GDP) due to unusually high real loan rates averaging 42.4 percent a year in 1981–82 (Velasco 1991).

Such wealth "compression" or shocks were clearly too large for the private sector net equity to absorb and were therefore transmitted to the banking system in the form of bad debts. Banks transmit their own losses in the economy through additional credit. They attempt to recover losses in two ways: by generating further credit or by widening spreads. The first approach involves additional lending or investments, in the hope that new credits will earn sufficient profits to cover existing losses. Credit expansion often includes the extension or rollover of bad loans to loss-making borrowers to cover up the extent of the damage of nonperforming loans (evergreening). Just as distressed borrowers are willing to pay higher interest rates to maintain liquidity in the face of deteriorating solvency, insolvent banks are apt to raise deposit rates to attract funds to maintain their own liquidity and a facade of solvency. Unless stopped, these banks increasingly will channel scarce resources to loss-making enterprises in an economy, thus distorting resource allocation further.

The inflationary impact of bank lending to loss-making enterprises was first grasped by Schumpeter (1934):

> This loss always occurs if the entrepreneur does not succeed in producing commodities at least equal in value to the credit plus interest. Only when he succeeds in so doing has the bank done good business—then and only then, however, is there also no inflation.

The work of Sundararajan and Baliño (1991) empirically confirmed the effect of banks increasing credit before and after a financial crisis. They found that total domestic credit increased in real terms, despite falls in real output and foreign exchange reserves.

The deterioration of bank portfolios and their rescue by central banks or the state have large monetary and fiscal implications because of feedback effects that lead to a vicious circle of macroeconomic instability. As demonstrated in the cases of Argentina and Chile, large current account and fiscal deficits required devaluation as part of the package of macroeconomic stabilization. Because enterprises and the public sector had large external debt, however, the borrowers suffered large foreign exchange losses from devaluation, with an immediate impact on the banks' portfolios. Central bank lending to rescue insolvent banks injected excessive reserve money into the system. A central bank can become insolvent if it acquires liabilities of greater market value than the capacity of its seigniorage to service. At that point the central bank can service its liabilities only by accelerating inflation (Fry 1991). Alternatively, the government can run higher fiscal deficits to finance the recapitalization of banks by borrowing from the central bank. Either method increases money supply, and unless there is accompanying tight monetary measures, domestic inflation exceeds international inflation, leading to further devaluation and enterprise losses (figure 1.2).

The second transmission mechanism of bank losses is the widening of spreads. Banks must raise their spreads to cover the nonaccrual of income from nonperforming loans. If the writeoff of nonperforming loans (provisioning) is also included, spreads have to widen further. Thus if nonperforming loan levels reach 20 percent of total loans, spreads might have to widen from an average of, say, 4 percentage points to as much as 12 percentage points (figure 1.3). Spreads

Figure 1.2 The vicious circle of financial distress

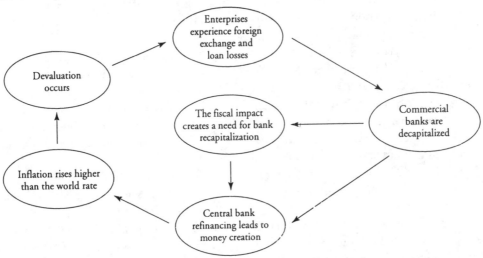

are increased either by reducing deposit rates, which leads to disintermediation from the banking system, or by raising lending rates to such punitive real levels that even good borrowers have incentives to become bad borrowers.

A Framework for the Resolution of Bank Distress

The pioneering work of Long (1987) and Hinds (1988) has cogently argued that macroeconomic imbalances, such as large fiscal and balance of payments deficits, sharp changes in relative prices, external shocks, and policy errors can lead to weak financial structures, large portfolio losses, and weak bank management and supervision. These factors in turn reduce the efficiency of resource allocation, causing

Figure 1.3 Spreads and nonperforming loans

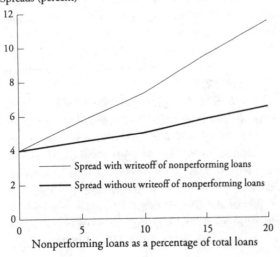

distressed borrowing, bank runs, capital flight, and monetary and price instability. Consequently, bank restructuring is a key element in achieving sustainable and stable growth. But as Hinds points out, bank restructuring makes sense only when coupled with a restructuring of the real sector in which inviable firms are closed and viable but troubled firms are restructured. The problems faced by banks in Eastern Europe have brought fresh insights to these views and new challenges to the process of bank restructuring.

A stock-flow–consistent approach to bank restructuring

The relationship between bank problems and the problems of the real sector is probably best depicted in a stock-flow–consistent matrix of sectoral and national accounts. A stock-flow–consistent analytical framework is used to examine the causes and effects because bank losses are not just flows but also evolve from changes in relative prices and their impact on the portfolio (stock) wealth of asset or liability holders. In this framework financial imbalances in one sector of the economy show up as potential losses in other sectors, causing major portfolio shifts that can disrupt and destabilize the economy.

Consider this example, using the flow of funds accounts for the Republic of Korea in 1990 (table 1.8). The economy is divided into four domestic sectors and one external sector. Deficits of expenditure over income in a sector are financed either by the drawdown of assets or by borrowing from other sectors. The deficits of the enterprise sector (17.0 percent of GDP) are financed by the surpluses of the household sector (11.4 percent), government (3.7

Table 1.8 Sectoral and national financial balances, based on the Republic of Korea's financial balances, 1990 (percentage of GDP)

Account	Households	Enterprises	Banks	Government	Domestic total	External funds	National total
Revenues	22.4	12.4	39.7	4.3	78.7	2.1	80.8
Expenditures	11.0	29.4	39.5	0.5	80.4	0.4	80.8
Surplus or deficit	11.4	−17.0	0.1	3.7	−1.7	1.7	0.0
Financed by:							
Buildup or drawdown of assets	−11.4		−11.5	−3.7	−26.7	−1.7	−28.4
Borrowing		17.0	11.4		28.4		28.4

Source: Bank of Korea 1992.

percent), banking (0.1 percent), and the external sector (1.7 percent).

Sectoral imbalances arising from a variety of causes thus need to be financed, and financing restrictions force adjustment in the economy due to the stock-flow consistency of the national accounts. For example, imbalances in the economy can be created either by large fiscal deficits, requiring financing by the banking system or externally, or by excessive spending by the enterprise or household sectors. These imbalances can be caused by changes in policy or relative prices, by external shocks, or even by bad enterprise and bank management (box 1.1).

The stock-flow consistency of this framework helps to conceptualize the diagnosis process by identifying the sources of financial imbalance that caused the losses in the banking system. The framework also helps policymakers think through the issues of loss allocation, because bank losses would have to be borne sooner or later somewhere in the economy.

Unfortunately, not enough data exist to construct this matrix for any actual country. Sectoral balance sheets for the enterprise sector and the government sector are not normally compiled in national income accounts. Even if government and enterprise balance sheets could be compiled, serious inconsistencies would occur because governments operate on a cash accounting basis while banks and enterprises usually prepare accounts on an accrual basis. Moreover, value-added flows are not consistent with the size of changes in the sector balance sheet items.

The stock-flow consistency of this model, however, helps to clarify several issues in bank distress that were sometimes confused in partial equilibrium analyses:

• *Bank restructuring cannot be executed independently of enterprise restructuring and budget reform.* Because of implicit or explicit state guarantees on the deposit base, bank losses ultimately become quasi-fiscal responsibilities of the state. At the same time, any recapitalization of the banking system that does not address the financial imbalance of the corporate sector would only invite another financial crisis.

• *Domestic losses cannot be passed on to the external sector unless there is external debt forgiveness or unilateral debt repudiation.* In fact, the cutoff of external funds resulting from the 1982 Mexican debt crisis stopped the growth of unsustainable debt accumulation by both the enterprise and the government sector in many developing countries in the 1980s. The net external resource transfer from servicing external debt created a large internal debt problem in a number of countries when governments and enterprises were initially unwilling to reduce consumption to bring the imbalances to sustainable levels.

• *Wealthholders disintermediated from domestic banking systems or engaged in capital flight to avoid losses from potential bank failure as well as from a potential wealth tax to pay for the national debt overhang.* This not only narrowed the domestic inflation tax base, which worsened the fiscal deficit, it also worsened the balance of payments. As is now well known, any central bank liquidity support during a banking crisis in an economy with an open account only results in loss of foreign exchange reserves.

• *An insolvent sector cannot rescue another insolvent sector.* Stability in the system requires that surplus resources be found to pay for the deficits in other sectors if the external sector is unwilling to lend new resources. In Chile and Malaysia, for example, the supply response arising from devaluation, liberalization in the real sector, and fiscal retrenchment generated sufficient growth from renewed foreign direct investment and a current account surplus to alleviate problems in the banking system. In Argentina and Yugoslavia, where normal seigniorage of the central banks was insufficient to service the large burden of net

---

Box 1.1 Rewriting the national balance sheet

The effects of bank losses can be demonstrated from the sectoral and national balance sheet presented in table 1.8. Suppose that in year one, growth slows and the enterprise sector begins to default on loans, equivalent to 10 percent of its loans. In the table loan losses would be equivalent to 1.7 percent of GDP (10 percent of enterprise borrowing of 17 percent of GDP). Assuming that these are all domestic loans, the losses would fall on either the banking system, as the major lender, or the government. In either case the surplus of the banking or the public sector would have to adjust by 1.7 percent of GDP.

If the losses are not recognized because of defective accounting, then all the losses would be reflected in the books of the banking system as impaired assets. These are financed by bank deposits. If the rate of losses carries on for three years, the banks would have carried impaired assets equivalent to 5.1 percent of GDP. If at that point the household sector loses confidence in the banking system and engages in capital flight, domestic savings would fall and the balance of payments would worsen, causing a further decline in domestic growth and worsening the enterprise losses and bank loan losses.

At that point the government can only stabilize the situation by raising domestic real interest rates (to stem capital outflows) or by recapitalizing the banking system. A market-based solution is possible if the failed banks are allowed to collapse, passing the losses on to the depositors. But this would worsen domestic savings and encourage disintermediation, including capital flight.

Consequently, the government may have to absorb the bank losses by either guaranteeing the banking system or recapitalizing it through an issue of bonds in exchange for the losses. Note that the losses have de facto become a quasi-fiscal deficit. Macroeconomic stability then depends on whether the government has the debt-servicing capacity to service its increased debt burden, equivalent to 5.1 percent of GDP. Assuming that the nominal interest rate is 10 percent, the government must bear an additional debt-servicing burden equivalent to 0.5 percent of GDP. If the government is unable to borrow domestically or internationally to finance the higher internal debt, then it may have to resort to either higher taxation or monetary creation.

Recent experience with loan losses in three Scandinavian countries indicated that loan losses averaged 5.5 percent of GDP between 1991–92 and that the government provided support to the banking system equivalent to 3.3 percent of GDP.

The national balance sheet and financial flows framework suggest that both stock and flow losses have to be taken into consideration. Stock-flow consistency suggests that there is no free lunch. If the external sector will not bear losses, then domestic bank losses must be borne elsewhere in the economy, initially in the public sector because of either government action or deposit insurance, but ultimately through higher taxation or monetary creation.

Source: IMF 1993.

---

foreign exchange liabilities, the central banks themselves became major sources of monetary instability, which eventually led to hyperinflation.

Bank restructuring, enterprise restructuring, and fiscal reform in transition economies

The stock-flow–consistent framework suggests that losses in one sector must appear in or be financed by other sectors. Thus the unwillingness of one sector to continue financing inefficient behavior in another sector could trigger massive balance sheet and flow adjustments. The rapid growth of domestic debt in many highly indebted countries after recourse to external debt was shut off in the 1982 debt crisis demonstrated how enterprises, governments, and banks all tried to mobilize internal resources to meet excessive expenditure commitments and to service their external debt. Private wealthholders, sensing that heavy taxation was inevitable in such an environment, stashed their capital abroad to avoid either a wealth or an inflation tax.

Nowhere was the interlocking relationship among banks, the budget, and enterprises so evident than in the formerly socialist economies of Central and Eastern Europe. Former President Gorbachev of the Soviet Union used to say that the workers pretended to work, and the state pretended to pay them. The institutional structure of the centrally planned economy is best portrayed in the "troika" model of budget, enterprise, and banking system, where every element is owned by the state (figure 1.4). The state based its budget revenue almost totally on resources extracted from the enterprises and the banking system. In 1989 tax collected from state enterprises (including sales tax) accounted for 89 percent of Soviet federal revenues. Prior to reform, enterprises extracted monopoly profits from consumers and banks extracted monopoly interest revenue from enterprises because enterprises were locked in to designated state banks.[1] Moreover, because enterprises acted as tax agents, there was no parallel revenue-collecting machinery to extract excise or consumer taxes (McKinnon 1991).

Figure 1.4 The troika model

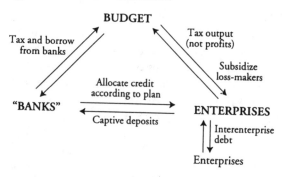

The old Soviet accounting system, which was designed to check compliance with plan rather than measure the profitability or solvency of enterprises, tended to overstate profits (measured according to internationally accepted accounting standards) by 12 to 15 percent, due mainly to underdepreciation and underallocation of costs (Enthoven, Sokolov, and Petrachkov 1992).

Liberalizing prices, deregulating the real sector, and moving the banking system into a two-tier structure had the effect of eroding the tax base in most transition socialist economies, particularly in terms of the enterprise tax. For example, the Chinese tax system allows the repayment of loans as a deduction on enterprise income tax. Between 1978 and 1988 total revenue from enterprises in China fell from 60 percent of government revenue to 25 percent, while government revenue fell from 34 percent of GNP to 21 percent (World Bank 1990). Subsidies to loss-making enterprises also became a heavier burden. The net revenue extracted from enterprises fell from 20 percent of GNP in 1978 to only 2 percent in 1988.

Giving enterprises greater autonomy in the liberalization phase also eroded monopoly profits and encouraged enterprises to evade taxation through spending on inventory, higher wages, and higher investment. The budget compensated for the loss of revenue by shifting the burden of investment financing to banks and to the retained earnings of enterprises. During 1986–89 budget financing of investments of Polish enterprises fell from 4.5 percent of GDP to 2.9 percent, while borrowing from banks rose from 6 percent to 20 percent of GDP.

The troika system was stable as long as enterprises were relatively efficient and output growth was expanding. But state-owned enterprises under central planning were inefficient—they invested in outmoded equipment, geared products toward the domestic market, and granted excessive wage increases. In China there was a clear positive correlation between decentralized enterprise "ownership" and productivity. The average annual growth rate of labor productivity during 1980–87 was 5.2 percent for state-owned enterprises, 12.3 percent for urban collectives, and 18.0 percent for rural town and village enterprises.

Moreover, as prices remained tightly controlled, losses began to increase. In Yugoslavia current losses of enterprises escalated from 0.2 percent of gross social product in 1984 to 14.3 percent by 1989 (National Bank of Yugoslavia 1990). In Romania losses of state enterprises were as much as 19 percent of GDP in 1989 (IMF 1990). In China as many as one-third of state enterprises were reportedly incurring losses in 1991. These losses were largely reflected in the books of the banks that lent to these enterprises. Moreover, because there was no inflation accounting during this period of high inflation, the government was overtaxing the inflation profits of the enterprises, especially through the sale of old inventory at historic costs. Even sound firms with surplus cash kept in banks were subject to severe inflation tax, because such demand deposits paid no interest.

Bank credit is not the only source of credit for enterprises. Because of suppliers' connections among enterprises, interenterprise credit is often more important than bank credit. Loss-making enterprises have often relied on credit from other enterprises to survive. Central bank attempts to tighten bank credit often have had the effect of temporarily increasing interenterprise credit. In Yugoslavia interenterprise credit rose from about 14 percent of total domestic credit in 1980 to more than 33 percent by 1988. In Poland interenterprise credit in June 1990 (at a time of tight liquidity) was one-and-a-half times larger than bank credit. Consequently, even sound enterprises can be dragged down because of losses on uncollectible interenterprise credit.

Other than the inheritance of enterprise loans at overstated book values, banks in transition economies also suffer from the following structural and institutional flaws:

- *Geographic and sector concentration.* Almost all the banks in Central and Eastern Europe suffer from geographic and sector concentration in their loan portfolio. This has exposed them to large shocks arising from the collapse of the Council for Mutual Economic Assistance market or from downturns such as a decline in agriculture.

- *Foreign exchange mismatches.* Yugoslav and Polish banks had large foreign exchange mismatches in their books because all foreign exchange proceeds were surrendered to the national bank, while the banks collected foreign currency deposits from residents. Unless the national bank is able to guarantee the liability exposures, such banks are highly vulnerable to exchange rate depreciations.
- *Shareholder-borrowers.* In Hungary, Yugoslavia, and the states of the former Soviet Union enterprise borrowers are also significant shareholders in banks. This was a major problem in Yugoslavia, and led to uncontrolled lending (chapter 9). There are now more than 1,800 banks in Russia, many of which are owned by borrower-enterprises and operated under an inadequate supervisory framework.
- *Segmentation of credit and deposit markets.* Most banks are still segmented into the enterprise financing market and the retail deposits and housing finance markets. Household deposits are largely concentrated in national savings banks, which lend substantially to finance housing at subsidized interest rates. With interest rate liberalization, most of these specialized banks with large portfolios of below-market yields became technically insolvent. These banks are only gradually diversifying their liabilities into the retail market.
- *Inadequate loan loss provisions.* Because of the strain on their budgets, most authorities in the transition economies are unwilling to concede to banks pretax provisioning for bad debts. Consequently, these banks generally have negligible loan loss provisions.
- *Inadequate legal and supervisory framework.* Most transition economy banks do not have a strong and clear legal framework to enforce financial discipline through debt recovery and liquidation procedures. Bank supervisory authorities are unable to enforce discipline on banks due to the lack of strong banking laws and the supervisory capacity to carry them out.
- *Lack of banking skills and outdated systems and procedures.* The inadequacies of accounting, legal, and supervisory frameworks all underscore the dire shortage of human capital. Bank skills in credit and project evaluation are grossly inadequate. The inefficiencies of the banks in providing speedy and

reliable payments and fund management compound the problems of the enterprises.

In market-based economies the relationships among banks, enterprises, and the budget have not been as sharply defined as in the troika, but variations of the negative features listed above have been evident. The prevalence of economic *grupos* in Chile, Colombia, and Spain, for example, created connected lending and a concentration of power that contributed to banking problems in these countries.

As the stock-flow–consistent framework demonstrates, the objective of bank restructuring is thus to rewrite the national balance sheet and profit and loss accounts such that economic efficiency, sound credit allocation, and macroeconomic stability are restored as an integral part of a national program.

The political challenge of bank restructuring lies in the difficult area of loss allocation. Bank losses are ultimately reflections of real sector losses in the enterprise and budgetary sectors, compounded by inefficiencies or fraud in the process of financial intermediation. The success of bank restructuring depends on the ability to allocate such losses to the rest of economy without suffering macroeconomic instability.

The Process of Bank Restructuring

Like financial sector liberalization, bank restructuring is a process, not an event (Caprio, Atiyas, and Hanson 1994). The techniques of this process are well defined, but their application depends on individual country conditions. The process of bank restructuring may be distilled into four main phases, some of which may overlap:

- Diagnosis.
- Damage control.
- Loss allocation.
- Rebuilding profitability and creating the right incentives.

The process of bank restructuring operates in a dynamic context, where techniques of restructuring can play major roles in changing the incentives within the economy. Chapter 2 discusses the problems of diagnosis and loss allocation, which lie more in the realm of political economy. Chapter 3 focuses on supervisory remedies for bank restructuring, the issue of damage control, and the building of safe and sound banking systems.

Annex 1.1 Bank problems in the 1980s

Africa

Ghana	In 1989 the government recapitalized ten state-owned and -controlled commercial banks that had suffered large foreign exchange losses and nonperforming loans. A nonperforming asset recovery trust was established to dispose of bad debt.
Guinea	In 1985 the government closed six state-owned specialized banks, with losses amounting to almost 97 percent of total assets.
Kenya	In 1989 eight failing institutions were merged into a "turnaround" bank, Consolidated Bank Ltd. The Kenya Deposit Protection Fund also was established. In 1992 the central bank had to intervene in two local banks.
Madagascar	In 1988, 25 percent of all loans were deemed irrecoverable and 21 percent more deemed "difficult to collect," compared with capital and reserves of less than 5 percent of assets.
Mauritania	In 1984 the five major banks had nonperforming assets ranging from 45 to 70 percent of their portfolios. The cost of rehabilitation was estimated at about 15 percent of GDP in 1988.
Senegal	Between 1988 and 1991 six commercial banks and a development bank were closed. A single asset recovery body took over the nonperforming assets and corresponding liabilities of the liquidated banks.
Tanzania	In 1987 the main financial institutions had arrears amounting to half their portfolio and implied losses were nearly 10 percent of GNP.

Asia

Bangladesh	In 1987 four banks accounting for 70 percent of total credit had an estimated 20 percent nonperforming loans.
Hong Kong	Between 1983 and 1986 the Commissioner of Banking had to take over or liquidate seven banks and deposit-taking companies.
Malaysia	Between 1986 and 1988 the central bank intervened in thirty-two deposit-taking cooperatives, four commercial banks, and four finance companies.
Nepal	In 1988 reported arrears of three banks accounting for 95 percent of the financial system averaged 29 percent of all assets.
Philippines	Between 1980 and 1987 the Central Bank closed 173 banks. The government took over $5.1 billion of foreign debt of the two largest banks, which were subsequently partially privatized.
Sri Lanka	State-owned banks, which make up 70 percent of the banking system, have estimated nonperforming loans of about 35 percent of the total portfolio.
Thailand	During 1983–84 fifteen finance companies and securities companies with assets of B 9.8 billion went under, and the rescue scheme cost B 8 billion. Between 1984 and 1987 three commercial banks had their capital reduced and recapitalized with assistance in low-interest loans from the central bank. The Thai Financial Institutions Development Fund was established to assist rehabilitation of problem institutions.

Latin America

Argentina	Between 1980 and 1989 the Central Bank intervened in ninety-three institutions, of which only seven were rehabilitated or sold. In 1990 more than 200 banks were in the process of liquidation. The restructuring process is proceeding.
Bolivia	During 1986–87 five banks were liquidated, and nonperforming loans reached an estimated 30 percent of total loans in 1987.
Chile	In 1981 the government liquidated eight insolvent institutions that held 35 percent of total financial system assets. In 1983 another eight institutions were taken over, accounting for 45 percent of system assets.
Colombia	Between 1982 and 1987 the central bank intervened in six banks, accounting for 24 percent of system assets.
Costa Rica	In 1987 public banks accounting for 90 percent of loans considered 32 percent of loans "uncollectible."
Uruguay	Between 1984 and 1987 the central bank intervened in five domestic banks and de facto "nationalized" 75 percent of total deposits.

Annex 1.1   Bank problems in the 1980s (continued)

Industrial countries

Australia	During 1989–90 two large state banks received capital injections from the government to cover loan losses.
Canada	Two small provincial banks failed in 1985, following the failure of a number of trust and loan companies.
Finland	The central bank took over control of the Skopbank, the apex bank for the Finnish savings banks, in August 1991. Several banks also suffered losses due to bad loans and share investments.
Japan	Banks have suffered from the sharp decline in the stock market (down 56 percent from its peak in 1987) and declines in real estate prices, with official estimates of nonperforming loans at ¥ 12.3 trillion ($120 billion) as of September 1992. Of this, ¥ 4 trillion was not covered by collateral. Several small trust banks had to be taken over by stronger banks. In August 1992 the government announced ¥ 10.7 trillion ($86 billion) of fiscal stimulation. The program included the endorsement of the establishment of a private entity (owned jointly by the financial institutions) to buy nonperforming loans of banks with real estate collateral.
Norway	The Central Bank provided special loans to assist six banks suffering from the recession that followed the oil bust of 1985–86, particularly from problem real estate loans. The state took control of three of the largest banks, partly through a government bank investment fund (NKr 5 billion),and the state-backed bank insurance fund had to increase capital to NKr 11 billion.
Spain	Between 1978 and 1983 fifty-one institutions holding one-fifth of all deposits were rescued. In 1983 the government nationalized Rumasa, a holding company controlling more than 100 enterprises and 20 small and medium-size banks.
Sweden	In 1991 the government had to inject SKr 5 billion ($800 million) into the state-controlled Nordbanken, and to guarantee a $609 million loan to save the largest savings bank.
United Kingdom	The Bank of England acquired Johnson Mathey, a key player in the gold market, recapitalized it, and subsequently sold it. The Bank of Credit and Commerce International, one of the largest bank frauds in history, was closed in 1991.
United States	Between 1981 and 1991 more than 1,400 savings and loans and 1,300 banks failed. The thrift crisis may have cost between $315 billion and $500 billion. The Resolution Trust Corporation acquired $357 billion of bad assets of thrifts by the end of 1991 and had disposed of $228 billion. The government granted $70 billion to strengthen the Federal Deposit Insurance Corporation.

Transition economies

Bulgaria	Nonperforming loans are reported to have exceeded 60 percent of assets.
Hungary	The government has included guarantees in the state budget to cover a portion of nonperforming loans.
Poland	A recent audit of seven state-owned commercial banks indicated that substandard loans accounted for 25 to 60 percent of assets.
Yugoslavia	According to a statistical survey of the National Bank of Yugoslavia, problem loans in 1988 amounted to 35 to 40 percent of banks' portfolios.

Source: World Bank 1989 (updated); *Financial Times,* various issues; *The Economist,* various issues; and other reports.

Annex 1.2 *Euromoney* top 500 banks: selected indicators, 1992
(percent)

Country group	Number of banks	Equity/asset ratio	Profit/asset ratio	Return on equity
Africa				
South Africa	6	4.91	0.78	15.32
Asia	46	5.19	0.63	11.96
China	5	2.07	0.50	17.29
Hong Kong	1	4.47	0.45	6.89
India	2	2.84	0.39	12.64
Korea, Rep. of	15	6.41	0.39	6.15
Malaysia	2	6.12	0.47	6.82
Singapore	5	8.78	0.92	10.93
Taiwan (China)	11	4.53	0.91	20.56
Thailand	5	6.32	1.04	14.37
Latin America	24	20.15	0.84	2.39
Argentina	3	14.37	−0.47	−12.91
Brazil	8	11.75	0.67	6.83
Mexico	7	7.68	0.55	4.22
Puerto Rico	4	12.30	1.23	10.25
Uruguay	1	24.29	0.00	0.00
Venezuela	1	50.49	3.06	5.97
Middle East and North Africa	23	7.95	1.00	9.08
Algeria	3	6.76	0.38	5.42
Bahrain	1	7.88	0.22	1.42
Iran	1	0.67	0.00	0.58
Israel	3	4.65	0.07	1.03
Jordan	1	6.53	0.68	10.44
Kuwait	1	9.74	1.42	n.a.
Qatar	1	12.13	1.99	n.a.
Saudi Arabia	5	7.61	0.94	19.34
Turkey	4	11.77	3.31	25.98
United Arab Emirates	3	11.70	1.00	8.43
OECD	392	4.64	0.33	5.69
Australia	8	5.89	0.62	9.58
Austria	7	4.10	0.29	5.56
Belgium	8	3.14	0.08	5.60
Canada	10	5.45	0.64	8.47
Denmark	6	6.25	0.19	2.80
Finland	5	5.15	−1.07	−22.30
France	23	3.53	0.23	5.41
Germany	41	2.82	0.15	4.40
Greece	3	3.12	0.44	14.70
Ireland	2	4.87	0.44	4.28
Italy	42	4.79	0.40	8.54
Japan	81	3.44	0.19	5.51
Luxembourg	1	0.95	0.23	8.10
Netherlands	6	4.25	0.39	6.80
New Zealand	1	4.65	−0.36	−5.77
Portugal	3	9.48	1.05	9.91
Spain	19	5.83	0.89	12.06
Sweden	5	3.12	1.00	15.44
Switzerland	11	5.94	0.45	5.94
United Kingdom	27	4.73	0.39	8.82
United States	83	6.00	0.39	5.72
Transition economies	9	6.82	0.87	12.39
Bosnia-Herzegovina	1	8.55	0.50	5.80
Bulgaria	1	4.41	0.83	18.74
Cuba	1	2.70	0.00	0.00
Czechoslovakia	1	4.70	1.38	29.28
Poland	2	10.04	4.05	39.12
Slovenia	1	9.11	−1.23	−13.31
Yugoslavia	2	8.24	0.58	7.07

Source: Euromoney 1992.

Note

1. Under Soviet-style funds management all current receipts of state enterprises had to be placed in the current account with a designated state-owned bank, on which little interest was earned. These enterprises were allowed to service interest, pay for inventory purchases, and pay wages from this account. Any surplus was transferred to the state in the form of taxes or dividends. Funds required for investment were allocated from the budget under the central plan or approved for bank borrowing under the credit plan, on which (after interest liberalization) market interest was paid. This explains the unusually high enterprise deposits in these banking systems and the high spreads earned by their banks. For example, 88 percent of Chinese enterprise deposits with banks were sight or current deposits (September 1989) and accounted for 36 percent of total deposits in banks. Even at the height of hyperinflation, 56 percent of Yugoslavian deposits were demand or sight deposits.

References

Bank of Korea. 1992. *Economic Statistics Yearbook*. Seoul.

BIS (Bank for International Settlement). 1990. "Large-Value Funds Transfer Systems in the Group of Ten Countries." Basle, Switzerland.

Blejer, Mario, and Adrienne Cheasty. 1991. "Measurement of Fiscal Deficits: Analytical and Methodological Issues." *Journal of Economic Literature* 29: 1644–78.

Bryant, Ralph. 1984. "The Progressive Internationalization of Banking." Brookings Institution Discussion Paper 14. Washington, D.C.

Caprio, Gerard, Izak Atiyas, and James Hanson. 1994. *Financial Reform: Theory and Experience*. New York: Cambridge University Press.

Davis, E. P. 1989. "Instability in the Euromarkets and the Economic Theory of Financial Crisis." Bank of England Discussion Paper 43. London.

de Juan, Aristobulo. 1987. "From Good Bankers to Bad Bankers: Ineffective Supervision as Major Elements in Banking Crises." Economic Development Institute Working Paper. World Bank, Washington, D.C.

Diaz-Alejandro, Carlos. 1985. "Goodbye Financial Repression, Hello Financial Crash." *Journal of Development Economics*.

Enthoven, Adolf, J. V. Sokolov, and A. M. Petrachkov. 1992. *Doing Business in the Russian Federal Republic and the Other Republics of the CIS: Managerial and Financial Issues*. Montvale, N.J.: Institute of Management Accountants.

Fry, Maxwell J. 1991. "Can a Central Bank Go Bust?" University of Birmingham International Finance Group Discussion Paper 91-09. Manchester School of Economic and Social Studies, Manchester, England.

Gaspari, Mitja. 1989. "Balance of Payments Adjustment and Financial Crisis in Yugoslavia." In C. Kessides, T. King, M. Nuti, and C. Sokil, eds., *Financial Reform in Socialist Economies*. Economic Development Institute Seminar Series. Washington, D.C.: World Bank.

Hinds, Manuel. 1988. "Economic Effects of Financial Crises." Policy Research Working Paper 104. World Bank, Washington, D.C.

Huh, Chan, and Sun Bae Kim. 1994. "Financial Regulation and Banking Sector Performance: A Comparison of Bad Loan Problems in Japan and Korea." *Economic Review* 2: 18–29. Federal Reserve Bank of San Francisco.

IMF (International Monetary Fund). 1990. *Recent Economic Developments, Romania*. Washington, D.C.

———. 1993. *International Capital Markets, Part II. Systemic Issues in International Finance*. Washington, D.C.

———. Various years. *International Financial Statistics*. Washington, D.C.

Long, Millard F. 1987. "Crisis in the Financial Sector." World Bank, Washington, D.C.

McKinnon, R. 1991. "Taxation, Money, and Credit in Liberalizing Socialist Economies: Asian and European Experiences." Stanford University, Department of Economics, Stanford, Calif.

Montes-Negret, Fernando. 1990. "An Overview of Colombia's Banking Crisis, 1982-1987." Background paper prepared for *World Development Report 1989*. World Bank, Washington, D.C.

Morris, Felipe. 1990. *Latin America's Banking System in the 1980s: A Cross-Country Comparison*. World Bank Discussion Paper 81. Washington, D.C.

National Bank of Yugoslavia. 1990. *Quarterly Bulletin*. Sarajevo.

OECD (Organization for Economic Cooperation and Development). 1992. "Bank Restructuring in Central and Eastern Europe: Issues and Strategies." *OECD Financial Market Trends* (February). Paris.

Park, Yung Chul, and Won Aun Park. 1992. "Capital Market, Real Asset Speculation, and Macroeconomic Adjustment in Korea." Organization for Economic Cooperation and Development, Paris.

Schuijer, Jan. 1992. *Banks Under Stress*. Paris: Organization for Economic Cooperation and Development.

Schumpeter, Joseph. 1934. *The Theory of Economic Development*. Cambridge, Mass.: Harvard University Press.

Sheng, Andrew. 1992. "Bad Debts in Transitional Socialist Economies." World Bank, Financial Policy and Systems Division, Washington, D.C.

Sundararajan, Vasudevan, and Tomas Baliño, eds. 1991. *Banking Crises: Cases and Issues*. Washington, D.C.: International Monetary Fund.

U.S. Bureau of the Census. 1991. *Statistical Abstract of the United States*. Washington, D.C.: Government Printing Office.

Velasco, Andres. 1991. "The Chilean Financial System, 1975–85." In Vasudevan Sundararajan and Tomas Baliño, eds., *Banking Crises: Cases and Issues*. Washington, D.C.: International Monetary Fund.

World Bank. 1989. *World Development Report 1989: Financial Systems and Development*. Washington, D.C.

———. 1990. *China: Between Plan and Market*. A World Bank Country Study. Washington, D.C.

———. 1991. *World Development Report 1991: The Challenge of Development*. Washington, D.C.

———. 1992. *World Development Report 1992: Development and the Environment*. Washington, D.C.

Yusof, Zaimal Aznam, and others. 1994. "Finanacial Reform in Malaysia." In Gerald Caprio, Izak Atiyas, and James Hanson, eds., *Financial Reform: Theory and Experience*. New York: Cambridge University Press.

CHAPTER 2

Bank Restructuring Techniques

Andrew Sheng

Bankers and policymakers often fail to respond effectively to evidence of an impending banking crisis. Bankers, for example, tend to engage in "cosmetic" behavior, evergreening bad credits, assetizing losses, and hiding material risks and losses from the public and from bank supervisors (de Juan 1987). Proper understanding of the scope and causes of bank losses necessarily precedes effective treatment and accurate prognosis. Although individual bank crises are triggered by specific events—such as bank runs, capital flight, or the disappearance of prominent bankers—such events only mark the point of public or official recognition of problems that have been building up over a long period.

Recognizing Failure

Proper diagnosis does not necessarily imply correct prognosis. In many cases bank supervisors are unable or unwilling to measure the true extent of bank losses, especially where inadequate accounting standards allow income to accrue on nonperforming loans or allow such loans to be rolled over. Many countries also fail to recognize the size of the problem, whether because of a lack of political will or because of a perceived inability to deal with such losses.

There are further incentives to hide losses or delay action. Private banks are reluctant to reveal losses because they fear government intervention and a run on banks. State-owned banks have no incentive to operate profitably since they lend largely to state-owned enterprises or in accordance with policy-based credit directives. Governments resist dealing with bank problems where they rely on the banking system as a source of taxation or finance for fiscal deficits. Where banks are controlled by political

interests, resolving problem banks becomes not a technical issue but a political one.

In other cases supervisors are reluctant to confront complex structural issues, such as fundamental changes in the law, that could involve issues of national history and political economy. An example is the political difficulties encountered in eliminating the geographical and functional segmentation of the U.S. banking system, where many believed in unit- or community-based banking and were deeply distrustful of nationwide banks.

In addition, there are few incentives for government agencies to deal with problems that involve political economy issues of bank ownership and control and of borrower and depositor property rights. For example, many central banks are more concerned with issues of bank compliance with credit allocation guidelines or monetary targets than with issues of solvency. Many developing countries interested in developing rural banking systems have required state-owned banks to open extensive rural branches even when these were operating at a loss. In such cases state-owned banks become pools of political patronage and employment generation.

Moreover, ownership and supervision of banks and other deposit-taking agencies may be diffused across different ministries or agencies with varying skills and powers of supervision. Central banks cannot always take action against banks owned by the ministry of finance. A weak bank superintendency may not be able to enforce bank supervision regulations against state banks whose chief executives are political appointees. Large rural banks may be outside the supervision of the ministry of finance or the central bank. Politicized credit unions have been a source of problems in many economies, notably Japan and Taiwan (China).

Where bureaucrats believe that problems are cyclical and not structural, some authorities engage in "regulatory forbearance"—allowing more and more ailing institutions to breach the law, hoping that time and economic recovery will resolve the problems. In the United States such behavior worsened the problem of moral hazard, since undercapitalized problem institutions have a competitive advantage over soundly capitalized institutions and are more likely to engage in high-risk activities (Brewer and Monschean 1992; chapter 4).

Although ignoring failure can go on for decades, the cumulative effects of weak intermediation, excessive overhead, loan losses, mismanagement, and fraud often surface during recessions, leading initially to illiquidity in the weaker institutions and ultimately to default and failure. The government is forced to deal with the problems when bank runs threaten systemic bank failure.

Defining insolvency

Because not all financial institutions have adopted market value accounting, which requires that all assets and liabilities be marked to market, two types of bank insolvency should be distinguished. A financial institution is in *economic* insolvency when the market value of its assets (capital and reserves, excluding the value of deposit guarantees) is lower than the market value of its (nonequity) liabilities (Kane 1985). A financial institution is in *accounting* insolvency when the accounting report of its net capital and reserves, according to generally accepted accounting principles, is negative. A financial institution *fails* when it is unable to meet its obligations and authorities intervene to restructure or liquidate the failed institution.

Many financial institutions are economically insolvent but appear to be accounting solvent because different laws and accounting standards allow such institutions to operate, often under a national deposit guarantee scheme. For example, if market-value accounting had been applied to OECD banks during the height of the international debt crisis in 1985–86, a number of them would have been judged both economically and accounting insolvent. Moreover, many accounting insolvent banks do not fail because the government intervenes through bailouts or other assistance.

There is therefore a significant time lapse between loss recognition and loss measurement and allocation. The lag occurs because the parties involved—bankers, supervisors, and policymakers—often refuse to acknowledge that losses have occurred. The difficult question of political economy is how to allocate the losses across different sectors and over time. Who pays for bank losses?

A recent example is the reluctance of authorities in the post–centrally planned economies to recognize the economic insolvency of state banks that had inherited loans to loss-making state enterprises. These banks have not suffered bank runs because they carry a state guarantee on deposits and are fully state owned. With massive changes in relative prices in these economies, the banks may continue to finance loss-making enterprises for years to come—further distorting resource allocation. In many countries policymakers have been reluctant to recognize these losses because of the large resources required to recapitalize these banks (Sheng 1992).

The major arguments against marking bank assets to market value are that there may be no markets in such assets and that thin markets may yield inaccurate valuations. Asset valuation is relatively straightforward in industrial economies, where established markets, valuation expertise, and set accounting and asset valuation standards are in place. Asset valuation is much more difficult for less-developed economies, where none of these conditions prevail.

Asset valuation—particularly the valuation of collateral—is crucial for loan provisioning and hence for basic bank solvency. In most countries real estate forms the bulk of bank collateral (box 2.1). The share of bank lending in real estate peaked at 37 percent in Malaysia and reached 42 percent of total loans in the United States. At the 35 percent level, the exposure of banks to real estate would be 350 percent of bank capital, assuming a loan-assets ratio of 80 percent and an 8 percent capital base. By the end of 1991, 15 percent of U.S. construction and development loans were noncurrent, three times higher than the average (U.S. FDIC 1991).

Measuring losses

Loss diagnosis involves four steps: analyzing the causes of bank losses, applying uniform accounting standards to measure these losses, assessing the condition of banks, and calculating the costs of restoring banks to capital adequacy or, alternatively, of liquidating them.

Box 2.1 Bank exposure to real estate

Since real estate (land and buildings) form the bulk of loan collateral, banks are particularly vulnerable to real estate price changes. In the United States about half of all loans from banks with holdings of less than $1 billion are collateralized by real estate; banks with assets of more than $1 billion have 35 percent of total loans secured by real estate. Declines in collateral value reduce bank profitability in two ways: an income effect, since the borrower may not be able to service debt, and a wealth effect, since the bank will have to provide for the shortfall between collateral value and estimated market value. Commercial property is particularly vulnerable to price fluctuations. All property loans have effective maturities of seven to ten years because average rental yields are low and property developers typically recover cash flow through property sales. Cyclical overbuilding, however, means that commercial property prices can fall by as much as 50 percent from peak to trough, as has occurred in Japan (1991–92), Malaysia (1984–86), and the United States (1989–92).

A bank with 35 percent exposure to real estate is rapidly decapitalized by a fall of 50 percent in collateral value over a three-year period. Assume that a bank lends 80 percent against estimated market value. If collateral value falls below the original loan principal by 10 percent in each consecutive year, a bank with an initial 8 percent capital-asset ratio would fall below the 2 percent level by the third year.

An important step in the diagnostic process is to improve bank accounting and auditing standards—especially loan classification and interest accrual standards—so that the degree of bank distress can be measured uniformly in all areas. Although there is no set of international standards for loan classification, two sets of criteria determine loan performance: the lag in servicing of loans and the profitability or performance of borrowers.

In most cases a loan is nonperforming if it has not been serviced in 90 to 180 days. Income on nonperforming loans should not be tallied in the profit and loss account, and realistic provisioning should be made against the likelihood of losses in the recovery of debt. In many countries markets for valuing loan collateral such as plants and equipment are absent. Prior to the establishment of special banking tribunals, courts in Pakistan took as long as ten years to deliver a judgment on debt recovery. Banks are also reluctant to make provisions where these are not tax-deductible against profits. Accordingly, the extent of nonperforming loans in many developing countries is grossly understated because of the lack of uniform, enforced accounting standards, and hence bank profits are overstated.

Even where reasonable accounting standards apply, banks generally have found ways to disguise the reporting of nonperforming loans. De Juan (1991) found that the most problematic loans in classification schemes are those that are reported as "current." Many banks in developing countries operate overdraft loans, which are recallable on demand. These cash loans, or even short-term loans, are in effect long-term loans, since they are almost always rolled over, often with the interest capitalized.

Depending on the financial reputation of the borrower, some banks provide such loans on an unsecured basis. In Colombia, when the Superintendency of Banks limited the exposure of banks to their related group of companies, some banks channelled funds to specially created subsidiaries in Panama that lent the money back to the related companies in Colombia (chapter 6). In other cases banks simply rescheduled or rolled over debt, providing fresh loans to service interest. In some developing countries banks have been known to exchange their bad debts with one another and to treat these as new loans, thus delaying the requirement of reporting nonperforming loans to the central bank.

The World Bank has published a set of guidelines for bank supervision that provide minimum standards of best practice for developing countries in loan classification and income accrual, accounting for debt rescheduling, credit concentration, and accounting disclosure along generally accepted accounting principles (World Bank 1993).

Causes of Losses

The causes of bank losses are as important as their value. A 1988 study by the U.S. Comptroller of the Currency found that U.S. bank failures could be attributed mainly to poor asset quality (found in 98 percent of cases) and poor management (90 percent). A weak economic environment was a factor in 35 percent of U.S. failures, and fraud was an issue in only 11 percent. In developing countries the economic environment may play a larger role—but probably not more than, say, 50 percent. In many financial crises—including severe decade-long cases (as in Argentina)—private banks with good management survived, indicating that bank losses are not inevitable and can be avoided through good risk management and adequate capital.

Banks incur losses as a result of bad debt, operational losses, speculation, inefficiencies, excessive taxes or regulation, and fraud. Thus bank losses reflect significantly the impact of changes in relative prices (asset prices, tax rates, interest and exchange rates) on a bank's operations and balance sheet. When such flow and stock losses exceed the bank's total capital and reserves, bank insolvency occurs. While losses can often be controlled or minimized with quality management, some changes in relative prices, such as taxes and exchange rate or interest rate controls, are outside a bank's control. Studies of the causes of bank insolvencies therefore must consider the behavior of bank management, borrowers, depositors, and policymakers in response to external shocks, policy changes, and sectoral imbalances.

Assessing a bank's standing requires setting objective standards of measurement, obtaining independent verification of bank operations (through auditors or supervisors), and providing full disclosure of results to all parties involved in bank restructuring: depositors, shareholders, bank employees, management, and supervisory authorities. The full extent of stock losses (historic losses at a point of time) and potential flow losses (estimated future performance if restructuring fails), as well as the implications of loss distribution, should be transparent to all parties, since perceptions of inequitable distribution of gains or losses, based on imperfect information, can sabotage any restructuring effort.

During the 1980s severe bank losses appeared in both industrial (Norway, Spain, the United States) and developing countries for a variety of reasons.

Credit losses

Bank losses cannot be attributed solely to external shocks. India, Kenya, and Pakistan all enjoyed several decades of uninterrupted growth, but each country's banking system has suffered problem loans for a variety of microeconomic and macroeconomic reasons. In India and Pakistan the credit allocation policies of state-owned banks played an important role. Banks were expected to maintain a large number of loss-making branches, particularly in rural areas, and to lend at below-market rates for economic and social welfare purposes. Such policy-based lending has been

responsible for a significant volume of loan losses. Banks made loans according to policy directives and were lax in their credit evaluation because they believed that the state would underwrite the loans. In Kenya several small banks and finance companies failed because of excessively liberal licensing policies in the early 1980s—policies that were intended to improve indigenous ownership in the finance sector. Weak management skills and fraud, complicated by the ownership of banks by political factions, led to the failure of several smaller institutions. These institutions were subsequently consolidated under the supervision of the central bank. A deposit insurance fund protected depositors from losses. In the aftermath of political change in Kenya in the early 1990s, several loss-making banks were closed.

Commodity shocks

Market-based banking systems with reasonable supervision standards in economies that depend on commodities—such as Malaysia (chapter 7), Norway, and Texas in the United States (chapter 4)—also suffered severely in the wake of the collapse of oil and gas prices in 1984–85. In the decade before the collapse, banks in these areas enjoyed high profits as business boomed. The boom created a bubble in real estate and other asset markets as speculation in property and shares surged, financed by banks in pursuit of higher profits. The asset bubble burst as commodity prices turned downward and inflation fell. The real value of debt increased relative to collateral assets, thus creating a spate of enterprise defaults. Governments in all three areas intervened through the central bank or a state deposit insurance fund.

Inherited portfolios

A number of banks created in the reform of banking systems in formerly socialist economies—such as the Czech and Slovak Republics, Hungary, and Poland—inherited large portfolios of nonperforming loans to state-owned enterprises. Since state-owned banks had no credit risks under a centrally planned economy, many of these enterprises were loss-making ventures. The quality of most of these loans remains highly suspect, but it has not been possible to estimate the losses accurately in the absence of stable prices. In 1990–91 many of these enterprises suffered trade shocks from the collapse of the trade arrangement through the Council of Mutual Economic Assistance, creating large loan losses for the banks.

Connected lending

Banks in Argentina, Chile, Colombia, and Spain suffered from a system in which banks were owned by large economic groups that also owned enterprises, with substantial bank lending to finance activities within the same group. The largest failure of such a group was the Rumasa group in Spain, which was nationalized in 1983 (chapter 5). Seventeen of the twenty Rumasa-owned banks had made loans of more than 73 percent of their total credit to related companies, which numbered more than 300 subsidiaries. Connected lending also brought about the failure of a small German bank, Schroder Munchmeyer, which was caught in excessive lending to its parent construction company in 1983.

Excessive regulatory taxes

Efforts by central banks to control inflation through noninterest-bearing statutory reserves or low-interest liquidity reserves reduce bank profitability and may eventually be passed on to depositors or borrowers through high spreads. In Argentina reserve requirements averaged 15.8 percent in 1987, and forced investments reached 50 percent of total deposits. In Yugoslavia regulatory costs in the form of statutory and liquidity reserves added nearly 20 percent to bank spreads in 1989. It has been estimated that financial sector taxation in selected Sub-Saharan African countries has averaged up to 10 percent of GNP (Chamely and Honohan 1990).

Excessive overhead

Developing country banks incur high administrative costs through overstaffing, excessive branching, and wasteful expenditures. Prior to restructuring, banks in Ghana incurred noninterest operating costs equivalent to 6 percent of total assets, compared with an average of 1 to 2 percent in OECD banks. These costs accounted for more than 75 percent of total interest income.

Interest rate mismatch

All banks suffer structurally from maturity mismatches in their portfolios. The U.S. savings and loan crisis was caused primarily by the maturity mismatch in the balance sheet of savings and loans, which invested in twenty-year or more fixed-rate mortgages but relied on short-term deposits at flexible rates. After short-term rates rose in 1980–81 the thrift industry had an estimated net insolvency of about $100 billion in 1982 (U.S. Treasury 1991).

Foreign exchange mismatch

The 1974 failure of Herstadtt Bank in Germany highlighted the dangers of mismatches in foreign currency positions. Inadequate management attention to such dangers could lead to large speculative losses, such as those reported by Bank Duta in Indonesia in 1990. Until 1989 in Poland and Yugoslavia, for example, banks took substantial amounts of foreign currency deposits from residents but surrendered these funds to their national banks. Since foreign exchange reserves were considerably smaller than external debt during most of the 1980s, these banking systems suffered large losses when the domestic currency was devalued.

Fraud

The more infamous cases of bank failures have been associated with fraud. Early cases of fraud such as Banco Ambrosiano (Italy, 1982), Johnson Matthey (United Kingdom, 1984), and BMF Hongkong (Malaysia, 1982) seem small compared with the spectacular closure of the U.K. Bank of Credit and Commerce International in 1991, where fraud and mismanagement may have caused losses of $5 billion to $10 billion out of total assets of $20 billion. In Guinea five state-owned banks—accounting for the bulk of the banking system's assets—were closed in 1985 when 78 percent of their assets were found to be fictitious (Tenconi 1989). Even in traditionally orderly markets such as Japan, cases of forged deposit certificates have caused large losses to the smaller trust banks.

Flawed liberalization policies

Many of the banking problems of the 1980s can be traced to poorly designed financial liberalization policies (Zahler 1993). Liberal entry rules and the expansion of new banks and deposit-taking institutions in the absence of adequate capital and managerial skills and sufficient supervision were responsible for failures in Argentina, Chile, Kenya, Spain, and Uruguay. Caprio, Atiyas, and Hanson (1993) found that the lifting of credit ceilings and deregulation of interest rates allowed banks to take excessive risks in areas where they had no prior experience, such as real estate. Sundararajan and Baliño (1991) conclude that the connection between financial reform and crises derives from an unstable macroeconomic environment, unsound liability structures of nonfinancial firms, and weaknesses in the institutional structure for banking.

Understanding the big picture

Thus banking problems have no single cause. Neither the monetary causes of banking crises according to the approach by Schwartz (1985) nor the business cycle models of Minsky (1977) and Kindleberger (1978) are fully explanatory. To blame solely management failure, policy mistakes, or a business cycle tendency to develop Ponzi-type bubbles would not suffice. A proper diagnosis calls for a thorough understanding of the policy and economic environment, the institutional framework, banking practices, the quality of bank supervision (if any), and the structure of incentives (box 2.2; Glaessner and Mas 1991).

Policymakers are becoming increasingly aware that perverse incentives can lead to bank failure if left unchecked. For example, recent evidence suggests that it was moral hazard—not simply bad luck or delayed closure—that led to the U.S. savings and loan crisis and increased its cost (Brewer and Monschean 1992). Excessive tax incentives to real estate, for example, generated a property bubble that led to oversupply and resulted in heavy real estate loan losses in U.S. banks. Delays in obtaining court orders to force debt repayment encouraged firms to default in times of tight liquidity. In some developing countries the total lack of enforcement of banking laws and regulations emboldened bank management to ignore laws and undertake speculative risks.

While there is consensus that adequate supervision and enforcement are required to maintain stability in a financial system, even the most sophisticated bank supervisors in advanced OECD countries have not been able to prevent bank failures completely. Bank supervision is thus a necessary but insufficient condition for bank stability. Supervisory authorities must pay greater attention to issues of sector and national imbalances that may destabilize the banking sector. Similarly, there is a need for overall national risk management (Sheng and Cho 1993).

Assessing Problem Banks

Once uniform accounting standards and the causes of losses are agreed on, the actual assessment of bank solvency takes place. Bank examiners in the United States use a uniform CAMEL rating system, which assesses *c*apital adequacy, *a*sset quality, *m*anagement, *e*arnings, and *l*iquidity (see chapter 3). In the absence of bank examiners, some bank supervisors use external auditors for an independent review of the financial condition of banks. In World Bank operations in the financial sector, special portfolio audits have been commissioned using international auditors under carefully designed terms of reference (box 2.3). Such audits should provide the bank

---

Box 2.2 Assessing the risk of bank failure

A review of the policy and institutional environment in which banks operate is a good start for the diagnostic process.

Policy environment
- Is there significant financial repression?
- Does the state own a large stake in the financial sector?
- Is there liberal entry into the financial sector?
- Is there a nonbank financial sector that is growing rapidly without supervision?
- Are credit allocation and forced lending policies hurting banks' autonomy in credit decisions?
- Are banks being taxed considerably higher than nonbanks?
- Are banks substantially owned by large enterprise groups?

Institutional environment
- Are the legal framework and judicial processes conducive to enforcement of debt recovery?
- Do domestic accounting and auditing standards meet internationally accepted accounting standards?
- Is information on credit and borrower performance available and transparent?
- Is there good bank supervisory capacity?
- Do supervisory authorities fully understand the problems facing the banking system?
- Is sufficiently trained bank management staff in place, for example, in foreign branches?
- Do bankers have a good understanding of the costs of intermediation and the sources of their profits and losses?

Box 2.3 Special audits

Terms of reference for special audits of banks should include:

Accounting diagnosis
- Assessment of the bank's portfolio under agreed uniform accounting standards and loan classification methodologies.
- Assessment of the bank's credit process, including the quality of information used in loan classification and estimation of provisioning.
- Evaluation of adequacy of provisioning.
- Analysis of profit and loss accounts, including cost of intermediation.
- Analysis of reliability of reported earnings and operating expenditures.
- Evaluation of credit concentration to largest borrowers and the extent of connected lending.
- Evaluation of contingent liabilities such as lawsuits, unfunded pension liabilities, guarantees, and exposure to futures and options.
- Restatement of the accounts (balance sheet as well as profit and loss accounts), including adequate provisioning for all known losses or adjustments on assets and liabilities, as well as off-balance items.
- Solvency assessment, including exposure to interest

rate, exchange rate, and maturity mismatches.
- Compliance with regulations, especially for capital adequacy.
- Review of internal controls and potential exposure to fraud.

Institutional diagnosis
- Review of bank's strategic plan to operate safely and efficiently in a competitive environment.
- An audit of the adequacy of management systems and staffing and training policies.
- Review of organizational responsiveness to operational and strategic needs.
- Assessment of credit policies and procedures.
- Assessment of treasury operations (asset and liability management capacity, including management of liquidity, interest rate, and exchange rate risks).
- Review of the management information system (ability to obtain reliable and timely accounting and strategic information for sound decisionmaking).
- Review of the efficiency and reliability of operational procedures, including computer systems.
- Review of the internal audit function.
- Role of board of directors in monitoring and supervising management performance.

---

supervisor with sufficient information to assess the basic causes of bank losses, a realistic (and independent) assessment of the size of losses, and suggested remedies.

Recent experience with portfolio audits in Central and Eastern Europe, where there has been great volatility in prices and policies, suggests that measurement of the extent of losses is still subject to significant variation. This is because the accounts of enterprises (the banks' main clients) are not yet maintained according to generally accepted accounting principles and auditing standards that conform to European Union requirements. Even where these standards have been attempted, international auditors have been unable to impose inflation accounting. As a result accounting information is quickly outdated under conditions of high inflation. A comprehensive audit, followed by regular and quick portfolio reviews, is required to establish the trend of losses in banks operating in such environments.

Since using external auditors can be costly, some countries have built up their own capacity for off-site surveillance and on-site examination. Such teams provide another assessment of banks' solvency, which may be grossly underestimated by bank management or even external auditors.

Loss Recognition and Allocation

An important watershed in the bank restructuring process is loss recognition, the point at which policymakers become convinced of the need to act despite the enormous challenges involved. This usually occurs when it becomes apparent that failing to act would not only jeopardize confidence in the banking system, it would also destabilize the macroeconomic environment. This stage cannot be reached until a sound assessment of past losses in the financial system has been completed, as well as a projection of future losses if the problems are not addressed.

As discussed in chapter 1, bank losses should never be underestimated. Underestimating the size of losses creates credibility problems later with the public and policymakers, and insufficient resources—financial or human—may be allocated to deal with the problem. Time and again, delays in recognizing failure and taking action have escalated the cost of failure resolution. For example, bank losses in Norway first surfaced in 1987, when eight commercial banks and seven savings banks began reporting losses. The banking system as a whole reported negative profits in 1988 (Solheim 1990). The banks initially relied on bank-funded commercial banks' and savings banks' guarantee funds, but by 1991 the funds were insufficient to deal with the widespread problems. The Norwegian government ultimately had to create a Government Bank Insurance Fund to deal with the problem (box 2.4).

Once bank losses have been recognized, they must be allocated. But who should bear the losses? Not necessarily the holders of bank obligations. Conventional thinking assumes that banking losses should be borne, in broad descending order, by borrowers, shareholders, fellow bankers, employees (in situations of liquidation), government, and depositors. The failure of banks is like market failure. By not allowing banks to collapse, and hence effectively passing the losses on to all holders of the failed banks' liabilities, there may be no equitable or fair method of allocating such losses. Loss allocation decisions generally have been made on the basis of the existing legal framework and the current conditions of political economy. Because most governments do not feel that depositors should lose, the least painful political option is for the government to bear the losses. But is this solution fiscally sustainable? Moreover, will a government bailout create problems of moral hazard? Each of the potential bearers of bank losses plays a role in determining the optimal form of bank restructuring.

Borrowers

Defaulting borrowers pay in terms of the liquidation of their collateral. If banks have difficulty collecting from bad creditors, they may pass the loss on to other borrowers by raising lending rates. Losses allocated too heavily to borrowers through high lending rates and rapid debt collection may cause even good borrowers to default, leading to a credit crunch that may retard growth and recovery. Even good borrowers have incentives to default if a government bailout

is likely—"when most everyone (who counts) is bankrupt, nobody is!" (Diaz-Alejandro 1985). Indiscriminate bailout of bad borrowers also may induce good borrowers to delay debt repayment, thus imposing higher bailout costs. And borrowers may have no incentive to repay if repayments can be delayed due to inefficient court enforcement of bankruptcy or debt recovery.

Shareholders

If losses are met by shareholder deposits of new capital or bank liquidation, shareholders would lose their wealth. But shareholders with political clout may not lose their shares if they induce a government bailout. In Colombia the central bank's injection of additional equity into the rescue of a bank preserved the shareholders' shares, although the shareholders lost controlling interest. In Sri Lanka shareholders were effectively protected from loss when the central bank injected liquidity into loss-making finance companies without requiring a reduction in capital. Before laws were changed in Malaysia and Thailand, initial bank restructuring efforts imposed only partial losses on shareholders. In Thailand finance company shareholders surrendered only 25 percent of their shares to the Ministry of Finance in return for lifeboat support, while in Malaysia central bank injections of capital into three commercial banks absorbed equivalent losses, protecting existing shareholders. Both countries subsequently required full capital reduction of losses before government assistance was made available.

Because of the principle that share capital should be at risk, it is now standard practice that bank losses should be written off against existing share capital and reserves before governments intervene. Where reduction of capital is governed by corporate law,

---

Box 2.4 Norway: An institutional solution

Norwegian commercial and savings banks' cumulative losses on loans and guarantees during 1987–90 amounted to NOK 35 billion. This followed six years of operating losses, attributable to falling property values, extensive business failures, and economic recession. These losses eroded the banks' two lines of defense, their own capital and the bank industry–financed guarantee funds. To strengthen bank safety the government created the Government Bank Insurance Fund (GBIF) with a capital of NOK 5 billion to provide support loans or to

directly acquire shares in banks. Between 1991 and 1992 the fund provided support loans and preference capital amounting to more than NOK 16.7 billion to six financial institutions, including three of the largest banks in the country. The fund generally injected capital into the banks to meet their statutory capital requirements, subject to agreement by the banks to improve their operating efficiency and return to sound banking.

Source: GBIF 1992.

however, that procedure may be extremely cumbersome and impractical—a bank supervisor's application to a court for reduction of capital would trigger an irreparable bank run. Accordingly, banking laws such as Spain's allow deposit guarantee funds to write off losses against existing capital before any investment in capital by the fund.

Other bankers

Industrywide cooperation in rescuing a single failing institution is now common practice. This may take the form of a larger, stronger bank taking over a weaker institution, either voluntarily or with some incentives provided by the central bank (such as a soft loan). Alternatively, the costs of liquidating a small bank can be distributed among the other, healthy banks. The issue of persuading other bankers to absorb losses of failed banks is an open one. In Europe and the United States policymakers have moved toward greater concentration in banking by providing incentives to profitable and well-managed banks to absorb smaller, failed banks. In the United States concentration of problem banks was encouraged through "phoenixes," "bridge banks," or management consignments. This process may work where banks still have a "franchise" value due to limited licensing, protection from competition, or valuable branches or networks, but liberalized entry policies in a number of countries are making the process less appealing. In the past large Japanese banks helped absorb weaker, smaller banks. There is now resistance to such moral suasion.

The technique of strong banks absorbing weak banks works in the exceptional failure or two, and where the rest of the banking system is reasonably strong and profitable. Where losses are larger and more widespread, the stronger banks often refuse to help because of the danger of contagion. There is potential for disaster when weak, state-owned banks take over failing private banks, as demonstrated by the Consolidated Bank of Kenya, which later ran into substantial difficulties.

Employees

Bank unions are generally among the strongest unions in a country and have a significant say in the resolution of failed banks. Making failed institutions more efficient often involves large staff cutbacks. In

the case of state-owned banks, employee action has delayed the process of privatization. The Argentine banking system has a labor force of 145,000, three times that of Malaysia with only twice that country's GDP. Restructuring state-owned Argentine banks became difficult because bank employees became a powerful lobby against the closure of banks, inflicting further losses on the budget.

Depositors

A common technique to keep weaker institutions solvent is to lower deposit rates while maintaining high lending rates. Where no explicit deposit insurance scheme exists, depositors may be willing to bear some losses, such as lower deposit rates, so long as the return of their principal is assured. Some countries have used the inflation tax to pass on losses to depositors, particularly through negative real interest rates on deposits. Deposit insurance schemes protect only the nominal value of deposits, not their real value.

Some depositors in low-inflation economies have borne losses where there has been no explicit deposit insurance scheme. When Thai finance companies failed in the early 1980s, authorities agreed to repay depositors only the deposit principal, without interest, over ten years, in installments of 10 percent a year. With average inflation of 5 percent a year, depositors bore real losses of about 50 percent. When deposit-taking cooperatives failed in Malaysia, the authorities agreed to repay the principal, 50 percent in cash over two to three years at a positive (but low) interest rate and 50 percent in equity or convertible bond in a licensed finance company that absorbed the assets of the failed cooperatives and whose shares were to be sold publicly (chapter 7). When the company was sold to a successful, publicly listed company in exchange for shares in 1991, some depositors ended up gaining from the exercise.

External creditors

Some losses can be passed on to the external sector if foreign creditors are willing to absorb some of the losses on their foreign currency loans to the country in which the failed banks reside. An innovative technique for recapitalizing rural banks using the discount value of the Philippine government's debt in the secondary market is described in box 2.5.

Box 2.5 Debt-equity swaps in bank restructuring

Some countries with external debt at discounts to their par value can use the discounts to recapitalize banks. Commercial banks in Ecuador, for example, bought the nation's foreign debt from the secondary market at a discount in U.S. dollars and sold these bonds to the central bank, which bought them in domestic currency at full face value. The commercial banks used the profits between the discount and the face value to recapitalize themselves.

A variation of this approach was used in the Philippines to recapitalize the rural banks, which owed substantial sums to the central bank. The Land Bank of the Philippines bought restructured seventeen-year U.S.

dollar promissory notes of the Philippine government at a discount from foreign noteholders. These were sold to the central bank at 100 percent par value, in pesos plus interest, subject to the Land Bank's participation in the Rural Bank Capital Enhancement Program. Under the program a rural bank places new capital funds with the Land Bank, and the Land Bank issues the rural bank a seven-year promissory note for double the funds received as capital injection. The rural bank then uses the Land Bank promissory note to liquidate debt to the central bank. The system essentially uses the discount "profit" to recapitalize rural banks and settle their debts to the central bank.

Government

Governments intervene in bank failures directly and indirectly through central bank assistance, guarantees of bank deposits, and tax writeoffs for bad loans. What share of bank failure losses should be borne by the public sector? Should the losses be absorbed by the treasury or by the central bank? In theory, the central bank is a part of the public sector, and there should be no difference between treasury and central bank financing of the losses. In practice, the source of financing can be critical in bank restructuring schemes, with the choice depending on the solvency of the central bank and the size of its foreign exchange reserves.

A traditional central bank—one with only noninterest-bearing monetary liabilities, high capital, and reserves represented mainly by foreign exchange assets—should have few problems absorbing bank failure losses. The stock of public sector savings (in the form of the net worth of the central bank) is reduced by the losses absorbed. Since the central bank can always earn seigniorage on its currency liabilities, it can absorb large bank losses. The central bank may, however, lose foreign exchange reserves—in the form of capital flight—if it issues reserve money to rescue banks. The losses from the failure of some small banks in Hong Kong in the early 1980s were absorbed against the reserves of the Exchange Fund.

For solvent central banks or currency boards with large reserves, bank losses can be absorbed with few monetary effects. Indeed, a central bank with large foreign exchange reserves and no external debt gains from a devaluation when large revaluation surpluses are created. These surpluses can be used to absorb the losses from banking failures.

On the other hand, central banks that have been weakened by excessive lending to the public sector, with large interest-bearing liabilities and net foreign exchange liabilities, do not have the capacity to absorb bank failure losses. These central banks run the risk of monetizing the losses through the growth of their monetary liabilities, generating an inflationary pressure that distributes the losses to the holders of currency and central bank liabilities. Large quasi-fiscal deficits incurred by monetary authorities were major causes of hyperinflation in Yugoslavia and Argentina (chapters 9 and 11).

Experience suggests that, where central banks do not have the capital and reserves to absorb bank failure losses, the treasury should absorb the losses. The treasury can finance bank failure losses by raising taxes, cutting spending, using the inflation tax, selling its real or financial assets, or borrowing (long-term) domestically or abroad. In all cases bank failure losses are passed on either to taxpayers or to the holders of public debt, including currencyholders.

Despite the range of possibilities in loss allocation, most governments choose the most politically palatable course, that of bearing the losses in the public sector through the central bank, a deposit insurance fund, or directly in the budget. One of the least successful methods, with a total lack of transparency, is to use the deposits of state enterprises to bail out weak banks or finance companies, as happened in Kenya during the 1980s. This approach hid the scale of losses in the banks and financially weakened the state enterprises.

As long as the state provides implicit or explicit deposit insurance for the banking system, bank losses greater than available bank capital are equivalent to an internal debt of the government that is being financed by short-term bank deposits. Accordingly, the capacity of the state to deal with bank losses depends on its debt capacity, the domestic growth rate, and the real interest rate paid on state debt. Governments in strong fiscal positions, with low debt or strong borrowing capacity and favorable access to foreign or domestic capital markets, may be able to finance bank losses by swapping the bad debts in the banks with government bonds. As long as they are able to borrow without significantly raising domestic real interest rates, crowding out the private sector, or disturbing monetary stability, the state will be able to transfer most of the burden of bank losses to the future. The losses are written off over time, with the burden borne largely by taxpayers. The dynamics of government debt and bank losses are examined in box 2.6.

On the other hand, governments that are already saddled with high fiscal deficits and that are paying high real interest rates may not have the capacity to deal with bank losses except through some form of inflation tax. These losses are spread through the economy on financial assetholders and often create distortionary resource allocation effects—which worsen the macroeconomic environment.

Rewriting the National Balance Sheet and Incentives Structure

As mentioned earlier, any effort by the state to address systemic bank losses must include a rewriting of the national balance sheet and incentives structure. Authorities have to decide where losses should be allocated and whether these losses should be allocated to a one-time *stock* adjustment or to a gradual adjustment over time through *flow* changes. Both techniques affect the net solvency of different sectors, with significant implications for the incentives structure in the economy.

This effect is best illustrated by reviewing sector and national financial balances (see chapter 1). For example, if total bank credit amounts to 20 percent of GDP and losses amount to 15 percent of total credit, then recapitalization of the banks would require resources equivalent to 3 percent of GDP. If the government decides to absorb bank losses through a bond-bad debt swap (sometimes called a carve-out), then the government would have to issue bonds equivalent to 3 percent of GDP to shift the losses from the banking sector to the government sector. If domestic interest rates are 10 percent a year, the additional cost to the budget is 0.3 percent of

---

Box 2.6 The fiscal impact of bank losses

Since bank losses are quasi-fiscal deficits, the cumulative losses in the banking system are equivalent to an internal debt of the state. The long-term consequences of running such internal debt can be projected using the following equation: the change in the government debt to GNP ratio (d) is equal to the primary (or noninterest) deficit of the public sector, less what is financed by seigniorage, plus the current debt ratio (d) times the average real interest rate on the debt minus the growth rate of GNP:

$$\text{Change in } d = (\text{primary deficit/GNP}) - (\text{seigniorage/GNP}) + d (\text{real interest rate} - \text{growth rate})$$

The quasi-fiscal deficit due to bank losses tends to increase the primary deficit. To the extent that the central bank is already financing bank losses through liquidity creation, the revenue that can be obtained from seigniorage is correspondingly reduced. The change in the overall debt ratio d will increase with the primary deficit or if the real interest rate exceeds the domestic growth rate. On the other hand, d will decline with inflation or high GNP growth.

The equation above helps explain the varying success of bank restructuring programs. In countries with rela-

tively low inflation, high growth, and low fiscal deficits or small surpluses, d may be declining over time. This category includes Malaysia, Spain, and Chile after the macroeconomic stabilization program.

On the other hand, countries with large primary deficits and excessive real interest rates allow their debt ratios to become unsustainably large, so much so that the debt can only be reduced through higher and higher inflation. This category includes Argentina, Chile in the early 1980s, and Yugoslavia. The growth of the domestic debt also rose sharply because of excessive real interest rates, ranging as high as 40 percent a year.

How d will perform depends on whether bank losses continues to flow or converge toward zero, provided the bank restructuring exercise has stemmed all future losses. Carve-outs have not worked well in many Eastern European economies in transition because the problem stems from the continuing flow of enterprise losses. As long as the real sector is still suffering from economic losses, lending to such enterprises will ultimately show up as bank or quasi-fiscal losses.

Source: Fischer and Easterly 1990.

GDP. Assuming that the government has a small fiscal deficit of, say, not more than 2 percent of GDP, such additional costs may be fiscally sustainable with no major monetary implications. There is no net impact on the domestic economy's solvency since the transaction has no foreign exchange implications.

If, however, the public sector has a large fiscal deficit of, say, 8 percent of GDP, and inflation is running at 30 percent a year, then the total fiscal deficit would be worsened by the additional debt-servicing costs of 0.9 percent of GDP (30 percent times 3 percent new bonds for the carve-out). At that point the government may be faced with the combined problems of a declining tax base (due to the losses of state-owned enterprises and consequent losses of banks, plus rising unemployment) as well as capital flight (by wealthholders concerned with higher taxation).

Thus different solutions involve some form of rewriting of the national and sectoral balance sheets and, by implication, the incentives structure. Carve-outs may recapitalize the banking system by shifting the burden to the state, but they also may create moral hazard incentives that worsen future banking losses. Moreover, without parallel reforms in the real sector, banks may continue to incur losses so long as they continue lending to the enterprise sector. Thus bank restructuring often must be accompanied by changes in the real sector and in the incentives structure. It is futile to engage in paper transactions that appear to address bank solvency but that do not address the fundamental causes of the losses.

Sustainable bank restructuring requires that the national balance sheet and incentives structure be rewritten so that the economy moves toward an open, competitive, and stable financial structure. Different countries have rewritten the national balance sheet and incentives structure in different ways. Bank restructuring works where concomitant measures have been taken to reform the real sector, accompanied by major changes in the fiscal and policy environment.

Liquidate or restructure?

A first key policy decision is whether a market-based solution or government intervention should be adopted (box 2.7). Market-based solutions are generally the most efficient, with least cost to taxpayers. For example, a natural market solution to a failed bank is liquidation without any protection for the depositors. This presumes that depositors were aware of and willing to absorb the risk of bank failure. In many countries deposit protection is afforded through a small deposit insurance scheme that helps small depositors but presumes that large depositors can take care of themselves.

Liquidation was the approach used in the case of the United Kingdom's Bank of Credit and Commerce International (BCCI) in 1991, when extensive fraud was uncovered. The bank was liquidated after negotiations for additional capital injection to recapitalize the bank failed. It was left to the liquidator of the bank to recover and distribute any remaining assets according to the law. If the process is applied according to the law, the depositors of the failed bank will suffer losses beyond any deposit coverage they had under the British deposit guarantee scheme.

Another option, particularly successful where the number of failed banks is small and there is "franchise" value, is to sell or merge the ailing banks, without government assistance, to other banks, including foreign banks or new entrants to the banking sector. This method was adopted in Spain and Thailand, where the capital was reduced to the extent of the losses and the bank was recapitalized by offering the shares to new shareholders (Sundaravej and Trairatvorakul 1989). In the Spanish case some of the larger banks that gained market share by absorbing smaller problem banks later got into trouble (chapter 5).

If private buyers cannot be found for a failed bank, experience indicates that liquidations are generally cheaper than keeping insolvent banks open. But in some African banking systems with dominant state-owned banks, such as in Ethiopia, Tanzania, and Uganda, loss-making banks have been kept open because they are the only payments mechanism and major savings mobilization systems in the country.

Box 2.7 Restructuring mechanisms

Market-based solutions
- Shareholder capital injection
- Sale or merger
- Privatization
- Liquidation without deposit compensation

Government intervention
- Nationalization
- Liquidation with deposit insurance
- Asset recovery trust
- Bank "hospitals"
- Supply-side solutions
- Forced conversion into bonds

Bank supervisors in a number of countries hesitate to liquidate banks because of either the "too big to fail" principle or because of the possible contagion implications. But the real fear is perhaps "too big to liquidate," where the costs of liquidation—in terms of economic disruption, political backlash, and failure of the payments system—would be too large. Such hesitation creates perverse incentives—liberal entry into banking without exit results in moral hazard behavior. The experience of the 1980s suggests that as the costs of bank rescues rose, more bank supervisors were willing to take the bold step of liquidation in order to break the moral hazard trap.

Market-based solutions cannot succeed, however, where the problems stem from market failure itself. As indicated earlier, such failures could have many causes, including restrictive practices, bad macroeconomic policies, and inadequate supervision. Once liquidation has been ruled out, government intervention becomes the next logical step.

Government intervention in the financial sector

Although market-based solutions were tried in most of the countries studied, government intervention in bank restructuring occurred in all eight. There are good reasons for government intervention in bank restructuring. First, unlike enterprise failure, bank failure involves thousands of deposit and loan contracts, which involve extremely high transaction costs through the normal process of liquidation or court resolution.

Second, since banks are both the custodians of private savings and operators of the payments system, bank failures carry the systemic risk of causing economic disruption and loss of confidence in the system itself. The externalities of bank failures are very large.

Third, the fact that banks are closely regulated compared with enterprises gives depositors an implicit (and sometimes explicit) public guarantee that the government will safeguard the value of deposits. Consequently, despite awareness of the dangers of moral hazard in the "too big to fail" doctrine, governments have intervened in almost all known cases of problem banks. Even after Chile's period of doctrinaire free-market policies (1974–80), for example, when the banking crisis emerged in 1981 the government not only gave an explicit guarantee on all bank deposits, it also assumed or guaranteed all private sector external debt to preserve international

credibility. In almost all the cases examined, the government (including the central bank) absorbed the bulk of bank losses in order to protect the depositors.

One of the two most drastic forms of state intervention is nationalization. Nationalization of banks was undertaken in the 1980s by Costa Rica, El Salvador, and Mexico. In Mexico the banks were nationalized in 1982 for populist reasons rather than for reasons of national exigency. Nationalization internalizes the losses of the banking sector into public sector debt, thus removing any doubt about the safety of private sector deposits in the banking system. Even though Mexico shared the same debt crisis as other heavily indebted countries, it avoided a crisis of bank runs (although not capital flight) because of the nationalization. The cost of avoidance of bank runs was inefficient credit allocation by state-owned banks. It was mainly to promote the more efficient allocation of resources that Mexican banks were privatized in 1990–91 (Barnes 1992).

Another drastic solution is hyperinflation followed by currency reform. Conceptually, hyperinflation erodes the real value of the bank debt of the enterprise and public sectors by passing all losses on to the depositors. Proponents of this strategy often cite post–World War II German hyperinflation, after which a successful currency reform placed the economy on a strong path of growth and recovery.

The hyperinflation approach was tried in the 1980s in Argentina, Poland, and Yugoslavia—although in each case it was the consequence of a number of factors, not a deliberate act of policy—and in each case it failed because the structural problems within each economy were not corrected (chapters 9 and 11). In all three cases hyperinflation was unable to erode external debt and only increased disintermediation from the banking system. In Poland and Yugoslavia, where a significant share of deposits with domestic banks were denominated in foreign currency, hyperinflation and the accompanying devaluation worsened the internal debt obligations of the governments because banks carried an implicit or explicit state guarantee on these deposits. The governments ended up owing large sums denominated in foreign currency to their own residents.

In the absence of inflation accounting, inappropriate decisions can be made based on distorted information. For example, in the immediate post-inflation period (1990) Polish banks and enterprises reported exceptionally high profits, derived from the sale of inventory—without adjusting for replacement costs—

and a sharp cut in real wages. The government also temporarily enjoyed a budgetary surplus because of a higher tax on the inflation profits of enterprises. But enterprise losses reemerged quickly after 1990 because state-owned enterprises did not restructure to internationally competitive levels, real wages increased, and lost inventory had to be replaced.

Thus a stock-flow–consistent framework suggests that even temporary erosion of the debt of the deficit sectors (the enterprise and public sectors) at the expense of the surplus (household) sector will not work. Structural adjustments to the asset side of the national balance sheet, that is, changes in the real sector, must accompany bank restructuring. Bank failures arise from structural imbalances in the real sector—such as large fiscal deficits or enterprise losses—and until these are addressed, financial restructuring alone will bring only temporary relief.

The lessons of the Argentine case are important (chapter 11). Argentina started and ended the 1980s with banking crises. The primary cause of the early 1980s crisis was financial liberalization in an era of lax fiscal discipline, overborrowing, and inadequate bank supervision. These failings were also common to neighboring economies, such as Chile and Uruguay. With the cutoff of external credit—due mainly to the debt crisis but also to the government's inability to bring its fiscal deficit under control—the economy reeled into hyperinflation in 1989. Since the state had reached the limits of its debt capacity, the only way to reduce its interest and debt burden was to force the conversion of commercial bank time deposits into cash (up to the equivalent of $500) and dollar-denominated ten-year bonds with two years' grace called Bonex. This unilateral writedown of public debt to the private sector was a major blow to the financial system, but it gave breathing space to the public sector to carry out other real sector reforms that gradually restored economic growth in 1991 and 1992. Brazil also was forced to adopt this drastic solution in 1990.

Sequencing of action

Bank restructuring cannot be undertaken independent of real sector (or enterprise) restructuring. Financial reforms made well in advance of real sector liberalization could lead to subsequent reversals as recapitalized banks continue to make loans to loss-making enterprises. The debate remains open, however, on whether the state should first deal with the enterprise-borrower problem (the supply-side solution) or with the banking problem.

If the state assists the enterprise-borrower sector first by directly injecting funds to restore the capital base of borrowers, then the bad debts of the banking system are correspondingly reduced by the amount of state aid. But state assistance to the banking system does not automatically mean that there will be a "pass-through" effect, in which the banks pass-through their state aid in the form of debt rescheduling, reduction, or writeoffs. Recent cases of bank restructuring, particularly in Eastern Europe, suffer from the complaint by distressed borrowers that the state bailed out banks and depositors at the expense of the enterprise sector.

Sundararajan (1992) suggests the following sequencing for financial sector reforms:

- A minimal system of prudential regulation, including enforcement, and recapitalization of the banking system.
- Key monetary control reforms and support for changes in money markets.
- The speed of liberalization of interest rates and credit controls depends on the pace of fiscal and external policies in achieving overall macroeconomic balance.
- A wide range of central bank operational reforms, including policy research, foreign exchange market operations, prudential regulation, clearing and settlement systems, public debt management, and accounting and bank reporting systems.

While this sequence is appropriate for the financial sector, real sector reforms—particularly in the enterprise, trade, and fiscal areas—are much more difficult to achieve because of entrenched political and institutional interests. In the transition socialist economies with newly created parliamentary processes, needed changes in legislation and the political debate over privatization and equitable distribution of former state property often get entangled in a morass of debate that delays resolution.

The national balance sheet approach suggests the following:

- Rewriting the losses of the banking sector will involve distributing losses across almost all other sectors—enterprise, banking, government, and even external.
- Rewriting the national balance sheet has to be done in such a way that sector balance sheets are stable, sustainable, and credible—shifting large imbalances to a fiscally unsustainable public sector would only inflate macroeconomic imbalances.

- The national balance sheet can only be stable if changes to the balance sheet (that is, flows) follow the right incentive structure—toward sound risk management, competition, and efficiency.
- Resolving sector or national losses requires fresh resources, but not necessarily additional debt. Thus borrowing externally to settle domestic liabilities could worsen the national balance sheet if external resources leak out in the form of imports or capital flight.

Governments faced with difficult choices can opt for a Schumpeterian supply side–oriented approach to generate additional resources to deal with bank losses, or use Keynesian demand management to extract the resources to do so.

Supply-side solutions

In two cases governments with a historical inclination toward industrial policy and strong fiscal capacity chose supply-side solutions to deal with potential bank problems. In the case of the former German Democratic Republic, the German government avoided problems, first, by restricting entry into the banking sector with high capital and licensing standards (Meinecke 1991; Siebert, Schmieding, and Nunnenkamp 1992). No new banks were created in the five Eastern Landes, and thus Germany avoided the problem of failure of new entrants, which has been a common problem in the rest of Eastern and Central Europe.

Second, the authorities "cleaned up" the assets of the former state banks of eastern Germany by issuing "equalization claims" to these banks and selling the cleaned banks to the larger banks in western Germany. The debt of eastern state-owned enterprises were "cleaned" with "equalization claims" or guarantees issued by the Restructuring Agency, all of which are backed by the federal government. As a result of these initiatives the eastern banking system can function without the burden of past bad debts, and the risks against future bad debts are controlled by private banks operating under market rules, as defined by German law (Meinecke 1991).

In its August 1992 package the Japanese government went for measures aimed at fiscal stimulation (box 2.8). Other than some advanced purchase of land from the banks by local authorities and a proposal to create a quasi-official agency to buy land that would have been held by banks as collateral against nonperforming loans, the package focused on the supply side. In other words, if the burden of nonperforming loans was due to slow economic growth, then a stimulation package aimed at improving public infrastructure would generate sufficient growth and profits for the banks to clean out their portfolios. This approach hinges on the belief that there is little wrong with the structure of the banking system that correct incentives, improved supervision, and fiscal stimulation would not cure. The incentive structure is also supply side, since the fiscal measures reward efficient producers so that profits are generated in the

---

Box 2.8 Japan: A supply-side solution

The Japanese rescue package of August 1992 was a supply-side solution aimed at stimulating the economy to relieve banks of their nonperforming loan burden. The package involved a total of ¥10.7 trillion ($86 billion), comprising ¥ 8.6 trillion of public works spending (including ¥ 1 trillion of advance purchases of land by local governments) and ¥ 2.1 trillion of lending for small firms and private capital investments. The lending and investment portion was designed to assist small firms suffering from the credit crunch as banks restricted credit to prime customers. Funding for the program came from the Ministry of Finance's Trust Fund Bureau, which is funded largely from postal savings. The government also asked the public utilities to accelerate investments of ¥ 700 million and to add ¥ 1.1 trillion from public funds for investment in shares.

The Japanese banks have established an asset holding company along the line of the Japan Bankers Association Investment Inc., an offshore vehicle established in 1987 to buy developing country debt from Japanese banks. The Cooperative Credit Purchasing Company was established by 162 financial institutions with a capital of ¥ 7.9 billion to buy land from banks' collateral portfolio at book or below-market prices, thus allowing banks to obtain tax relief on the writeoff of nonperforming loans. By March 1993 the company had bought 229 nonperforming loans worth ¥ 681.7 billion at an average discount of 34 percent.

In December 1994 the Bank of Japan announced the creation of a special "rescue bank," using for the first time resources of the Bank of Japan to bail out two insolvent credit associations in Tokyo. Of the ¥ 40 billion capital of the rescue bank, half was provided by the Bank of Japan and half by private banks. The Deposit Insurance Agency will provide ¥ 40 billion to cover the losses of the failed institutions.

Source: Numachi 1993; Sasaki-Smith 1994.

system. The banks will still try to enforce financial discipline by weeding out the loss-makers and using their profits to write off the bad loans.

Flow and stock solutions

Government intervention in ailing banking systems involves one of two key approaches—flow or stock solutions (box 2.9). Depending on the degree of bank distress, intervention can involve a variety of these approaches, including a combination of flow and stock solutions.

Flow techniques. Flow solutions have worked quite well in most mild cases of banking distress. Where real sector problems are the result of a temporary shock and governance of banks, enterprises, and the civil administration are fairly effective, flow solutions can be useful. The most common flow technique is central bank liquidity support at subsidized rates. For example, the low interest rate regime in the United States from 1991–93 was largely responsible for recapitalizing the domestic banking system. Between 1991 and 1993 net interest income and writeback of provision for loan losses each accounted for about half of the factors contributing to the recovery of U.S. banks' earnings (Bank of Japan 1994).

Such techniques have high monetary costs because liquidity support for loss-making banks are expansionary in nature and counter the need for tight monetary policy, particularly when the economy is also undergoing a period of structural adjustment. On such occasions bank supervision responsibilities conflict with the central bank's own monetary policies. Some Latin American economies, such as Chile, have separated bank superintendency from the central bank to ensure that each objective is carried out independently and objectively.

The second most popular flow technique is to permit higher spreads, allowing the banks to pass the

loss burden on to either the borrowers (through higher lending rates) or the depositors (through lower deposit rates). Some countries try to protect borrowers by placing lending rate ceilings on loans, which forces the losses on the depositors. In 1980–81, when the Republic of Korea's heavy industrialization program stalled in the face of the international recession and large debt-servicing problems surfaced in the banking system, the authorities chose not to raise interest rates, which would have been the orthodox stabilization solution. Instead they lowered deposit and lending rates to negative real levels for two consecutive years in order to reduce the real burden of debt on Korean enterprises—and passed the losses on to the depositors. Korea was also able to impose a financial repression tax on depositors because of tight exchange controls. The negative effect was the retardation of financial deepening in Korea for a number of years, as well as the emergence of a large curb market, which had to be addressed separately.

In contrast, Chile was unable to impose a repression tax in the 1981 crisis because of an open capital account. In order to keep savings within the country, abnormally high real interest rates prevailed—averaging 46 percent a year in real terms during 1981–85—thus exacerbating the distress of borrowers. Similar conditions applied in Argentina and Yugoslavia. A repression tax would not have worked in Yugoslavia because of the foreign currency deposits in Yugoslav banking systems. Attempts to impose heavy financial repression taxes to pay for bank losses would have led to either disintermediation or capital flight.

Another flow solution is to deregulate banking to permit banks to engage in businesses outside their traditional avenues of income, in areas such as securities trading, investment banking, credit card and travel services, and even insurance. Deregulation is still proceeding in a number of countries, but in most cases deregulation should not be attempted without adequate supervision. There are high learning costs associated with new entrants into the banking business or diversification into new businesses. In Spain a large number of the new entrants into the banking industry in the late 1970s failed in the early 1980s. In the United States thrifts were allowed to diversify out of fixed-rate home mortgages into commercial and industrial loans, including commercial real estate, and many failed because of insufficient understanding of the risks associated with these loans. Community-based thrifts were taken over by new entrepreneurial groups that took more speculative

---

Box 2.9 Flow and stock solutions

Flow solutions
- Central bank liquidity support at subsidized rates
- Allow high spreads—use of inflation tax
- Regulatory and accounting forbearance
- Deregulation to allow new income sources

Stock solutions
- Carve out bad assets to central agency
- Capital injection by private or public sector
- Liquidation

risks under the umbrella of the nationwide deposit insurance scheme. In addition, supervision of these thrifts was relaxed in the early 1980s in the first flush of deregulation, resulting in greater exposure of the thrift industry to fraud, connected lending, and excessive risk.

Flow solutions work well in a market-based environment where the degree of economic insolvency is fairly small. The most promising environment for flow techniques is one where the capital adequacy of the problem bank is below statutory levels but is still positive, at between 0 and 2 percent of risk assets. Under such conditions, and assuming that bank spreads can be increased to the extent that banks have a good chance of regaining positive economic solvency within two or three years, flow solutions can work. But allowing spreads to widen runs the risk of increasing real lending rates to a level where even good borrowers begin to fail, or if the burden is passed on primarily to depositors in the form of lower negative deposit rates, there is a danger of systemic disintermediation. Worse, overall bank efficiency can suffer where high spreads are allowed, since the rent from high spreads can easily be consumed through higher operating costs instead of being used to charge off bad debts and build up capital.

Stock techniques. The stock solution involves three techniques that address the balance sheet and capital adequacy of the banks. If the problem bank is considered viable over the long run, then restructuring could involve a capital injection by either the public or private sector. If the bank is not considered viable, it should be liquidated, and depositors paid through the deposit insurance fund. The third technique, adopted in Chile, Ghana, and Spain, is to carve out the bad debts of banks in exchange for government

bonds or central bank liabilities. Alternatively, the bad assets can be retained in the books (with a government guarantee) and debt recovery becomes the responsibility of the banks.

There are two basic models for the carve-out approach: the U.S. Resolution Trust Corporation (RTC) and the Spanish Guarantee Fund. The RTC is essentially a liquidation arm of the federal deposit insurance system (chapter 4). It centralizes the disposal of assets of failed thrifts in a corporation run by the U.S. Federal Deposit Insurance Corporation (FDIC). Diagnosis, damage control, and discussions on the ailing banks are still the responsibility of the FDIC. Funding for the RTC is wholly an obligation of the U.S. government.

The Spanish Guarantee Fund acts as a bank "hospital," with the deposit insurance scheme serving as the vehicle for rehabilitation and liquidation (chapter 5). Before the fund steps in, all bank losses are applied against the existing paid-up capital according to the "accordion" principle, so that existing shareholders bear the first tranche of bank losses. Thus the balance sheet of the problem bank is collapsed (like an accordion) depending on the size of the losses. Funding was initially provided jointly by the Bank of Spain and the commercial banks, but later the main financial burden was absorbed by the central bank.

The carve-out technique has two structural models: debt workout by the banks and a total carve-out to a restructuring (debt collection) agency (box 2.10). Both techniques try to separate problem banks into "good bank-bad bank" components. Bad assets are concentrated into a "bad bank," with specialized staff to deal with the problems. The remaining assets are hived into a new institution—supported with

---

Box 2.10 Should carve-outs be handled by a centralized restructuring agency or left to the problem banks?

There is ongoing debate over the best model for asset and debt recovery: a decentralized debt workout by banks or transfer of bad debts to a centralized workout agency. Debt workout by banks assumes that the banks have sufficient skills and resources to deal with their problems. Although banks have the best information on the problems of their borrowers, they may not have the skills required to address these problems. Bank workouts work well with case-by-case resolutions that have little economywide impact. No changes in the law are required. This was the solution adopted in the Polish bank restructuring exercise.

The centralized asset recovery agency approach permits a consolidation of skills and resources in debt

restructuring and workout within one agency. Funding can be concentrated in one agency with state guarantee, such as the German Treuhandanstalt or the U.S. Resolution Trust Corporation. Laws may have to be changed, however, to allow transfer of debt rights to a state agency. This approach works well where large debt threatens normal operations of the banking system and centralization allows banks to concentrate on their normal banking business. A private sector variant of this is the Japanese Cooperative Credit Purchasing Company, established by Japanese banks to buy nonperforming loans from individual banks at market price.

adequate capital—so that the "good bank" can be revitalized and eventually sold to the private sector.

The appropriate technique depends on each country's institutional, legal, and market conditions. Both schemes work well where the legal framework is strong, where there is a large pool of bank professionals to staff the complex restructuring and liquidation work, and where the size of the problem is not systemic in nature. One of the most common complaints about centralized institutions is that they become administrative bottlenecks in the resolution of banking problems, particularly where asset transfers are embroiled in legal suits.

Stock solutions, particularly the carve-out, only buy time for problems in the real sector to be addressed, and hopefully correct the resource allocation and financial stability conditions that jeopardize other efforts at macroeconomic stabilization.[1] Stock solutions appear to be very straightforward, with a financial engineering exercise that cleans the banks at one stroke and transfers all the bad debts to the state. Successful carve-outs, however, have required extremely large budgetary resources. Both the U.S. RTC and the German Treuhandanstalt operate in well-established market economies, with strong liquidation and debt recovery laws and skilled bank turnaround specialists. Such budgetary and human resources are not available to many developing countries.

An insolvent institution cannot be rescued by another insolvent institution. Merging two weak institutions such that their combined capital is still negative is not a long-term solution. Similarly, a bad debt carve-out at the banking system level will not solve the problem if the central budget cannot mobilize sufficient resources to service the additional debt burden. Many developing country banking crises ultimately are a fiscal crisis. If the state can generate sufficient resources to pay for the losses of the banking system through additional taxes, spending cuts, or borrowing, then there is sufficient time for the state to tackle the root causes of bank losses—whether at the institutional level, within the banking system, or in the real sector. But if the fundamental problems stem from the fiscal imbalance itself, or if the state cannot mobilize sufficient tax resources to service the bank losses without resorting to inflationary financing, then the carve-out may itself become destabilizing. The public will not believe that the public sector has tackled the roots of the problem and may engage in capital flight, further exacerbating the problem of bank instability.

The fiscal issue became very clear from the eight cases studied. In the two industrial country cases, Spain and the United States, fiscal issues were not a fundamental problem. Both economies had modest fiscal deficits that could be increased through additional borrowing or fiscal adjustments that were not disruptive to the stability of the financial system. But the six developing countries studied—Argentina, Chile, Colombia, Ghana, Malaysia, and Yugoslavia—all suffered from reduced access to foreign financing when the international debt crisis broke in 1982. Almost all had weak fiscal positions (including large quasi-fiscal deficits) at the beginning of the banking problems. In several, large fiscal deficits were a major cause of the problems in the banking sector. Fiscal and external account adjustments in each country had severe effects on both domestic growth and the stability of the banking system. In Argentina and Yugoslavia central bank losses from foreign exchange losses were so high that such losses were eventually monetized, resulting in hyperinflation. The vicious circle of high debt, capital flight, recession, unemployment, and widening fiscal deficits eventually led to loss of monetary control.

In Chile, even though central bank losses were high from the absorption of bank losses, the correction of the central government deficit through tax reform and radical reform (including privatization) of the social security system generated sufficient surplus in the budget not to disturb monetary balance. Together with devaluation, trade liberalization, and the opening of the economy to foreign direct investment, the real economy turned around sufficiently to restore stability in the banking system without a recurrence of inflation (chapter 10).

Some form of stock solution involving direct government intervention is probably inevitable when the economic insolvency of the banking system is greater than 2 percent of risk assets.[2] The calculation of the fiscal cost to the government depends on the size of the domestic and foreign debt, the total fiscal and quasi-fiscal deficits, and the costs of servicing such debt. Experience suggests that countries with moderate debt levels and deep financial markets—which allow the government to obtain financing at low costs and long maturity—are likely to weather financial crises better than governments with shallow financial markets. For example, in 1987 Malaysia had external debt and fiscal deficit ratios comparable to those of Argentina (75 percent and 8 percent of GDP, respectively), but Malaysia had already begun to deal decisively with its bank restructuring through direct central bank assistance to ailing banks in a noninflationary manner (chapter 7). The solution lay in high domestic saving rates (28.0 percent of GDP in 1989, compared with 5.2 percent for Argentina) and a deep domestic financial market that allowed domestic borrowing with up to thirty years' maturity. In contrast, as domestic disintermediation occurred, debt-servicing burdens became unsustainable in high-inflation economies with shorter maturities and higher real interest rates.

The fiscal costs of bank restructuring can be calculated from the following example. Country A is a post–centrally planned economy in transition to a market economy. Its domestic debt to GDP ratio is 47 percent and its foreign debt to GDP ratio is 28 percent, with an annual fiscal deficit of 7 percent. Domestic bank credit to the private sector amounts to 30 percent of GDP. Recent studies indicate that the banking system has nonperforming loans totaling at least 20 percent of its portfolio, equivalent to 6 percent of GDP. If the government undertook a carve-out, the fiscal costs would depend on the level of interest paid on the government bonds. Current lending rates are 17 percent a year, while bank deposit rates are 12 percent, slightly below the inflation rate. Assuming that the government wished to issue bonds at a rate equal to the deposit rate, the annual fiscal cost would be about 0.7 percent of GDP (12 percent times 6 percent). This would require a minimum 5 percent increase in revenue or an equivalent reduction in expenditure, considering that total government revenue is only 14 percent of GDP. This approach provokes the usual arguments against taking any action in bank restructuring:

- The government cannot afford the losses.[3]
- The banks should be able to make profits in the future to regenerate their capital.
- Since the banks are responsible for the losses, they should do the cleaning up themselves.

What the authorities did not realize was that real interest rates began to rise as bank losses accumulated because depositors demanded a risk premium from what they perceived as a potentially unsafe banking system. The combination of rising losses (adding to the quasi-fiscal deficits) and rising real interest rates, as well as declining growth due to misallocation of resources, would increase the ratio of total debt to GNP (d) until it reached unsustainable levels (Fischer and Easterly 1990; see box 2.6).

There is no alternative in macroeconomic stabilization efforts to privatization, cutting back government spending to sustainable levels, allowing real sector liberalization in trade, opening to foreign direct investment, and a synchronized package of monetary and financial reforms to generate the growth that brings economic growth (and hence the level of d) back to a sustainable level.

Box 2.11 Bank restructuring mechanisms

U.K. model (Lifeboat Fund, 1974)
- Funded by large clearing banks and the Bank of England.
- Initial liquidity support for viable secondary banks.
- Failed banks liquidated.
- Bank of England took over a failed bank that was subsequently privatized; losses were borne by the central bank.

U.S. model (deposit insurance)
Federal Savings and Loans Insurance Corporation (until 1989)
- Acquisition or merger.
- Income maintenance program.
- Accounting forbearance.
- Phoenix and bridge banks.
- Management consignment.
Resolution Trust Corporation (after 1989)
- Concentration of failed assets in RTC.

- Liquidation or sale of banks to private sector.
- Losses borne by RTC (funded by federal guarantee).

Spanish model (bank "hospital" and carve-out mechanism)
- Accordion principle.
- Joint funding by commercial banks and the Bank of Spain.
- Deposit Guarantee Fund buys bad assets.
- Provides banks with guarantees and long-term soft loans.
- Sale of banks to the private sector.
- Nationalization of the Rumasa group.

Chile variation
- Central bank issues bonds to buy bad assets, with buyback schedule.
- Central bank loans to banks converted into equity.
- Sale of banks to the private sector.

Models of Bank Restructuring

Beginning in the 1970s, several models of bank restructuring appeared (box 2.11). The first industrial country model was the market-based flow solution adopted in the U.K. secondary banking crisis of 1973–76. A Lifeboat Fund was created with joint liquidity funding by the large clearing banks and the Bank of England. Twenty-three "fringe" banks, of which eighteen were deposit-taking institutions and five were authorized banks, were badly affected by the 1973–74 recession, with a number overspeculating in the property market. Most were reconstructed or merged into other companies, while a few eventually were liquidated or placed into receivership. None of the major clearing banks were affected. Total support was £ 1.2 billion, equivalent to 40 percent of the total capital reserves of all English and Scottish clearing banks. The primary burden of losses was borne by shareholders of the failed institutions, with some liquidity support from the Lifeboat Fund. Some residue losses arising from the takeover of one bank and subsequent resale were absorbed by the Bank of England.

The Thailand Financial Institutions Development Fund, created in 1981, was one of the first developing country bank restructuring institutions (Sundaravej and Trairatvorakul 1989). It was modeled partly on the U.K. model, with funding from mandatory contributions from financial institutions and borrowing from the Bank of Thailand. The fund is managed by the Bank of Thailand. It is not a deposit insurance scheme, but it has the flexibility of using its funds to recapitalize (buy equity in) problem financial institutions or of giving financial assistance to depositors of problem banks.

The United States has the most complex and comprehensive deposit insurance scheme. The scheme, which is market funded but government guaranteed, was established in the 1930s after the massive bank failures of the Great Depression. The scheme is unique in that it fostered the freedom of entry and operations of more than 29,000 deposit-taking institutions, mostly small and with state or national charters. Since these operate in highly geographically and functionally segmented markets within the United States, the scheme institutionalized the orderly exit of failed banks without disrupting depositor confidence. Supervision of deposit-taking institutions is divided among a complex of state and federal agencies (chapter 4). The system functioned well until the 1980s, when excessive competition, changes in market structure, speculation in real estate, mismanagement and fraud, and inadequate supervision led to unprecedented failures, first in thrifts and then in banks.

The Federal Savings and Loans Insurance Corporation (FSLIC), which became defunct in 1989 when it became insolvent, applied a number of market-based but government-assisted acquisition and merger solutions to deal with failed thrifts. Liquidation and direct deposit payout was often the last-resort solution. The preferred method was acquisition of the failed institution, followed by merger or sale of the "cleaned" institution to a private buyer. When FSLIC resources were inadequate to do stock cleanups it resorted to income maintenance programs in which it made up the income shortfalls between the yield on the assets of the failed bank and the market yield agreed with the buyer. These later turned out to be extremely expensive solutions, since the FSLIC bore most of the risks of subsequent failure.

When the number and size of thrift failures continued to increase in the second half of the 1980s, the FSLIC began to create "phoenix" or "bridge" banks by consolidating failed thrifts for subsequent resale. The corporation also engaged in management consignments, where the management of problem banks was give to bidders or established banks with proven management records. By 1989, however, thrift losses had became so large that the FSLIC became insolvent. It was dissolved and the funds were reconstituted in the Saving and Loans Insurance Fund under the charge of the Federal Deposit Insurance Corporation (FDIC) (chapter 4).

The FDIC used broadly similar techniques of purchase and assumption in dealing with problem banks, but because it had greater resources than the FSLIC—both financially and managerially—it was able to supervise and manage the rising number of failed and problem banks in an orderly manner. The 1989 Financial Institutions Reform, Recovery, and Enforcement Act delegated to the FDIC the responsibility of running the thrift insurance fund, which was also in charge of the newly created Resolution Trust Corporation (RTC). The RTC was created because the number of failed thrifts and their assets had grown so large that it was administratively and legally overwhelming for the FSLIC to handle. The RTC was given the task of managing and resolving failed thrifts in a market-based and orderly manner that would minimize government losses. In mid-1990 the RTC had more than 200 institutions under "conservatorship," that is, as ongoing businesses to be sold in part or whole; and another 200 under receivership, that is, for liquidation in full or in part. By the end of 1991 the RTC had assumed more than $357 billion in assets of failed thrifts and disposed of $229 billion.

The RTC asset disposal model was adopted by Ghanaian authorities, who created the Nonperforming Asset Recovery Trust (NPART) in 1989 to deal with the recovery and disposal of bad debts and their collateral. NPART is still engaged in asset disposals.

Asset recovery trusts are useful where the number and size of banks' bad assets are so large that they are administratively cumbersome to handle in a decentralized manner. Asset recovery trusts also can be a useful transitory tool where enterprise restructuring and debt recovery specialists are scarce and court procedures do not enforce quick debt recovery and disposal of collateral.

Problems with asset recovery trusts can occur because the information capital of banks on their borrowers often is destroyed or lost in the transfer. The transfer of rights of banks over their borrowers to the asset recovery trust may not be legally perfect, and the detailed knowledge of hidden assets of borrowers by individual banks may not be passed on to the trust, thus inhibiting the debt recovery process. Thus it is not yet entirely clear whether centralized asset trusts or decentralized debt recovery is preferable.

The Spanish Guarantee Fund—created in 1980—was a major institutional improvement over the U.S. and U.K. models since it embodied explicit intervention by the government with a recognized "carve-out" technique. Instead of intervening at the margin through liquidity support (as in the U.K. model) or purchase, assumption, and resale through the deposit insurance fund (as in the U.S. model), the fund operated as a bank hospital. Funding was shared by the larger commercial banks and the Bank of Spain, but the supervision and referral of problem banks to the hospital was left to the Bank of Spain. The technique used was, first, the application of the accordion principle: a full capital reduction to the extent of losses so that the shareholders bore the brunt of the losses; and second, the fund would purchase the bad assets in exchange for bonds. Sometimes the fund provided guarantees or longterm soft loans to the problem institution, but once the institution was "cleaned up" it was resold to the private sector, sometimes to foreign banks interested in entering the Spanish market (chapter 5).

The carve-out technique was widely adopted in a number of countries, notably Chile, Colombia, and Ghana and more recently in Hungary, Slovenia, and the Czech and Slovak Republics. The Chilean banking crisis of 1975–85 was one of the most severe in the 1980s. The government intervened in thirteen of twenty-five domestic banks (including two of the largest banks) and six of eighteen financial companies, covering 45 percent of total bank loans. Nonperforming loans reached as high as 113 percent of total bank capital and reserves by May 1983 and bad loans sold to the central bank amounted to 24 percent of total loans.

The Chileans began addressing their banking crisis by converting emergency loans to banks into equity, including heavy central bank subsidies to banks and finance companies to allow rescheduling of loans. A major step was the central bank purchase of bad loans, initially up to total bank capital and reserves, by swapping them for noninterest-bearing central bank bonds, with a repurchase schedule of 5 percent buyback every six months for ten years. In 1984, with a deepening crisis, this method was revised to cash purchase of bad loans up to 150 percent of capital and reserves. Loans sold for cash had to be rebought over ten years at a 5 percent real rate. Assisted banks could not declare dividends until the central bank's debt was fully repaid.

The Chileans forced the problem banks to increase their capital, first from existing shareholders, then from new subscribers. When private sector interest failed to develop, the state development agency Corfo bought equity (Corfo was limited by law to 49 percent equity ownership). Corfo's shares were to be resold to the private sector within five years, with any unsold balance to be transferred back to shareholders that had contributed to the equity increase.

The Chilean technique was quite successful—the banking system stabilized and the economy recovered after massive structural adjustments in the fiscal and trade sectors. But the burden of bank losses fell almost exclusively on the central bank, which in August 1985 held bad debt purchases of $2.36 billion and internal debt equivalent to 44 percent of GDP.

The Philippines also successfully applied the bad debt carve-out in relieving the Philippines National Bank and the Development Bank of the Philippines. About 104 billion pesos—including $5.1 billion of external debt—equivalent to 16.6 percent of GDP were transferred to the national government in 1986 (Lamberte 1989). Both banks were then restructured and partially privatized.

While the carve-out remains a popular technique, it is not always the best solution. In Malaysia, Thailand, and the United Kingdom the bad assets were retained in the banks' books and central bank assistance was provided in the form of loans (Thailand and the United Kingdom) or equity (Malaysia).

In the 1985–88 Malaysian banking crisis the central bank intervened in four of thirty-nine banks, four of forty-seven finance companies, and thirty-two of thirty-five deposit-taking cooperatives involving M\$ 9.4 billion, or 10.4 percent of total deposits. Total financial institution losses in 1985–86 totaled 4.7 percent of 1986 GNP. To handle the crisis, emergency legislation empowered the central bank to freeze the deposits of failed deposit-taking cooperatives and merge twelve failed cooperatives into one licensed finance company. The central bank provided soft loans to assist the rehabilitation and refund of depositors, who received 50 percent in cash and 50 percent in shares in the "phoenix" finance company. The central bank also provided M\$ 672 million in equity to the four banks and four finance companies, as well as soft loans of M\$ 1.3 billion. More recent cases of bank restructuring, particularly those in Eastern Europe, are discussed in chapter 3.

Conditions for Successful Bank Restructuring

The choice of the appropriate restructuring mechanism depends on several key factors: the size of the losses and the political economy of loss allocation, the legal and institutional framework, problems of the real sector, and the effectiveness of the implementing agency. Timing is also important. The urgency of the pending problems, the pressure brought on by specific events or macroeconomic policy considerations, and the proper sequencing and policy mix also affect the choice and outcome of bank restructuring schemes.

The objective of bank restructuring—to restore sustainable bank solvency and profitability—is related to the restoration of solvency and viability of the real sector. If the real sector continues to suffer large losses, the banking sector cannot be isolated from such losses, and may be a culprit in continuing to finance real sector losses. Successful bank restructuring calls for a recognition of these losses and imple-

mentation of measures for damage control. Bank restructuring is therefore often part of a larger package of macroeconomic stabilization and reform.

As a general rule, if banking problems are detected early, with a reasonably stable macroeconomic environment and effective administrative and supervisory machinery, flow solutions will be adequate to deal with banking system that still have 0 to 2 percent capital-asset ratios. If problems are allowed to deteriorate beyond this level, a combination of stock and flow solutions will have to be implemented, depending on the size of the distress. A summary of the conditions for successful bank restructuring are listed in box 2.12.

Middle- and high-income countries with good accounting standards, ample resources, and effective bank supervision agencies (whether in the central bank, bank superintendency, or deposit insurance agency) have been able to restructure their banks reasonably successfully. In dealing with problem banks, these countries adopted bank restructuring in tandem with enterprise and fiscal reforms, and it was the success of real sector reforms that generated the resources to clean up the banking system.

In Malaysia, Spain, and the United States the borrowing capacity of government (including the credibility of the central bank) was such that absorbing bank losses as part of the budget or as a quasi-fiscal deficit within the central bank did not disturb monetary stability and hence did not lead to inflation. In all three countries bank losses were partly due to disinflation or asset compression, as competition, corrections for overlending, and falling real estate prices created large losses in parts of the banking system, particularly in the more highly geared, managerially weaker new entrants.

The other five countries (Argentina, Chile, Colombia, Ghana, and Yugoslavia) all suffered

---

Box 2.12 Conditions for successful bank restructuring

- Clear links with enterprise restructuring.
- Stable macroeconomic environment.
- Strong political will.
- Effective restructuring agency.
- Transparent accounting standards.
- Legal framework favoring financial discipline.
- Incentives favoring private sector growth and competition.
- Cadre of professional bankers (domestic or foreign).
- Effective bank supervision and enforcement.

from large external debt overhangs that developed in the early 1980s. Ghana was able to embark on a path of macroeconomic adjustment after 1983 with substantial external aid. The success of its fiscal reforms generated a primary surplus that, together with external aid, allowed a carve-out to be executed in the banking system to remove bad debt from the banks without generating any monetary pressure.

Chile and Colombia both suffered from the effects of rapid liberalization in the financial sector, resulting in overlending and the shocks of the cutoff of external resources after the 1982 debt crisis. Colombia was able to maintain growth and absorbed the losses within the central bank. The shock to Chile was significantly larger, and the carve-out imposed an extremely large burden on the central bank that has yet to be eliminated, despite the restoration of strong growth.

Argentina and Yugoslavia demonstrate the problems of attempting bank restructuring without dealing with structural issues. In Yugoslavia the experimentation with self-managed enterprises that both owned and borrowed from banks was a structural failure. Banks that were owned by worker-managed enterprises could not impose financial discipline on loss-making enterprises and instead became the transmission mechanism of massive resource misallocation. Even though the federal government did not ostensibly have any fiscal deficits, the quasi-fiscal losses of the national bank and the losses of enterprise-owned banks were huge by any standard. Such losses could not even be removed through hyperinflation. The political difficulties of dealing with such losses were inherent in the regional fragmentation that occurred in 1990.

Argentina began and ended the 1980s with economic and banking crises. In both cases the credibility and sustainability of fiscal discipline was at stake. With the cutoff of external financing, the government resorted to internal financing and borrowed heavily from the banking system. The central bank incurred large losses from its net foreign liabilities, and attempts to impose monetary stability failed because monetary policy could not overcome fiscal indiscipline. In the end the banking system channeled more than half its resources to funding the fiscal deficits of the government and the quasi-fiscal losses of the central bank. Disintermediation was massive despite real interest rates exceeding 30 percent a year. In the end even hyperinflation could not

wipe away the fiscal burden. The government had to remove its debt burden by transferring its banking debt into dollar-denominated long-term debt, which reduced the fiscal debt-servicing burden and passed the losses to the future. Finally, massive privatization and efforts in fiscal, trade, and enterprise reform—including a major currency reform in 1991—turned the tide of confidence and restored stability in the Argentine economy.

These eight cases demonstrate the importance of political will, or in the language of structural adjustment loans, "ownership" of the adjustment program. Since much of bank debt is in domestic currency, external aid and technical assistance are neither necessary nor sufficient conditions for successful bank restructuring. But where there are large overhangs of external debt, external debt restructuring can relieve the government's debt-servicing burden, and hence its capacity to absorb further internal debt arising from bank restructuring.

The importance of a single effective restructuring agency—whether in the central bank, ministry of finance, or another agency—is demonstrated by the gaps and conflicts in supervision in a number of cases. The creation of deposit insurance schemes with insufficient resources or legal powers to deal with the problems can be disastrous. These institutions give the illusion of a responsible agency without the substance. Deposit protection agencies in Kenya and the Philippines were not provided with sufficient resources to deal with the rising level of bank problems, and in the end the rescuer had to be rescued. This was also the fate of the U.S. FSLIC.

This chapter has demonstrated the importance of diagnostics and loss allocation. Having determined the sources of losses of the banking system, an appropriate mix of policies and measures has to be found to deal with the losses. Where the state has preferred to preserve the stability of the banking system and the nominal value of bank deposits, banking system losses are ultimately state obligations. Resources—in the form of renewed growth, savings, and fiscal revenue—will have to be found to pay for the losses. The rewriting of the national balance sheet has to be undertaken in such a way that the incentives structure does not permit a repeat of bank failure. Such a rewriting involves fundamental change in the efficiency and productivity of the real sector. Unless the real sector returns to growth and stability, there may be insufficient resources to remove the bad debts from the banking system.

Notes

1. Financial transactions to relieve enterprises or banks of bad debts also have incentive problems. If relief of the debt burden hardens the budget constraint for enterprise and bank management, this is a positive development. This appears to have been the case in the Republic of Korea. If debt relief encourages moral hazard behavior, as appeared to have occurred in many Latin American countries, bailouts may have very high costs.

2. Recent U.S. experience suggests that banks are economically insolvent (negative capital) when accounting (capital) solvency falls below 2 percent of risk assets. Accordingly, the 1992 Federal Deposit Insurance Improvement Act mandates that supervisory authorities take statutory action against banks when their capital adequacy falls below 2 percent.

3. Fiscal revenue from bank profit taxes in a number of Eastern European economies in transition was as much as 15 percent of total revenue. But such profits were calculated before adequate provisions were made for bad debt, so that banks were overtaxed and decapitalized by bad accounting.

References

Bank of Japan. 1994. "How U.S. Commercial Banks Dealt with the Asset-Quality Problem." *Quarterly Bulletin* (May). Tokyo.

Barnes, Guillermo. 1992. "Lessons for Bank Privatization in Mexico." Policy Research Working Paper 1027. World Bank, Washington, D.C.

Brewer, Elijah, and Thomas Monschean. 1992. "Ex Ante Risk and Ex Post Collapse of S&Ls in the 1980s." *Economic Perspectives* (July/August). Federal Reserve Bank of Chicago.

Caprio, Gerard, Izak Atiyas, and James Hanson. 1993. "Financial Reform Lessons and Strategies." Policy Research Working Paper 1107. World Bank, Washington, D.C.

Chamely, Christophe, and Patrick Honohan. 1990. "Taxation of Financial Intermediation." Policy Research Working Paper 421. World Bank, Washington, D.C.

de Juan, Aristobulo. 1987. "From Good Bankers to Bad Bankers: Ineffective Supervision and Management Deterioration as Major Elements in Banking Crises." Economic Development Institute Working Paper. World Bank, Washington, D.C.

———. 1991. "Does Bank Insolvency Matter? And What to Do About It?" Economic Development Institute Working Paper. World Bank, Washington, D.C.

Diaz-Alejandro, Carlos. 1985. "Goodbye Financial Repression, Hello Financial Crash." *Journal of Development Economics.*

Fischer, Stanley, and William Easterly. 1990. "The Economics of the Government Budget Constraint." *World Bank Research Observer* 5(2):127–42.

GBIF (Guarantee Bank Insurance Fund). 1992. *Annual Report.* Norway.

Glaessner, Thomas, and Ignacio Mas. 1991. "Incentive Structure and Resolution of Financial Institution Crises: Latin America Experience." Latin America Technical Department Technical Paper. World Bank, Washington, D.C.

Kane, E. J. 1985. *The Gathering Crisis in Deposit Insurance.* Cambridge, Mass.: MIT Press.

Kindleberger, Charles P. 1978. *Manias, Panics, and Crashes: A History of Financial Crises.* New York: Basic Books.

Lamberte, Mario. 1989. "Assessment of the Problems of the Financial System: The Philippines Case." Background paper prepared for *World Development Report 1989.* World Bank, Washington, D.C.

Meinecke, Hans-Dieter. 1991. "The Restructuring of the East German Banking System." Deutsche Bundesbank, Berlin.

Minsky, Hyman P. 1977. "A Theory of Systematic Fragility." In E. I. Altman and A. W. Sametz, eds., *Financial Crises: Institutions and Markets in a Fragile Environment.* New York: Wiley.

Numachi, T. 1993. "The Cooperative Credit Purchasing Co., Ltd." World Bank, Financial Policy and Systems Division, Washington, D.C.

Sasaki-Smith, Mineko. 1994. "The Bank of Japan's New Bailout Scheme." Morgan Stanley, Tokyo.

Schwartz, Anna J. 1985. "Real and Pseudo-Financial Crises." In Forrest Capie and Geoffrey Wood, eds., *Financial Crises in the World Banking System.* New York: St. Martin's Press.

Sheng, Andrew. 1992. "Bad Debts in Transitional Socialist Economies." World Bank, Financial Policy and Systems Division, Washington, D.C.

Sheng, Andrew, and Yoon Je Cho. 1993. "Risk Management and Stable Financial Structures." Policy Research Working Paper 1109. World Bank, Washington, D.C.

Siebert, Horst, Holger Schmieding, and Peter Nunnenkamp. 1992. "The Transformation of a Socialist Economy: Lessons of German Unification." In Georg Winckler, ed., *Central and Eastern Europe: Roads to Growth.* Washington, D.C.: International Monetary Fund.

Solheim, Jon A. 1990. "The Banking Crisis in Norway." Paper presented at the Economic Development Institute seminar on financial sector liberalization and regulation, June, Boston.

Sundararajan, Vasudevan. 1992. "Financial Sector Reforms and their Appropriate Sequencing." International Monetary Fund, Monetary and Exchange Affairs Department, Washington, D.C.

Sundararajan, Vasudevan, and Tomas Baliño, eds. 1991. *Banking Crises: Cases and Issues.* Washington, D.C.: International Monetary Fund.

Sundaravej, Tipsuda, and Prasarn Trairatvorakul. 1989. "Experiences of Financial Distress in Thailand." Policy Research Working Paper 283. World Bank, Washington, D.C.

Tenconi, Roland. 1989. "Restructuring of the Banking System in Guinea." Background paper prepared for *World Development Report 1989.* World Bank, Washington, D.C.

U.S. Comptroller of the Currency. 1988. "An Evaluation of the Factors Contributing to the Failure of National Banks." Washington, D.C.

U.S. FDIC (Federal Deposit Insurance Corporation). 1991. *Quarterly Banking Profile, Fourth Quarter.* Washington, D.C.

U.S. Treasury. 1991. "Modernizing the Financial System." Washington, D.C.

World Bank. 1993. "Bank Supervision: Suggested Guidelines." Financial Policy and Systems Division, Washington, D.C.

Zahler, Roberto. 1993. "Financial Sector Reforms and Liberalization: Welcome Address." In Shakil Faruqi, ed., *Financial Sector Reforms in Asian and Latin American Countries.* Economic Development Institute Seminar Series. Washington, D.C.: World Bank.

CHAPTER 3

Resolution and Reform: Supervisory Remedies for Problem Banks

Andrew Sheng

Banking is essentially a service business of intermediation. Banks fail because of human errors or faults, whether fraud, mismanagement, poor policies, or inadequate supervision. The human element in banking looms so large that bank supervisors often blame bank failures on bank management—and in certain cases they may be absolutely right. But the simultaneous eruption of so many bank failures internationally in the 1980s suggests that there are larger macroeconomic reasons for widespread bank distress. It is no coincidence that bankers worldwide engaged in a credit frenzy, creating the environment for and conditions of loss. As chapters 1 and 2 indicated, the roots of bank failure are multifaceted, with structural, systemic, policy, and managerial dimensions.

At the most basic level, banks intermediate between two sets of contracts—deposit contracts between depositors and the bank and loan contracts between borrowers and the bank. In addition to these savings mobilization and credit allocation function,

banks transmit funds on behalf of their customers—the payments system function. Bank failure is fundamentally the contractual failure of a bank to honor its obligations to its depositors and results primarily from the related failure of borrowers to honor their contracts to the bank (counterparty risks) or from the impact of market changes on the bank's net worth (market risks).

Moreover, since any financial transaction involves payment and settlement, there are risks associated with settlement and operations. Liquidity risk is a major problem in any market that dries up in times of uncertainty. Legal risks occur when property rights are uncertain or undefined. A computer failure may delay payment or accounting, thus subjecting some party to loss. Finally, systemic, aggregation, or interconnection risks occur when the failure of one party triggers systemwide failure through contagion. Financial market risks are defined in box 3.1.

All financial products are essentially contracts involving the exchange of property rights or value.

Box 3.1 Financial market risks

Counterparty credit risks—the risk that the counterparty will fail to fulfill the (credit) contract. The size of the loss is the replacement cost of the contract in the market.

Market risks—risks arising from market price changes, such as interest rate risk, exchange rate risk, and commodity price risk.

Settlement risk—the risk that one party (or agent bank) will not settle or deliver final value when settling a contractual obligation.

Operating risk—losses due to inadequate internal controls, procedures, and operating equipment, software, and systems.

Liquidity risk—losses that result if forced to sell under illiquid market conditions.

Legal risk—losses caused by uncertainties in the legal definition of obligations or court reversals of commonly understood obligations, such as the legal obligations of multilateral netting.

Aggregation risk—sometimes called systemic or interconnection risk. Failure of one party triggers failure elsewhere in system (for example, contagion).

Source: Federal Reserve Board, Federal Deposit Insurance Corporation, and U.S. Comptroller of the Currency 1992.

Financial markets trade these contracts between different parties. Bank supervision, in a narrow sense, involves ensuring that banking contracts are honored and enforced according to legal guidelines. Since market transactions involve the risks listed above, market participants (banks and their clients) and bank supervisors must be concerned with risk management.

This chapter explores the techniques of bank failure resolution and restructuring. Specifically, it looks at damage control at the microeconomic level, the need to rebuild bank profitability and create the right incentives for monitoring a sound financial base, and finally the need to address the critical link between bank and enterprise restructuring.

Controlling Damage through Supervision

Bank supervision has four objectives:
- Competition and operational efficiency.
- Safety and soundness.
- Monetary policy and allocative efficiency.
- Protection of small depositors (equity).

Problem banks develop for a variety of reasons, macroeconomic as well as microeconomic. Overcapacity in banking, excessive competition, operational inefficiencies, repressive taxation, structural rigidities, portfolio concentration, speculation, mismanagement and fraud, external shocks, policy mistakes, and inadequate supervision all contribute to bank insolvency and poor performance.

Some objectives of bank supervision are conflicting: many government-directed credit policies with welfare objectives impose costs, risks, and perverse incentives on banks with disastrous impacts on their net worth. Similarly, tight monetary policies that require banks to maintain large non–interest bearing statutory reserves tend to erode banks' profitability. There is a tradeoff between safety and efficiency. Some bank supervisors allow the banking system to be concentrated in banking cartels, which generate higher profits and capital through monopoly profits that can cushion the system against periodic external shocks. Smaller and less-capitalized banks could easily be absorbed by the stronger banks during a recession. Bank solvency is protected at the expense of competition and efficiency.

Supervisors who are concerned with competition and efficiency may have exit mechanisms already built into the system. The deposit insurance scheme in the United States, for example, permits the orderly exit of inefficient institutions without disrupting

the system as a whole. Without such mechanisms in place, bank crises may last much longer than necessary (Zahler 1993).

In many countries the rising demand to protect small depositors and ensure systemwide stability has been extended—through the "too big to fail" principle—to an implicit or explicit guarantee of the entire deposit base. This need to protect depositors, and consequently the banking system, generates the dangers of moral hazard, the socialization of losses, and the privatization of gains. Hence the drive to strengthen supervision of the financial sector to avoid the high costs of bank failure and disruption. This push for stronger supervision has paralleled the trend toward financial sector liberalization and seems contradictory to a key lesson of the 1980s—that even the most sophisticated bank supervisors have been unable to prevent bank failures.

What then, is the role of the modern bank supervisor? The supervisor's primary role is damage control and getting the incentives right. Banks are in the business of risk intermediation, but the deposit insurance schemes that are in place around the world have led to bank risk-taking that is asymmetric: speculative risks are taken for private gain at public cost. Where financial sector liberalization programs have failed to take account of this asymmetry, reforms have generally failed. Banking crises have convinced policymakers of the need to level the playing field and to evenly match risks with rewards or punishments. A corollary of this objective requires bank supervisors to minimize moral hazard behavior, connected lending, conflicts of interest, fraud, and mismanagement. Accordingly, financial sector liberalization is going through a phase of re-regulation, with broader coverage extending not only to the banking sector but also to nonbank financial intermediaries. International cooperation in financial sector supervision also has become necessary as financial services become globalized.

Bank supervision in the 1990s may focus on national risk management: setting the rules of the game for financial intermediaries in such a way that risks are taken with an adequate level of capital (Sheng and Cho 1993). In other words, financial intermediaries should be free to engage in asset liability management that allows them to diversify their risks by region and by sector while matching their interest rate and exchange rate risks, so long as they are supported by a level of capital sufficient to cushion them against their risk profile.

Thus bank supervision helps banks (and other financial intermediaries) define and better manage their risks, given their capital adequacy. To supplement the safety and soundness of the system, supervision should be augmented by a lender-of-last-resort system or some form of deposit insurance (Talley and Mas 1990). Damage control of ailing financial institutions begins with diagnostics—the assessment and evaluation of problem institutions.

Assessing problem banks

Most bank supervisors have broadly adopted the U.S. CAMEL method of assessing bank performance: *c*apital adequacy, *a*sset quality, *m*anagement quality, *e*arnings, and *l*iquidity. The Canadian Office of the Superintendent of Financial Institutions has refined this system to CAMELOT, adding the quality of *o*perations and *t*reasury management (McPherson 1992).

Capital adequacy. Since the Basle Committee on Banking Supervision agreed on a uniform standard of risk-weighted capital adequacy of 8 percent (adopted internationally at the end of 1992), most developing countries are moving toward the 8 percent target. There is, however, a tendency to regard this standard as a maximum rather than as a minimum. Most developing country banks require a substantially higher capital base, together with higher standards of loan or asset provisioning, because of their higher risks. It should be remembered that until deposit insurance was introduced in the 1930s, U.S. banks had capital-asset ratios well above 20 percent in the nineteenth century and between 15 and 20 percent until the 1930s. (The substantial variation in the capital-asset ratios of international banks can be seen in annex 1.2.)

There is not only significant international variation in capital-asset ratios, but also varying definitions of capital. Some regions, for example Latin America, report much higher capital-asset ratios than the OECD average, but provisions against bad loans may be considerably lower. In other countries hidden reserves are not disclosed in published balance sheets, so international comparisons may be misleading. The Basle Committee is still working on the proper level of capital adequacy for market and interest rate risks, including the difficult area of derivatives and off–balance sheet liabilities.

The quality of capital is only as good as the quality of asset or loss provisioning. Where asset provisioning is inadequate, high nominal capital-asset ratios are deceptive. Thus the correct cushion against nonearning or nonperforming assets is non–interest bearing liabilities. A simple rule of thumb to ensure stability is that total core capital (excluding interest-bearing subordinated loans) plus total provisions against nonperforming loans should at least equal the total stock of nonperforming loans (Sheng 1991).

Asset quality. The greatest danger to capital erosion is poor asset quality. Asset quality is based on the quality of credit evaluation, monitoring, and collection within each bank. What assets are at risk? Are assets too concentrated in one geographical or economic sector? Is there connected lending? Are there hidden losses "below the line?" Are losses hidden in bank subsidiaries and affiliates? Are there unreported fraud losses? Have apparently diversified loans been collateralized on a single large asset? Have adequate provisions been made against potential losses in the asset portfolio? These are some of the questions that supervisors should ask bank management.

Asset values are subject to greater potential losses in a volatile price environment, not simply from the changes in supply or demand, but also from the illiquidity in markets of certain assets during times of stress. For example, when markets are thin, as in a newly introduced government bond market, bond prices can fall sharply if there are no market makers or if the economy is uncertain. Thus, even if the credit risks on a particular financial instrument are low, the holder may still be subject to significant liquidity and interest rate risks.

Bank supervisors should improve the accounting treatment or value measurement of various assets and liabilities, both tangible and intangible. Values (and thus risks) of derivatives are also conceptually difficult to quantify and measure. As Goldstein and Folkerts-Landau (1993, p.23) emphasize, "rapid expansion of, and concentration in, a particular banking activity often signals both a weakening of internal controls and an underassessment of credit risk."

Management quality. In a world of uncertainty and asymmetric information, bankers' judgment on risks is as important as bank supervisors' judgment on the competence and integrity of bank management. The bank supervisor's job is not to second-guess the banker, since any involvement in credit decisions (directly or indirectly through credit allocation guidelines, for example) would compromise the bank supervisor's objectivity. Moreover, good behavior cannot be legislated (Lin 1992). Still, bank supervisors should ensure that the managers of public savings have professional training and experience, that sound procedures and controls are in place, and that succession plans exist for key management. For example, boards of directors should be fully informed of the operations and performance of their banks and be held responsible for management's compliance with banking laws and regulations. There should be good internal audit and controls, and timely and accurate information should be provided to management to assess the risks of the bank.

Recent developments that hinder management's ability to monitor risks include the growing area of derivatives, which in nominal terms are almost the size of the on–balance sheet assets of the global banking system. A number of banks have made substantial profits from such trading, but bank supervisors and industry experts share a common concern that some institutions do not fully understand how and why such profits were made, and worry that the institutions did not have the proper management tools and internal controls to monitor the risks involved.

Earnings. The potential problems of financial institutions often are reflected in their earnings performance. Many developing country banks run into difficulties because of excessive operating expenses. In Ghana, for example, the operating expenses of state-owned banks were almost 75 percent of gross interest income in the late 1980s (chapter 8). Banks were overstaffed and maintained unprofitable branches for reasons of prestige or under government direction. In OECD countries operating costs are 65 to 70 percent of gross income (including noninterest income), with provisions for loan losses set between 15 and 20 percent and pretax profits between 12 and 20 percent. OECD banks earn about a third of their gross income from noninterest sources, particularly foreign exchange trading and fees. The average return on assets for the top fifty U.S. banks was 0.95 percent in 1988, nearly four times that of the top fifty Japanese banks and roughly twice that of the top fifty European banks. Return on equity of U.S. banks in 1988 was 18.4 percent, compared with 12.5 percent for the Japanese banks and 10.3 percent for the European banks (*American Banker* 1990). The performance ratios of U.S. national banks are shown in table 3.1.

Of particular importance to bank earnings is the income accruals policy on nonperforming loans and the stringency of loan loss provisioning. Supervisors

Table 3.1 Performance indicators of U.S. national banks, 1986–91
(percent)

Indicator	Performance ratio
Return on equity	7.7
Return on assets	0.5
Net interest income on assets	3.5
Noninterest income on assets	1.6
Noninterest expense on assets	3.5
Loss provisioning/assets	1.0
Loss reserves/loans	2.5
Loss reserves/noncurrent loans	71.4
Net loan loss/loans	1.3
Loss provisioning/net loan loss	131.7
Real estate loans/total loans	35.2
Noncurrent loans/total loans	3.5
Noncurrent real estate loans/real estate loans	3.7
Equity capital/assets	5.9

Source: U.S. Comptroller of the Currency 1992.

should ensure that minimum standards are followed and that banks do not engage in "cosmetic accounting," such as the elaborate rescheduling of nonperforming loans to make the loans appear to be performing. In the early 1980s in Colombia, for example, banks opened subsidiaries in Panama to bypass domestic lending guidelines so that problem loans would escape supervisory attention (chapter 6).

Liquidity. Liquidity is generally not a major problem for sound banks in a reasonably competitive banking system, and weak banks often can replenish liquidity by bidding up interest rates. The recent banking crises suggest that in many cases liquidity crises have their roots in solvency problems. No international standard exists for measuring liquidity, since liquidity depends on an individual bank's financial position, the depth of domestic money and capital markets, and the willingness of the central bank to supply liquidity to banks. The Basle Committee has developed a framework for liquidity that attempts to measure and manage net funding requirements, market access, and contingency planning (Basle Committee on Banking Supervision 1992; Musch 1992).

In many developing countries—including many post–centrally planned economies—problems within the national payments system have created large "floats" (items being cleared) that tie up huge amounts of bank liquidity. In early 1993 float and clearing items in the Russian banking system totaled 55 percent of the monetary base. This created a credit crunch for enterprises that could only be relieved by central bank credit. Supervisors may be able to bolster bank liquidity by improving the efficiency of national check clearinghouses or automating the large-value interbank transfer systems.

Operations. Because banks operate the national payments system, they are vulnerable to the systemic risks of failures of banks within the payments system or even from technical operating system failures. Many banks today are so dependent on computers and telecommunications that they cannot tolerate more than a day-long shutdown of their computer equipment. When the computer system of the Bank of New York failed in 1990, for example, it threatened to delay settlement and payment of all transactions in New York. The New York Federal Reserve Bank had to inject additional liquidity into the market until the technical failure was resolved. Bank supervisors must ensure both that technical backup facilities are in place for individual banks and that systemwide operations for the payments system are protected from technical failures.

Banking has become highly dependent on technology—not only for global operations, but also for information processing, funding arrangements, and market arbitrage. Accordingly, bank management must pay close attention to the robustness of operating systems and management information systems, which are critical to risk management. A system failure that coincides with large market volatility could destroy a bank's capacity to avoid losses in the interim.

Treasury management. Partly because of the need to "save" on capital, and also because of financial innovations and market deepening, banks have increasingly relied on non–credit based income to boost earnings. For example, income from treasury operations and noninterest income accounts for as much as half of gross bank income in Switzerland. The risks in treasury operations are mainly interest rate and exchange rate risks. But with the increasing role of derivatives (options and futures)—which involve off–balance sheet exposures—bank supervisors are becoming increasingly concerned with exposure to third parties (reputation and counterparty risks), which may unravel when one party in the chain of market transactions fails to honor its contracts.

Some money-center banks have transformed their operations from a lending function to a market transaction function, generating revenue from money market instruments, bonds, derivatives, and foreign exchange trading rather than from credit generation. In doing so, these banks have transformed their internal risk management procedures, concentrating on the return on capital that factors in benchmark yields, duration (maturity of instrument), and counterparty exposure. Bank supervisors must understand the risk management systems that are in place and ensure that these systems are fully understood at the treasury, chief executive, and board levels of the bank.

Early warning signals

A common complaint about banks is that their performance is not transparent to the public, and often not even to the bank supervisor. Formal bank supervision entails both off-site surveillance and analysis of bank reporting and performance and regular on-site inspection (World Bank 1993). Irregular inspection may result in a failure to detect early warning signals. During 1985–86, for instance, when many banks in the U.S. state of Texas began to fail as a result of overlending, the number of inspections was halved due to budgetary and staff constraints (chapter 4).

Deregulation, globalization, and financial innovation have allowed banks to evolve into complex organizations that span the world geographically and across different product lines. Banks have become involved in insurance, securities firms, and fund management, including commodities and futures trading. While such diversification of assets could reduce risks, in a number of cases—notably the U.K. Bank of Credit and Commerce International (BCCI) case—the inadequacy of coordinated supervision has perpetuated fraud. The ability of bank supervisors to supervise financial conglomerates across legal and geographical boundaries will be a major challenge in a global banking environment (Corrigan 1992). Bank supervisors will have to better understand the financial commitments of the banking core to the nonbanking (and probably unregulated) wings of the financial conglomerates. Some of these new activities could be driven by "regulatory arbitrage" to avoid detection of overleveraging or fraud. Thus what appears to be a minor new item about the involvement of a bank in a distant offshore company could turn out to be a major source of losses.

Early warning systems can be improved through the installation of commercial software for off-site surveillance and bank analysis. Still, such programs are no substitute for alert analysis of bank indicators from a variety of sources (box 3.2). "Soft" indicators—such as market talk or anonymous letters reporting fraud and mismanagement—are particularly indicative that a bank may be at risk. The BCCI case is a classic example of the gaps in international

---

Box 3.2 Early warning signals of a problem bank

- Weak or uninformed board of directors and a dominant chief executive.
- Poor lending practices.
- Late submission of bank returns and reports.
- Problems in affiliates, related companies, or large customers.
- Rapid staff turnover and changes in top management.
- Change in auditors.
- Rapid growth in assets.
- Liquidity problems.
- Deposit rates higher than market.
- Market talk.
- Public complaints.
- Ostentatious spending.
- Use of political influence.

---

supervision that delay detection of extensive fraud and mismanagement over a number of years.

Although off-site surveillance is important and the use of external auditors can strengthen supervision of financial intermediaries, there is no substitute for on-site inspection of banks—if only to provide direct evidence to bank supervisors of problems on the ground. Moreover, external auditors may face conflicts of interest since they are paid by banks, and may not be trained to detect fraud. Bank examiners can assess the validity of market talk about cosmetic accounting, connected lending, or speculative losses. Examiners also can gather evidence that may be used in later legal actions. In a number of instances the lag between reports of potential fraud by auditors and subsequent action to obtain evidence has resulted in the destruction of such evidence.

Approaches to damage control

The purpose of damage control in supervisory action is to minimize bank losses once they are detected. In almost all cases inspection teams should be sent in as soon as possible to determine the extent of the damage. Where laws prevent direct bank inspection, external auditors should be commissioned to provide an independent view of the losses. Four rules should guide damage control efforts.

Strengthen or change management. Because of the high leverage in the banking business, shareholders face lower risks as losses increase, and consequently the greatest risks are borne by depositors or by the deposit guarantee fund. Thus shareholders and management have incentives to disguise losses and to take

speculative risks to cover up such losses. Where fraud is suspected, management should be changed, since untrustworthy managers have incentives to escalate the fraud and run before supervisory action is taken. Many bank supervisors hesitate to change management because current managers have the best information on the state of the bank, whereas new managers will need time to learn. Moreover, there is often a punitive desire to make the existing management responsible for collecting the bad debts that they made.

Bank supervisors tend to forget that, where fraud or corruption in credit decisions is present (such as taking commissions on loans or connected lending), managers have every incentive to hide or escalate losses. This is partly because jail sentences are not commensurate with the scale of bank theft. Managers go to jail whether they have stolen $10,000 or $100 million, and the larger the losses, the greater the need for public rescue—thus implicating the supervisors in some form of coverup. The Malaysian central bank governor succinctly expressed the Malaysian experience with problem bank management: "Never let monkeys look after bananas" (Bank Negara Malaysia 1987).

Double your estimate of losses. Bank accounting is not transparent to the public or to the bank supervisor, mainly because losses can stem from a variety of causes that may not be uncovered until stern supervisory action has been taken. Aristobulo de Juan, a bank supervisor who helped resolve Spanish banking problems in the early 1980s, asserts that final losses are always double the previous estimates (de Juan 1991). His experience, borne out in a number of other countries, is that external auditors' estimates of losses are almost always double those of the bank management, bank inspectors' estimates are at least double those of the auditors, and final losses on liquidation are double those estimated by the bank inspectors.

Delayed loss recognition is partly the result of wishful thinking—the hope that things will recover in the next quarter or accounting period. The underreporting of losses in the previous accounting period by bank management or auditors undercuts their credibility, and hence there are incentives not to report large variations. In addition, the evaluation of nonperforming loans is a judgment, and actual writeoffs could be substantially higher. Experience in Finland and Norway suggests that writeoffs of nonperforming loans ultimately could be as high as three-quarters of book value. As conditions deteriorate, and the net worth worsens, the bargaining position of the problem bank weakens and sale of assets under time pressure forces further losses. Recent U.S. experience suggests that even under conservative accounting, liquidation losses averaged as much as 17 percent of book value for failed banks and thrifts.

BCCI is an example of the escalation of losses. Initial press reports suggested that the bank's capital was totally eroded. Later estimates escalated to $5 billion of total assets of $20 billion, and recent estimates suggest that more than $10 billion may have been lost. Another example comes from Norway, where problems in the banking system were detected in 1988 but losses continued to escalate until 1992. The banks only began to recover in 1993. Asset deterioration occurs partly as a result of management deterioration and breakdown of controls. In cases of fraud involving banker-borrower collusion, borrowers may abscond with or deny the validity of collateral. When banks get into trouble, borrowers have incentives to seek legal loopholes to delay or renege on payment because they see an end to their debt-servicing commitment. Thus, where collateral documentation has been weak, the bank (or its liquidator) can collect only after protracted court proceedings—which result in further losses.

Act sooner, not later. Experience suggests that the sooner supervisory action is taken, the lower will be the costs incurred. The U.S. thrifts crisis illustrates the enormous costs of delayed action, in this case the result of reluctance to absorb the losses in the loosely regulated environment of the early 1980s. The economic insolvency of the thrifts might have been only about $100 billion if all assets had been marked to market in 1982 (U.S. Treasury 1991). But after more than 1,400 thrifts disappeared from the market as a result of liquidations and mergers in the 1980s, government efforts to bail out the industry cost at least $315 billion (U.S. GAO 1989).

The larger losses due to delayed action are not attributable solely to the time cost of initial losses (the stock problem). In many cases—particularly in post–centrally planned economies—flow problems are more to blame, arising from the structural difficulties of transforming loss-making state enterprises. As long as banks continue to lend to these loss-makers, the deterioration in net worth will compound. This failing can only be resolved through determined damage control and radical restructuring. Since 1990 Hungarian authorities have engaged in four rounds of recapitalizing loss-making state banks.

Obtain support for supervisory action. Problem banks hold public funds. Where explicit deposit insurance schemes or implicit central bank support of the banking system are present, commercial bank losses in excess of bank capital are quasi-fiscal deficits. Consequently, action taken by bank supervisors must be carefully explained both to the public and to policymakers. Bankers who are likely to lose their jobs and shareholders who are likely to lose the value of their shares are quick to blame inadequate or misguided bank supervision. Thus it is important for the public to understand that the primary objective of supervisory action is to protect the safety of public deposits and that losses often are caused by poor bank management and inadequate action by shareholders—particularly where shareholders have been unwilling to augment capital to save the problem bank.

Damage control inevitably means that the bank supervisor has to intervene in problem financial institutions. The degree of intervention depends on the seriousness of the situation, and also on the legal powers available to the supervisor. A typical sequence of events is listed in box 3.3.

Depending on the legal powers available to bank supervisors, some countries use moral suasion to get bank management to take corrective action. In the United States, where legal powers are clearly defined, a memorandum of understanding about corrective action is signed by the bank supervisor and the problem bank. Failure to comply with the conditions of the memorandum can trigger a series of supervisory actions, such as cease and desist provisions. These may require the problem bank to cease certain loss-making activities, such as foreign exchange trading or buying junk bonds. In other countries central banks can prohibit further branching or the granting of new loans. Access to the money market can be denied, and central bank discounting facilities can be withdrawn. These actions control the problem bank's access to funds and limit the damage that the bank can inflict on other financial institutions and depositors.

Box 3.3 Bank supervisors' damage control options

- Guide management action and reporting.
- Draft memorandum of understanding with board of supervisors.
- Cease and desist action.
- Restrict central bank lines and trading limits.
- Change management and board of supervisors.
- Appoint adviser or conservator.
- Assume control.
- Increase capital.
- Initiate liquidation.

If the provisions of the memorandum of understanding or any legal provisions are violated, U.S. regulators may remove or suspend specific persons from participating in the affairs of the bank. Alternatively, a penalty can be levied on banks or bank managers for violations of regulations or orders. A U.S. bank manager found guilty of certain violations can be disbarred permanently from employment in any bank. In other countries this punishment is enforced largely through moral suasion, where licenses are withheld if unfit persons are found managing a deposit-taking institution.

Criteria for intervention

Once a bank supervisor intervenes in a financial institution, whether by appointing an adviser (in most countries) or conservator (in the United States) or by assuming control directly, the public considers the government responsible for the deposit liabilities. Thus intervention is not a step to be taken lightly. In the past the decision to close or intervene in a bank has been left largely to the bank supervisor. The 1991 U.S. Federal Deposit Insurance Corporation Improvement Act, however, put in place a series of measures that would compel regulatory action when bank capital falls below certain levels.

The act mandates prompt corrective action when a bank becomes critically undercapitalized, defined as the point at which its capital and reserves fall below 2 percent of risk assets. This threshold is both a general rule of thumb about levels of "near insolvency" and an empirically verifiable danger threshold. According to the 2 percent criteria, the margin of error in the measurement of accounting solvency (according to generally accepted accounting principles) should not exceed 2.5 percent if risk assets account for 80 percent of total assets. In other words, undermeasurement of losses of 2.5 percent of risk assets would wipe out the capital of a bank with only a 2 percent capital-asset ratio. Minor falls in the return on assets of a bank due to nonperforming loans could quickly decapitalize a bank according to market-value accounting.

Under the 1991 act significantly undercapitalized banks—defined as those having less than 3 percent core capital and 6 percent risk-weighted capital—would have to restrict their pay and bonuses, and bank regulators could force the election of new directors and the sale of units of the problem bank. Banks with core capital of less than 4 percent and risk-weighted capital of less than 8 percent would have to restrict dividend payments, limit asset growth, face curbs on activities, and file a plan to increase capital (table 3.2).

Rehabilitate or close?

One of a bank supervisor's most difficult tasks is calculating the costs and benefits of bank rehabilitation or closure. In the mid-1980s governments rescued large problem banks because of the "too big to fail" principle, thus extending deposit insurance coverage to almost 100 percent of the deposit base. Now there is consensus that only banks that are critical to the payments system, and whose failure could trigger systemic failure, should be intervened in and perhaps not allowed to fail. This approach suggests that bank supervision should focus on a core of high-quality "failproof" banks that are directly involved in the high-value, time-critical payments transfer and clearing system. Smaller banks and nonbank financial intermediaries whose failure would not jeopardize the payments system should be allowed to fail, to rid the market of inefficient institutions. Indeed, the current view is that supervisors should not aim to prevent bank failures (Quinn 1991).

There is, however, a body of opinion that functioning institutions may have a higher market value (and thus a lower cost of bailout) than immediate closure would produce. Different countries use different institutional mechanisms to make this difficult decision. In the United States the Federal Deposit Insurance Corporation (FDIC) decides whether to intervene. The FDIC cannot choose a method that is more expensive than liquidating the bank and paying off the depositors. A purchase and assumption route is taken if it will save the FDIC substantial time and administrative costs over liquidation and deposit repayment and if the sale price of a failed bank will be higher than its liquidation value.

In Belgium an Intervention Fund Committee comprising bank representatives has to satisfy itself that offering support would be less costly than reimbursing depositors after a winding up. In Malaysia an advisory panel to the central bank—comprising members of the central bank, ministry of finance, attorney general, a representative of the bankers association, and another private sector member—advises whether the central bank can invoke certain powers to rescue a failing institution.

The decision to rehabilitate or close depends on the institutional framework, the legal powers and

Table 3.2 U.S. regulatory action under the 1991 Federal Deposit Insurance Corporation Improvement Act

Capital status	Risk-weighted capital[a]	Core capital[a]	Mandatory and discretionary actions
Well capitalized	10 percent	5 percent	• Cannot make any capital distribution or pay a management fee to a controlling person that would leave the institution undercapitalized.
Adequately capitalized	8 percent	4 percent	• Same as above.
Undercapitalized	Less than 8 percent	Less than 4 percent	• Subject to increased monitoring. • Must submit a capital restoration plan. • Asset growth is restricted. • Approval required for acquisitions, branching, and new lines of business.
Significantly undercapitalized	Less than 6 percent	Less than 3 percent	• Must increase capital. • Interest rates paid on deposits restricted to the prevailing rates in the region. • Asset growth is restricted; reduction of total assets may be required. • May be required to elect a new board of directors.

Critically undercapitalized	4 percent	Less than 2 percent	• Must be placed in conservatorship or receivership within ninety days.
			• Prohibited from the following without FDIC approval:
			  – Entering into any material transaction other than in the usual course of business.
			  – Extending credit for any highly leveraged transaction.
			  – Making any material change in its accounting methods.
			  – Paying excessive compensation or bonuses.

a. Ratio of capital to assets.
Source: Nakajima and Taguchi 1993.

resources available to intervene, and the ultimate cost to the government. The steps involved, however, broadly include the following:

• Determining the size of bank losses (the degree of insolvency). Conservative estimates should be made according to the "double losses" rule described above.
• Calculating the net deficit, estimating the time frame of recovery and assuming that new capital is available.
• Determining loss allocation—to shareholders, the need for (and costs of) staff retrenchment, and the burden to be borne by the restructuring agency (central bank, deposit insurance agency, or ministry of finance).
• Estimating the fiscal impact of depositor bailout, assuming that government will engage in either a carve-out or flow solution.
• Is there a franchise value? If so, this can be added to the capital of the insolvent bank.
• Is there a market for bank shares with other banks or new shareholders?

Recent U.S. experience indicates that the resolution process starts with a diagnosis, typically involving an information package and asset valuation review. After this, an information meeting is arranged with potential acquirers of the failed bank or the remaining assets, with those interested performing a "due diligence" examination of the failed institution (box 3.4).

A failed bank has four basic pieces: a deposit franchise; market assets—such as bonds and cash—that can be disposed of easily; banking assets—such as loans—that cannot be valued easily; and problem assets—such as nonperforming loans and real estate—that are worth less than book value and have high carrying costs. The franchise value of banks is difficult to assess. But the scarcity of bank licenses in a number of countries and the existence of large branch networks often generate significant franchise value. In Spain, for example, foreign banks were willing to acquire problem banks from the Deposit Guarantee Fund in order to gain entry into the Spanish market. The Bank of Thailand was able to recapitalize problem banks by selling off shares to well-capitalized nonfinancial institutions that wanted to acquire a strategic stake in banks. In Norway the Government Bank Insurance Fund effectively "nationalized" the banks by injecting capital into problem banks. Bank privatization had to await the restoration of the banks to health, and by early 1993 a number of them had begun to generate small profits.

Experience from a number of countries suggests that the net insolvency of problem banks should be determined in a transparent and legally enforceable manner. In the Philippines shareholders of failed banks taken over by the Central Bank have successfully disputed the valuation of the net capital shortfall, impeding the efforts of bank supervisors working on the failing banks. Once the net losses of the problem bank have been established, the appropriate technique of bank restructuring should be chosen based on the initial conditions, an assessment of the flow of future losses, and the need to sequence reforms.

The Longer View: Rebuilding Bank Profitability

Prevention is obviously better than a cure. Financial distress is not a historical inevitability—it can be avoided through a combination of supervision, sound macroeconomic policies, and effective financial institution-building. As the financial liberalizations of the 1980s show, liberalization in the absence of a consistent and adequate macroeconomic policy framework may be unsuccessful or even counterproductive (Gelb and Honohan 1989). Drastic surgery—carving out bad loans or rehabilitating banks—will not be sustainable if the underlying causes of bank distress are not removed. A number of conditions must be met if bank restructuring is to be successful (box 3.5).

Stable macroeconomic environment

A stable macroeconomic and financial environment is crucial to financial reform. Countries with high inflation often witness severe disintermediation from the banking system and distorted allocation of resources. High inflation, the accompanying devaluation, and high real interest rates create uncertainty and large wealth losses in the economy, which worsen financial distress. Open capital accounts permit volatile capital flows and make monetary and macroeconomic management even more difficult.

The massive banking problems of the 1980s drive home the message that inappropriate macroeconomic and regulatory policies contribute to bank fragility. As many banking crises showed, the competitive pressures unleashed by financial liberalization, while increasing efficiency, also carry risks, because banks and other financial institutions alter their behavior to ward off institutional downsizing (IMF 1993). Asset price bubbles—and their subsequent deflation—had their origins in excessively lax monetary and supervisory policies during the early phase of the boom, and in excessive restrictiveness thereafter.

As discussed in chapter 2, the banking system can generate losses that are ultimately quasi-fiscal deficits because of the implicit or explicit state guarantee on the deposit base. In macroeconomic terms the sustainability of such losses is based on the sustainability of the total public deficit and debt. In highly indebted countries that had external financing cut off,

Box 3.5 Conditions for rebuilding bank profitability

• Stable macroeconomic environment
• Relationship with enterprise restructuring
• Removal of tax and regulatory distortions
• Legal and accounting reform
• Market and institutional deepening
• Getting the incentives right
• Professional competence and ethics

reliance on internal debt financing resulted in money creation and high inflation. Distressed borrowing—first by enterprises, then by banks, and ultimately by the state—forced up real interest rates beyond sustainable levels. Where such real rates paid by the state exceed the real growth rate and the growth rate of noninterest tax revenue, the total public debt grows exponentially and becomes unsustainable, leading to hyperinflation or debt default (see box 2.6; Fischer and Easterly 1990).

In the end, a number of countries achieved macroeconomic stability (together with restoration of stability in the banking sector) only when the government was able to generate a primary surplus that allowed the total public debt ratio (including the stock of recognized or unrecognized bank losses) to stabilize or decline over time. The anchor of macroeconomic stability is fiscal discipline, where the need for public borrowing does not crowd out funding for private investment or overextend the nation's external debt capacity. Sound domestic and external debt management strengthens monetary control, deepens the capital market, and reduces inflationary pressures.

Relationship with enterprise restructuring

A financial system cannot remain profitable over the long run at the expense of the real sector. In many countries—and especially in the post–centrally planned economies—bank distress is a direct consequence of enterprise insolvency. By failing to address bank distress, governments worsened resource allocation and macroeconomic stability, as banks continue to pump resources into loss-making enterprises to keep themselves afloat. Consequently, bank restructuring must be accompanied by a credible package of real sector reforms that address the causes of enterprise and borrower losses.

For example, countries that suffered from the "Dutch disease" of overvaluation of the exchange rate, such as Chile (1976–80), Colombia (1980–84), and Malaysia (1980–84), saw the profitability of domestic industries erode as imports grew, experienced a decline in the profitability of exports, and saw investment turn toward nontradables such as real estate and share speculation. The correction of the exchange rates in these countries helped restore enterprise profitability, since domestic agriculture and industries became able to compete once again with imports and were able to create new markets for exports.

On the other hand, rapid trade liberalization in previously protected markets such as Ghana and Poland removed the high rents earned by inefficient state-owned enterprises, creating large losses as firms struggled to adjust to the new competitive environment. State banks that had lent heavily to these enterprises were unable to avoid large losses.

Combining bank restructuring with enterprise restructuring will be particularly important in the post–centrally planned economies because the enterprises will require significant resources during the transition to a market-based environment. The adjustment costs during this period, which could severely decapitalize the banks in these countries, may be unavoidable (Sheng 1992).

Removal of tax and regulatory distortions

Tax and regulatory distortions in the financial sector worsen resource allocation. In Turkey, for example, 26 percent of the lending rate in 1983 was attributable to a direct tax on interest or reserve costs on banks, thus pushing the cost of intermediation higher (Hanson and Rocha 1986). In Ghana the tax rate on banks was higher than that for nonfinancial enterprises (chapter 8).

Discriminatory tax rates between banks and nonbank financial intermediaries also have created unfair competition. For example, development banks, finance companies, and money market funds may not have to maintain statutory reserves with the central bank, and therefore their cost of funds may be significantly lower than that of commercial banks. Such sectors of the market enjoy significant competitive advantage, and yet the commercial banks would bear the brunt of the credit risks if they were to fund these nonbank financial institutions excessively. The recent exposure of Japanese banks to stocks and property was relatively limited, but if the exposure to nonbank financial institutions is included, this exposure was considerably greater.

In essence, tax and regulatory reforms entail removing financial repression and desegmenting the financial system. This requires the removal of excessive regulation of interest rate and credit allocation policies, including dismantling of interest rate controls, freeing entry into investment banking and capital market activities, reducing quasi-fiscal burdens such as excessive reserve requirements, liberalizing exchange rate controls, and removing credit quotas, targets, and ceilings. Taxation on domestic intermediation of funds should be harmonized to create a level playing field for competition.

Legal and accounting reform

Legal and accounting reforms should ensure that financial transactions and financial institutions are as transparent as possible, with laws and court procedures that enforce financial discipline. Domestic accounting standards should be brought in line with international accounting standards so that domestic bank efficiency can be compared with international standards. Accounting disclosure and audit standards should facilitate public and supervisory understanding of the performance trends of financial institutions so that the market can appraise the true value of these institutions' net worth.

Prudential standards must be simple, comprehensive, and educational (Butsch 1992). They should not be a substitute for internal controls of banking institutions, but should educate financial institutions and the public to be aware of their risks. Moreover, legal impediments to debt recovery, including bottlenecks in court proceedings or defects in the law, should be remedied so that banks can impose financial discipline on borrowers. In Hungary courts were unprepared—both technically and in terms of capacity—to deal with the growing number of bankruptcies and liquidations required under the new banking and commercial law of 1992. As of September 1992, the debt of companies under liquidation or bankruptcy proceedings by financial institutions amounted to 110 billion forints, or nearly 90 percent of the classified bad debt reported by banks (National Bank of Hungary 1992). In many countries where debt recovery was delayed by cumbersome court procedures, special tribunals were established to expedite the process. In 1993 Pakistan took the unusual step of publishing the list of major defaulters to state-owned banks to induce them to repay.

Market and institutional deepening

Market and institutional deepening calls for basic improvements in the financial infrastructure. This involves two major areas: the creation of active money and capital markets (to allow markets to function smoothly and price the market value of financial assets at a competitive level) and the enhancement of the operating efficiency of the payments system (such as check clearing and electronic fund transfer mechanisms).

Improvements in money and capital markets strengthen macroeconomic management because the central bank is able to use more efficient indirect instruments of monetary management and the budget can be financed in a more transparent manner. Better money and foreign exchange markets also improve the market skills of banks, particularly their short-term liquidity management. With deeper capital markets, the budget gains access to longer-term funds at market rates, reducing the need to repress the banking system for funds. Development of a government bond market creates a benchmark yield curve for domestic interest rate determination while providing a stable and noninflationary source of financing for the budget (Emery 1993).

Development of the securities market provides long-term equity financing for the corporate and banking sectors, reducing their gearing and therefore strengthening their capacity to absorb higher risks and external shocks. As such markets develop, specialized funds such as venture capital, mutual, and property funds can be established to mobilize funds for higher-risk investments.

Improving the timeliness and certainty of payments transmission, clearing, and settlement generally reduces the liquidity pressures in an economy (Summers 1992). It also imposes financial and accounting discipline on participants in the financial system and allows the bank regulator to detect quickly those institutions that have difficulties meeting their payments or that are operationally inefficient. The inefficient payments and settlement system that was used in the post–centrally planned economies prevented central banks from engaging in more active monetary measures to stabilize inflation. In active, global, and twenty-four-hour trading of financial markets, central banks have become more aware of the systemic risks arising from the possible disruption or failure of money and capital market payment, clearing, and settlement systems.

Another area of financial deepening is the development of nonbank financial intermediaries, which help to spread risk and transform maturities. Encouraging the development of contractual savings institutions, such as life insurance companies, pension and provident funds, and social security schemes, would promote long-term finance that strengthens the capital market.

Getting the incentives right

In recent years policymakers have become aware of how distorted incentive structures can lead to massive waste and inefficiency. A policy framework that attempts to alleviate bank distress must take into account the incentives of all parties concerned—bank managers, bank equity and liability holders, and regulators. Such a framework should strive to preserve financial discipline and induce cooperative solutions (Glaessner and Mas 1991). In other words, the incentives structure should induce bank management and shareholders to take preventive action before bank distress occurs, and also force timely action on the part of regulators to act before distress becomes too costly.

In principle this logic is irrefutable. In practice, because laws are enacted periodically, the incentive structures built into laws and institutions may quickly become obsolete because of rapid market changes. Therefore the design of incentive and institutional structures should take into consideration cyclical factors and random shocks. For example, deposit insurance may be useful in preventing bank runs, but it also has proven quite costly in terms of moral hazard costs.

Thus a fundamental principle in the design of a safe and sound financial system is the avoidance of asymmetry between risk and rewards. Bankers must always have their own capital at risk so that they will not engage in speculative behavior at large social costs. Bank supervision should not supplant bank management judgment, and overregulation runs the twin risk of bank management and depositor complacency and risk aversion, so that high-yielding projects may not be funded, leading to lower long-term growth. Moreover, a high level of bank supervision is equated with a full or extensive government guarantee of the deposit base.

Another lesson from recent experience is that bank supervision is useless if there is insufficient enforcement. Policy credibility influences public behavior. Despite the extensive failure and high losses of many African banks due to mismanagement or fraud, few bankers have been charged or jailed. Thus bank supervision has bite but no teeth. Incentives alone will not create a sound financial system, but strong disincentives should be built in so that rewards are evenly matched with the risks of punishment.

Professional competence and ethics

The soundness and efficiency of the banking system ultimately is only as good—or bad—as the professional competence and ethics of the people who operate and supervise the system. Even the best bank supervisor cannot prevent the failure of a system where bankers cannot tell a good borrower from a bad borrower, as in the highly distorted price environments of the post–centrally planned economies. Bad bankers cannot become good bankers if they do not receive training in credit skills and the accounting and legal framework does not allow them to enforce debt recovery. And good supervisors can become bad supervisors if they supplement their income by "taxing" or borrowing from bankers.

Strong institution-building therefore depends on devoting significant resources to building skills and strengthening controls within individual banks. The bank regulator or central bank can facilitate this by encouraging private involvement in the development of selected institutions, such as bankers associations and training centers, credit rating agencies, and credit information sharing bureaus (Gibeault 1993). As international supervisors recognize, "the self-discipline of banking institutions must be reinforced" (Butsch 1992).

A central dilemma of financial supervision in a global financial market with twenty-four-hour trading is that the regulatory framework is a patchwork of national policies. Global financial conglomerates are evolving that can engage in significant international regulatory and tax arbitrage, moving funds to take advantage of information asymmetry and market opportunities. Most of these movements have legitimate market reasons, but predatory measures—such as acting in concert—are increasingly being taken in small markets by big players that are outside the jurisdiction of any single regulatory authority.

Much has been achieved through international cooperation in banking supervision. Difficulties naturally arise in cooperation across functional lines, such as cooperation with securities and insurance regulation. Nevertheless, the long-term health and stability of the global financial system depends on the integrity and fairness of the market operators—the intermediaries themselves.

Bank and Enterprise Restructuring in the Post–Centrally Planned Economies

World Bank operations to assist the post–centrally planned economies with bank restructuring are currently under way in a number of countries, including Bulgaria, Hungary, Poland, Romania, Slovenia, and the Baltic states. As discussed in chapter 1, the intermingling of roles between the budget, state-owned banks, and state-owned enterprises suggests that the move toward a market-oriented financial system will require a careful sequencing of the disengagement of public roles from private functions. The crucial elements of bank and enterprise restructuring are listed in box 3.6.

First, state-owned enterprises have to shed their social welfare functions (housing, child care, and other benefits for workers and their households) and concentrate on efficient production.

Second, state banks have to disengage themselves from the quasi-fiscal function of providing funding—both working capital and investment—to the budget and to state-owned enterprises, especially loss-making enterprises. As long as banks are burdened with such quasi-fiscal roles, they cannot intermediate savings and investment efficiently, and controlled interest rates do not reveal the true market price of credit and savings.

Third, the budget must not rely on the taxation of banks and state-owned enterprises to finance itself (McKinnon 1991). Neither should the budget continue to protect inefficient state-owned enterprises by providing massive subsidies—including monetary creation—to maintain economic growth. The rapid rise in inflation resulting from monetary creation to finance loss-making enterprises or rescue failing banks has been the bane of many governments in the post–centrally planned economies.

Fourth, the time and pace of price reform is important. Rapid price reforms immediately cause huge losses and reveal inefficiencies in state-owned enterprises, resulting in massive losses to the banks that finance

them. Not all price reforms are negative. For example, trade and exchange rate reforms were principal elements of the reform package that allowed Polish, Czech, and Hungarian firms to adjust to export markets, thus reducing the losses that would have occurred had access to such markets been denied.

Much of the debate on the correct sequencing of bank and enterprise restructuring in these countries is colored by the controversy over privatization of banks and enterprises. While privatization is not an end in itself, it is a powerful means of improving efficiency in the production of goods and services and of strengthening social and democratic institutions (Snoy 1992). There is no question that privatization helps in two key areas: adjusting the incentives structure (moving toward more efficient production) and improving the financial balance (capital adequacy) for economic agents. Still, whether mass privatization should be pursued all at once or through intermediate steps, such as corporatization, is an empirical question that can only be answered by each country's legal, institutional, political, and historical precedents.

While the process of bank restructuring will vary from country to country depending on initial conditions and financial structure, several principles and objectives should guide the design of bank restructuring programs:

- The financial condition of the banks needs to be improved so that they can efficiently intermediate funds. Bank losses often reveal themselves in large spreads, leading to both negative real deposit rates and high real lending rates. Banks should be "cleaned" so that spreads narrow to revive saving and investment. The cleaning-up process would facilitate the privatization of banks, including meeting minimum capital adequacy requirements.
- Since bank losses generally stem from lending to loss-making enterprises, the debt burden of enterprises must be relieved to improve their recovery and income generation capacity and facilitate privatization of state holdings and general economic restructuring. Related to the problem of bank restructuring is the issue of "pass through"—how debt relief for the banks can be passed through to the enterprises to facilitate their restructuring and recovery. Restructuring also must reduce the backlog of enterprises in liquidation or bankruptcy, since these tie up scarce economic resources.
- The burden of past losses of state enterprises and banks should be shared by the state, nonstate bank shareholders, borrowers, and depositors.

Box 3.6 Preparing for reform

The following steps must guide bank and enterprise restructuring efforts:
- Determine the size of losses—the stocks and flows.
- Choose a centralized or decentralized debt restructuring solution.
- Reduce flow losses resulting from continued exposure to loss-making enterprises and thereby improve intermediation.
- Determine whether the writeoff of enterprise debts will be done by banks or by the state.
- Determine whether to restructure banks before privatization and restructuring of enterprises.
- Determine the appropriate role of banks in enterprise restructuring.

The rationale for using state funds to relieve banks of their stock of nonperforming loans is to improve the allocation of scarce resources. The higher the level of state assistance, the greater the burden of losses that is shifted to taxpayers, instead of to future borrowers or depositors or current shareholders. The "carving out" of bad debt through swaps of bad debts for long-term bonds spreads the costs over several years.

- It must be determined how the losses can be absorbed by the budget without threatening fiscal discipline and macroeconomic stability. In many post–centrally planned economies it is unclear how the state can finance such losses given these countries' tenuous fiscal situation. This is further complicated by governments' heavy reliance on tax revenues from state-owned banks.
- The choice of restructuring options may depend not only on the fiscal cost, but also on time and administrative costs. For example, pushing numerous failed debtors into bankruptcy proceedings without established court procedures and trained personnel will create bottlenecks that allow asset values to deteriorate as banks await court decisions. Thus solutions should foster competition and transparency and avoid overly bureaucratic measures.
- Finally, bank restructuring must address incentives in such a way as to prevent excessive debt leveraging, avoid weakening credit discipline, allow market forces to operate on a level playing field, and improve competition, resource allocation, and risk management. Any scheme that preserves monopolies or oligopolies (state or private) will only perpetuate existing distortions and increase future costs of resolution. The restructuring scheme should improve incentives that reward competition and efficiency and punish agent behavior that raises social costs.

The diagnosis process requires clear identification of the causes of the losses in the banking system, including the proper measurement of losses—using international accounting standards—in both banks and enterprises. Recent experience in Eastern Europe suggests that portfolio audits of banks do not reveal the true size of losses because the fundamental problems stem from enterprise losses, which are difficult to measure in the absence of complete price reform and enterprise restructuring, particularly the lack of clear ownership of property rights. Thus losses will continue to flow until these issues are resolved.

The inability of supervisory authorities to impose damage control in many post–centrally planned economies stems from the limited resources and capacity of these authorities. Bank supervisors have been preoccupied with the need to draft banking legislation, develop off-site surveillance capacity, and produce basic banking regulations and standards. Examination capacity is limited to a few inexperienced inspectors whose ability to regulate the rapidly growing banking sector is at best rudimentary. In many cases damage control measures are limited to the gradual withdrawal of central bank funding to loss-making state banks and to canceling licenses when fraud or wrongdoing is suspected. In the absence of a comprehensive bank supervision framework, many supervisors face the daunting task of resolving large loss-making banks, which are structurally linked with loss-making enterprises. In many cases these supervisors have neither the financial nor the human resources to deal with the problems.

Absorbing quasi-fiscal losses

Since the state generally provides an explicit or implicit guarantee on deposits in the predominantly state-owned banking system, losses in these banks are quasi-fiscal deficits. The ability of the budget to bear such losses can be determined using the Fischer-Easterly equation for the change in the government debt to GNP ratio (d) (see box 2.6):

$$\text{Change in } d = (\text{primary deficit/GNP}) - (\text{seigniorage/GNP}) + d\,(\text{real interest rate} - \text{GNP growth rate}).$$

The primary deficit is worsened by the quasi-fiscal losses of the banking system, which can be financed through seigniorage. Consider a post–centrally planned economy at the early stage of reform:

Primary deficit/GNP before banking losses	2.0 percent of GNP
Credit to state-owned enterprises	70.0 percent of GNP
Average nonperforming loans	25.0 percent of total credit
Equivalent "carve out" bond to stabilize banking system (70 times 0.25)	17.5 percent of GNP

Quasi-fiscal losses of banking system:
Carve-out bond at x

interest rate on government

debt, say 10 percent a year	1.8 percent of GNP
Seigniorage	2.5 percent of GNP
Real interest rate	0.5 percent a year
Growth rate	−1.0 percent of GNP
Inflation	9.5 percent a year

Using the equation above,

$$\text{Change in } d = [2.0 + 1.8] - [2.5]$$
$$+ d[0.5 - (-1.0)] = 2.75 \text{ percent x } d$$

The total sustainable debt ratio d increases with the primary deficit (including quasi-fiscal losses of the banking system), with the real interest rate paid on debt, and when growth becomes negative. If interest rates are liberalized during this process, and distressed borrowing raises the real interest rate to, say, 10 percent a year, then change in d would increase correspondingly to 13.9 percent. In other words, a rising real interest rate would make the public sector debt burden unsustainable.

A central issue in bank and enterprise restructuring has been the reluctance of governments to liberalize interest rates for fear that the fiscal condition would run out of control. At the same time, reluctance to deal with bank and enterprise losses—because of the politically unacceptable levels of unemployment that would result—has worsened the macroeconomic environment and delayed the adjustment process.

If the quasi-fiscal (flow and stock) losses are too large for the budget to absorb in a single carve-out, how should the losses be allocated? The troika model (chapter 1, figure 1.4) suggests that bank restructuring cannot be undertaken without corresponding reforms in the fiscal and enterprise sectors, including accompanying changes in the legal, accounting, and regulatory frameworks. One approach is spelled out in the recent Chinese reforms, announced in the October 1993 Third Plenum of the Chinese Communist Party. At the banking level all policy-based loans will be removed from the banking system and transferred either to the budget or to specialized policy-based banks. This frees the banks to become profit-motivated institutions. At the enterprise level state-owned enterprises will be corporatized (made into legal entities with equity capital, initially entirely state owned) and run according to market principles.

The budget will be reformed by introducing a value-added tax and other direct forms of taxation to reduce the overreliance on enterprise taxes.

Diagnosis and prognosis

The first point to recognize is that banks are dealing not only with historical (stock) losses, but also with flow losses arising from continued loans to loss-making enterprises. In many post–centrally planned economies nonperforming losses occur partly because of the lack of accounting standards to measure such activity. Guidelines used by auditors to assess loans should be consistent with the guidelines issued by both bank supervisors and tax authorities. Auditors often may agree with the bank supervisors, but without the agreement of tax authorities—and tax allowance for bad debt provisions—the banks are unwilling to provide for nonperforming loans.

Second, losses mount because there is no legal framework for debt recovery. In a number of countries authorities were preoccupied with drafting a banking law and neglected to strengthen court procedures to deal with debt recovery. Moreover, the administrative and technical capacity of the courts to deal with massive liquidation and bankruptcy proceedings is extremely limited. Bankers, lawyers, borrowers, and judges have little experience with complex debt resolution, particularly where losses have to be allocated. Banks are reluctant to write off debt because doing so could lead them to become severely capital impaired. Tax authorities are reluctant to allow banks to make extensive provisions for fear of further eroding the tax base. Courts and lawyers have few legal precedents for adequate decisionmaking. Enterprise managers cannot preserve the value of assets so long as decisions on resolution are pending. Finally, policymakers cannot make decisions unless they are empowered to act.

Thus the bad debt problem is likely to worsen unless there are institutional and policy solutions to problem enterprises and borrowers. In essence, banks and enterprises are suffering from a lack of clarity in ownership and management of real sector resources. As privatization was delayed, enterprises and borrowers having liquidity problems became accountable to no one, since management did not have the authority or resources to correct liquidity or solvency issues and banks could not exercise financial discipline since they did not have sufficient capital or managerial skills to write off bad debts or convert loans to equity.

Consigning problem borrowers to bankruptcy and liquidation courts only worsened the process of problem resolution since the courts also had no experience with these issues. This led to gridlock, and in the meantime assets deteriorate in value while awaiting decisions on resolution.

The design of the enterprise resolution problem requires a good database on the structure of the nonperforming loans. Data on classified loans should be made available, broken down by class of enterprise, size of enterprise, economic sector, and the level of provisioning for each class. There should also be an industrywide study on whether bank losses are due to poor internal credit procedures or excessive overhead expenditure. A cost-of-intermediation study would also reveal what caused the rise in intermediation spreads and whether banks can respond by reducing overhead costs in the face of loan deterioration and declining business.

Centralized and decentralized solutions

Loan losses often are highly concentrated in a few large loss-making enterprises and economic sectors (box 3.7). If such concentration exists, the design of the bank and enterprise restructuring program will be very different from one where loan losses are widely dispersed. Concentration in a few large enterprises or sectors suggests that the problems be dealt with at a specialized or centralized level, whereas a widely dispersed bad debt problem may require decentralized solutions.

There has been lively debate over centralized and decentralized solutions to the bad debt problem throughout Central and Eastern Europe. Opponents of centralized solutions fear that centralization would reimpose bureaucratic solutions, delay privatization, and give central planning powers back to the public sector. Proponents of centralization argue that banks are not equipped to deal with enterprise restructuring and that decentralized restructuring would give a blank check to banks to waste funds on behalf of the state. Both arguments have some validity, and the appropriate solution depends on the conditions prevailing in each country. A summary of the major advantages and disadvantages of each approach is shown in table 3.3.

Damage control and the need for sound intermediation

Any restructuring scheme must address how to limit the flow of future losses in the banking system. Centralizing bad debts in a debt restructuring agency is one way of moving bad debts off the books of the banks, but this approach would require fiscal resources that may not be available to many post–centrally planned economies.

The Polish and Hungarian experiences suggest that giving senior bank management greater autonomy and discretion seems to improve bank performance, although the results are not uniform. Where state banks are excessively burdened by inherited bad loans and no solutions are in sight, some banks may engage in greater speculative lending, with further losses borne ultimately by the state.

Corporatization is not enough if the underlying weaknesses of credit procedures and lack of internal controls have not been corrected. Supervision of banks must be tightened. Without clear changes in the ownership of banks—whether to the private sector (domestic or foreign) or to a specially formed state holding company—no single institution will be able to exercise full shareholder rights to control losses.

An institution-building program to strengthen internal bank controls, credit procedures, debt skills,

---

Box 3.7 Concentration of nonperforming loans

Recent evidence suggests that bad debt in post–centrally planned economies tends to be highly concentrated. In Romania in 1992, four sectors accounted for almost three-quarters of nonperforming loans and about half of interenterprise arrears. In three sectors, twenty companies accounted for nearly two-thirds of the total loans and bad debt in their sector. The largest enterprise in each sector accounted for more than a third of that sector's bad debt. Moreover, about 100 companies accounted for more than three-quarters of bad loans.

In Poland in 1991, more than 80 percent of the bad and doubtful loans of the nine state-owned banks were exposures to state-owned enterprises. The twenty largest borrowers in each bank accounted for about 40 percent of their total assets. The fifty-eight largest companies in the classified loans category account for 11 percent of total sales, 5 percent of total budget revenue, 7 percent of total subsidies, and 6 percent of total employment. Thus resolving these loss-making enterprises would have a considerable impact on growth, employment, fiscal expenditure, and future bank profits.

Source: World Bank sector studies.

Table 3.3 Centralized and decentralized approaches to bank and enterprise restructuring

Centralized	Decentralized	Comments
Bad debts transferred to one agency	Banks responsible for bad debts	Depends on banks' capacity to absorb bad debts
Focused approach—restructuring skills are concentrated	Bad debt resolution integrated with banks' normal operations	Depends on skill levels in banks
Ideal where bad debts are concentrated in a few large enterprises or sectors	Ideal for dispersed small-borrower problems	
Frees banks to concentrate on serving healthy customers	Scale of enterprise problem cannot be divorced from normal bank operations—carve-out would leave banks as empty shells	
Legal change required to transfer property rights to agency	No legal change required—banks operate under debt recovery law	Transfers of claims to agency could be legally problematic, and information could be lost on transfer of debt
Budget bears brunt of losses	Banks are more likely to be more careful in debt recovery, since their funds are involved	Neither solution may have a hard budget constraint as long as ownership rights are unclear
Could create a bureaucratic bottleneck	Banks could be paralyzed because the size of bad debts overwhelms their capacity	Incentives structure must be clear—enterprise management, banks, and budget must find a solution that is practical and entails the least social cost

and overall management—complemented by international banking expertise wherever possible—should be developed for each country. This program should strengthen audit skills and disclosure requirements, such as the need to disclose accounts according to international accounting standards. In Poland, for example, the "twinning" of nine state-owned banks with foreign banks to strengthen bank management appears to have helped prepare some of the banks for eventual privatization. Indigenous banking skills also were developed by licensing foreign banks to operate in the domestic market, adding skills, techniques, and technology, as well as competition. Enterprise restructuring and capital market development were assisted by the creation of specialized development institutions, such as the Polish Development Bank, which were better equipped to engage in corporate finance work than the commercial banks.

It is wrong to assume that the banking sector is so critical to intermediation that it is the only source of credit. In many post–centrally planned economies the banking sector has been constrained from granting new credit to state-owned enterprises because of management caution and official credit restraint. Enterprises have relied instead on internally generated earnings, interenterprise credit, export sales, and joint ventures with foreign enterprises. In China, the Czech Republic, Hungary, and Poland foreign direct investment has been a major source of capital and know-how for corporate transformation. China also has boosted corporate investment by developing stock markets in Shenzhen and Shanghai and floating shares in Hong Kong. In Russia and Yugoslavia liberal bank licensing laws allow enterprises to own banks to finance their own businesses, creating several problems for the future.

The use of interenterprise credit presents a difficult challenge to bank and enterprise restructuring. Such credit can rise to the level of money supply during a period of tight money. Significant efforts to net such credits were attempted in China and Romania. Because of the large potential losses in such lending, interenterprise credit can bring down good enterprises as well as loss-making ones.

Loss allocation—should the budget bear it all?

The interlocking nature of the post–centrally planned bank and enterprise problem requires that a restructuring strategy be formulated by a high-level interagency committee comprising representatives of the budget ministry, the ministry in charge of privatization, the enterprise sector, the law ministry, the central bank, supervisory authorities, the banks, and the private sector.

In Hungary a banking supervision committee—comprising representatives of the State Banking Supervision, the National Bank, the Ministry of Finance, the State Holding Company, and representatives of the banking and enterprise sectors—was established to advise the government and undertake measures that would coordinate and strengthen bank supervision during restructuring. Such a committee focuses attention on the fact that bank and enterprise restructuring has to be an across-the-board effort. No bank and enterprise restructuring program can be successful without consensus from all parties concerned.

The early debate in some countries over whether the banks or the budget should bear bad debt losses was unproductive since all banks and enterprises belonged to the state at the early stages of transformation. Delays in the removal of the bad debts only worsened the problem. Governments initially tried to avoid absorbing losses in the budget by allowing banks to widen their spreads and generate profits from the inflation tax. This worsened incentives for debt recovery because banks found it easier to generate credit than to recover bad debts. As bank positions deteriorated with the collapse of the Council for Mutual Economic Assistance market, many Central and Eastern European economies had no choice but to act.

Requiring the government to issue bonds to carve out (or at least isolate) the nonperforming loans of the banks raises two issues that are usually hotly debated: the coverage issue and the fee or buyback issue. Both essentially involve the size of the state's share of the debt burden.

Coverage. The first problem, determining the size of the nonperforming loans, depends on the criteria chosen. Conceptually, all classified loans should be fully provisioned, and if banks are undercapitalized the government should recapitalize the banks by issuing bonds at the market interest rate sufficient to cover the capital shortfall. But since the definition of classified loans is still debated (since the value of collateral and the flow of future losses are by no means certain), the true size of the bond issue is subject to considerable variation. Budget officials are likely to argue on the basis on "affordability"—that increasing state debt during the transformation will likely substantially worsen the fiscal position.

On the other hand, the banks and state holding companies that wish to privatize the banks argue that the banks should be cleaned up as much as possible. The state can avoid making an early decision by offering a blanket guarantee on nonperforming loans during the transition period, an approach that creates no immediate cash flow implications. Many governments avoid this path, however, because of the moral hazard risks implied.

Given that the flow of losses will continue until the enterprises are restructured or privatized or until macroeconomic and price stability has been achieved, there will be a continuing burden on the state. The Czech and Slovak Federal Republic had to recapitalize the Bank for Consolidation at least twice since its formation. Hungary had to engage in a loan consolidation scheme in 1992, despite guaranteeing 50 percent of the inherited bad loans as late as 1991.

With respect to coverage of the carve-out, there should be only one uniform criteria for nonperforming loans, to be agreed on by the banks, the auditors, the supervisory authorities, and the tax authorities as early in the process as possible. This makes the process more transparent and equitable in terms of treatment by different banks. Having different definitions of coverage for different bad debts of different periods would generate different incentives for the banks. Banks would be tempted to overstate certain categories of classified loans in order to receive preferential treatment.

Buyback. The second issue is whether the state should reduce its burden by requiring a "buyback" feature or imposing a fee or tax on the banks that benefit from recapitalization. Banks or their shareholders would be required to buy back from the state the after-tax value of the bonds, since the bonds must be repaid from after-tax profits.

If the fee or buyback is levied on the banks, then the cost of the recapitalization effort is reduced by the net present value of the fee or buyback feature. In other words, the banks have been given an asset that is also a liability, the net effect of which may be zero depending on the size of the buyback. This will not have the effect of recapitalizing banks in order to improve their intermediation, since the banks may pass the full extent of their burden onto borrowers or depositors by widening spreads.

The net effect is the same if the fee or buyback is levied on the bank shareholders, except that the banks' balance sheet would improve at the expense of the shareholders. But to the extent that the shareholders force the banks to generate higher dividends to repay the fee or the buyback, the "intermediation improvement" effect is correspondingly reduced. Imposing the buyback on the shareholders also creates a new class of shares because all existing shares become subject to the "lien" of the buyback. This would hamper future efforts at privatization because new shareholders will not want to share in the loss and old shareholders will want the newcomers to bear some of the burden of past losses.

A more common method of avoiding the buyback is for the state to increase the capital of banks (through ordinary or preferred shares) to the extent of estimated losses. The increased share capital dilutes the equity of existing shareholders, and the bad debts can be written off against the enlarged capital base of the banks (or against the preferred share element) on a parri passu basis. The state benefits from the bank recapitalization through future dividends or from the sale of such shares. The state can also use this opportunity to reduce the extent of bank shareholdings of enterprises that are also substantial borrowers from their banks.

It should be recognized that the budget cannot bear the complete losses of the banking system all at once. Nor is the true size of the losses fully determined at this stage since it depends on other factors, such as the macroeconomic environment. Still, if the government wants to improve intermediation in the banking system, it has to decide what level of net resources it wishes to allocate to bank recapitalization. The net effect can be reduced if the government decides to issue bonds at a below-market interest rate, since these bonds will have to priced at market value.

There is therefore a clear tradeoff between the extent of state contribution (in the stock of bonds) and the benefits in the improvement of bank intermediation. Since different banks price their spreads differently depending on the assistance they receive, the method of recapitalization is critical. In other words, the method of recapitalization will have incentive effects that may defeat the whole objective of recapitalization.

Privatization before restructuring?

Should state-owned banks be privatized before or after restructuring? Experience with privatization, particularly where foreign investors are involved, indicates that such exercises should be as credible and transparent as possible. If banks are privatized (or minority shares sold to the public) before a clean-up, the state may have to pay for larger clean-ups at a later stage.

Poland successfully privatized some banks after a period of restructuring and twinning, where foreign banks advised state banks on privatization and internal reorganization. Other post–centrally planned economies have had problems privatizing banks before restructuring because foreign banks are cautious about investing in banks with uncertain asset quality. In such cases the state would gain more from privatization if the banks were restructured before flotation.

The role of banks in enterprise restructuring

To what extent should banks be involved in the restructuring of their problem borrowers? Banks have perhaps the best concentration of skills—however limited—and information on enterprise performance and behavior, and through their long association with enterprises have considerable supervisory power because of their control of credit.

Because enterprises in these economies have large employment and social welfare responsibilities, however, the banks do not have the political backing to engage in massive restructuring that would entail retrenchment of labor, nor do they have the resources to finance new long-term investments, since their own deposit base has very short maturity.

In addition, commercial banks in the West—unlike investment banks—have never been significantly involved in financing corporate restructuring. Supervisors in the post–centrally planned economies who enforce the traditional separation between commercial banking and the corporate sector also have built into the banking law safeguards against banks taking too much equity in enterprises.

As discussed earlier, bank and enterprise restructuring requires a rewriting of the national balance sheet, redistributing gains and losses. Successful restructuring strengthens financial balances in all domestic sectors. The issue is whether short-term bank funding is the correct mechanism to resolve fundamental issues of enterprise inefficiency and hence national losses. A related question is whether the state should absorb the losses of both the enterprise and banking sectors through debt carve-outs or their equivalent.

The failure of the enterprise and banking sectors in these economies has much to do with the grossly overleveraged financial structures of central planning, which centralized all risks (and ownership) in the hands of the state. Given the distorted and inefficient pricing structure that prevails in these economies, requiring the banks to provide more debt to nascent private sector enterprises or overleveraged state enterprises cannot improve their overall financial position.

The long-run solution must come from redressing the debt-equity ratios of key sectors, moving them to a more viable and sustainable position. This implies that the domestic economy requires more capital—namely, savings, foreign investment, or retained earnings—rather than more debt. The banking system cannot provide long-term investment capital for enterprises, only short-term working capital. But it can help the restructuring process by imposing financial discipline, reducing transaction costs through intermediation, and helping to weed out inefficient enterprises.

The solutions to enterprise restructuring have to come from the generation of domestic equity, either from privatization or from removing trade and distributional barriers to market entry, which would foster domestic savings in the form of private entrepreneurial retained earnings. Encouraging foreign direct investment also helps. Fostering capital and equity markets clearly supplements this effort.

The development of restructuring enterprises should be left to investment banks, which can be created through joint ventures with foreign investment banks with expertise in such restructuring. Resolving the real sector will require supply-side solutions, which cannot be undertaken by inducing the banking system to direct credit to large loss-making ventures. Such credit would put the short-term deposits of the banking system at risk levels that would destabilize the economy in the long term.

The transformation of previously state-owned factors of production toward market orientation requires that economic decisions ultimately be decentralized to the marketplace. As stated earlier, bank restructuring is ultimately about building sounder financial structures and clearer property rights. The process of bank restructuring, diagnosis, damage control, loss allocation, and getting the incentives right is essentially about the definition of property rights and obligations. Hence, rewriting the national balance sheet will require a closely coordinated effort of reforms in all sectors, in which commercial banking is only one component. And because many institutional changes are involved, the process will necessarily take time.

Conclusion

We are witnessing a dramatic integration of the post–centrally planned economies with the international market economy. This transformation will bring with it enormous challenges of bank and enterprise restructuring. As stated earlier, this volume is not a definitive guide for bank supervisors, encompassing all the ideas and experiences related to the phenomenon of financial distress. A wide range of ideas have been brought together to show how complex the origins and effects of the problems are, and how difficult the solutions. There has never been a single, quick solution to financial distress. What this volume hopes to show is that there are common approaches and integrated processes, taking into account the need to be consistent in rewriting the national balance sheet, along with important institutional, legal, and commercial changes in markets, products, and human skills, that could lead to the design of better restructuring programs.

References

American Banker. December 27, 1990.
Bank Negara Malaysia. 1987. *Annual Report 1986.* Kuala Lumpur.
Basle Committee on Banking Supervision. 1992. *International Developments in Banking Supervision.* Basle, Switzerland.
Butsch, Jean-Louis. 1992. "The Role of Banking Supervisory Authorities in the Prevention of Systemic Risk." Paper presented at the seventh international conference of banking supervisors, October 7–9, Cannes.
Corrigan, E. Gerald. 1992. "Strengthening International Cooperation between Banking Supervisors." Paper presented at the seventh international conference of banking supervisors, October 7–9, Cannes.
de Juan, Aristobulo. 1991. "Does Bank Insolvency Matter? And What to do About It?" Economic Development Institute Working Paper. World Bank, Washington, D.C.
Emery, Robert. 1993. "Developing a Government Bond Market." Financial Sector Development Department Technical Paper. World Bank, Washington, D.C.
Federal Reserve Board, Federal Deposit Insurance Corporation, and U.S. Comptroller of the Currency. 1992. "Joint Report to the Senate Banking Committee." Washington, D.C.
Fischer, Stanley, and William Easterly. 1990. "The Economics of the Government Budget Constraint." *World Bank Research Observer* 5(2):127–42.
Gelb, Alan, and Patrick Honohan. 1989. "Financial Sector Reforms in Adjustment Programs." Policy Research Working Paper 169. World Bank, Washington D.C.
Gibeault, Jean. 1993. "Credit Risk Bureaus." Financial Sector Development Department Technical Paper. World Bank, Washington, D.C.
Glaessner, Thomas, and Ignacio Mas. 1991. "Incentive Structure and Resolution of Financial Institution Crises: Latin America Experience." Latin America Technical Department Technical Paper. World Bank, Washington, D.C.
Goldstein, Morris, and David Folkerts-Landau. 1993. "The Growing Involvement of Banks in Derivative Finance: A Challenge for Financial Policy." In *International Capital Markets, Part II: Systemic Issues in International Finance.* Washington, D.C.: International Monetary Fund.
Hanson, James, and Roberto Rocha. 1986. "High Interest Rates, Spreads, and the Costs of Intermediation." Industry and Finance Series 18. World Bank, Washington, D.C.
Hove, Andrew C. 1994. "Resolving Failed Banks." Paper presented at the eighth international conference of banking supervisors, October 12, Vienna.

IMF (International Monetary Fund). 1993. *International Capital Markets, Part II: Systemic Issues in International Finance.* Washington, D.C.

Lin See Yan. 1992. "Financial Reform in Malaysia: The Institutional Perspective." Bank Negara Malaysia, Kuala Lumpur.

McKinnon, R. 1991. "Taxation, Money, and Credit in Liberalizing Socialist Economies: Asian and European Experiences." Stanford University, Department of Economics, Stanford, Calif.

McPherson, Donald. 1992. "Reformation of the Regulatory Framework for Financial Institutions in Canada." World Bank, Financial Policy and Systems Division, Washington, D.C.

Musch, Erick. 1992. "A Framework for Measuring and Managing Liquidity." Paper presented at the seventh international conference of banking supervisors, October 7–9, Cannes.

Nakajima, Zenta, and Hiroo Taguchi. 1993. "Toward a More Stable Financial Framework: Long-Term Alternatives." Bank of Japan, Institute of Monetary and Economic Studies, Tokyo.

National Bank of Hungary. 1992. "Monthly Report, September." Budapest.

Quinn, Brian. 1991. "Techniques for Dealing with Problem Banks." In P. Downes and R. Vaez-Zadeh, eds., *The Evolving Role of Central Banks.* Washington, D.C.: International Monetary Fund.

Sheng, Andrew. 1991. "Bank Supervision: Principles and Practice." Economic Development Institute Working Paper. World Bank, Washington, D.C.

———. 1992. "Bad Debts in Transitional Socialist Economies." World Bank, Financial Policy and Systems Division, Washington, D.C.

Sheng, Andrew, and Yoon Je Cho. 1993. "Risk Management and Stable Financial Structures." Policy Research Working Paper 1109. World Bank, Washington, D.C.

Snoy, Bernard. 1992. "Privatization and Financial Sector Reform in Central and Eastern Europe." Paper presented at the Colloquium of Association Internationale de Droit Economique (AIDE), Budapest.

Summers, Bruce J. 1992. "The Role of the Central Bank in Developing Payment Systems." Paper presented at the nineteenth SEANZA central banking course, November, Tokyo.

Talley, Samuel H., and Ignacio Mas. "Deposit Insurance in Developing Countries." Policy Research Working Paper 548. World Bank, Washington, D.C.

U.S. Comptroller of the Currency. 1992. "Remarks of William P. Bowden, Jr. on National Banks in the United States." *Quarterly Journal* 11(1): 51–61. Washington, D.C.

U.S. GAO (General Accounting Office). 1989. *Thrift Failures.* Washington, D.C.

U.S. Treasury. 1991. "Modernizing the Financial System." Washington, D.C.

World Bank. 1993. "Bank Supervision: Suggested Guidelines." Financial Policy and Systems Division, Washington, D.C.

Zahler, Roberto. 1993. "Financial Sector Reforms and Liberalization: Welcome Address." In Shakil Faruqi, ed., *Financial Sector Reforms in Asian and Latin American Countries.* Economic Development Insitute Seminar Series, Washington, D.C.: World Bank.

CHAPTER 4

The United States: Resolving Systemic Crisis, 1981–91

Andrew Sheng

The United States has the largest banking system in the world, with 29,000 mostly small, regionally restricted deposit-taking financial intermediaries and more than $5 trillion in assets. With 12,500 commercial banks, the United States has about ten times as many banks per capita as the other countries in the Group of Ten combined. Japan has only 150 commercial banks, and the United Kingdom 600 licensed deposit-takers (Miller 1991). The United States also has what is probably the most complex statutory regulatory regime in existence (table 4.1). Deposit insurance in the U.S. banking system is comprehensive—covering all deposits under $100,000—and practically universal.

Because the United States traditionally has favored a unitary, rather than an interstate, branch banking

system, the deposit insurance and regulatory regimes created in the 1930s were designed not only to promote stability, but also to facilitate orderly exit. Despite the advanced supervisory system, however, there were 1,100 commercial bank failures and 630 thrift (savings and loan institutions) insolvencies requiring official intervention during the 1980s. The number of thrift institutions fell by more than 30 percent and banks by about 14 percent through market-driven consolidation within the industry, officially assisted resolutions, and occasional liquidation. This record of instability was unparalleled since the banking crisis of the 1930s, when 4,370 banks failed between 1933 and 1940—4,000 of them in 1933 alone. By 1991 U.S. taxpayers had contributed at least $80

Table 4.1 Regulatory mechanisms for U.S. depository institutions as of June 30, 1990

Institution	Number	Assets (billions of U.S. dollars)	Share of total assets of depository institutions (percent)	Regulatory agency
Commercial banks	12,502	3,360.0	66.7	Office of the Comptroller of the Currency: "National" banks Federal Reserve Bank: Bank holding companies and state-chartered members of the Federal Reserve System Federal Deposit Insurance Corporation: National and state-chartered, federally insured, nonmembers of the Federal Reserve State agencies
Savings banks insured by the Bank Insurance Fund	461	233.4	4.6	Federal Deposit Insurance Corporation
Thrifts and other savings banks[a]	2,878	1,251.7	24.8	Office of Thrift Supervision: All institutions insured by the Savings Association Insurance Fund, including most state-chartered thrifts State agencies
Credit unions	13,102	195.3	3.9	National Credit Union Administration
Total	28,943	5,040.4	100.0	Five federal and fifty state agencies

a. As of December 31, 1989.
Source: U.S. GAO 1991; U.S. Treasury 1991.

billion to "cleaning up" the thrift industry, with still more demands to follow. In addition, the 1991 FDIC Improvement Act approved $70 billion to recapitalize the Bank Insurance Fund operated by the Federal Deposit Insurance Corporation (FDIC). How could a debacle of this magnitude occur in a system of this size and sophistication, where no less than five federal and fifty state regulatory agencies oversee deposit-taking activities, and where comprehensive deposit insurance has existed for more than fifty years?

The Origins of Failure

Many of the reasons for the exceptional number of failures are common to other banking systems in distress. Nevertheless, the U.S. case merits special comment because of its sheer cost in nominal terms and the lessons it holds for developing countries with less sophisticated banking systems. This chapter focuses on two main groups of institutions: the roughly 3,000 thrifts with one-quarter of total depository system assets and the 12,000 commercial banks with two-thirds of system assets. Although their problems evolved differently—and the thrift industry crisis unfolded earlier—they share a legacy of cyclical and structural weaknesses. Specifically, they faced drastic changes as technological innovation fostered competition, they operated in a regulatory environment replete with overlaps and gaps, their operating freedom was segmented both functionally and geographically, and they suffered the moral hazard risks of a comprehensive deposit insurance umbrella. These structural weaknesses were exacerbated by cyclical factors when the U.S. economy entered a recession in 1980–81, emerged with a period of strong growth, and then entered another recession in 1990.

There were, however, important initial qualitative differences between the problems of thrifts and those of banks. First, structural differences affected their ability to adapt to changing market conditions. Thrifts were historically fixed-rate mortgage lenders with variable deposit rate liabilities and thus were subject to massive interest rate risks, whereas banks faced less severe maturity mismatches and had greater investment flexibility. As a result the thrift industry suffered a systemwide technical insolvency of truly crisis proportions during 1980–83, when U.S. domestic interest rates rose to unprecedented levels. By contrast, the commercial banking system, despite more than 1,000 bank failures during the 1980s, remained both solvent and profitable. The

few hundred bank failures prior to 1989 were resolved comfortably within the resources of the FDIC and had no discernible real economic or financial impact. It was not until the end of the decade—when the magnitude of large bank failures threatened to bankrupt the deposit insurance fund for banks—that uncomfortable parallels with the early thrift crisis arose. Moreover, the decrease in profitability and increase in the domestic loan losses of the banks grew as the economic recession that began in 1990 continued. This provoked a very real fear of a domestic credit crunch and further deflationary consequences.

There are also important similarities in structural weakness, which came to the fore in the second half of the 1980s. Unlike their European counterparts, the U.S. bank and thrift systems are highly segmented functionally, geographically, and in terms of regulatory oversight. Furthermore, until the mid-1980s deposit interest rate ceilings under Federal Reserve Regulation Q constrained the ability of banks and thrifts to attract personal savings.[1] These ceilings heightened the competition between the two types of institutions for domestic savings and encouraged the growth of money market funds and other deposit substitutes. Specifically, the banks lost their franchise value in the 1980s and sought to regain market share within the confines of regulatory corsets. Even though Regulation Q was eventually removed, the built-in structural rigidities impeded the banks' and thrifts' ability to make a smooth adjustment to a world of unstable relative prices or to accommodate to competitive changes in domestic and international markets, including the rapid pace of technological innovation that began in the 1970s.

During the 1970s and 1980s the banks lost their franchise on the payments mechanism, low-interest deposits, and loans to commerce and industry due to technological innovation and competition from credit card companies, money market funds, insurance companies, mortgage pools, and pension funds. From 1960 to 1994 the depository institutions' share of financial intermediary assets fell from 39 percent to about 29 percent (Edwards and Mishkin 1995). In 1960 bank loans to commerce and industry were nearly ten times the size of the commercial paper market. By 1989 that ratio had fallen to just under 1.5 times. Demand deposits of banks fell from 60 percent of total deposits to less than 20 percent over the same period. Competition also came from foreign banks. Between 1983 and 1990 the percentage of commercial and industrial loans provided by foreign banks rose from 20 percent to just over 29 percent.

Another factor contributing to the problems of banks and thrifts was the extensive financial deregulation in the early 1980s, which coincided with an increase in deposit insurance coverage. These developments allowed greater bank gearing and expanded portfolio diversification. They also encouraged new entrants and promoted rapid growth. These sudden changes also encouraged higher risk-taking and speculation by some institutions in highly leveraged transactions and real estate. For most of the decade this speculative expansion was underpinned by an unusually long period of domestic economic growth promoted by the free market, supply-side economic philosophy and policies of the Reagan administration. At the same time, deposit insurance coverage was extended widely through the "too big to fail" principle when regulatory authorities intervened to save a number of large institutions. Brokered deposits and "pass-through coverage" also overextended insurance coverage. Consequently, extensive moral hazard risks arose at a time when regulatory oversight—particularly, but not exclusively, of the thrifts—was relaxed due to budgetary cutbacks.[2]

These cumulative factors—loss of franchise, deregulation and intense competition, geographical and functional segmentation, moral hazard, and gaps in regulation—reinforced losses rooted in macroeconomic and microeconomic factors. The combined effects of regional economic downturns, poor bank management, imprudent lending practices in foreign debt and then real estate, and, in the case of thrifts, extensive fraud, generated unprecedented losses in the U.S. banking system. A structural risk asymmetry existed: the government had an open-ended obligation to protect deposit liabilities during a period when banking asset values were exposed to volatile market forces and private sector mismanagement.

The System of Depository Institutions

The United States has no national banking system, making it unique among industrial countries. Reflecting the populist mood of the country against the concentration of wealth and power, the banking and the thrift systems were designed with two aims: to prevent market concentration by preserving regional and functional markets and to ensure safety and soundness under industry-financed deposit protection, which was mandated by the federal government and ultimately guaranteed by it as well. Historically, thrifts were organized primarily as mutual associations, and they provided long-term, fixed-interest, predominantly residential mortgages for their local communities. Accordingly, their asset base was more specialized than that of commercial banks and their overall interest rate risk significantly higher. The legislative foundations for this system were laid in the 1930s in response to the failure of more than 4,000 U.S. banks. Despite the evolution of bank and thrift holding companies as vehicles for circumventing statutory restrictions on functional and geographic diversification, until the 1990s no nationwide branching system had evolved.

Regulatory overlaps and gaps

The supervisory system allows for regulatory overlap and regulatory arbitrage because banks and thrifts can be chartered by federal or state authorities. Over time, however, the balance of supervision has fallen on the federal government, largely because of the federal guarantee backing the industry-financed deposit insurance. Each of the four principal federal supervisory agencies has an extensive off-site surveillance system backed by selective on-site examination processes. These agencies employed some 6,800 examiners at the end of 1989, 1,500 more than at the low point in 1984.

The Office of Thrift Supervision authorizes national thrifts and savings banks, whereas the Office of the Comptroller of the Currency, an agency of the U.S. Treasury, charters national banks. The term *national bank* refers to a bank chartered by federal agencies. Since 1989 the Office of Thrift Supervision has regulated virtually all thrifts.[3] The Board of Governors of the Federal Reserve System (the central bank) supervises bank holding companies; its regional Federal Reserve Banks are also responsible for state-chartered banks that are members of the Federal Reserve System and that have access to the central bank discount window and lender-of-last-resort facilities.[4]

Deposit insurance falls under the purview of the Federal Deposit Insurance Corporation (FDIC). The FDIC also supervises, often jointly with state chartering agencies, its state-chartered member banks that do not belong to the Federal Reserve System. Until August 1989 there was also a Federal Savings and Loan Insurance Corporation (FSLIC), which all federally chartered thrifts were obliged to join and to which most state-chartered ones also belonged.[5] A

Savings Association Insurance Fund, maintained separately within the FDIC and financed by the thrift industry, was created in 1989 to replace the old deposit insurance fund beginning in August 1992. In the interim, thrift deposit insurance was provided by the newly created Resolution Trust Corporation (RTC). The RTC was financed partly with federal funds and was charged with taking over and resolving thrifts that failed after August 1989.

Geographical segmentation in the system is enforced through limitations on interstate banking and limitations on intrastate branching. The McFadden Act of 1927 allows states to restrict or prevent branching, and since most states do not permit entry into their territory through branches of banks from another state, interstate branching is effectively prohibited. The need to attract out-of-state capital to assist in resolving local banking problems has led to some relaxation of these restrictions, however. By 1991 almost all states permitted interstate banking by bank holding companies owning local banks through state-chartered subsidiaries. To enable banks and thrifts to grow out of their problems, most states also relaxed their limits on intrastate branch banking by banks headquartered in their states. Nevertheless, laws still prevent interstate bank branching throughout the United States. Reform proposals introduced by the U.S. Treasury in 1991 would have allowed nationwide branching by banks. Most of these highly controversial recommendations, however, failed to receive the necessary congressional approval.

Functional segmentation is mandated by the Banking Act of 1933 (the Glass-Steagall Act), which prohibits all Federal Reserve members from engaging in investment banking activities, particularly from dealing directly in underwriting or purchasing securities (except for certain government issues). Moreover, the act prohibits any person or company that issues, underwrites, sells, or distributes securities from taking deposits from the public. U.S. money center banks therefore cannot engage in investment banking and securities activities that are open to European banks. While this functional segregation made sense when banks had an exclusive "franchise" in deposit-taking activities, this profit base was eroded substantially in the 1970s. Money market funds and other deposit-substituting innovations offered by investment banks and nonbanks now also capture domestic savings. Consequently, functional segmentation also has eroded in recent years as federal authorities relaxed or reinterpreted

Glass-Steagall provisions to permit limited securities activities. Moreover, some state-chartered banks have enjoyed more freedom anyway. The U.S. Treasury's 1991 reform proposal would have abolished Glass-Steagall restrictions.

Deposit insurance encouraged moral hazard behavior

The two deposit insurance funds created in the early 1930s, FSLIC (for thrifts) and FDIC (for commercial banks), virtually eliminated bank runs in the United States, but their intrinsic flaws emerged during the 1980s. For example, banks pay deposit insurance premiums on a flat-rate basis, regardless of the different risks inherent in each bank. Furthermore, the insurance coverage per account was raised from $40,000 to $100,000 in 1980, a fourfold increase in real terms from the original $2,500 set in 1933.[6] By relaxing the definition of deposit coverage to include "brokered" deposits, thrifts and banks were able to finance growth from access to savings nationwide.[7] Furthermore, the deposit insurance scheme was implicitly extended to cover 100 percent of the deposit liabilities of thrifts and banks, with few exceptions, under the "too big to fail" principle. Regulators decided not to allow some larger banks to fail and guaranteed all deposits—the bailout of Continental Illinois in 1984 is a notable example. And in the case of official thrift resolutions, it was also common practice to protect all deposits.

The FSLIC actually had to be closed in late 1989 after a failed attempt to recapitalize it under the 1987 Competitive Equality Banking Act. It wound up with the largest corporate deficit ($87 billion) ever reported (U.S. GAO 1990). At the same time, the commercial banks' insurance fund in the FDIC was renamed the Bank Insurance Fund. Consequently, at the end of 1989 the FDIC and RTC together were providing deposit insurance coverage to 12,706 commercial banks, 476 state-chartered and 20 federally chartered savings banks, and 2,878 federally and state-chartered thrifts (U.S. Treasury 1991).

Macroeconomic Developments

The structural weaknesses in the U.S. banking system were exacerbated by cyclical factors. During the 1970s inflation rose as a result of successive oil shocks. As part of the recycling of petrodollar surpluses, banks began their aggressive lending to developing countries. Deregulation in the securities, telecommunications, airline, and natural gas markets generated more competitive pressure in the economy. As competition from savings banks, real estate trusts, mutual funds, and pension and insurance funds began to erode the banks' market share, they responded by diversifying out of traditional bank lending activities, mainly through the creation of bank holding companies.

The escalation of thrift failures in the early 1980s was a consequence of the 1979–82 recession. In late 1979 the Federal Reserve severely tightened monetary policy in an effort to curb inflation. Treasury bill rates rose to nearly 16 percent a year in 1981, compared with an average of 10 percent in 1979 (5.5 percent in 1977). These events, combined with a sudden, sharp increase in world oil prices, acted as a brake on the economy. Concurrently, the steep appreciation of the dollar during 1981–84 affected the international competitiveness of U.S. firms, which were already hurt by rising financial and fuel costs. Dollar appreciation also had an adverse impact on the U.S. agricultural sector. When the economic slowdown in 1979–80 was followed almost immediately in 1982 by the worst recession since the 1930s, unemployment rose and business bankruptcies reached a post–World War II high. Growth in real gross national product (GNP) dropped from 1.9 percent in 1981 to –2.6 percent in 1982 (table 4.2).

The U.S. economy was sufficiently large and diversified to absorb these shocks, and it rebounded to enjoy steady economic growth from 1983 to the end of the decade. Nevertheless, different sectors and regions were affected at different times with varying severity by changes in the business cycle and relative prices. Regional economic recessions, in turn, adversely affected banks and thrifts in those areas. In particular, declining prices and exports of U.S. farm products resulted in a sharp deterioration in agricultural land values, leading to the failure of Midwest farm banks in the early and mid-1980s. Similarly, from 1982 to 1988 nominal domestic oil prices fell by 57 percent, with severe impact on oil-producing states in the South and Southwest. Thrifts and banks had expanded aggressively in these areas on the basis of oil wealth accumulated in the late 1970s. In Texas, for example, thrift assets increased from $35 billion in 1982 to $85 billion in 1985 (U.S. Treasury 1991).

In addition, tax incentives stimulated real estate construction in 1982, with an across-the-board impact on residential and commercial property development. The speculative boom in property was financed by liberal lending by thrifts, which sought to grow out of their problems. But when nominal interest rates fell to their lowest levels in 1987, a serious general overcapacity was exposed. This oversupply, on top of regional economic recessions, created pressure on bank asset and collateral values. First in the South and Midwest and subsequently in the Northeast and Southwest, each episode of localized economic downturn had a direct impact on local banks and thrifts, which were virtual captives given their inability to diversify risks through nationwide branch operations. In 1987, for example, 90 percent of bank failures

Table 4.2 Macroeconomic indicators, 1979–90
(percent unless otherwise specified)

Year	Real growth in GDP	Current account/ GDP	Terms of trade (1980=100)ᵃ	Inflation rateᵇ	Government balance/GDP	Certificate of deposit (CD) deposit rate	Prime lending rate	Exchange rate (U.S. dollars/ Special Drawing Rights)
1979	2.1	0.0	105.5	11.3	–1.4	11.2	12.7	1.3
1980	–0.1	0.0	100.0	13.5	–2.8	13.0	15.2	1.2
1981	2.0	0.2	110.4	10.3	–2.6	15.9	18.9	1.1
1982	–2.5	–0.2	110.0	6.2	–4.3	12.3	14.9	1.1
1983	3.7	–1.2	121.2	3.2	–6.0	9.0	10.8	1.0
1984	7.0	–2.7	123.1	4.3	–4.7	10.4	12.0	0.9
1985	3.6	–3.1	124.3	3.6	–5.3	8.0	9.9	1.1
1986	3.0	–3.4	135.7	1.9	–5.0	6.5	8.3	1.2
1987	3.8	–3.6	130.2	3.7	–3.3	6.9	8.2	1.4
1988	4.4	–2.7	146.8	4.0	–3.2	7.7	9.3	1.3
1989	2.5	–2.1	150.1	4.8	–2.8	9.1	10.9	1.3
1990	0.8	–1.7	98.5	5.4	–4.0	8.2	10.0	1.4

— Not available.
a. Ratio of the index of average export prices to the index of average import prices.
b. Consumer price index.
Source: World Bank data; IMF, various years.

occurred in states that still prohibited or at least limited intrastate branching (U.S. GAO 1987).

Beginning in 1983 the national economy grew steadily by borrowing. The supply-side economic philosophy of the period brought cuts in income tax rates and led to rising fiscal deficits. These budget shortfalls averaged 5 percent of GNP during 1982–86, nearly double the level in the previous five years. At the same time, household savings declined from 5.0 percent of GNP to 3.8 percent in the 1980s. As corporate savings also fell in response to increased competition, the net savings rate dropped to only 3.0 percent in the 1980s, less than half of its historical average of 7.5 percent (Harris and Steindel 1991).

In the face of this relaxed fiscal stance, tight monetary policy sought to keep real interest rates high—they averaged 4.5 percent a year from 1983 to the end of the decade—compared with the negative rates that had prevailed during the late 1970s. Short-term rates remained above those of the country's key competitors until the closing years of the decade, which induced capital inflows that financed the rising fiscal and current account deficits. As domestic consumption rose with tax cuts and a favorable exchange rate, the United States experienced the longest uninterrupted economic expansion in postwar history from 1983 to the end of the decade. Unemployment and inflation fell to levels not seen since the early 1970s. Prosperity was accompanied by a prolonged bull market in company shares, rapid appreciation of property values, securitization of debt, and a boom in corporate mergers and acquisitions. Many of these were financed by high-leverage transactions and innovative junk bonds.

The high interest rate environment also intensified competition for new deposits from nonbank and new financial institutions. To create a more level playing field, Regulation Q retail deposit rate ceilings were relaxed beginning in 1980 and eventually eliminated. Although these moves improved liability management, the endowment effect of cheap deposit liabilities was permanently eroded for both banks and thrifts. They saw a steady decline in aggregate financial strength throughout the decade.

There were, therefore, two broad phases to the U.S. bank and thrift crisis. In the early 1980s the thrift industry, whose assets were primarily long-term fixed-rate mortgages, became technically insolvent following the sudden jump in U.S. interest rates. Their costs of funds increased sharply, yet most of them did not have the freedom to offer adjustable rate mort-

gages until 1980. With their variable lending rates, commercial banks were not as seriously affected by interest rate risks, except for a few mutual savings banks in the Northeast.[8] For the most part, however, bank failures were confined to specific geographic regions, involving mainly small banks in agricultural and oil-producing states.[9] They did not have systemic ramifications and were easily managed by the well-capitalized FDIC. Local banks with generally conservative management and adequate capital and reserves were able to weather their temporary distress.

In the face of wholesale thrift insolvencies, and with an increasing number of small bank failures, pressure mounted to deregulate. Encouraged by the popular antipathy toward government interference characteristic of the Reagan administration, legislators and regulators complied in the early 1980s. Consequently, the general outlook for banks and thrifts changed markedly in the mid- and late 1980s. Sustained growth nationwide and growing competition prompted banks and thrifts to expand credit rapidly, relax credit assessments, and engage in imprudent leveraging and outright moral hazard.

Many banks, especially the larger ones, had problems arising from a particular exposure. In the late 1970s banks had enjoyed a large expansion in petrodollar deposits from oil-exporting countries following their windfall oil price increases. A significant amount of this wealth was placed with U.S. money center banks in the Eurodollar markets. It financed large-scale lending to developing countries at a time when U.S. domestic lending opportunities were diminished by the impact of the U.S. recession. By 1983 international business accounted for one-third of U.S. banks' net income. Between March 1981 and September 1982, when the Mexican debt crisis occurred, U.S. banks' exposure to developing countries rose 76.1 percent, to $220.7 billion. Their exposure to twelve highly indebted countries more than doubled, rising from $43.4 billion to $91.1 billion. After 1982, however, this debt became a drag on large banks' profitability as loan arrears and losses mounted. Banks were driven back to the domestic market in search of higher-yielding investments and fee-based income to boost earnings, support loan loss provisioning, and replenish eroding capital.

A 1988 study by the Office of the Comptroller of the Currency revealed that of 171 bank failures between 1979 and 1987, the poor economic environment was a contributing factor in only 35 percent of the cases. And in no case was it the principal cause of failure. Poor bank management, on the other hand, was apparent in 90 percent of the failures. In the thrift industry, where macroeconomic externalities played a greater role in early failures, failures after 1985 were attributed primarily to fraud, gross mismanagement, and extensive speculative investments. Failures increased sharply and were qualitatively different during the second half of the decade.

The thrift crisis, 1980–83

With continued higher costs of funds against an asset base that was tied to fixed-rate lending, the thrift industry become insolvent virtually overnight. Between 1980 and 1983, 470 thrifts failed. The net insolvency of the thrift industry was estimated at $100 billion in 1982 if the assets were marked to market (U.S. Treasury 1991). The FSLIC had insufficient resources to cope with across-the-board depositor pay-offs and liquidations. Because the technical insolvency of the thrifts was systemic, a stock solution would have placed too high a cost on the budget (and on taxpayers) in a political climate that favored budget cutting. Congress consequently adopted a flow remedy to allow thrifts to grow out of their problems. The Depository Institutions Deregulation and Monetary Control Act of 1980 gradually eliminated Regulation Q interest rate ceilings, raised the deposit insurance ceiling to $100,000, and permitted federally chartered thrifts to offer adjustable rate mortgages.[10] In 1982 the Garn-St. Germain Act accelerated the pace of liberalization, authorized certain capital forbearance measures, and permitted emergency interstate acquisition of failed thrifts (U.S. GAO 1987).

Federally chartered thrifts obtained greater access to funding through (insured) brokered deposits, and they were allowed to convert from mutual status to limited liability companies. In addition, authorities pressured troubled but solvent thrifts into "supervisory" mergers without financial assistance from the FSLIC, while market forces induced more than 400 voluntary mergers in 1981 and 1982 alone. Regulators also granted an array of special capital and regulatory forbearance measures that permitted thrifts to stay in business, sometimes for years, even though they were insolvent.[11] Nevertheless, between 1980 and 1983 more than 850 thrifts were closed or merged, mostly through industry consolidation and a few officially managed liquidations (Barth, Bartholomew, and Bradley 1990). When nominal interest rates declined after 1982, the positive impact on thrift profitability appeared to justify the liberalization. Modest positive

Table 4.3 Selected data for federally insured thrifts, 1980–90

Year	Number	Deposits (billions of U.S. dollars)	Earnings (billions of U.S. dollars)
1980	4,005	503.2	—
1981	3,785	519.9	–6.2
1982	3,349	560.5	–5.9
1983	3,183	671.1	2.6
1984	3,136	784.5	1.0
1985	3,246	843.9	3.7
1986	3,220	890.7	0.1
1987	3,147	932.6	–7.8
1988	2,949	971.5	–13.4
1989	2,878	945.7	–17.6
1990	2,699[a]	885.1	–6.5[a]

— Not available.
a. As of June.
Source: U.S. Treasury 1991; U.S. OTS, various years.

aggregate earnings resulted between 1983 and 1985 (table 4.3).

Bank and thrift problems, 1985–89

As late as June 1987, nine U.S. money center banks still held two-thirds of all U.S. banks' claims on fifteen heavily indebted countries, an amount equivalent to 113 percent of their total capital. From 1985 to 1989 U.S. banks managed to reduce the ratio of direct loans to developing countries from 5.9 percent of total loans ($96.6 billion) to 3.3 percent ($66 billion), and they began large-scale loan loss provisioning in 1987. Data on U.S. banks' loan losses on developing country debt is not available, but in 1987 the large money center banks made loss provisions of $20.7 billion on their developing country portfolios, causing the first annual loss for the U.S. banking system as a whole.

The banks are still charging off their developing country debt, a large component of which was sold in the secondary market, rescheduled, or forgiven under Brady debt initiatives. In 1991, 13.4 percent of net loans to foreign governments and institutions was charged off, so that by the end of 1991 such loans totaled $26.3 billion, or less than 1.3 percent of total loans.

The developing country debt burden had a long-run impact on the banking industry as a whole. When the international debt crisis erupted in 1982, U.S. banks turned homeward for growth and earnings prospects in order to build reserves against prospective losses on their developing country loans. In the face of heavy competition, they tried to maximize returns on equity by engaging in off–balance

Table 4.4 Selected financial ratios for commercial banks, 1930–89

(percent)

Ratio	1930–39	1970–79	1980–89	1980–84	1985–89
Equity/ assets	11.88	6.39	6.11	5.96	6.22
Loans/ assets	29.43	53.73	57.75	54.71	59.94
Loans/ equity	2.48	8.41	9.45	9.18	9.64
Reserves/ loans	—	1.33	1.78	1.14	2.20
Loans/ deposits	33.92	65.00	74.15	69.67	77.42
Return on assets	0.46	0.77	0.61	0.69	0.55
Return on equity	3.84	12.09	9.94	11.65	8.77
Net interest margin	1.85	3.00	3.32	3.20	3.41
Net loan chargeoffs/ loans and leases	—	0.39	0.82	0.57	0.99
Net loan chargeoffs/ net income	—	26.86	78.39	45.04	108.96

— Not available.

Source: U.S. Treasury 1991.

sheet and contingent liability transactions. They also increased consumer lending, high-leverage transactions, and domestic real estate lending. By the end of 1990 their exposure to domestic real estate had risen to about 36 percent of total loans, compared with 31 percent in 1980. Noninterest income also doubled between 1982 and 1989 to the equivalent of 15 percent of interest income, while off–balance sheet activities doubled in dollar terms from 58 percent of bank assets to 116 percent.

The financial strength of banks has steadily eroded since the 1930s (table 4.4). Average equity-asset ratios, for example, declined from 11.9 percent in the 1930s to 6.1 percent in the 1980s. Regulatory efforts to raise and harmonize international capital adequacy standards prompted a small increase in the second half of the 1980s. Returns on assets and equity also declined as net loan chargeoffs rose to the unprecedented level of 109 percent of net income between 1985 and 1989. During 1990–91 U.S. banks provisioned $66 billion on loan losses, equivalent to more than 190 percent of their net income. This occurred despite widening net interest margins, which reached their highest level (3.41 percent) ever during the second half of the 1980s.

Of particular concern were debt overhang and real estate loan exposure. During the 1980s the U.S. corporate sector engaged in widespread overleveraging. With the liberalization of several big industries, mergers and acquisitions rose sharply as industries simultaneously engaged in massive competition and consolidation. Debt-financed acquisitions through leveraged buyouts and the issue of junk bonds (subordinated debt) became fashionable. Tax incentives favored debt creation, while defense against takeovers resulted in corporations retiring their own equity.

Between 1984 and 1990 U.S. corporations built up $400 billion in debt, raised $650 billion in securities markets, and retired $640 billion of equity. This pushed corporate debt-to-assets ratios to 32 percent, double the leverage ratios in the early 1950s (Frydl 1991). Similarly, household debt increased as household savings declined and consumption increased. The ratio of household debt to household assets rose from 38 percent in 1980 to more than 52 percent in 1990. Home mortgages rose by $1.3 trillion.

For the banks, however, the greatest exposure was in real estate loans. By the end of 1991 real estate accounted for 41.5 percent (by value) of total loans, compared with 2.7 percent for highly leveraged transactions. Noncurrent real estate loans amounted to 4.6 percent of total real estate loans, compared with 7.6 percent for highly leveraged transaction debt and 12.3 percent for developing country debt (table 4.5).

The real estate overhang was serious because excessive capacity was pervasive. The commercial office vacancy rate in 1991 reached 18 percent, compared with less than 4 percent in 1980, while returns on commercial property turned negative. The failure of large developers such as Olympia and York continued to threaten the profitability of the large banks.

Although the number of bank failures declined to 108 in 1991 (table 4.6), the assets of failed banks jumped to $66 billion, compared with $19 billion in 1990. At the same time, the assets of problem banks

Table 4.5 Noncurrent loan rates at year-end, 1983–93

(percentage of total assets)

1983	1984	1985	1986	1987	1988	1989	1990	1991	1992	1993
1.96	1.97	1.87	1.94	2.46	2.14	2.30	2.94	3.02	2.54	1.61

Source: U.S. FDIC, various issues.

Table 4.6 Problem indicators, 1985–91

Indicator	1985	1986	1987	1988	1989	1990	1991
Unprofitable FDIC-insured commercial banks (as a percentage of total)	17.1	19.8	17.7	14.6	12.5	13.4	10.8
Problem commercial and savings banks	1,140	1,484	1,575	1,406	1,109	1,046	1,069
Failed or assisted FDIC-insured commercial banks	118	144	201	221	206	159	108
Assets of failed banks (billions of U.S. dollars)	—	—	10.1	49.8	30.2	18.7	66.2
Assets of problem commercial and savings banks (billions of U.S. dollars)	237.8	335.5	358.5	352.2	235.5	408.8	611.1
Noncurrent loans and leases plus real estate owned/ total assets of FDIC-insured commercial banks	1.87	1.95	2.46	2.14	2.26	2.90	2.99

— Not available.
Source: U.S. FDIC, various issues; Federal Reserve Bank of Kansas City 1992.

rose by 50 percent to $611.1 billion, accounting for 17.8 percent of total bank assets.

The thrifts, for their part, tried to expand out of their residential mortgage enclave during the mid-1980s. Deregulation, easy access to funds, and a federal deposit guarantee encouraged an influx of entrepreneurs to take over ailing thrifts, often with little requirement to commit new capital. The thrifts' ownership structure also changed. By the mid-1980s more than half the thrifts were full-fledged, profit-motivated, limited liability companies; in 1980, 73 percent had been mutual institutions with home ownership as their sole communal goal. They advanced aggressively into direct real estate investments—especially commercial and industrial real estate—and industrial and commercial loans, in which they had little expertise. Once-conservative thrifts invested heavily in junk bonds in search of higher yields without fully understanding the risks involved.[12] Thrift failures were conspicuously high among the new entrants and where aggressive new management abandoned conservative lending policies.

By mid-decade the overall situation among depository institutions was deteriorating rapidly despite continued economic growth. The combination of eroding margins, higher-risk lending, regulatory forbearance, and intense competition among banks, thrifts, and other financial institutions began to take its toll. Regional economic factors also continued to play an important role, especially in oil-producing regions as oil prices fell. The FDIC reported 322 bank failures during 1980–85; there were nearly 800 during 1986–89 (table 4.7). In the energy-producing region of the Eleventh Federal Reserve District, which includes Texas, 265 banks failed between 1988 and 1989, nearly one-fifth the number of banks in the district.[13] Nine of the ten

largest Texan bank holding companies received FDIC assistance. Furthermore, in 1988—when 221 FDIC-insured banks with assets of $53.7 billion failed—the corporation reported its first-ever operating loss. The incidence of large bank failures was rising, and bank holding company failures were beginning to drain the resources of the FDIC.

Similarly, the number of thrifts requiring deposit protection and official resolution increased markedly as accumulated credit problems materialized. These failures were qualitatively different from the earlier episode since they could not be attributed to the interest rate mismatches of the early 1980s. Nearly three-quarters of the 631 official thrift resolutions recorded from 1980 through 1989 occurred after 1984 (table 4.8). The FSLIC was virtually insolvent by early 1989 and was wound up in August.

Response to the Crisis

In the face of rising failures, the regulatory agencies adopted market-based and innovative measures to restructure ailing institutions.

Table 4.7 Bank failure resolutions, 1980–89

Year	Purchase and assumption	Insured deposit transfer	Insured deposit payoff	Open bank assistance	Total
1980	7	0	3	1	11
1981	8	0	2	3	13
1982	35	0	7	8	50
1983	36	0	9	3	48
1984	62	12	4	2	80
1985	87	7	22	4	120
1986	98	19	21	7	145
1987	133	40	11	19	203
1988	164	30	6	21	221
1989	175	22	9	1	207
Total	805	130	94	69	1,098

Source: U.S. Treasury 1991.

Table 4.8 Thrift failure resolutions, 1980–90

Year	Liquidations	Mergers and acquisitions	Management consignment program[a]	Conservatorships	Total
1980	0	11	0	0	11
1981	1	27	0	0	28
1982	1	62	0	0	63
1983	5	31	0	0	36
1984	9	13	0	0	22
1985	9	22	23	0	54
1986	10	36	29	0	75
1987	17	30	25	0	72
1988	26	179	18	0	223
1989	7	1	0	37	47[b]
1990	0	0	0	315	315
Total	85	413	95	352	946

a. Only lasted from 1985–88.
b. Includes ten resolutions by the FSLIC before August 9, 1989, when the Financial Institutions Reform, Recovery, and Enforcement Act was passed, although only eight are accounted for under liquidations and mergers and acquisitions.
Source: U.S. OTS, various years.

FSLIC and FDIC intervention

The regulatory response to the thrift crisis, however, showed an initial preference for deferring realization of market value losses. Officials urgently needed to avoid liquidations or costly restructuring because the insurance fund (FSLIC) had a book net worth of only about $6 billion in 1981. This would have completely evaporated if the fund had continued to provide financial assistance to failed institutions. On the banking front, however, circumstances were different. Liquidation of large banks was abjured largely on a "too big to fail" basis, exemplified early in the decade when federal authorities took control of Continental Illinois Bank (1984). By contrast, smaller bank failures, although regionally disruptive, were resolved comfortably with the then-ample resources of the FDIC, and generally without liquidation.[14]

In general, the FSLIC preferred low-cost or no-cost interventions that conserved its cash. These included the Management Consignment Program, which placed troubled and poorly run thrifts under the management of other institutions or individuals at no cost to the FSLIC. Introduced in 1985, the program was discontinued in 1988 because franchise values tended to deteriorate. Hired management did not have enough financial incentive to restructure the institutions quickly and adequately for resale. In the early years, the Federal Home Loan Bank Board also merged groups of insolvent thrifts into new institutions—"phoenixes"—with new management and provided some recapitalization (Silverberg 1990). But with the number of thrift insolvencies rising to more

than 100 a year in 1984–85, the FSLIC shifted emphasis.

The FSLIC tried to keep thrifts open long enough to arrange mergers or acquisitions. Keeping some troubled thrifts afloat required regulatory forbearance, including capital augmentation and income maintenance techniques as enticements to new owners.[15] However, these techniques became very costly because some of the acquisitions required additional assistance later.[16] The thrifts were simply too insolvent to recover, a fact that was particularly evident among some of the resolutions arranged in December 1988. New investors often were not required to put up much cash, while the FSLIC filled the net worth hole with special financing instruments. Although these arrangements conserved the FSLIC's cash and permitted the new investors to borrow against future revenue streams, they frequently left the agency with contingent liabilities. Hurried transactions have been criticized for the competitive advantage they gave to thinly capitalized thrifts and for their failure to promote sound management of acquired assets, which were sweetened with government guarantees covering yields and capital values (Fogel 1990).

With larger resources, and a relatively lower level of problems in the banking sector, the FDIC had authority to provide "open bank assistance" to avert failures. This assistance involved preventive intervention before closure, which usually included cooperative assistance from the Federal Reserve in the form of emergency credits for temporary liquidity purposes.[17] Banks were kept open if the FDIC felt that their operations were essential to the community. Where failures did occur, FDIC law required bank regulators to choose a method of resolution that was less costly than liquidating the institution and paying off depositors. However, the method chosen did not necessarily have to be the least costly remedy. The Garn-St. Germain Act relaxed even this requirement and expanded the authority for open bank assistance. The law also empowered the FDIC to permit emergency interstate acquisitions of failed institutions.

Most often, however, the FDIC arranged purchases and assumptions, similar to thrift mergers and acquisitions (see tables 4.7 and 4.8). Purchases and assumptions involved cash contributions covering the shortfall of assets over liabilities (less the premium paid by the acquirer). In later years the agency sometimes substituted interest-bearing notes. Although acquirers recapitalized the banks, the FDIC might contribute some new capital as well. Beginning in

1986 the fund pursued "whole bank" purchases and assumptions more aggressively because "clean bank" carve-outs of all bad assets were draining its resources. When whole-bank transfers became more difficult to arrange, the FDIC introduced "small loan" purchases and assumptions, whereby acquirers agreed to take a package of smaller loans, including some nonperforming ones. By the early 1990s, with the increasing number of large bank failures, the FDIC was running out of resources to undertake even these resolutions. At this point the General Accounting Office, the auditing and investigative arm of the U.S. Congress, recommended establishing a formal early closure policy. The agency was keen to reduce the average rate of loss (16 percent of total assets) incurred by banks that failed between 1985 and 1989.

In March 1990 FDIC assistance to ailing institutions became subject to three key criteria: all proposals had to be considered with a competitive bidding process, institutions requesting assistance had to agree to unrestricted "due diligence" review by all potential acquirers cleared by the FDIC, and bidders had to establish quantitative limits on guarantees so that the FDIC could assess the cost of each proposal.

Regulatory forbearance

Outright capital and regulatory forbearance for ailing depository institutions was another important feature of bank restructuring. It supported the efforts to avoid liquidation, even though resolution costs ultimately rose as a result. Regulators and supervisors not only allowed forbearance of capital requirements, but relaxed accounting standards as well. In addition, budgetary cutbacks reduced the number, frequency, and quality of examinations in the earlier years, although vigilance increased toward the end of the decade. This laxity ultimately increased the scope and magnitude of losses. It also made the task of resolving failures more difficult because franchise values deteriorated with the increasing severity of distress.

In the case of thrifts the FSLIC actually reduced net worth requirements from 5 percent, to 4 percent, and then to 3 percent in 1982. Beginning in 1983 the agency relied increasingly on outright exemptions. Furthermore, the FSLIC used capital augmentation instruments such as net worth certificates and income maintenance certificates to boost accounting capital. In 1986 the FDIC adopted formal capital forbearance measures, mainly to assist the temporarily distressed Midwest banks heavily exposed to the agricultural and energy sectors. It extended the scope of the program in 1987.

Technically insolvent thrifts were able to stay in business for years because they could rely on historic book-value rather than marked to market, generally accepted accounting principles. Similarly, developing country debt was not marked to market for the money center banks. Thrift regulators made an additional mistake by introducing special regulatory accounting principles. Among their many shortcomings, the principles permitted consistent overvaluation of delinquent or nonperforming loans and property in depressed real estate markets and greatly enhanced the value of intangible goodwill on balance sheets. Under these special accounting rules, apparent income could be boosted so much that insolvent thrifts appeared to be highly profitable. More than half the failed thrifts that were resolved in 1988, when the principles were suspended, had been accounting insolvent for more than three years, and more than 70 percent had been insolvent on a more stringent "tangible" capital basis (Benston and Kaufman 1990).

Regulatory reform

The concept of official "conservatorship" gained support in the 1987 Competitive Equality Banking Act, which empowered the FDIC to establish short-life "bridge" banks to operate banks already in receivership. Bridge banks allowed early settlement of losses against uninsured depositors and creditors, preserved some franchise value (although holding company creditors and shareholders lost their investments), and permitted a clean sweep of management (Mires and Spong 1988). By the end of 1989 the FDIC had become sole shareholder in five bridge banks that successfully reprivatized formerly unmarketable banks (including two large Texas bank holding companies). The Financial Institutions Reform, Recovery, and Enforcement Act of 1989 expanded conservatorship authority for both banks and thrifts to allow reorganization and restructuring of mostly insolvent institutions not yet in receivership. Although outright nationalization is not considered a viable option in the United States, these techniques place control under the temporary stewardship of federal authorities and in some cases allow a temporary public equity stake when institutions are sold to the private sector.

In late 1989 the U.S. Congress was forced to overhaul the insurance and regulatory system for thrifts because the FSLIC was bankrupt. The

Financial Institutions Reform Act liquidated the FSLIC, established a new oversight agency—the Office of Thrift Supervision—and reorganized the deposit insurance fund. The legislation also created the Resolution Trust Corporation (RTC) to handle imminent thrift failures. The RTC, which was given six years to clean up the thrift industry mess, became an interim deposit guarantor. To finance the bailout, the RTC could borrow $20 billion through general Treasury bond financing and contributions from federal home loan banks. It could also issue $30 billion of special Resolution Finance Corporation bonds, using zero-coupon Treasury bonds as collateral.

Congress optimistically expected the RTC to use the proceeds of rapid asset disposition to cover the underwriting of new thrift conservatorships and the warehousing of the bad assets it acquired. Income from future thrift resolutions and bond sales were also supposed to support the RTC's program. Between August 1989 and the end of 1990, 531 thrifts, with $271 billion in assets, failed. At the end of April 1991 the RTC still had 219 thrifts in conservatorship and 375 in receivership, with more likely to follow. Through May 1991 the RTC reported total estimated losses of $55 billion incurred from the disposal of 396 insolvent thrifts, for which asset sales and collections totaled $163 billion.

With the onset of a recession in 1990 and a deep slump in real estate markets throughout much of the country, failures were costing more and resolutions and asset disposition were harder to arrange. The RTC returned to Congress in 1990 for more funding, finally receiving authorization for $78 billion in early 1991. By the end of 1991 the RTC had seized $357 billion in assets, had sold and recovered $228 billion, and had remaining assets of $129 billion to be sold.

The Financial Institutions Reform Act also reregulated in some important areas, and it increased insurance premiums for both thrifts and commercial banks to generate additional billions for the Savings Association Insurance Fund and the Bank Insurance Fund by the mid-1990s. The minimum tangible capital standard for thrifts was set at 3 percent of total assets, a standard that was achieved by the end of 1994. Also, thrifts were directed to increase their level of housing assets, and the ratio of commercial real estate loans to capital was restricted. State-chartered thrifts were limited to the same type and amount of real estate equity investment as federally chartered ones, and thrifts in general were restricted in the quality of corporate debt securities they could purchase.

Costly bank failures also were mounting, a problem that only increased with the depth of the recession. Significantly, just over half the failures in 1989 were among national banks, rather than state-chartered ones, and nearly all of those were in the Southwest (65 percent in Texas alone). The 12,593 FDIC-insured banks earned $1 billion less in the first quarter of 1990 than they had in the first quarter of 1989. This drop resulted mainly from higher provisioning for domestic credit losses (U.S. FDIC *Annual Report* 1990). Net loan chargeoffs were nearly 50 percent greater than a year earlier, and the ratio of troubled assets continued. Aggregate performance was affected disproportionately by banks in the Northeast, where Mexican loan chargeoffs and real estate loan losses took a heavy toll. As the economy slipped into recession at the end of 1990, there were 1,012 problem banks (10 percent of the total), and 11 percent of all banks—including 20 percent of the largest with assets in excess of $10 billion each—were unprofitable.

On November 27, 1991, Congress passed the FDIC Improvement Act, a compromise that addressed few of the reforms the administration requested. The act included the following provisions:

- Authority for the FDIC to borrow $70 billion from the Treasury to replenish the Bank Insurance Fund.
- Rules enabling regulators to act quickly when a bank's core capital falls below 2 percent of risk assets and to replace management and limit the asset growth of "critically undercapitalized" banks.
- Rules requiring ailing banks to suspend dividend payments.
- Restrictions on the Federal Reserve's ability to provide credit to ailing banks.
- Some rollback of deposit insurance coverage on brokered deposits and deposits of U.S. banks abroad.
- Requirement that foreign banks taking insured deposits be locally incorporated.
- Reduction of the number of state-chartered banks authorized to underwrite and sell insurance.

The legislation failed to address the Treasury's proposals to allow banks to underwrite securities and thereby remove the functional segmentation between investment banking and commercial banking established by the Glass-Steagall Act (*The Economist*, 30 November 1991).

Conclusion

When the Financial Institutions Reform Act was first proposed in February 1989, the administration claimed that the thrift cleanup would cost the taxpayers $60 billion.[18] A subsequent independent estimate of deposit fees and taxes for 1988–99 placed the figure at $150 billion, or about 3 percent of gross domestic product for 1988 (Hill 1990). Failed bank resolutions cost the industry, through the FDIC, a mere $17 billion during 1985–89, although large outlays continued in 1990 and 1991. The 1991 FDIC Improvement Act provided the FDIC with another $70 billion in borrowing powers to deal with the problem banks.

Apart from these costs, there were long-run market consequences as well. Delays in the resolution of failing financial institutions slowed the pace of asset disposition and shifted risk—first from individual institutions to the industry through the mechanism of the insurance fund, and then to the government. In addition, selective sale of interstate acquisition privileges in a structurally segmented system transferred costs to competing institutions. Regulatory forbearance prevented normal market shrinkage by inhibiting exit. Solvent and comparatively healthy institutions were forced to compete with undercapitalized or virtually insolvent ones that could afford to price liabilities and assets unrealistically. Tax benefits to acquirers shrank the pool of prospective buyers to those to whom they were an attractive incentive. The extent of deposit insurance encouraged moral hazard behavior by depositors, managers, and directors, and effectively substituted public capital for private capital.

The U.S. case raises important issues regarding the timing of loss recognition and failure resolution. Proponents of market-value accounting, the Securities and Exchange Commission among them, argue that marking the value of assets to market forces discipline on financial institutions because losses are recognized more promptly, thereby ensuring prompt management and regulatory action and ultimately reducing the cost of failure resolution. Historic accounting, by contrast, gives banks more time to recognize losses on bonds and loans, since it can always be argued that markets for bank loans are not perfect and the valuation of bank loans should be judgmental.

This debate is particularly interesting because bank balance sheets are clearly subject to both interest rate risks and credit risks, which are interrelated. Even credit risks can be "reduced" to an interest rate risk since the higher the credit risks, the lower (or even negative) the interest rate yield on bank loans, which reduces the value of bank loans. Opponents of market-value accounting argue that the uncertainties (and errors) of measuring such risk are high, and therefore time should be given to allow more accurate assessment of such valuation. The weight of evidence definitely points toward market-value accounting, however, as financial markets converge and price volatility increases. A clear case for market-value accounting is the need for higher capital for financial institutions to cushion against risks, not whether such risks are measured accurately under such accounting.

On the positive side, public attention has focused on the fundamental structural problems of the U.S. system. Restrictions on geographic and functional diversification have been eased, if not eliminated. Industry consolidation continues: since 1985, 5,400 banks, thrifts, and credit unions have been absorbed or eliminated. Roughly 10 percent of thrifts account for about 70 percent of total industry assets, whereas 11 percent held 60 percent of the total in 1979. Similarly, 70 percent of commercial bank assets are held by less than 3 percent of banks, and the trend of mergers of large money center banks has continued, the most recent being the merger of Chase Manhattan and Chemical Bank.

The U.S. case demonstrates the difficulties of resolving failures in a system consisting of a large number of geographically and functionally segmented financial institutions. While a federally guaranteed and industry-financed deposit insurance scheme was by and large successful for more than fifty years in preventing bank runs, the large losses of recent years show that quasi-public capital (in the form of the federal deposit guarantee) is not a substitute for sound private capital.

Clearly, after a long history of growth, banking capital in the United States became severely eroded relative to the risks and the competition from new players. The franchise for low-cost deposits in operating the payments mechanism was eroded by the invasion of credit cards and the evolution of deposit substitutes from mutual funds, insurance companies, and securities houses. There was also greater competition from foreign banks in the U.S. market. The banks and thrifts responded by taking higher risks, including derivatives and new, off–balance sheet activities that incurred higher costs and losses when the economy began to slow down.

Several observations can be made:

- Even the most sophisticated bank regulation and examination did not prevent large-scale bank failures. Banks are subject to structural flaws and cyclical changes in the economy. If tax incentives push the economy toward real estate, banks are likely to make mistakes in both industrial and developing countries.
- Bank losses are quasi-fiscal deficits, even in highly private, market-based economies. Even though the U.S. banking system remains almost entirely in private hands, a large percentage of bank losses was financed by budget appropriations or borrowings by the insurance funds under Treasury guarantee.
- Inadequate resources and powers postponed timely decisionmaking, and in the end the state suffered from the inefficient actions of an insolvent rescuer (FSLIC) trying to rescue insolvent intermediaries.
- Ill-timed and ill-conceived deregulation contributed substantially to the problems or exacerbated difficulties precipitated by changes in business cycles. The relaxation of supervisory vigilance and sound bank accounting principles contributed to the accumulation of losses greater than those initially reported.

From these observations, two lessons can be drawn:

- During economic liberalization, anticompetitive regulations should be removed to promote competition, but regulations against conflicts of interest, fraud, and moral hazard should be strictly enforced.
- The costs of delayed action demonstrate that the sooner action is taken, the better. To some, delays in action reflected the gridlock of overlapping supervisory authorities and the absence of political will to confront the issues. But in the U.S. case, once the will was manifested, considerable national resources were harnessed, backed by professional skills, to deal with the problems. Few developing countries have either the will or the capacity to deal with banking problems in this manner.

Notes

1. Regulation Q interest rate ceilings for deposits in commercial banks were introduced in the 1930s, and were imposed on thrifts in the mid-1960s to dampen competition among them. The deposit rate ceiling for thrifts, however, was set at a margin above the level for commercial banks to preserve thrifts' competitive advantage in collecting small savings deposits. As inflation rose during the 1970s, Regulation Q proved a serious constraint on both types of institutions, resulting in disintermediation.

2. For example, between 1983 and 1985, when many Texas banks were building up bad assets, bank examinations were halved (U.S. FDIC Annual Report 1990).

3. The Office of Thrift Supervision was created in 1989 under the Financial Institutions Reform, Recovery, and Enforcement Act to replace the Federal Home Loan Bank Board, which had been responsible for national chartering, regulation, and oversight.

4. Although the Federal Reserve is the primary regulator of bank holding companies, their subsidiary banks are usually supervised by the Office of the Comptroller of the Currency or the FDIC.

5. The FSLIC was financed by the Federal Home Loan Bank System, thus linking the insurance and oversight functions. The Federal Home Loan Bank Board had an inherent conflict of objectives since it was both a regulator of thrifts and a promoter of the housing industry and widespread home ownership.

6. By 1990 the FDIC covered 75 percent of deposits in insured banks, compared with 65 percent in 1970 and only 45 percent in 1934.

7. Specialist brokers arranged deposits nationwide for thrifts for a fee. Deposits were broken down into insurable amounts so that they could be covered by FDIC's $100,000 limit per account. "Pass through" coverage brought pension and insurance funds into the deposit network as well.

8. Mutual savings banks were insured by the FDIC but had interest risks similar to the thrifts and suffered the same consequences of tight monetary policy. Failures among a few state-chartered mutual savings banks in the Northeast following a property price slump tapped FDIC resources, but their loan loss and net worth problems proved more short-lived than those of the thrifts. Fourteen mutual savings banks with $17.4 billion in assets received FDIC assistance between 1978 and 1983.

9. Banks in a twelve-state, predominantly agricultural area accounted for more than half of bank failures in 1985, following the collapse of farm land prices and widespread foreclosures, but these Midwest farm banks rebounded in 1987 (Hefferman 1988).

10. California had already allowed its state-chartered thrifts this privilege. This new freedom had an immediate positive impact on the structure of thrift balance sheets and consequently on earnings.

11. These included lower capital and liquidity requirements, liberal lending limits on real estate loans, deferrals on loan losses, large tax-free transfers to loan loss reserves, special treatment of tax loss carryforwards, revaluation of premises and other property, recording mutual fund assets at cost rather than at market value, liberal valuation of intangible assets, less frequent use of enforcement action, and ready access to Federal Home Loan Bank advances (ABA 1988).

12. By mid-1990 federal rescuers held a portfolio of $3.7 billion in junk bonds acquired from failed thrifts.

13. The banks in the district lost $1.0 billion in 1986, $2.7 billion in 1987, and $2.2 billion in 1988.

14. Only eighty-five thrifts were liquidated between 1980 and 1989, nearly half of those in 1987 and 1988. Similarly, the FDIC paid off depositors in only 244 cases between 1971 and 1989, and 94 of those cases occurred during 1980–89. In the entire history of the FDIC only $2.8 billion had been spent for

this purpose. In a limited number of bank and thrift cases, insured deposit transfers were used when depositor payouts were imminent but a healthy institution was willing to pay a premium for the insured deposits, and perhaps some assets.

15. The Garn-St. Germain Act authorized net worth certificates, issued by thrifts in exchange for FSLIC promissory notes, which were used to boost thrift capital to the minimum requirement.

16. Thrift-assisted mergers involved some, but not necessarily all, of the following additional measures: capital loss protection of a negotiated "covered" portion of assets; yield guarantee subsidies or income maintenance agreements, which shifted interest rate risk to the FSLIC; and indemnification for legal expenses incurred from lawsuits or contingencies arising from the failed thrift. They also might include loss-sharing of asset disposition, gain sharing, tax allowances, buyout options allowing the FSLIC to purchase covered assets, warrants for shares in assisted thrifts, and marked to market payment for covered assets or for goodwill booked for covered assets (Seidman 1990).

17. The FDIC's open bank assistance programs incurred losses of $11.2 billion from inception in 1933 to the end of 1988. The greatest costs were in the 1980s, with cases like Continental Illinois (1984), BankTexas Group (1987), and First City Bancorporation (1988).

18. By the time the legislation passed in August, the initial program provided $166 billion over ten years to resolve 191 thrifts, at a direct nominal expense to taxpayers of $90 billion. In April 1990, however, the General Accounting Office estimated that the projected nominal budget outlays would amount to at least $315 billion (U.S. GAO 1990). This estimate subsequently rose to $400 to $500 billion.

References

ABA (American Bankers Association). 1988. "The FSLIC Crisis: Principles and Issues." Washington, D.C.

Amel, Dean F. 1989. "Trends in Banking Structure Since the Mid-1970s." *Federal Reserve Bulletin* 75 (March): 120–33.

Barth, James R., Philip F. Bartholomew, and Michael G. Bradley. 1990. "Determinants of Thrift Institution Resolution Costs." *Journal of Finance* 45 (July): 731–54.

Benston, George J., and George G. Kaufman. 1990. "Understanding the Savings-and-Loan Debacle." *Public Interest* 99 (Spring): 79–95.

Brumbaugh, R. Dan, and Robert E. Litan. 1989. Joint testimony before the Subcommittee on Financial Institutions Supervision, Regulation, and Insurance of the Committee on Banking, Finance, and Urban Affairs, U.S. House of Representatives, September 19, Washington, D.C.

Brumbaugh, R. Dan, Andrew S. Carron, and Robert E. Litan. 1989. "Cleaning Up the Depository Institutions Mess." *Brookings Papers on Economic Activity* 1. Washington, D.C.

Corrigan, Gerald. 1989. "A Perspective on Recent Financial Disruptions." *Federal Reserve Bank of New York Quarterly Review* 14 (Winter): 8–15.

———. 1990. "Reforming the U.S. Financial System: An International Perspective." *Federal Reserve Bank of New York Quarterly Review* (Spring).

Edwards, F. R., and F. S. Mishkin. 1995. "The Decline of Traditional Banking: Implications for Financial Stability

and Regulatory Policy." *Federal Reserve Bank of New York Economic Policy Review* (July): 27–42.

Federal Reserve Bank of Kansas City. 1990. *Banking Regulation, Its Purposes, Implementation, and Effects.*

———. 1992. "Commercial Bank Performance, 1991." *Financial Industry Trends.*

Felgran, Steven D. 1988. "Bank Participation in Real Estate: Conduct, Risk, and Regulation." *New England Economic Review* (November-December): 57–73.

Fogel, Richard L. 1990. "Failed Thrifts: Resolution Trust Corporation and 1988 Bank Board Resolution Actions." Statement of the Comptroller General, General Government Programs, before the Committee on Banking, Finance, and Urban Affairs, U.S. House of Representatives, April 2, Washington, D.C.

Frydl, Edward J. 1991. "Overhangs and Hangovers: Coping with the Imbalances of the 1980s." *Annual Report.* Federal Reserve Bank of New York.

Gregorash, George, Eileen Maloney, and Don Wilson. 1987. "Crosscurrents in 1986 Bank Performance." *Federal Reserve Bank of Chicago Economic Perspectives* (May/June): 23–35.

Harris, Ethan S., and Charles Steindel. 1991. "The Decline in U.S. Savings and its Implications for Economic Growth." *Federal Reserve Bank of New York Quarterly Review* 15 (Winter): 1–19.

Heffernan, Peter J. 1988. "Nothing is Forever: Boom and Bust in Midwest Farming." *Federal Reserve Bank of Chicago Economic Perspectives* (September/October).

Hill, Edward W. 1990. "The S&L Bailout: Some States Gain, Many More Lose" *Challenge* 33 (May/June): 37–45.

Holthus, C.G. 1989. Statement of the President-Elect of the American Bankers Association before the Subcommittee on Financial Institutions Supervision, Regulation, and Insurance of the Committee on Banking, Finance, and Urban Affairs, U.S. House of Representatives, September 20, Washington, D.C.

IMF (International Monetary Fund). Various years. *International Financial Statistics.* Washington, D.C.

Johnson, Manuel H. 1989. Testimony of the Vice Chairman, Board of Governors of the Federal Reserve System, before the Subcommittee on Financial Institutions Supervision, Regulation, and Insurance of the Committee on Banking, Finance, and Urban Affairs, U.S. House of Representatives, September 19, Washington, D.C.

Kaufman, George. 1990. "Crisis Spreads: Make FDIC Insurance Redundant." *Challenge* 33 (January/February): 13–17.

Melichar, Emanuel. 1986. "Agricultural Banks Under Stress." *Federal Reserve Bulletin* 72 (July): 437–48.

Miller, Randall. 1991. "Testimony on Mergers." U.S. Office of the Comptroller of the Currency Bulletin (December). Washington, D.C.

Mires, Ralph E., and Kenneth Spong. 1988. "The Death of a Bank: Assuring an Orderly Transition." *Banking Studies* special issue, "Problem Banks," Federal Reserve Bank of Kansas City.

Seidman, L. William. 1990. Testimony of the Chairman, FDIC, on FSLIC Resolution Fund Appropriations for Fiscal 1991, before the Subcommittee on Housing and Urban Development, Veterans Administrations, and independent agencies of the Committee on Appropriations, U.S. Senate, May 23, Washington, D.C.

Silverberg, Stanley C. 1989. "U.S. Banking Problems in the 1980s." World Bank, Financial Policy and Systems Division, Washington, D.C.

————. 1990. "The Savings and Loan Problem in the United States." Policy Research Working Paper 351. World Bank, Washington, D.C.

Spong, Kenneth. 1988. "Assistance for Problem Banks." *Banking Studies* special issue, "Problem Banks," Federal Reserve Bank of Kansas City.

U.S. FDIC (Federal Deposit Insurance Corporation). Various years. *Annual Report*. Washington, D.C.

————. Various issues. *Quarterly Banking Profile*. Washington, D.C.

U.S. GAO (General Accounting Office). 1987. "Thrift Industry Forbearance for Troubled Institutions, 1982–86." Washington, D.C.

————. 1990. Statement by the Comptroller General of the United States before the Committee on Banking, Housing, and Urban Affairs, U.S. Senate, April 6, Washington, D.C.

————. 1991. "Deposit Insurance and Strategy for Reform." Report GGD-91-26. Washington, D.C.

U.S. OCC (Office of the Comptroller of the Currency). 1988. *Bank Failure: An Evaluation of the Factors Contributing to the Failure of National Banks*. Washington, D.C.: U.S. Treasury.

————. 1990. "Condition of the Banking System 1989." U.S. Treasury, Division of Industry and Financial Analysis, Washington, D.C.

U.S. OTS (Office of Thrift Supervision). Various years. *Annual Report*. Washington, D.C.

U.S. RTC (Resolution Trust Corporation). 1990. "Conservatorship Institutions Post Slight Decline in First Quarter Operating Losses." Press release. Washington, D.C.

————. 1991. *RTC Review* (April).

U.S. Treasury. 1991. *Modernizing the Financial System: Recommendations for Safer, More Competitive Banks*. Washington, D.C.

White, Lawrence J. 1990. "Problems of the FSLIC: A Former Policy Maker's View." *Contemporary Policy Issues* 8 (April).

————. 1991. *The S&L Debacle: Public Policy Lessons for Bank and Thrift Regulation*. New York: Oxford University Press.

CHAPTER 5

Bank Restructuring in Spain, 1977–85

Andrew Sheng

The Spanish banking crisis was the most serious to hit the OECD countries after the U.K. secondary banking crisis of 1974–76. The crisis spanned 1977–85 and affected 52 of the country's 110 banks; most were small and medium-size firms that together accounted for more than 20 percent of total deposits. Twenty banking institutions related to the Rumasa industrial conglomerate had to be resolved through a special nationalization and reprivatization program introduced in 1983. The rest were resolved through the Deposit Guarantee Fund, and most were absorbed by domestic and foreign banks. Twenty-one of the non-Rumasa banks had to be recapitalized by the fund before they could be resold, and only three small banks were actually liquidated. In only a few cases did private banks absorb troubled institutions without extensive official intervention. The seven largest Spanish banks survived with limited damage and played an important role in absorbing a number of the failed institutions.

As with other banking crises, Spain's banking problems resulted from a combination of the oil shock of 1973–74, inappropriate policy responses to these shocks, and rapid liberalization and expansion of the banking sector without adequate regulation and supervision. Institutional factors such as the extensive ownership of banks by industrial conglomerates and bad bank management were also responsible. The crisis was costly to resolve. For example, the government expected to be repaid only 25 percent of a 400 billion peseta ($2.5 billion) interest-free loan that it extended to the Rumasa holding company as part of the plan to salvage the Rumasa banking group (de Juan 1985). One estimate placed the net cost of the crisis at 1,581 billion pesetas (in constant 1985 prices), or 5.6 percent of 1985 GDP, of which 1,216 billion pesetas (77

percent) was borne by either the Deposit Guarantee Fund or the Bank of Spain (Cuervo 1988).

As in other cases, Spain's banking crisis followed a period of strong economic growth in the 1960s and early 1970s. The death of General Francisco Franco in 1975, however, unleashed several years of social, political, and economic transformation. The transition to democracy did not permit decisive adjustment to the oil shocks. Between 1975 and 1979 the peseta appreciated by more than 35 percent in real terms, the stock of external debt doubled, and real wages increased by 9 percent. Although the banking crisis peaked in 1982 and 1983, losses had been accumulating throughout the 1970s and early 1980s, exacerbated by the impact of rising oil prices, double-digit inflation, and rigidities in the labor market and productive sectors, which undermined the profitability and solvency of enterprises.

Problems in the banking system began to surface in 1977 when the Bank of Spain noticed that rising liquidity problems in some cases hid much larger solvency problems. One of the most striking features of the crisis was the extent to which failed banks had exceeded permissible levels of loan concentration to related parties and risk concentration to single persons or entities. The initial response to the emerging problems was slow, partly because the legal framework for banking was antiquated. The central bank initially had neither the legal power to intervene nor adequate powers to impose and enforce sanctions against wrongdoers. The Deposit Guarantee Fund was established in 1977, but this too proved inadequate to deal with the unfolding crisis.

The Banking Corporation was created in 1978 to take control of and, where possible, reorganize troubled institutions. Financed half by private banks and half by the Bank of Spain, the corporation lacked the legal means to recapitalize insolvent institutions and proved an inadequate mechanism for dealing with impending crises. As a result the Deposit Guarantee Fund was reconstituted as a legal entity in 1980. The new fund, still jointly financed, provided not only managerial and administrative oversight of failed banks but also direct recapitalization. The amount of deposit insurance coverage was also increased. By law fund ownership had to be divested within one year of takeover, promoting prompt resolution and resale of five of the fund-controlled banks to foreign institutions and twenty-two to domestic banks by late 1985. This process inaugurated a prolonged period of structural reform in Spanish banking that continued into the 1990s. The fund has become an important model for bank restructuring in many other countries because of its flexibility, efficiency, fairness, and realistic approach to protecting the public interest in the banking system.

Structural Adjustment and the Financial System

In the 1960s Spain embarked on a series of indicative development plans along the French model, with a heavy emphasis on industrialization. This energy-intensive investment was seriously affected by the oil shocks of 1973 and 1979. Although the country enjoyed one of the highest growth rates in Europe in the early 1970s—annual GDP growth peaked at nearly 8 percent in 1972—real growth fell to 0.5 percent in 1975 and the economy entered a period of stagnation during which growth did not exceed 2 percent a year. Reaction to the first oil shock was delayed by the political transition following Franco's death. Real wages were allowed to rise to avert social unrest, and the real exchange rate appreciated by more than 35 percent between 1975 and 1979. As fiscal deficits began to widen, inflation exceeded 24 percent in 1977 and did not fall below double digits until 1985 (table 5.1).

The dramatic changes in the economy coincided with a period of liberalization and rapid expansion in the banking sector, which financed the growing indebtedness of enterprises. Spanish businesses, buoyed by the steady growth of the 1960s, faced major structural adjustments in the 1970s, with rising energy costs, increasing competition, and rigidities in the labor market structure impeding their ability to reduce real labor costs. In addition, enterprises began to face higher financial intermediation costs as a result of tighter monetary policies introduced to curb inflation. Higher real interest rates, declining liquidity, and slower growth all led to a deterioration

Table 5.1 Macroeconomic indicators, 1970–89
(percent unless otherwise specified)

Year	Real growth in GDP	Current account/GDP	Terms of trade (1980=100)[a]	Inflation rate[b]	General government financial balance/GDP	Bank nominal interest rate[c]	Exchange rate (pesetas/U.S. dollar)
1970	4.1	2.2	153.1	5.7	0.7	n.a.	70.0
1971	4.6	2.0	159.8	8.2	–0.6	n.a.	69.4
1972	8.0	1.1	155.8	8.3	–0.2	n.a.	64.2
1973	7.7	0.8	146.4	11.4	0.8	n.a.	58.2
1974	5.1	–3.6	108.2	15.7	–0.3	n.a.	57.6
1975	0.5	–3.3	117.9	16.9	–0.5	n.a.	57.4
1976	3.3	–3.9	114.0	14.9	–1.0	n.a.	66.9
1977	3.0	–1.6	108.0	24.5	–1.3	14.0	75.9
1978	1.4	1.1	114.9	19.8	–2.3	15.0	76.6
1979	–0.1	0.6	114.7	15.7	–2.1	15.7	67.1
1980	1.2	–2.4	100.0	15.6	–2.5	17.1	71.7
1981	–0.2	–2.6	85.1	14.5	–3.8	16.7	92.3
1982	1.2	–2.4	91.3	14.4	–5.4	16.4	109.8
1983	1.8	–1.6	86.8	12.2	–4.6	16.7	143.4
1984	1.8	1.3	89.3	11.3	–5.3	16.9	160.
1985	2.3	1.7	89.8	8.8	–6.9	15.8	170.0
1986	3.3	1.7	104.6	8.8	–6.0	14.6	140.0
1987	5.5	0.0	98.3	5.3	–3.2	15.7	123.4
1988	5.0	–1.1	103.0	4.8	–3.3	15.3	116.4
1989	4.8	–2.9	105.5	6.8	–2.8	16.3	118.3

a. Ratio of the index of average export prices to the index of average import prices.
b. Consumer price index.
c. Does not include regulated or special rates for private banks. Rates are averages of selected rates for commercial discounts, credits, and loans.
Source: IMF and World Bank data; Bank of Spain.

in stock market values, putting heavy pressure on collateral values and on banks holding large portfolios of corporate stock.

Until the mid-1970s Spain's banking sector was highly profitable, benefiting from a protected market and a rapidly growing economy that averaged 7 percent annual growth during 1961–74. Interest rates on loans and deposits were regulated, market entry was severely restricted (and foreign banks were entirely excluded), and chartering of new branches was heavily constrained until 1977. Moreover, domestic banks were forced to allocate substantial funds to priority investments; as late as 1985, 48 percent of banks' resources were still regulated. Commercial and industrial banks were functionally separated.

Under pressure from the Bank of Spain, important reforms occurred in 1969, 1974, 1977, and 1981 that aimed to open the system to greater competition. In 1969 interest rates were freed for foreign deposits, interbank operations, loans of more than three years, and domestic liabilities with maturities of more than two years. Reforms in 1974, 1977, and 1981 rationalized the rate structure until all rates were free except those on liabilities of less than a year (or less than six months for deposits over $6,500 equivalent). This led to competitive innovation as new financial instruments were introduced. After the 1971 and 1974 reforms it was easier to open new banks and new branches. In 1977 foreign banks were admitted. Although they were restricted to having three offices nationwide, foreign banks brought new instruments to the market. Bank specialization was abandoned in 1977, and gradual reduction of forced investment began. At the same time the creation of a money market led the Bank of Spain to rely more heavily on open market operations—rather than reserve requirements and rediscount facilities—to facilitate and broaden monetary control. The money market expanded beyond a simple interbank market to include nonbanking institutions, many of them private.

Banking regulation, however, remained outmoded, focusing on compliance with legal requirements and technical ratios—not uncommon where banking systems have been repressed. Moreover, until the mid-1980s most regulatory and disciplinary power rested with the Ministry of Finance rather than with the Bank of Spain. In addition, the 1946 Banking Law (which remains the principal banking legislation) and the penal code did not provide an appropriate basis for action against wrongdoers. Information disclosure was also inadequate, especially in light of the transition to freer markets. These shortcomings were particularly unfortunate given the growth of large industrial conglomerates (in the case of Rumasa, within a nonbank holding company structure) and the large number of related nonbank financial companies created to sustain the ownership structure of new or acquired banks. The complex of related companies together with creative accounting techniques obscured the real consolidated financial position of banks and their customers from bank examiners, as bank managers struggled to survive in the new competitive environment.

Under these economic, financial, and regulatory conditions, liberalization had a grave impact on the viability of many banks because of the timing and manner of bank competition and expansion it generated. Specialization gave way to multipurpose banking. Although the banking sector became more sophisticated and innovative, many new entrants lacked professional experience, adequate financial backing, and in some cases the ethical standards expected of sound bankers. None of the banks created during the financial liberalization of the 1970s survived as independent institutions, and 90 percent of the banks involved in the banking crisis were created between 1973 and 1978.

There were three types of unstable banks: self-financing (those with an artificial structure that had concentrated risk primarily in finance for the acquisition of their own assets); medium-size banks that had extended an imprudent concentration of risk to their controlling groups to finance speculative investments, often in related companies; and larger institutions hurt by the impact of persistent economic crisis on their enterprise borrowers (Alvarez Rendueles 1983). Industrial banks, for example, had greater investment freedom than savings or commercial banks and built their asset portfolios by raising high-cost funds.[1] They prospered during the period of rapid economic growth but were unable to disengage quickly from their narrow base of lending to highly indebted industries when prosperity ended.

The era also saw expansion and growth through the formation of large industrial bank groups. Existing banks often were purchased with only a small down payment; the balance was covered by debt and in some cases banks were bought with credits extended by the acquired bank itself. The relatively inexpensive deposit base was used for speculative investment in banks whose purchase prices were often highly inflated. In the hands of the new owners banks directed credit to related companies and to sharehold-er companies and individuals to have access to funds to repay their debts, including those incurred to pur-chase the bank in the first place. Complex networks of related financial entities developed through intricate lending schemes and cross-ownerships, sometimes with other banks. Lending limits to single borrowers could be evaded easily.

Such growth could be sustained only with further speculation and higher borrowing. Nonbank compa-nies were formed to sustain the quoted prices of banking companies in the hope that stock market appreciation would vindicate the valuation of the original bank acquisition. The sharp decline of the Spanish stock market during 1974–80 led banks and their related or controlling groups to turn to real estate investment. Speculation in real estate, initially fueled by growing tourism, was expected to produce earnings sufficient to cover the interest owed to banks on the loans that they had granted to related entities, as well as other loans whose investment returns dete-riorated in the depressed economic climate. When the oversupply retarded property prices the banks were forced to renew loans and capitalize interest arrears to the borrowers to ensure their own survival. Banks that were connected to industrial concerns through cross-holdings were dragged into further bad credits. "Good" bankers became "bad" bankers to cover their own mistakes (de Juan 1987).

This unsound competitive expansion occurred in a market environment in which many retail deposit rates were still regulated, so that competition occurred mainly over market share—through aggres-sive branching—and, where possible, by bidding up interest rates on wholesale deposits. The number of bank offices more than tripled between 1973 and 1983, while the number of people employed in bank-ing rose from 150,000 in 1975 to more than 180,000 by 1980. Financial intermediation costs rose as a result. Net interest margins, for example, rose from 3.45 percent in 1974 to 4.45 percent in 1978 and had only fallen to 4.33 percent by 1980 (Cuervo 1988). Operating expenses, equivalent to 2.55 per-cent of average domestic liabilities in 1974, had risen to 3.53 percent by 1979.

Higher margins coincided with higher real inter-est rates at a time when falling sales margins and the indebted capital structure of industry led to liquidity and debt-servicing difficulties. Although banks' real lending rates were negative or flat until 1980, they had reached a positive real rate of more than 5 per-

cent by 1984, clearly exacerbating the liquidity prob-lems of enterprises. Nonperforming enterprise loans accumulated, followed by distress borrowing. Enterprises consumed their capital, leading to wide-spread business failures that had a direct impact on bank solvency. In a now-familiar vicious circle, banks continued to raise interest rates in order to increase margins. They had to compensate for falling income and the high level of forced investment, and to gener-ate surpluses for increasing their loan loss provisions. Predictably, higher financial costs caused even worse problems for enterprises.

Response to the Crisis

The initial response to the growing crisis was a simple deposit insurance scheme—the Deposit Guarantee Fund, introduced in November 1977. The fund's principal objective was to insure small deposits and avoid the threat of massive deposit withdrawals that could spark a systemwide panic. The scheme provid-ed deposit insurance of 500,000 pesetas (nearly $10,000) per depositor. Administered as an account within the Bank of Spain, the scheme was funded equally by the central bank and by participating com-mercial banks, who paid a one-time premium amounting to 1 peseta per 1,000 pesetas of deposit liabilities. Because the fund could only be used where banks had been closed and were going to be liquidat-ed, it was of little real assistance in resolving problem banks. A mechanism was needed for facilitating restructuring and resale rather than closure. Moreover, as the scale of bank problems mounted the inadequacy of the insurance guarantees became clear. The limit was raised first to 750,000 pesetas per depositor in 1980, then to 1.5 million pesetas in 1981.

To improve flexibility in handling individual bank crises, the Banking Corporation was established in March 1978 to supplement the deposit insurance function of the Deposit Guarantee Fund. Equally funded by private banks and the Bank of Spain, the corporation was empowered to take over and tem-porarily administer insolvent banks (sometimes through ownership) but not to recapitalize them. Once a bank confronted a crisis, the Bank of Spain would restrict and apply conditions to its liquidity support. Under pressure, controlling shareholders either had to recapitalize the bank or pass control to the Banking Corporation at a nominal price. The corporation then took over administration of the bank, began to rationalize operations, and searched for a buyer. The corporation's main purpose was to restore banks' viability. Even though bank operations and management improved under this system, the corporation faced a serious dilemma because it could not inject new capital in the institutions, most of which had lost their entire capital at least once. Forcing banks to the brink of closure without the means to restore solvency undercut the corporation's ability to sell them off again.

The Bank of Spain began to tighten supervision and control during this period. It devoted more attention to loan and investment analysis and to asset quality. In addition, the bank implemented an early warning system that, among other things, forecast income and expenditures for each bank and detected deviations. There were important improvements in information disclosure as well.

The Deposit Guarantee Fund

In 1980 the Deposit Guarantee Fund was restructured and its powers substantially increased. A royal decree redefined the fund's objective by empowering it to "carry out all the operations deemed necessary to reinforce the solvency and operation of the banks, in defense of the interests of the depositors and of the fund itself." The fund became a separate public entity operating under private law. Its expanded powers included not only administration of the enlarged deposit insurance scheme but also the ability to purchase any bank assets at book value, make deposits at any rate or term, and provide various guarantees to acquiring institutions. It was also authorized to assume bank losses in order to restore solvency and facilitate sale within a maximum term of one year. Moreover, the fund could inject new capital in order to restore equilibrium to insolvent institutions.[2] In its new form the fund supplanted the Banking Corporation, which had not had the means to restore solvency to banks, making it difficult to find buyers for the banks it took over.

The fund pursued its principal objectives of protecting depositors and restructuring banks for prompt sale even where there were undesirable tradeoffs, such as further concentration in the Spanish banking industry. By mid-1985 the number of banks had fallen from 110 to 90, for example, and 85 percent of the total deposits of the system were held by eight Spanish banking groups (de Juan 1985). The fund maintained its identity as a functionally specialized, mixed (public-private), autonomous institution with a clearly delineated mandate throughout this consolidation and contraction. In the Rumasa case, however, the fund was used only for those purposes for which it had a comparative advantage, namely provisional administration and disposition. The capital deficiencies of the Rumasa group were handled through a comprehensive nationalization and reprivatization effort. In the end the fund participated directly or indirectly in the rescue of twenty-nine banks during 1978–85 (table 5.2) and in the administration and final sale of twenty banks previously owned by the Rumasa group.

An eight-member board of directors oversaw the fund's operations. The board consisted of four private bankers appointed by the Ministry of Finance and four representatives from the Bank of Spain. The vice governor of the Bank of Spain chaired the board, voting only in the case of a tie. Among its duties and responsibilities, the board could request external audits of member banks, including their holding and related companies. This structure—combined with the close relationship of the fund and the Bank of Spain—mitigated the likelihood of bureaucratization and politicization and fostered a public perception of fairness (annex 5.1). The fund coordinated its operations closely with the central bank, particularly in the early and final stages of intervention. The fund also worked closely with the bank in designing the financial packages that were the basis of negotiations for the resale of banks to other banking institutions. It worked speedily and efficiently, selling most of the banks it acquired within one year, and frequently within six months.

Rescuing the banks. Once the Bank of Spain requested that the fund intervene, the fund followed a number of steps in dealing with each problem bank. Before that request was made, the Bank of Spain provided emergency liquidity support to the problem bank. In some cases the Bank of Spain determined that a bank was viable if remedial actions were taken and agreed to a plan of action that might include an injection of capital from shareholders and short-term central bank liquidity support. In other cases the central bank identified and assessed the extent of insolvency and demanded recapitalization by existing shareholders before inviting fund intervention.[3] The Bank of Spain also permitted fund appraisers to collaborate in the assessment so that preliminary estimates of the steps necessary to resolve the bank's crisis could begin before the fund took complete control.

Table 5.2 Interventions by the Deposit Guarantee Fund, 1978–85

Bank	Date of initial intervention	Date of sale	Buyer
Navarra	January 1978	—	Closed for liquidation (May 1978)
Cantabrico	February 1978	July 1980	Banco Exterior de Espana
Meridional	April 1978	July 1981	Banco de Vizcaya
Valladolid	December 1978	March 1981	Barclays Bank
Granada	January 1979	December 1980	Banco Central
Credito Comercial	January 1979	January 1980	Banco de Vizcaya
Asturias	February 1980	November 1980	Banca March
Lopez Quesada	April 1980	June 1981	Banque Nationale de Paris
Promocion de Negocios	April 1980	November 1981	Banco de Bilbao
Catalan de Desarrollo	May 1980	May 1980	Banco Espanol de Credito
Industrial del Mediterrano	July 1980	January 1981	Banca Catalana
Occidental	July 1981	July 1982	Banco de Vizcaya
Comercial Occidental	July 1981	July 1982	Banco de Vizcaya
Descuento	November 1981	July 1983	BCCI Holding (Luxembourg)
Pirineos	December 1981	—	Closed for liquidation (December 1981)
Union	March 1982	April 1982	Banco Hispano Americano
Prestamo y Ahorro	March 1982	April 1982	Banco de Vizcaya
Mas Sarda	March 1982	April 1982	Banco de Bilbao
Levante	October 1982	July 1983	Citibank/Banco Zaragozano
Catalana	November 1982	May 1983	Group of fourteen banks
Industrial de Cataluna	November 1982	May 1983	Group of fourteen banks
Industrial del Mediterraneo	November 1982	May 1983	Group of fourteen banks
Barcelona	November 1982	May 1983	Group of fourteen banks
Gerona	November 1982	May 1983	Banca March
Alicante	November 1982	May 1983	Banco Exterior de Espana
Credito e Inversiones	November 1982	May 1983	Banco Central
Simeon	December 1983	a	Banco Exterior de Espana
Urquijo-Union	July 1985	a	Banco Hispano Americano
Finanzas	September 1985	a	The Chase Manhatran Bank

— Not applicable.

a. The fund did not arrange these rescues, but it did collaborate in the financial reorganization.

Source: Deposit Guarantee Fund; Cuervo 1988.

Shareholders unwilling to inject new capital faced the prospect of no new liquidity support from the Bank of Spain and possible suspension of their bank's charter. Under such pressure they had no choice but to relinquish control of their banks to the fund. An exceptional amendment to the General Corporate Law lowered the quorum of shareholders required to approve necessary capital increases. This enabled the fund to act quickly and decisively once the Bank of Spain requested its intervention in an insolvent bank.

Transfer of control occurred at a shareholders assembly convened no later than seven days after the Bank of Spain requested it. The Bank of Spain informed shareholders of the extent of losses and the impact of writeoffs on the capital and reserves of the institution. If the bank had no net worth—that is, all the capital was lost—and shareholders would not recapitalize it, the fund would pay a nominal 1 peseta per share (more if the capital had not been completely eroded). Once the fund had gained full control through this first phase of the "accordion" operation (simultaneous reduction and increase in capital), it could subscribe the new capital needed to restore the bank's viability. The accordion operation served two

objectives: amortizing potential losses in the bank and penalizing shareholders by diluting or writing off their participation (de Juan 1985). In some cases the fund obtained control only after applying the accordion to the holding company.

The new capital requirements were determined not only on the basis of losses suffered through write-offs, but also by taking into account the amount of deposit liabilities the bank had under normal operating circumstances. Thus the fund effectively replenished the original equity and pre-panic level of deposits. If further funds were needed, the fund could purchase assets, offer guarantees or counterguarantees on behalf of the restructured bank, grant long-term loans at subsidized rates, or permit temporary regulatory forbearance. The fund also immediately replaced all top executives with trusted professionals. The new management introduced administrative reforms, improved operational efficiency, and enhanced the marketability of the resuscitated institution. In any event, all action taken by the fund was predicated on the assumption that the revived banks would continue to be viable after the fund's support ceased and the bank's liabilities to the fund were eliminated.

The fund subscribed substantial new capital in those banks with solvency problems (annex 5.2). Only three banks showed no change in their original capital. In nineteen cases more than 50 percent of original capital was written off, and in thirteen of those cases almost all initial capital was lost. Among the nineteen, only four received capital increases from the fund that were less than the amount of their initial capital endowment. In two cases the fund replaced capital fully to maintain the size of the bank, and in the remaining thirteen cases the banks received more than the amount of their original capitalization from the fund. The capital increases subscribed by the fund, however, represented only a fraction of the resources used to restructure insolvent banks, the greatest cost being the purchase of nonperforming loans. Because the fund normally acquired a substantial portion of the nonperforming assets of insolvent banks, it was in charge of selling all the assets transferred to it, usually during a period beyond that of its provisional administration of the rescued bank.

When a suitable buyer for an insolvent bank could be found immediately, the fund tried to sell the bank right away in order to avoid loss of confidence in the institution and further erosion of the deposit base. In other cases a comprehensive external audit by a recognized accounting firm was completed and potential buyers identified. The Bank of Spain and the fund together prepared the basis for the private offering. The prospectus included at the very least a summary of how the fund acquired the bank, action taken to restore its solvency, a clear definition of the fund's objectives in selling the bank, and a statement of maximum value and the specific conditions under which problem assets could be carved out by the fund. This last element was the main adjustment factor in ensuing negotiations. The basis of the offer detailed the financial support offered by the fund and the Bank of Spain, including loans, subsidized interest rates, and terms; exemptions to technical coefficients (regulatory forbearance); and any other information deemed relevant, such as guarantees against "hidden liabilities." It also required that the purchaser renounce future claims or legal actions against the fund resulting from differences that might arise between expected and realized returns on assets, and it stated the availability of additional information and the final date for receipt of bids.

The prospectus was circulated to a select group of domestic and foreign institutions, who were invited to make counterproposals that were submitted to the fund's board of directors. Once the board selected an offer, it had to communicate the decision to the Ministry of Finance, which had fifteen days to exercise its option to buy the shares in cases where the national interest was affected. This two-stage process provided a check and balance to the restructuring efforts.

The special case of Rumasa. Rumasa, a Spanish holding company comprising more than 300 subsidiaries, owned 20 small and medium-size banks and 100 productive industrial or commercial enterprises. The rest of its offshoots were mainly investment trusts and their instrumentalities, created to obscure both risk concentrations and ultimate ownership of various companies. The conglomerate was involved primarily in the beverage, hotel, commercial, construction and property, and financial services industries. Four major companies comprised 51 percent of the group, while sixteen companies accounted for 71 percent of turnover. All the companies were highly leveraged and, according to official estimates, the holding company had a substantial negative net worth. Operating losses were increasing. The subgroup of banks was the source of finance for Rumasa's development.

Starting in the early 1960s, when the banking sector was opened to limited competition from local and regional banks, Rumasa began to acquire local banks. It continued to build its banking group over the next twenty years. It pursued an aggressive acquisition strategy in the early 1970s involving inflated stock market valuations for the target banks. Rumasa also bought banks that were facing difficulties. By 1983 seventeen of the Rumasa banks had extended more than 73 percent of their total credit to the private sector, concentrated with Rumasa and its related companies. At the time of the expropriation in 1983 the banks showed a negative capital of about 21 billion pesetas ($146.4 million equivalent).

Because of the magnitude of the Rumasa problem and the close relationships between its banks and nonfinancial companies, this case was handled differently from the others. If the fund had intervened to rescue the banks, most of the productive enterprises would have failed because of their excessive indebtedness. In addition, it was not considered an appropriate disposition of fund resources (half of which came from the banking system) to apply them to the rescue of nonfinancial companies. Moreover, the employment impact of such large-scale enterprise failures—

Rumasa employed 50,000 people, 11,000 of them in its banks—presented a major public policy challenge. Consequently, in early 1983 the government decided to nationalize (expropriate) the holding company and its related businesses.

Administration of the holding company was entrusted to the Department of National Heritage, a government department, which followed a two-pronged strategy. First, it took effective control of all the companies, some of which were discovered weeks after the holding company had been expropriated. Second, it developed a plan to sell the companies as soon as possible. The Rumasa group was separated into subgroups for this purpose: two large productive companies, small and medium-size productive companies, and banking institutions. An external audit of all companies began immediately, and a conservative management strategy was followed as the sale program progressed. First Boston, an international investment bank, was entrusted with the sale of large companies and acted as an adviser to the government regarding any offer to purchase the small and medium-size companies. Management and sale of the banks rested with the fund, which in this case acted solely as manager. Productive companies were sold rapidly, sometimes to foreign investors, because the government assumed enough of the companies' bad debts to make the enterprises viable. The largest Rumasa bank was sold to a foreign consortium, and two others were sold to domestic investors. The remaining seventeen banks were purchased by and divided among the seven largest Spanish banks. The banking system played an important part in this salvage operation, not only by acquiring the Rumasa banks but also by bearing some of the financial losses.

Twelve banks, for instance, purchased low-interest (9.5 percent) twelve-year government bonds and accepted 13.5 percent interest-bearing deposits from Rumasa banks. This debt instrument provided the main source of funds for the government's long-term (twelve-year) interest-free loan, amounting to 400,000 million pesetas ($2.5 billion equivalent), to the Rumasa holding company. That loan was channelled to the Rumasa banks to repay the loans they had made to other Rumasa entities. In addition, the Bank of Spain extended credits of 400,000 million pesetas, at 8 percent interest, to the Rumasa banks before they were sold. These banks therefore enjoyed a 5.5 percent margin between the cost of funds from the Bank of Spain and the income from their deposits with the twelve Spanish banks. This amount would be amortized over twelve years and repaid as the government's twelve-year debt issue matured. In effect, the government would repay the twelve Spanish banks; they in turn would repay the deposits of the former Rumasa banks; and those institutions would repay their outstanding credits from the Bank of Spain (de Juan 1985).

Sharing the costs

In all cases shareholders suffered the first losses by losing their equity. Except for the three small liquidated banks, depositors and other creditors did not suffer directly from the crisis.[4] The balance of the losses were absorbed jointly by the largely private banking system, the government, and the Bank of Spain. In the case of the banks controlled by the Deposit Guarantee Fund, the losses were shared in equal parts by the Bank of Spain and the banking system, reducing the system's technical reserves. Contributions from the banking community to the fund amounted to 1.2 per 1,000 of liabilities in domestic and foreign currency per year, equivalent to 10 percent of annual profits. By December 1984 these contributions totaled about $0.5 billion, too little to absorb all the losses. Additional borrowing from the Bank of Spain was necessary, which totaled about $2.9 billion. The Bank of Spain loans were long term with a 7.25 percent annual interest rate. According to the fund's estimates, and assuming that no additional banks require its intervention in the period considered, its reserves will be sufficient to repay the Bank of Spain loan completely by the end of the 1990s.

In the Rumasa case, costs to the government included the annual interest on its twelve-year debt issue, less whatever it recovered from the Treasury loan to Rumasa. In addition, the government had to underwrite the financing cost of the Bank of Spain loans to the Rumasa banks in excess of what the bank would have lent to cover ordinary deposit withdrawals. Costs to the banking community included the difference (4 percent) between the interest paid to the Rumasa banks on their deposits and the interest earned from the public debt issue held by banks, which would decrease over time.

In addition, the public shared in the losses through higher lending rates and lower deposit rates imposed by the banks to cover the cost of the insurance premiums to the fund. Taxpayers also assumed a loss from the larger financial burden of new public debt issues arising from the crisis and from the higher inflationary tax resulting from the central bank's credits to the fund.

The big-bank problem

Another challenge to the banking system loomed, however. In the late 1980s some of Spain's largest banks also were confronted with the need to clean up their loan losses and deal with other problems. Given the Bank of Spain's gradualist approach, it was only after the crisis in the other banks had been tackled that attention turned to the big banks.

Although some banks were in a worse position than others, most of their problems stemmed from five principal difficulties:

- Loan losses from their extensive relations with industry.
- Losses from their controlling interests in banks that the authorities had persuaded them to buy because of overlapping directorships or close relations, but in which the Deposit Guarantee Fund had not intervened.
- Excessive overheads.
- Loans to developing countries, which were affected by the new rules on provisioning for country risk.
- Lapses in pension fund accruals to cover retirement plan contingencies. The Bank of Spain forced the banks to constitute the necessary reserves.

It is difficult to quantify the massive provisions made in the late 1980s by several of the biggest banks, but it is clear that profitability was squeezed as a result. In at least two cases banks were forced to suspend dividend payments. Between 1986 and 1988 three large banks constituted provisions and charged off amounts (totaling $6 billion) that were nearly double that of the three best-performing big banks. In addition to tapping their normal operating profits, some banks had to liquidate and sell off nonbanking assets in order to finance the provisioning effort.

Despite these problems Spanish banks remain highly profitable because of Spain's continued economic prosperity and because of their access to relatively cheap deposits and their ability to lend at relatively high rates. In 1991, for example, two of the larger banks were among the five most profitable banks in the world. In 1989 the lending margin for Spanish banks was equivalent to 4.4 percent of total bank assets, the highest of any European Community member except Greece or Portugal. Net profits

amounted to 1.52 percent of total assets in 1990, a slight decrease from the previous year but above the 1.4 percent reported in 1988 (*Financial Times*, 23 May 1991).

Conclusion

The institutional reforms adopted in Spain to deal with the banking crisis evolved rapidly as financial conditions deteriorated. Although the authorities initially underestimated the extent and depth of the banking crisis and provided only limited deposit guarantees, they soon developed a fair, flexible, and pragmatic approach to resolving individual bank crises. Moreover, they were realistic in assessing the appropriate limits of the Deposit Guarantee Fund's capabilities by separating the problems of the Rumasa group from the scope of fund intervention.

Substantial improvements in the legal and accounting frameworks and in bank regulation and supervision have flowed from the crisis as well. Law 13 (1985) reduced the amount of compulsory investment by banks and addressed matters of capital adequacy and financial disclosure. Royal Decree 1144 (1988) regulates the creation of new banks and the installation of foreign banks. Law 26 (1988) enhances official intervention and enforcement powers, while Law 19 (1988) compels external audits of all financial institutions supervised by the Bank of Spain. In addition, an outpouring of central bank circulars have refined and clarified supervision and regulation.

The Spanish crisis was manageable, limited to 20 percent of banking system deposits and 21 percent of total net worth. The largest private commercial banks, together with the Bankers' Association, were able to assist substantially in resolving the fate of nearly all the smaller failed banks, albeit under considerable state pressure. Competition in the home market from foreign banks also provided an incentive for Spain's private commercial banks to acquire recapitalized Spanish banks, sometimes even by assuming losses in the short run.

Indeed, the banking crisis of 1977–85 spurred a fundamental restructuring in the Spanish banking industry, resulting in fewer but larger institutions. This is reflected in the fact that in 1990 the largest seven Spanish banks accounted for 61 percent of total bank assets, 47 percent of all deposits, and 63 percent of all bank loans. The presence of more foreign banks added a competitive impetus to innovation as well, although they generally did not fare well against the domestic competition in the years following the crisis.

Mergers with and acquisitions of the smaller banks by the larger solvent ones did not lead, however, to needed rationalization in the domestic banking system. Even the spate of bank mergers in 1988 and 1989—a movement endorsed by the government—was followed by a period of relative self-satisfaction within the Spanish banking community. Interest rates remained high, resulting in higher retail margins than in almost all other European countries. The resulting high profits compensated for enduring problems: namely, the ingrained inefficiency of high staff levels and too many branches and imposition of tight monetary policies, including high reserve requirements and continued compulsory investments. In addition, the pressure to provision against past losses has been compounded by the need to improve capital levels to internationally accepted standards. Consequently, the prospect of greater competition within a unified European market promises far greater rationalization, more consolidation, and broader diversification for Spanish banks in the 1990s.

Annex 5.1 Organization of the Deposit Guarantee Fund

The board of directors of the Deposit Guarantee Fund has many functions, including informing and advising the Bank of Spain on all matters regarding the operation of the fund, determining the best ways of achieving its objectives, and preparing and approving the fund's financial statements. The board informs the central bank which banks face financial difficulties possibly requiring fund intervention. It also determines the form of payment of annual premiums paid into the fund by the banks, sets the requirements for admitting new banks to the fund, and informs the public of any change in membership. It requests external audits of member banks, decides the frequency and extent of those audits, and also may request external audits of related companies. In addition, it can suspend payment of deposit guar-

antees to any depositor directly related to the financial difficulties of a bank. Furthermore, the board can approve the purchase of assets by the fund from a bank facing financing difficulties (so long as such purchases avoid a further involvement of the fund) without precluding further requests to the bank management to take additional remedial actions. Also, the board requests advances from the Bank of Spain to the fund when needed.

The fund is organized in three departments: legal, administration and control, and asset management. The Legal Department can initiate legal or criminal action against previous administrators of banks under intervention or temporary administration by the fund. The fund always tries to minimize its losses by maximizing recovery of assets purchased at book value from an insolvent bank and by repossessing any guarantees received as collateral for nonperforming loans. The Legal Department supports these efforts and defends the interests of the fund and of the banks under its control or liquidation. Finally, the department is legal counsel for the other departments.

The Department of Administration and Control is responsible for the internal administration of the fund and of those companies temporarily owned by it as a result of asset purchases. It controls and recovers claims acquired by the fund, maintains timely records, and services obligations of fixed assets (for example, property taxes). In addition, the department coordinates the sale of assets with other departments, including reprivatizing banks. It also prepares the annual budget and financial plan of the fund, including requests for advances from the Bank of Spain.

The Asset Management Department is responsible for the effective administration and sale of all assets received by the fund but not directly related to banking activities (for example, industrial firms). It evaluates their financial viability, minimizes further financial commitments by the fund, and tries to sell the best assets quickly. It tries to improve less attractive assets while searching for possible buyers. It also appraises, or subcontracts appraisal of, the fixed assets in the fund portfolio.

Annex 5.2 Deposit Guarantee Fund control and subscription of new values
(millions of pesetas)

Bank	Means of acquisition	Initial capital	Writeoffs against capital value	Capital increase	Final capital	Capital increase/ initial capital
Cantabrico	1 peseta per share	764	267	795	1,292	1.04 *
Meridional	1 peseta per share	1,125	1,012	1,102	1,125	0.90
Valladolid	1 peseta per share, plus 700 million pesetas to cancel debt of previous owners	2,200	1,100	4,400	5,500	2.00
Granada	1 peseta per share	2,247	786	3,054	4,515	1.36
Credito Comercial	Controlled through its holding banks	776	0	0	776	0.00
Asturias	—	936	468	936	1,404	1.00
Lopez Quesada	—	1,621	810	3,100	3,911	1.91
Promocion de Negocios	—	1,444	722	1,444	2,166	1.00
Catalan de Desarrollo	—	2,625	2,625	3,000	3,000	1.14
Industrial Mediterraneo	—	2,100	1,050	2,500	3,550	1.19
Occidental	1 peseta per share	4,630	4,621	7,000	7,009	1.51
Comercial Occidental	Controlled through its holding banks	1,625	1,621	500	504	0.31
Descuento	1 peseta per share	2,250	2,245	2,500	2,505	1.11
Union	50 percent of the nominal price of each share	7,723	0	0	7,723	0.00
Prestamo y Ahorro	Controlled through its holding banks	2,256	2,233	1,500	1,523	0.66
Mas Sarda	—	2,283	1,529	3,000	3,754	1.31
Levante	1 peseta per share	1,992	1,990	5,500	5,502	2.76
Catalana	—	5,754	5,748	15,344	15,350	2.67
Industrial de Cataluna	Controlled through its holding banks	4,258	4,254	4,500	4,504	1.06
Industrial del Mediterraneo	Controlled through its holding banks	3,550	3,543	3,500	3,507	1.00
Barcelona	Controlled through its holding banks	568	567	1,137	1,138	2.00
Gerona	Controlled through its holding banks	397	0	0	397	0.00
Alicante	Controlled through its holding banks	1,594	1,592	2,500	2,502	1.57
Credito e Inversiones	1 peseta per share, controlled through holding banks	1,595	1,592	3,500	3,503	2.19

— Not applicable.
Source: Deposit Guarantee Fund; Larrain and Montes-Negret 1986; author's calculations.

Notes

This chapter is based principally on Larrain and Montes-Negret (1986) and Cuervo (1988).

1. Industrial banks were permitted to lend up to 10 percent of their total resources (own funds and borrowed ones) to a single borrower. Given that capital adequacy was set at a 10 percent gearing ratio, in practice total exposure to a single customer could reach up to 110 percent of capital. The limits on lending to a single borrower were far less liberal for commercial banks, with maximum exposure reaching as much as 33.75 percent of capital.

2. One limitation involving the deposit insurance system is the asymmetry resulting when a depositor has a claim in a bank that is liquidated by the fund. In contrast to cases where the fund resells banks, in liquidation depositors receive only the portion of their deposits covered by the guarantee—100 percent up to 1.5 million pesetas. Any remaining balance is included among outstanding claims against the net proceeds of the liquidation. In other cases, however, all deposits are insured independently of their size, since the fund insures the solvency and continued operation of rescued banks. This distinction was of little consequence during the banking crisis, however, because only three small banks were liquidated.

3. The Bank of Spain's assessment included the quality of a bank's loan portfolio, concentration of loans and credits to related parties, and estimates of losses and of new capital needs. In most cases, however, a realistic assessment could not be made until the fund had taken control of the bank because cosmetic accounting methods were used by management to obscure the magnitude of the bank's problems.

4. In the cases of liquidation, large creditors shared in the losses to the extent that the portion of deposits above 1.5 million pesetas (which was uninsured) could be recovered only from the net proceeds of liquidation.

References

Alvarez Rendueles, Jose Ramón. 1983. "El Tratamiento de las Crisis Bancarias en España." In *Crisis Bancarias: Soluciones Comparadas*, seminario desarrollado en la Universidad Internacional Menendez Pelayo, en colaboración con la Asociación Española de Banca Privada, Julio, Santander.

Cuervo, Alvaro. 1988. *La Crisis Bancaria en España 1977–1985*. Barcelona: Editorial Ariel.

de Juan, Aristobulo. 1985. "Dealing with Problem Banks: The Case of Spain." Paper presented at the seminar on central banking, International Monetary Fund, July 1–12, Washington, D.C.

———. 1987. "From Good Bankers to Bad Bankers: Ineffective Supervision and Management Deterioration as Major Elements in Banking Crises." Economic Development Institute Working Paper. World Bank, Washington, D.C.

Financial Times. 1991. "Spain." May 23.

Larrain, Mauricio, and Fernando Montes-Negret. 1986. "The Spanish Deposit Guarantee Fund." World Bank, Financial Policy and Systems Division, Washington, D.C.

Lopez-Claros, Augusto. 1989. "Growth-Oriented Adjustment: Spain in the 1980s." *Finance and Development.* 26 (March): 38–41.

Minsky, Hyman P. 1982. "The Potential for Financial Crises." Working Paper 46. Washington University, Department of Economics, St. Louis.

CHAPTER 6

Structural Weaknesses and Colombia's Banking Crisis, 1982–88

Fernando Montes-Negret

Signs of an impending crisis in Colombia's banking system first appeared in 1981 when the country's terms of trade began to deteriorate, resulting in large loan losses. Seven banks—accounting for about a quarter of the total assets of the Colombian system—failed in the ensuing crisis of 1982–88. Superficially, their failure was part of a classic boom-bust economic cycle that began in the mid-1970s. The business cycle explanation, however, is inadequate. Until the crisis Colombia had enjoyed relatively long-term economic stability. Real growth decelerated sharply from a peak of 8.5 percent in 1978 to 0.9 percent in 1982, though it was never negative during the 1980s. Furthermore, foreign-controlled banks in Colombia withstood the distress far better than their domestic competitors, largely because they were managed more conservatively and had a larger capital base. And most financial intermediaries, such as development finance companies and savings and loan corporations, also were generally resilient. (Most of the failures in the nonbanking sector were concentrated among finance companies, where substantial fraud and other abuses occurred.)

Rather, the Colombian crisis was the result of structural weakness in the banking system, high corporate leverage, inadequate bank supervision, and fundamental policy misjudgments, which exacerbated the effects of the business cycle. Two distinctive features of the Colombian crisis are the linkages of banks with industrial conglomerates, or groups (*grupos*), and the large losses incurred by the Colombian banks' offshore affiliates and subsidiaries.

The restructuring of the Colombian banking system required government-financed recapitaliza-tion—including outright nationalization of some banks—and assistance to nonbank financial intermediaries and enterprises. Because Colombia had a strong fiscal and external position, the authorities were able to resolve bank failures and introduce a macroeconomic stabilization program more success-fully than many other countries that experienced banking crises. Although adjustment policies initially exacerbated the loan loss and cash flow problems of the banking system, in the end improved public finances supported the restructuring effort and restored public confidence.

Macroeconomic Background

Major macroeconomic developments and policy decisions affected the financial system's performance over three stages: the coffee boom of 1975–80, the domestic and international recession of 1981–85, and the recovery of 1986–88. During the first phase a large and unexpected improvement in the terms of trade triggered sustained growth. Real GNP growth more than doubled, from around 2.5 percent in the early 1970s to an annual average of 5.4 percent during 1976–80, peaking at 8.5 percent in 1978 (table 6.1). International coffee prices rose from $0.65 a pound in 1975 to $2.35 in 1977, boosting export revenues from $635 million to $2 billion by the end of the decade. Net international reserves rose tenfold in five years, reaching $5.6 billion in 1981.

The increase in prosperity, however, was accom-panied by rising inflation, which reached a peak of 33 percent in 1978. Authorities fought inflation with tight monetary policy and a crawling peg exchange rate mechanism, which resulted in a cumulative total real appreciation of 27 percent between 1974 and 1982. Monetary policy comprised two major measures: the introduction in 1977 of a marginal minimum legal reserve requirement of 100 percent on demand deposits, with higher requirements on other deposits, and a central bank, dollar-denominated cash certificate issued to exporters at favorable interest rates to neutralize any inflation pressures from export proceeds. Both measures affected banks' profitability. The legal reserve requirement reduced the money multiplier, lowered profits, weakened capitalization, and made money scarce and expensive. The cash certificates encouraged disintermediation because banks were still subject to interest rate controls. Overvaluation of the exchange rate encouraged imports and reduced domestic competitiveness, with widespread consequences for all economic sectors.

This mix of policies was imposed on a highly leveraged and interconnected banking and corporate system that was augmented by largely unregulated offshore activities. The consequences were disastrous. The economic boom encouraged a sharp rise in corporate borrowing to finance investment and speculative activities. Corporate debt soared to more than 70 percent of total liabilities in the first half of the 1980s, compared with 24 percent in 1950 and about 50 percent at the end of the 1970s. Such high debt ratios were the result of readily available subsi-

dized credit, tax biases favoring debt accumulation, and legal disincentives to retain earnings. The heavy concentration of ownership in the corporate sector reinforced the drive toward debt leveraging. New equity issues were limited so that existing shareholders could maintain their controlling interest, controlling the large groups with high debt and low equity. Where groups also controlled banks, these banks provided a captive source of financing for groups seeking to expand. Moreover, restrictive monetary policies and an overvalued exchange rate encouraged foreign borrowing, since foreign loans were available at lower interest rates.

The banking system responded by rapidly expanding credit. Overall growth in the banking system was 39 percent in 1977, but private commercial banks expanded credit by 48 percent. Forced investments and limits on lending to individual borrowers encouraged banks to book loans abroad.[1] Foreign subsidiaries of Colombian banks handled the foreign borrowing of Colombian corporations, frequently directing the lending to related parties. The proceeds of some loans were illegally repatriated to Colombia, where they financed takeovers or highly leveraged projects that were unlikely to generate foreign exchange in the short run, if at all. High-risk currency mismatches appeared in the balance sheets of banks' related companies and caused the quality of bank portfolios to deteriorate.

Table 6.1 Macroeconomic indicators, 1975–88
(percent unless otherwise specified)

Year	Real growth in GNP	Current account/ GNP	Fiscal budget/ GNP	Terms of trade [a] (1980=100)	Inflation rate [b]	Nominal interest rate [c]	Real interest rate	Change in industrial output	Change in agricultural output	Real exchange rate [d] (December 1986=100)
1975	2.3	−0.8	−0.2	79.2	23.1	25.2	1.7	1.2	5.8	87.5
1976	4.7	1.4	1.0	117.6	20.2	28.1	6.6	4.4	3.1	83.5
1977	4.2	2.3	0.6	154.4	33.1	26.7	−4.8	1.4	3.3	75.1
1978	8.5	1.4	0.7	118.2	17.8	28.8	9.4	10.0	8.1	74.9
1979	5.4	1.8	−1.0	113.2	24.6	33.4	7.0	6.1	4.8	71.5
1980	4.1	−0.5	−1.9	100.0	26.6	35.3	6.9	1.2	2.2	73.1
1981	2.3	−5.2	−3.0	90.5	27.5	37.3	7.7	−2.6	3.2	71.4
1982	0.9	−7.5	−4.8	96.4	24.6	38.0	10.8	−1.4	−1.9	66.2
1983	1.6	−7.2	−4.3	94.5	19.8	33.7	11.6	1.1	2.8	64.4
1984	3.4	−3.3	−4.4	99.0	16.1	34.8	16.1	6.0	1.8	69.9
1985	3.1	−5.3	−3.3	98.3	25.0	35.2	8.1	3.0	1.6	80.0
1986	5.8	1.1	−1.6	99.9	18.9	31.0	11.0	5.9	3.4	95.0
1987	5.4	0.9	−0.7	70.3	23.3	31.1	6.3	6.2	6.4	97.3
1988	3.7	−1.6	−1.3	68.1	28.1	33.9	4.5	2.2	2.6	97.4

— Not available.
a. Ratio of the index of average export prices to the index of average import prices.
b. Consumer price index.
c. For 1975–79, rate on 120-day Certificados de Abono Tributario (CATs). For 1980–88, rate on 90-day certificates of deposit.
d. Colombian pesos to U.S. dollar.
Source: Montes-Negret 1990; IMF, various years.

Financial Sector Structure and Policies

The Colombian financial system is a paradox: concentration prevails amid competition and the public sector dominates amid private sector oligopoly. Of the twenty-six commercial banks, nine publicly owned ones accounted for 63 percent of the banking system's total assets at the end of 1987. (Four of the nine were nationalized after 1982.) Private bank ownership is concentrated in a few powerful conglomerates, with the five largest financial groups controlling half the combined equity of commercial banks, finance companies, housing banks, and trade finance companies.

During the 1950s and 1960s the Colombian financial sector was severely repressed. The government controlled interest rates, determined credit allocation, and subsidized directed credits through the rediscount mechanism of the central bank. These policies impeded efficient resource allocation and domestic mobilization of savings and led to the growth of a large curb market.

Financial sector liberalization in the 1970s increased competition and domestic savings and resulted in the creation of savings and loan corporations. These corporations eroded the market share of the banks from 57 percent in 1976 to 46 percent in 1988. The monetary reform in 1974 further opened the financial sector in order to improve monetary control and rein in the growing curb market. Commercial banks' access to the central bank was restricted primarily to lender-of-last-resort facilities, although access to other sources of funds was enhanced. The minimum legal reserve requirement was lowered, and banks were allowed to offer attractive interest rates. Market-determined interest rates were gradually adopted to sustain a positive real interest rate structure. Limits on the growth of commercial bank loans also were abolished.

The introduction in 1975 of the "Colombianization" policy, however, retarded domestic competition. Foreign investment in banks was forbidden, and existing foreign banks had to convert to mixed ownership, with at least 51 percent of capital held by Colombians. As a result concentration increased in the large domestic conglomerates. The lack of competition hampered innovation and technological change, and banks' market share fell in a number of financial services.

A significant development during this period was the internationalization of Colombian banks, a result of the rise in international bank lending to develop-

ing countries in the late 1970s. This lending allowed banks to expand their offshore and international activities—particularly in Panama, where supervision was minimal. There were several reasons for this international expansion. First, offshore subsidiaries allowed banks to circumvent the functional separation of commercial and investment banking because their Panamanian subsidiaries could participate in syndicated lending and other international money market operations. Second, the small size of the banks' capital base ($524 million at the end of 1981) restricted their capacity to lend, particularly to large projects and on an unsecured basis to individual clients. Thus even though Colombian law restricted capital-liability ratios to 1:10, Panamanian affiliates and subsidiaries sometimes registered capital-liability ratios of 1:20 or more. Third, the export boom and the associated surplus in foreign exchange encouraged capital outflow and overseas expansion. Overseas investments amounted to 80 percent of the capital and reserves of the domestic Colombian banking system at the end of 1984. By the end of 1986 Colombian banks had three branches, twenty-three subsidiaries, and eighteen affiliates abroad.

Colombian supervisory authorities did not fully appreciate the additional risks incurred by this expansion overseas, nor did they recognize the magnitude of loan concentration to related parties or the extent of exchange control violations. In most cases the loans funding the overseas subsidiaries and affiliates were obtained through international borrowing secured by guarantees furnished by the parent banks. These credit supplements were registered mostly as foreign loans in Colombia or were brought in illegally to finance takeovers or domestic speculation.[2] The offshore entities also overextended themselves in syndicated lending to regional sovereign borrowers, assuming large liquidity risks. As a result these offshoots compromised the solvency of their parent banks.

The risks were not wholly overseas, however. A study of the banks' past-due loans as of 1987 suggests that such loans were highly concentrated by industrial sector and by company. Almost a third of past-due loans were owed by eleven manufacturing companies; two of them were state owned. One company accounted for a third of the past-due loans owed by these companies. The manufacturing sector's debt-servicing difficulties reveal not only flawed financial structures, but also inefficient production and management. These past-due loans were highly concentrated in the banking sector: 76 percent (by value) of the loans were held by six banks, five of which eventually required government assistance of some kind.

Finally, a major flaw in the Colombian banking system was the quality of its capital base. In 1980 local banks were allowed to include as part of their capital the difference between the market and historical value of their fixed assets. By 1984 more than half of total bank equity was accounted for by the revaluation component, thus eroding the capacity of the banks to absorb bad asset and other losses.

Crisis and Resolution

The boom ended in 1981 with the onset of the international recession, with coffee revenues and nontraditional exports falling sharply. The effects of the overvaluation of the peso and the decline in exports initially were cushioned by an increase in oil exports and by the high levels of accumulated external reserves. Imports continued at unsustainably high levels, however, despite restrictive policies introduced in 1982. At first the authorities chose to postpone fundamental adjustment, hoping the economy would grow out of its difficulties through expansionary fiscal and monetary policies. This strategy swelled the deficit of the overall nonfinancial public sector to 6.7 percent of GDP in 1984.

These deficits were financed by external borrowing, central bank loans to the government (until 1983), and capital gains taxes on foreign currency and gold holdings. But the net services deficit in the balance of payments deteriorated markedly after 1980—sliding from a deficit of $74 million to almost $1.7 billion in 1983, and $2 billion thereafter—as a result of record-high international interest rates and higher interest payments on Colombia's rapidly growing external debt.[3] Net capital inflows also dropped, from about $2.2 billion in 1982 to $0.9 billion in 1984, because of the debt crisis, loss of confidence in Colombian banking operations, and the corporate sector's efforts to repay foreign currency debts. Government spending, regional relief funds, extensive rediscount facilities for distressed private manufacturing enterprises, and substantially lower legal reserve requirements on bank deposits generated excess liquidity, which accelerated external reserve losses. By 1984 the central bank's international reserves had dropped to 32 percent of their 1981 level (table 6.2). The current account turned from a slight surplus in 1980 to a deficit of 10.8 percent of GDP in 1983.

Table 6.2 International reserves and domestic liquidity, 1980–88

(percent unless otherwise specified)

Year	External debt (millions of U.S. dollars)	Net international reserves (millions of U.S. dollars)	Change in M1	Change in M2	Change in monetary base
1980	6,941	5,356	—	—	—
1981	8,716	5,630	—	—	—
1982	10,306	4,891	25.4	24.6	17.7
1983	11,412	3,078	24.7	29.8	13.5
1984	12,039	1,796	23.4	24.5	18.3
1985	14,241	2,068	28.2	34.4	25.9
1986	15,364	3,479	22.8	28.8	28.2
1987	17,008	3,451	32.9	28.0	31.5
1988	17,001	3,811	25.8	23.4	26.9

— Not available.

Source: Montes-Negret 1990; World Bank data.

Inflation moderated from 27 percent in 1981 to 16 percent in 1984, thanks to the stabilization program adopted and the continued high unemployment (13 percent in 1984). But sticky interest rates, the crowding-out effect of public sector borrowing, and higher risk premiums in anticipation of a peso devaluation resulted in high real rates of interest on time deposits (between 10 percent and 12 percent) and loans (11.0 percent to 14.5 percent). This compounded the loan quality problems of banks and their overindebted corporate customers—the number of which rose sharply with higher real lending rates (table 6.3).

The first indication of serious banking troubles came in June 1982 when the authorities intervened in Banco Nacional, which accounted for 2.3 percent of total bank assets, and subsequently liquidated it. Small depositors were reimbursed. Other creditors received soft loans and, along with the central bank, were to be repaid through asset recovery and sales. Because the bank had engaged in highly speculative ventures and had concentrated loans in companies of Grupo Colombia, the controlling conglomerate, its problems were attributed to the abuses of a new class of bankers that had appeared following the 1974 liberalization. Although the episode was treated as an isolated event, rumors persisted of problems elsewhere. Indeed, in October 1982 the government was forced to declare a twenty-four-hour economic emergency and nationalize the private Banco del Estado (3.5 percent of total banking assets) after it had exhausted its liquidity lines from the central bank. Although relatively small, Banco del Estado was an important regional bank whose restoration was considered important to public confidence. This bank also had concentrated loans to

Table 6.3 Banking system indicators
(billions of pesos unless otherwise specified)

Year	Total equity[a]	Net revaluation of bank assets	Loan provisions	Substandard loans	Substandard loans/total equity (percent)	Total bank credit	Total past-due loans	Past-due loans in foreign currency/ total past-due loans[b] (percent)	Return on total capital[c]
1975	9.8	0.85	0.69	3.55	29.18	59.75	1,550	32.58	—
1976	12.4	1.05	0.31	5.87	40.76	76.66	3,410	56.74	—
1977	16.4	1.40	1.00	6.48	33.43	96.12	2,900	35.10	—
1978	22.1	3.59	1.10	7.90	30.74	117.46	3,600	30.19	—
1979	29.4	7.07	1.51	10.12	29.27	152.11	4,400	37.25	—
1980	41.5	11.41	2.11	16.80	35.40	233.89	6,220	27.56	—
1981	54.0	19.15	3.05	27.77	45.78	319.19	9,440	24.01	13.8
1982	70.7	28.34	7.24	57.07	70.48	389.92	21,680	21.80	5.6
1983	84.7	37.46	12.15	83.25	83.94	514.08	40,060	19.06	5.5
1984	86.8	42.95	23.43	148.51	144.10	585.94	95,490	35.17	6.3
1985	34.1	56.26	90.70	192.80	298.41	768.80	140,100	46.27	−6.3
1986	163.9	63.49	103.49	216.40	68.91	956.60	156,800	40.62	4.0
1987	196.2	74.70	116.69	224.82	55.13	1,217.66	158,800	41.81	10.0
1988	285.7	120.26	63.06	185.64	42.91	1,583.49	101,430	9.47	7.6

— Not available.
a. Includes paid capital, legal reserves, contingent reserves, revaluations, exchange rate adjustments, callable capital, and bonds forcefully converted into equity ± accumulated profits and losses.
b. Commercial banks only.
c. Average of six-month figures.
Source: Montes-Negret 1990.

related parties and ignored legal and prudential regulations, and losses proved greater than originally estimated. This rescue set a precedent for the extension of public deposit insurance coverage to the entire banking system—a precedent that had important fiscal consequences as the crisis unfolded.

Improving institutional responses

The problems of Banco Nacional and Banco del Estado marked only the first phase of Colombia's banking crisis and demonstrated that Colombia was not prepared to deal with extensive bank distress. The decree nationalizing Banco del Estado, however, marked a turning point. The decree introduced a code of conduct for bank managers, prohibiting lending to shareholders or related parties that would endanger the liquidity or solvency of the banks. It also prohibited the use of funds to finance speculative takeovers and cross-ownerships in excess of legal limits and imposed sanctions for assisting in tax evasion or for supplying misleading information about the financial condition of institutions. The decree also applied sanctions for violating prudential regulations and for engaging in unorthodox business practices, and made management subject to criminal prosecution and severe penalties.

The decree also allowed the government to nationalize any insolvent financial institution without compensating those responsible for the failure so long as

normal liquidity support from the central bank had been exhausted or normal procedures for intervention and liquidation might jeopardize public confidence. In addition, the government was empowered to appoint new boards of directors and management, assume and capitalize the bank's obligations with the central bank, purchase the shares of previous shareholders, and define the mechanism to determine the price of shares and allow the future sale of nationalized institutions. Finally, the decree introduced financial sector reform measures, including empowering the government to broaden ownership of financial institutions by setting limits on individual and group participation and mandating gradual divestiture of stakes above these ceilings.

A number of other initiatives were introduced in 1983 and 1984 to strengthen the financial and corporate sectors. An enterprise capitalization fund was created to provide preferential credit for purchasing new shares or convertible bonds in highly leveraged but viable companies. A comprehensive and voluntary mechanism was established to restructure private corporate debt. An innovative capitalization fund was created in which banks could invest up to 7 percentage points of their legally mandated reserves in central bank bonds to rediscount loans at preferential interest rates for the purpose of selling new bank shares. Preferential credits were provided to buyers of financial institutions' repossessed assets. Lower reserve requirements and higher interest rates on forced investments boosted the profitability of financial intermediaries (Vargas and others 1988).

Though helpful, these initiatives did not avert further bank failures. In 1983 Colombia's second largest commercial bank, Banco de Bogota, sustained serious loan losses from its Panamanian operations, sovereign debt exposure, and loan concentration. It also suffered from losses incurred by the controlling Grupo Bolivar, which was engaged in an expensive defense against an unfriendly takeover by Grupo Sarmiento-Angulo. Reluctant to nationalize the bank because of its size, the Monetary Board allowed competing financial groups to endorse the bank's shares to a trust fund administered by a state-owned bank. The authorities wanted to avoid further concentration in the banking system and hoped to obtain additional capital, which would resolve the ownership struggle. The central bank provided a cash advance as partial payment of the estimated value of the shares being put into trust. The advance would be canceled once the trust fund sold the shares to the public, but in the meantime the two competing groups received a subsidized credit. The government appointed a new board and reconfirmed the existing management. The scheme did not work as planned, however, because the shares in trust for sale to the public were too expensive given the bank's inability to pay dividends.

At this point Colombian authorities faced several challenges. They had to undertake an economic stabilization program. They needed to obtain additional external credits to roll over the external public debt. And they had to replenish the banks' lost capital, preferably without further nationalizing and without bailing out owners and managers as they had in the case of Banco de Bogota.

Resumed growth

Coffee prices rebounded in the second half of 1985 after a well-implemented adjustment plan introduced in late 1984 began to restore economic growth (Garay and Carrasquilla 1987). A drastic reduction in the public sector deficit was followed by a rapid correction of the overvalued peso through an accelerated crawling peg. The government budget moved from a deficit of 4.2 percent of GDP in 1985 to a surplus of 0.2 percent in 1986. Government revenues increased by almost 50 percent in 1985 because of improved collection, a broader tax base, and new taxes (notably an import surcharge). An improved current account surplus of 1.3 percent of GDP in 1986 relieved Colombia's reliance on external financing and curbed

the depletion of international assets. Nominal peso devaluation reached 43 percent against the dollar between March and December 1985, amounting to a real devaluation of 28.5 percent in 1985 and 38.0 percent between 1985 and 1986. Prices increased only moderately, restrained by excess industrial capacity, a good harvest, subsidized foodstuffs from Venezuela, lower international commodity prices, falling international interest rates, and continued tight wage and monetary policies.

Although this reversal of fortune provided authorities with the resources to undertake bank restructurings, monetary and exchange rate policies also increased pressures on the banking system. As observed in other banking crises, real interest rates on bank loans continued to be high, reflecting distress borrowing by enterprises, higher risks, and tight liquidity. Moreover, the depreciation of the peso created large foreign exchange losses for banks and enterprises with net foreign debt, increasing not only their liabilities but also their debt servicing burden. At its peak in 1985, past-due debt in foreign currency amounted to 46 percent of total past-due loans.

Banco de Colombia

Amid its economic stabilization efforts, the government was forced to rescue Colombia's oldest and largest commercial bank, Banco de Colombia (18 percent of total bank assets), which was embroiled in the fraudulent investment practices of its controlling Grupo Grancolombiano. This was the most complex bailout, involving 168 financial and nonfinancial companies—real and on paper. Public savings invested in two investment funds managed by the group had been used to finance costly takeovers of large manufacturing companies in the food processing, cement, and steel sectors, all sensitive to the business cycle. The fund managers manipulated the publicly quoted price of the underlying companies in 1981 by selling shares to group-related companies for less than the funds had paid for the shares in 1980. The resulting run on the funds led Banco de Colombia to extend large credits to group-related companies so that they could repay or purchase additional shares from the funds. When the related companies could not repay the bank, Colombian authorities intervened to stem a liquidity crisis. Grupo Grancolombiano was forced to absorb the losses in the investment funds and compensate defrauded investors. In 1983 the Superintendency of Banks replaced the bank's management, and subsequently the government forced the controlling shareholders to establish a trust fund pledging the shares of the group's holding company, Cingra, to back the loans made by Banco de Colombia to group-related companies. Banco de Colombia was then able to reverse some of its loan loss provisions and ended 1983 with a profit.

This intervention, however, merely postponed Banco de Colombia's day of reckoning. External auditors appointed in 1983 found massive irregularities stemming from illegal and unaccounted foreign exchange transactions, a large concentration of delinquent loans that had been rolled over to related, unprofitable, or nonviable enterprises, and lack of provisions against expected losses from unsecured, nonperforming loans (particularly to textile, automotive, and cotton-producing companies, all suffering from the economic downturn). By September 1985, 42 percent of the bank's total loans were nonperforming (equivalent to about 2.5 percent of GDP). Banco de Colombia's small net capital produced a gearing ratio of 38:1, nearly four times the legal limit of 10:1, and its net financial margin was negative. Moreover, the different financial companies of the Grupo Grancolombiano held one-third of all the external debt of Colombia's financial system.

The government initially assumed a substantial amount of overdue dollar-denominated and domestic public sector debts, ordered the sale of group enterprises to repay the bank, and attempted to reschedule Banco de Colombia's foreign debt. The central bank provided liquidity support, but attempts to recapitalize the bank failed when Banco de Colombia's accumulated losses reached more than twice its equity by the fourth quarter of 1985. The bank was nationalized in 1986 after losses had amounted to $356 million, of which 69 percent was attributable to its Panamanian operations. The government used the Spanish "accordion" technique to shrink capital to one centavo per share and then capitalized the 3 billion pesos ($15 million) of outstanding loans from the central bank. In addition, it subscribed 60 billion pesos ($300 million) of callable capital, and the new guarantee fund supplied additional soft credits. Because of continued mounting losses resulting from rapid peso devaluation, the callable capital did not have a positive financial impact. In 1988 the central bank issued dollar-denominated bonds to hedge the bank's rescheduled foreign exchange liabilities.

By far the most costly of the resolutions, Banco de Colombia highlighted the worst cases of abuse of fiduciary responsibility and fraud. But other failures shared some of the same characteristics. The share of substandard bank portfolios in the total portfolio rose from an average of 7 percent during 1975–80 to 24 percent in 1984. Loans in foreign currency traditionally accounted for a large share of all past-due loans, but their share and value jumped in 1984 to roughly ten times the level in 1981, and nearly doubled again in 1985. In 1985 officials found that the past-due foreign exchange loans of insolvent banks exceeded $450 million (almost half of all past-due loans), putting at risk Colombia's dwindling net international reserves and threatening the success of the urgent new international syndications. For example, two of the Panamanian offshoots had loan exposures exceeding $1 billion (Caballero 1988).

The guarantee fund

It was against this background that Congress, at the end of 1985, finally legislated a guarantee fund, which provided a means for resolving institutions short of full-scale nationalization or liquidation. One mechanism was "officialization," with private management but de facto official ownership. Under officialization shareholders were able to retain a minority stake while the fund took majority control. The government's deposit guarantee was proportional to its capital stake. Once the capital stake reached 51 percent the funds to officialize the bank came from either the fund or the central bank, but there was no budgetary outlay. The fund also helped rescue financial institutions by subscribing additional equity, extending loans, purchasing real or financial assets, arranging repurchase agreements, assuming domestic and external liabilities, offering guarantees, insuring deposits, and administering viable institutions. The fund was prohibited from assuming losses when purchasing bank assets and did not receive a capital endowment. It was placed under the oversight of the Superintendency of Banks, with a view to eventual self-financing through insurance premiums. In practice the fund relied on fees, insurance premiums, bond subscriptions by banks and development finance companies, and loans from the National Coffee Fund, guaranteed by the central bank.

Further insolvencies

Three small banks were officialized toward the end of the crisis in 1986. Banco de los Trabajadores, with 0.4 percent of total banking system assets, suffered recurrent liquidity problems between 1983 and 1985. The guarantee fund intervened because more than 40 percent of the bank's loan portfolio was nonperforming, its financial margin was insufficient to cover operating costs, and controlling shareholders failed to raise sufficient new capital. Banco Tequendama, accounting for 0.7 percent of banking system assets, was more problematic because it was a Colombian-Venezuelan joint venture. More than half its business was denominated in foreign currency and was concentrated in financing trade between Colombia and Venezuela. Credit lines shrank as a result of the 1982 debt crisis and Venezuela's balance of payments difficulties, exacerbating the inherent instability of the bank, which relied on costly and unstable deposits from Colombian agencies. Normal liquidity support and emergency interim subsidies failed to stabilize the bank. Nonperforming assets were roughly 65 percent of total assets, and by the end of 1985 the bank had lost almost three times it capital. Its limited scope of business and the unknown extent of problems in its partially owned Venezuelan subsidiary and its office in Curaçao made the restructuring difficult. Finally, Banco del Comercio also had serious management problems and could not compete adequately. It engaged extensively in intrabank deposits and guarantees in foreign currency with foreign subsidiaries in Panama and Montserrat. Between 1982 and 1985 nonperforming assets increased from 7 percent of total assets to 20 percent. When a recapitalization effort failed, the guarantee fund pared down the balance sheet, purchased bad assets (16 billion pesos) with a bond yielding 24 percent a year, and subscribed new capital of more than 6 billion pesos.

In addition, between 1982 and 1984 the Superintendency of Banks intervened in a number of consumer finance companies, and in 1987 it intervened in or liquidated five development finance companies and eight finance companies. Most of these were part of financial conglomerates built around insolvent commercial banks. Other finance companies also received financial support from the guarantee fund, although they were not officialized.

Conclusion

The 1984 economic adjustment program was quite successful. By 1986 the current account had returned to surplus, aided by higher coffee prices and petroleum and coal exports. The fiscal position went from a deficit of 3.5 percent of GDP in 1985 to a surplus of 0.6 percent in 1986. With confidence and private investment restored, growth recovered to 5.8 percent in 1986 and 5.3 percent in 1987. These environmental factors, aided by bank restructuring, further reduced the stock of nonperforming loans and restored bank profitability. By 1988 substandard loans as a percentage of total loans fell to 12 percent, compared with a peak of 25 percent in 1984. The ratio of substandard bank loans to capital and reserves dropped to just under 43 percent in 1988, compared with 144 percent in 1984. Between 1982 and 1987 the government provided more than 150 billion pesos—about $750 million at the 1986 exchange rate, or 2 percent of GNP—to recapitalize financial institutions.

On the regulatory front, the Superintendency of Banks revised rules covering loans to related parties, set limits on loans to single borrowers, and improved bank capital and reserves by transferring substandard or nonperforming loans to the guarantee fund. Raising the loan loss provisioning requirements also improved capital ratios. Institutional and legal mechanisms were established to facilitate future bank restructurings and assistance to distressed financial intermediaries and nonfinancial enterprises, and to protect the deposits of small savers.

The Colombian case was not a generalized banking crisis. It involved only seven of twenty-six banks and affected at most one-quarter of bank assets, compared with 60 percent of bank assets in the Chilean case, for example. The situation unraveled over a relatively long period (1982–87), and the equity base and bank profitability had already weakened before then. Although the downturn of the business cycle might have precipitated the bank failures, the high concentration of banks' loan portfolios was the most important reason for the insolvencies. Contributing factors include weak supervision before the crisis, along with inadequate legal and institutional arrangements and excessive government regulation in the form of low-yielding, large forced investments and relatively high legal reserve requirements. Fraud, bad credit decisions, undercapitalization of banks and their corporate customers, the failure of overseas affiliates and subsidiaries, and increasing operational and financial costs also played a part.

Notes

This chapter is an abbreviated version of Montes-Negret (1990).

1. Forced investments amounting to 16.5 percent of bank loans were channeled to agriculture and represented a substantial subsidy to the state. Banks held securities of the central bank, but these yielded only 8 percent at a time when nominal rates ranged from 28 to 38 percent. In 1984 the yield was raised to 15 percent, but the additional 7 percent return had to be used for loan loss provisioning. By booking loans abroad, banks could reduce the base of computation for forced investments. Foreign currency lending was finally excluded from the base of computation in December 1987.

2. In addition, Colombian banks were authorized to purchase trade-related, legally registered loans of their overseas subsidiaries. These purchases were funded with credits provided by the same international bank that had originally extended the loan to the Panamanian offshoot. This enhanced the influence of international banks in negotiating syndicated loans to Colombia.

3. The external debt doubled from $6.8 billion in 1980 to $12.3 billion in 1984.

References

Arango, M. A. 1988. "El Sector Industrial y las Deudas de Dudoso Recaudo del Sector Fianciero." DCI, Banco de la Republica, Bogotá.

Banco de la Republica. 1986. *Fondo de Garantias de Instituciones Financieras, Antecedentes, y Normas Basicas.* Bogotá.

———. 1988a. "La Recuperacion del Sistema Financiero." Notas Editoriales, *Revista del Banco de la Republica* 58(693).

———. 1988b. "Orientacion del Sistema Financiero y sus Resultados." Notas Editoriales, *Revista del Banco de la Republica* 727(May).

Caballero, Carlos. 1988. "La Experiencia de Tres Bancos Colombianos en Panama." *Coyuntura Economica* 18(1).

Carrizosa, Mauricio. 1986. *Hacia la Recuperacion del Mercado de Capitales en Colombia.* Bogotá: Bolsa de Bogotá.

Colombia. 1986. "La Nacionalización del Banco de Colombia y el Grupo Grancolombiano: Antecedentes y Justificación." Economia Colombiana, *Revista de la Contraloria General de la Republica.*

Garay, Luis, and Alberto Carrasquilla. 1987. "Dinamica del Desajuste y Proceso de Saneamiento Economico en Colombia en la Decada de los Ochenta." *Ensayos Sobre Politica Economica* 11. Banco de la Republica, Bogotá.

IMF (International Monetary Fund). Various years. *International Financial Statistics.* Washington, D.C.

Jaramillo, J. C. 1977. "Sector Externo." *LIV Informe Anual del Gerente a la Junta Directiva.* Segunda Parte, Banco de la Republica, Bogotá.

———. 1982. "La Liberación del Mercado Financiero." *Ensayos Sobre Politica Economica* 1(March). Banco de la Republica, Bogotá.

Lee, Martha. 1983. "Comentarios a la Reforma del Sistema Financiero." *Ensayos Sobre Politica Economica* 4(December). Banco de la Republica, Bogotá.

Montes-Negret, Fernando. 1990. "An Overview of Colombia's Banking Crisis: 1982–88." Background paper prepared for *World Development Report 1989.* World Bank, Washington, D.C.

Montes-Negret, Fernando, and Alberto Carrasquilla. 1986. "Sensibilidad de la Tasa de Interes Activa de los Bancos a Cambios en los Parmetros de Politica y Estructura." *Ensayos Sobre Politica Economica* 10(December). Banco de la Republica, Bogotá.

Ortega, Francisco J., and Rudolf Hommes. 1984. "Estado y Evolución de la Capitalización de Bancos y Corporaciones Financieras." *Banca y Finanzas* 186(December).

Vargas, H., M. Lee, F. Montes-Negret, and R. Steiner. 1988. "La Evolucion del Sistema Financiero en los Ultimos Años." *Revista del Banco de la Republica* 731. Bogotá.

World Bank. 1989. *World Development Report 1989: Financial Systems and Development.* New York: Oxford University Press.

CHAPTER 7

Malaysia's Bank Restructuring, 1985–88

Andrew Sheng

Sharp deflation in the Malaysian economy in 1985–86 precipitated large losses among a number of financial institutions, most notably four (of thirty-nine) commercial banks, four (of forty-seven) finance companies, thirty-two (of thirty-five) deposit-taking cooperatives, and thirty-three illegal deposit-taking institutions. Losses among the unregulated deposit-taking institutions were relatively small; those sustained by the banks and finance companies—which were supervised by the central bank—and the deposit-taking cooperatives were far greater. Between 1985 and 1987 those forty institutions lost roughly 3.1 billion ringgit (M$), equivalent to 4.7 percent of gross domestic product (GDP) in 1986. Losses were distributed more heavily among the lightly supervised deposit-taking cooperatives, whereas bank losses amounted to only 2.4 percent of total deposits in 1986. This suggests that deficiencies in oversight and delay in recognizing the magnitude of the portfolio problems of nonbank financial intermediaries were chiefly to blame for this short-lived crisis. Restructuring, while costly, was aided by sound structural adjustment in the Malaysian economy, specifically fiscal retrenchment and currency depreciation. Economic recovery brought a return to enterprise profitability, a high level of national savings, and adequate foreign exchange reserves to cushion the system against international economic shocks.

Structure of the Financial System

Malaysia has a relatively broad and deep financial system consisting of thirty-nine commercial banks (twenty-two domestic, sixteen foreign, and one Islamic), forty-seven licensed finance companies, twelve merchant banks, and seven discount houses. There are also several specialized financial intermediaries, including development banks, building societies, provident funds, and insurance companies. Foreign banks account for a quarter of total bank loans and one-fifth of total bank deposits. At the end of 1987 assets of the financial system totaled M$203 billion, equivalent to 269 percent of gross national product (GNP) (table 7.1).

The degree of monetization, measured as the ratio of broad money to GNP, was 0.94 in 1986, comparing favorably with that of the Republic of Korea (0.94), the United States (0.82), the United Kingdom (0.77), and Australia (0.73). Malaysia also has active foreign exchange and capital markets and a liberal exchange control regime that allows free convertibility of the ringgit with all major foreign currencies. The Kuala Lumpur foreign exchange market has an average monthly turnover of M$20 billion, and the Kuala Lumpur stock exchange—which reported a market capitalization of M$97.1 billion ($37.8 billion) in the first half of 1988—is one of the most active stock exchanges in the developing world. In 1986 equities amounted to 24 percent of total financial assets, about the same proportion as in Canada but far greater than in Korea (4 percent) or Taiwan, China (9 percent).

Licensed deposit-taking institutions, which accounted for 70 percent of total financial system assets at the end of 1987, are under the direct supervision of Bank Negara, the central bank. The central bank has two bank supervision departments, one for off-site monitoring and the other for on-site examinations. Banks are constrained from acquiring shares without the central bank's permission and from

Table 7.1 Assets of the Malaysian financial system

(billions of ringgit)

Type of institution	Annual change		Assets at end-1987	Share of total assets (percent)
	1986	1987		
Banking system	11.3	11.0	140.6	69.3
Monetary institutions	9.0	9.6	110.0	54.2
Central bank	3.8	3.8	24.2	11.9
Commercial banks[a]	5.2	5.8	85.8	42.3
Nonmonetary institutions	2.3	1.4	30.6	15.1
Finance companies	1.8	1.6	21.3	10.5
Merchant banks	0.1	0.0	6.3	3.1
Discount houses	0.4	−0.2	3.0	1.5
Nonbank financial intermediaries	5.4	6.4	62.4	30.7
Provident, pension, and insurance funds	4.6	4.8	42.0	20.6
Employees Provident Fund	3.8	3.8	32.3	15.9
Other provident funds	0.4	0.3	3.5	1.7
Life insurance funds	0.4	0.6	4.7	2.3
General insurance funds	0.0	0.1	1.5	0.7
Development finance institutions[b]	0.3	0.2	4.6	2.3
Savings institutions[c]	−1.2	0.4	7.2	3.6
Other financial intermediaries[d]	1.7	1.0	8.6	4.2
Total	16.7	17.4	203.0	100.0

a. Includes the Islamic bank.
b. Includes all development banks.
c. Includes the National Savings Bank and deposit-taking cooperatives.
d. Includes building societies and capital market funds.
Source: Bank Negara Malaysia.

making property investments except for operating needs. The central bank also supervises the forty-seven licensed finance companies, traditional providers of consumer and housing finance. Other financial institutions are supervised by various agencies. For example, all deposit-taking cooperatives are under the authority of the Ministry of National and Rural Development, while some development banks are supervised by the Ministry of Public Enterprises and others by the Ministry of Finance. Although the system is comprehensive, it applied varying degrees of supervisory stringency to different types of depository institutions and failed to rein in a handful of illegal deposit-taking institutions, whose number increased rapidly during the economic prosperity of the 1970s and early 1980s.

As the economy prospered during the early 1970s the banking system expanded rapidly. Incomes rose with favorable commodity prices and the advent of substantial oil revenues, and national savings increased sharply, contributing to the rapid growth of savings in the banking system. Asset growth also accelerated, from an average annual rate of 19.1 percent in the first half of the 1970s to 24.4 percent in the second half. Growth stayed at double-digit rates until 1984, falling sharply to 7 percent by 1987. The value of loans grew by an average of 23 percent a year during 1975–84. The number of bank branches

more than doubled, from 336 to 770 between 1970 and 1986, and employment in banking quadrupled, exceeding 40,000 people at the end of 1985. The larger domestic banks also began to expand abroad, boasting forty-five foreign branches at the end of 1986 and foreign assets of M$11.2 billion (15 percent of all assets).

Nonbank financial intermediaries accounted for 31 percent of the assets of the Malaysian financial system at the end of 1987. The bulk of these assets was held by provident and pension funds and the National Savings Bank, whose assets were primarily in government bonds or deposits with the banking system. During the 1970s, however, deposit-taking institutions and some deposit-taking cooperatives emerged as quasi finance companies, collecting deposits to finance a range of business activities while remaining outside the supervisory authority of the central bank. The unlicensed deposit-taking institutions acted as pawnbrokers or credit and leasing companies and took deposits from the public illegally to fund their lending and investment activities. Cooperatives, by contrast, operated under a legal loophole permitting them to take deposits from their members (who simply paid a small fee). The Department of Cooperative Development, which was responsible for supervising 3,000 cooperatives, was not equipped to monitor the thirty-five deposit-taking cooperatives, whose complex operations expanded rapidly during the 1970s. These cooperatives had diversified out of traditional consumer finance and had acquired more than 1 million members, 600 branches, and total deposits exceeding M$4 billion. There was no lender-of-last-resort facility for these cooperatives, which frequently did not observe the mandated 25 percent liquid deposit ratio.

Macroeconomic Background

Malaysia is a small, open, middle-income, oil-exporting country. The Malaysian economy historically has been sensitive to changes in the terms of trade (figure 7.1); its external trade to GNP ratio was 130 percent in 1987. Well-endowed with natural resources, it is the largest exporter of rubber, palm oil, tin, and tropical hardwoods; an important producer of cocoa and pepper; and a net exporter of crude oil and natural gas. Manufacturing accounted for 23 percent of GDP and manufactured exports for 45 percent of gross exports in 1987. In 1988 GNP reached $31.6 billion ($1,869 per capita).

The government, considered a model of cautious economic management, has a stated policy of maintaining a current account surplus, strong external reserves, and low inflation. In the 1960s Malaysia enjoyed steady real GDP expansion averaging 5.2 percent a year, while inflation remained at less than 1 percent a year. During the 1970s the economy grew by an average 8 percent a year in real terms, with

GDP growth peaking at 9.3 percent in 1979, but inflation rose to an average of 6 percent, peaking at 11.1 percent in mid-1981 (table 7.2).

During 1979–81 Malaysia witnessed its sharpest deflation since the post–Korean War recession of 1952–53. In 1981, in light of its strong financial position and to counteract the impact of the severe international recession that had begun in 1980, the government embarked on a countercyclical policy intended to build up infrastructure and the industrial base. The policy relied primarily on external borrowing. Federal government development expenditure rose from an average of M$3.0–4.0 billion a year during 1977–79 to a peak of M$11.5 billion in 1982, resulting in a deterioration in the federal fiscal deficit to 18.7 percent of GNP (figure 7.2). The terms of trade deteriorated by 10.2 percent as commodity prices fell in 1981–82, and the current account went from near balance in 1980 to a deficit of M$8.4 billion, or 6.0 percent of GNP, in 1982. The net result was a tripling in the foreign debt from M$10 billion in 1980 (matched by equal foreign exchange reserves) to M$31.8 billion at the end of 1983 (49 percent of GNP). The debt service ratio worsened at the same time, as international bank lending declined in 1982–83, making a countercyclical policy financed by external borrowing unsustainable.

The government undertook a stringent structural adjustment program in 1983 to reduce the fiscal and balance of payments deficits and to control the growth of external debt, especially the expenditure and debt incurred by the nonfinancial public enterprises. Temporary recovery in commodity prices during 1983–84 and the resulting revival of GDP growth to 7.8 percent in 1984 contributed to the success of the adjustment effort. The overall fiscal deficit fell to 9.5 percent of GNP in 1984.

Beginning in the second half of 1985, however, global commodity prices dropped sharply, and they continued to fall in 1986. Crude oil prices fell 62 percent from their peak, and palm oil prices fell 57 percent, to below the cost of production. Terms of trade worsened by 4.5 percent in 1985 and by 15.5 percent in 1986. Total export income fell by 2.6 percent in 1985 and 5.9 percent in 1986. Real GDP growth became negative (–1.0 percent) in 1985 for the first time since 1975, while nominal GNP declined by 2.9 percent in 1985 and 7.9 percent in 1986. Cutbacks in public spending exacerbated the decline in GNP, which for the first time declined for two consecutive years in current terms. As revenue

Figure 7.1 Terms of trade and current account deficit, 1970–88

(percent change)

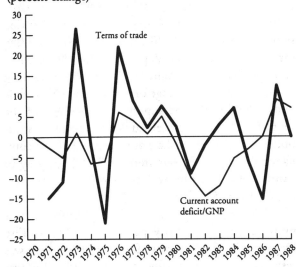

Source: IMF, various years.

Table 7.2 Macroeconomic indicators, 1970–89
(percent unless otherwise specified)

Year	Real growth in GDP	Current account/GNP	Terms of trade[a] (1980=100)	Inflation rate[b]	Government balance/GNP	Deposit interest rate	Exchange rate (ringgits/ U.S. dollar)
1970	6.0	0.1	77.0	1.8	−3.7	—	3.1
1971	5.8	−0.8	70.8	1.6	−7.7	—	2.9
1972	9.4	−1.7	59.4	3.2	−9.0	—	2.8
1973	11.7	0.6	72.3	10.6	−5.5	—	2.5
1974	8.3	−2.4	81.6	17.3	−6.0	—	2.3
1975	0.8	−2.2	68.8	4.5	−8.4	—	2.6
1976	11.6	2.1	76.9	2.6	−7.1	5.5	2.5
1977	7.8	1.3	84.7	4.8	−8.5	5.2	2.4
1978	6.7	0.3	81.3	4.9	−8.0	5.1	2.2
1979	9.3	2.1	99.0	3.7	−8.3	5.5	2.2
1980	7.4	−0.6	100.0	6.7	−13.8	6.2	2.2
1981	6.9	−4.5	86.4	9.7	−19.8	9.7	2.2
1982	5.9	−6.0	80.6	5.8	−18.7	9.8	2.3
1983	6.3	−5.3	79.9	3.7	−14.0	8.0	2.3
1984	7.8	−2.3	87.0	3.9	−9.5	9.5	2.4
1985	−1.0	−0.9	79.2	0.3	−7.9	8.8	2.4
1986	1.2	−0.2	64.8	0.7	−11.2	7.2	2.6
1987	5.3	3.5	77.4	0.9	−8.2	3.0	2.5
1988	8.8	2.1	77.8	2.0	−4.5	3.5	2.7
1989	8.8	−0.2	77.6	2.8	−5.1	4.6	2.7

— Not available.
a. Ratio of the index of average export prices to the index of average import prices.
b. Consumer price index.
Source: IMF, various years; World Bank data.

declined, the overall fiscal deficit increased again in 1986, to 11.2 percent of GNP, after the modest recovery in 1985. Again, the government cut spending, bringing development expenditure down to M$3.2 billion in 1987, the lowest level since 1979.

The government also decided to allow the exchange rate to depreciate freely in order to bring

Figure 7.2 Fiscal deficit and nominal GNP growth, 1976–88
(percent change)

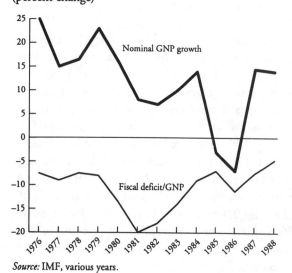

Source: IMF, various years.

about an adjustment in the balance of payments. The ringgit depreciated by 16.7 percent against its composite from September 1985 (Plaza Accord) to the end of 1986. Despite the rise the depreciation caused in import costs, inflation fell sharply to 0.7 percent in 1986, compared with 9.7 percent in 1981.

On the real side of the economy, major shifts occurred in the direction of domestic investment during the halcyon years of the second half of the 1970s and the early 1980s—when real GDP grew at an average rate of 8.6 percent, the exchange rate was strong, and foreign investment flowed in. Exchange rate appreciation brought a shift toward the nontradable sector. Strong corporate profits and speculation drove the Kuala Lumpur stock exchange composite index from 100 in 1977 to a peak of 427 in early 1984.

Bank lending to property acquisition and development was stimulated by the influx of foreign workers allied to inward investment in the petroleum industry and other areas of the economy. Demand for office and residential rental properties caused prices to triple between 1975 and 1983. In 1986 the number of completed property developments in Kuala Lumpur alone was five times the number in 1983. In 1983, at the height of the property boom, prime commercial property in Kuala Lumpur was valued at M$450 a square foot, with a monthly rental of M$3.20 a square foot, but by 1986 overbuilding and forced selling drove values down to M$180 and rental prices to M$0.90 a square foot. By the end of 1986 total new banking system loans to real estate amounted to 55 percent of total new loans, compared with 32 percent in 1980. The share of property loans in total bank loans outstanding rose from 26 percent at the end of 1980 to 36 percent at the end of 1986.

The 1985 slowdown brought a sharp contraction in cash flow for many Malaysian companies. Incomes declined dramatically in the face of falling commodity prices, weak export sales, and poor domestic demand. Companies fell behind in debt repayments, while their committed outflows, particularly in the property sector, continued to drain resources. Share prices dropped 60 percent from their 1984 peak, and total market capitalization fell 44 percent, to M$46.7 billion in 1986. Inflation had fallen to almost zero, and the growth rate of narrow money (M1) became negative by the end of 1984. Broad money (M3) growth also slowed sharply to 3.6 percent by 1987, the slowest rate in fifteen years (figure 7.3).

As liquidity began to tighten in the early 1980s with the decline in commodity prices, the banking system's loans-to-deposits ratio rose from an average of 75 percent in the 1970s to 90 percent in 1983. Private sector expenditure initially was slow to adjust to the declining income, resulting in a drawdown of savings. Annual growth of deposits in the banking system fell sharply, from 20 percent in 1984 to 4 per-

cent in 1986. For the corporate sector, excluding deposits from the oil sector, growth in deposits was –19.2 percent at that time. Faced with threats to their survival, many cash-strapped enterprises engaged in distress borrowing, paying exceptionally high rates for funds in order to meet temporary liquidity shortfalls. By 1985 the real rate of borrowing had risen to an unprecedented 11.8 percent, compared with 2.0 to 3.0 percent in 1981 (figure 7.4). The growth of bank loans moderated to 6 percent at the end of 1986, compared with 37 percent in 1980.

The combination of tight liquidity, low inflation, and a dramatic decline in share and property prices brought into focus the financial overcommitments of many entrepreneurs. Those who had built up their gross assets through speculation in shares and property, financed through excessive gearing, were caught in a triple squeeze: they faced a sharp decline in income flows, a collapse in asset values, and a rise in the cost of debt service. As the slowdown in the economy gathered momentum during 1985, tightening liquidity combined with bad economic news to cause nervousness among depositors.

The Impact of Recession on the Financial System

The dangers of rapid expansion into new areas of growth without fully understanding the implications first became evident in 1982, when Bumiputra Malaysia Finance (BMF) nearly failed. BMF, the Hong Kong finance company subsidiary of Malaysia's

Figure 7.3 Money supply and real GDP growth, 1970–88
(percent change)

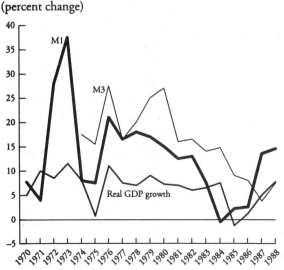

Source: Bank Negara Malaysia.

Figure 7.4 Real interest rate and real GDP growth, 1980–88
(percent)

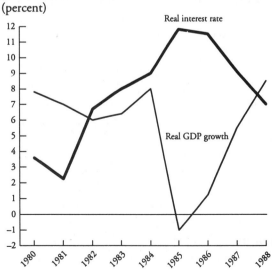

Source: Bank Negara Malaysia.

largest domestic bank, had extended M$2.4 billion in loans to several Hong Kong corporations and individuals. When borrowers defaulted on the loans, the parent bank absorbed the losses, and Malaysia's national oil corporation, Petronas, became the largest shareholder by injecting fresh capital into the bank. Petronas bought M$1.26 million in loans from the bank; the remaining M$1.0 billion in nonperforming loans was written off in 1983, constituting one of the largest losses in the history of Malaysian banking. But the warning that the BMP episode signaled of events to follow went unheeded, especially when economic performance rebounded during 1983–85.

Banks

By mid-1985 financial problems had reemerged. In July the failure of Overseas Trust Bank in Hong Kong prompted rumors about problems in a large domestic Malaysian bank, sparking a run on its branches. Although the panic was quelled, this was the first such incident in Malaysia since the mid-1960s. In September Setia Timor Credit and Leasing, a small leasing company engaged in illegal deposit-taking, failed. The first failure among the deposit-taking institutions, it sparked isolated runs on several licensed finance companies. The panic withdrawals were halted quickly. But in December 1985 Pan-Electric, a large, publicly listed company in Singapore, collapsed, causing widespread panic that led to an unprecedented three-day closure of the Kuala Lumpur and Singapore stock exchanges. A run then occurred on a medium-size finance company associated with businessmen—later arrested—who also had interests in Pan-Electric. Bank Negara provided market liquidity, the run subsided, and an experienced professional was appointed to manage the finance company. Nevertheless, sporadic bank runs throughout 1986 culminated in the failure of the twenty-four deposit-taking cooperatives in July and August. At that point there was danger of systemic financial failure, a possibility that persisted for the remainder of 1986.

The traumatic events of 1985–86 were as much a shock to bank management as to their borrowers. Throughout the previous two decades, the Malaysian banking system had enjoyed rising profits, with pretax profits peaking in 1984 (figure 7.5). During the period of uninterrupted growth and rising property (and hence security) values, bad loans were negligible. As late as 1983 specific and bad debt provisions aver-

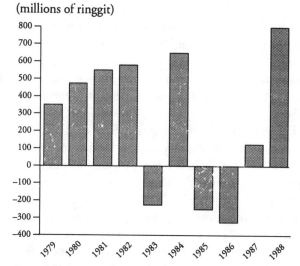

Figure 7.5 Banking system pretax profits, 1979–88
(millions of ringgit)

Source: Bank Negara Malaysia.

aged only 1.0 to 1.5 percent of total loans. Foreclosed property could easily be sold at values higher than the outstanding loans that financed them. However, with M$37.3 billion wiped off stock market capitalization and property prices falling under pressure of distress sales, the banks faced rising levels of nonperforming loans and bad and doubtful debts in 1985–86.

To identify the impact of the recession on the banking system, the central bank in 1985 introduced uniform guidelines for financial institutions on the treatment of nonaccrued income, or interest-in-suspense. At the beginning of the crisis in 1984 bad debt provisions and interest-in-suspense were only M$2 billion, or 3.5 percent of the total loans of the banking system (table 7.3). At 2.3 percent, bad debt provisions were not out of line with international standards, such as those for the major British clearing banks. By the end of 1988, however, total interest-in-suspense and bad debt provisions amounted to M$11.7 billion, or 14.5 percent of the gross loans of the banking system. These provisions covered approximately 47 percent of total nonperforming loans, a relatively high level compared with the average provisions of 25 to 40 percent for the international banks exposed to highly indebted countries. The fastest-rising component was interest-in-suspense, indicating private sector difficulties in servicing debt during the recession. Between 1984 and 1988 interest-in-suspense grew at an average annual rate of 73 percent, from M$664 million to M$5.9 billion, while bad debt provisions rose at a slower rate of 42 percent, from M$1.3 billion to M$5.7 billion.

Table 7.3 Outstanding interest-in-suspense and bad debt provisions, 1984–88
(millions of ringgit)

Year	Interest-in-suspense	Bad debt provisions	Total as a share of total loans (percent)
1984	664	1,346	3.5
1985	1,500	2,493	5.6
1986	2,844	4,056	9.7
1987	4,242	5,188	12.9
1988	5,932	5,722	14.5

Source: Bank Negara Malaysia, various years.

These large provisions ultimately cut bank profits across the board. Even the best-managed foreign banks showed substantially lower profits and several reported large losses, which they covered through fresh injections of capital. Four medium-size domestic banks were the most severely affected, mainly by heavy losses from their involvement in the property sector. All four banks were relative newcomers: one, whose license had been issued in 1979, was majority state owned; two had been restructured within the previous ten years from branches of foreign banks; and the fourth was a joint-venture bank. The four banks collectively had expanded their loan base aggressively between 1980 and 1985, increasing their market share from 7.2 percent to 8.8 percent by the end of 1985. But mismanagement, fraud, overstretched managerial resources, and poor internal procedures and controls had led to lax control over costs and a rapid rise in nonperforming loans. The central bank stepped in to change the management and the boards of directors, and to arrange for capital injections, including direct infusions from the central bank in three cases.

Licensed finance companies

Of the forty-seven licensed finance companies, traditional providers of consumer and housing finance, those that aggressively lent to finance real estate development were particularly vulnerable. Finance companies lagged behind commercial banks in building professional expertise in commercial credit operations and were slower to restrict loans to the property sector. Problems also occurred disproportionately among new entrants. Consequently, the industry was hit rather severely by the downward spiral in property prices and economic performance. By 1984 eleven finance companies had reported losses totaling M$17 million (of industry profits of M$227 million). Eight of these firms had started operating between 1979

and 1985. By 1987 losses had risen to M$252 million. The central bank assumed control of four companies unable to inject new capital to cover their losses. Many of the others had strong shareholders (one-third were subsidiaries of banks) and were able to cover their capital deficiencies.

Nonbank financial intermediaries

Setia Timor's inability in September 1985 to meet its deposit withdrawals was the first sign of serious financial distress among deposit-taking institutions. Press reports stating that directors and staff of a few deposit-taking institutions had absconded with funds highlighted the problem of illegal deposit-taking institutions, which attracted deposits by paying interest rates of 24 to 36 percent a year compared with the 8 to 10 percent offered in the formal banking sector. During 1985–87 the central bank investigated thirty-three failed, illegal deposit-taking institutions involving 8,000 depositors and total deposits of M$49 million.

Nervousness among depositors spread to the deposit-taking cooperatives as well. In early 1986 Kosatu, with M$156 million in deposits from 53,000 members in sixty-seven branches, suspended payments. The thirty-five deposit-taking cooperatives, which had started in the 1960s as a slow-growing, grassroots network, diversified and grew rapidly during the 1970s. They moved into property and share investment, often in companies connected with board members or staff. Expansion was spearheaded by the largest among them, the Cooperative Central Bank, and largely unrestrained due to the absence of reserve requirements and lack of enforcement of the 25 percent liquid deposit requirement. Audit reports were sometimes as much as two years late. The thirty-two deposit-taking cooperatives that ultimately were investigated by Bank Negara had 106 related companies ranging from newspapers to cosmetics distributors.

Almost all the cooperatives were affected by the recession, including the Cooperative Central Bank, with 363,749 members and total deposits of M$1.5 billion. Its 1987 audited accounts showed accumulated losses exceeding M$726 million and a capital deficiency of M$652 million. The bank was placed in receivership, and the government made available a standby facility of M$323 million to meet liquidity needs. By the end of 1987 thirty-two deposit-taking cooperatives, accounting for M$3.1 billion in deposits (an estimated 77 percent of total cooperative deposits), were under investigation by or under the supervision of Bank Negara.

The insurance industry also suffered from the recession. At the end of fiscal 1986 fourteen of sixty-one insurance companies did not comply with the minimum solvency requirement of 20 percent of their net premium income. Inspection by the Office of the Director-General of Insurance revealed that solvency problems had been compounded by the underprovisioning of outstanding claims reserves, bad debts from poor agency collection, and declining investment values for quoted securities and landed properties. As part of the effort to coordinate supervision of the financial system, the duties and responsibilities of the director-general of insurance were transferred from the treasury to the central bank in April 1988.

The Response

The bank restructuring exercise was approached from two fronts: monetary and regulatory. The objectives, however, were sometimes contradictory. Tighter monetary policy raised interest rates but also increased the level of nonperforming loans in the banking system. On the other hand, institutional adjustments at the microeconomic level could not be achieved without macroeconomic changes, both in terms of monetary policy and regulatory guidelines. A main objective of monetary policy was to ease the contractionary effects of fiscal retrenchment and the deterioration in the balance of payments. However, Bank Negara had considerable difficulty reducing the abnormally high real rates of interest, even when deposit rates fell in 1987. The bank had to make major adjustments to meet both objectives, including some monetary and prudential deregulation to promote greater efficiency in the banking industry.

Economic and monetary measures

In 1985–86 Bank Negara introduced a series of policy measures designed to address the macroeconomic impact of the recession on the banking system. Of key macroeconomic importance was the move to allow the currency to find its own foreign exchange level, with only some intervention to stabilize sporadic speculation. Other measures included extensive reform of the bank's export credit refinancing scheme to promote exports, a reduction in the liquidity and statutory reserve ratios of the commercial banks to lower their effective cost of funds, and the creation of a M$1 billion investment fund to shift bank lending out of real estate to the productive (tradables) sectors of agriculture, manufacturing, and tourism. The bank also introduced a more flexible interest rate regime by freeing deposit rates and encouraged the establishment of a secondary mortgage market to securitize long-term housing loans.

While distressed bank borrowers were forced to pay high real interest rates, the banking system was generally unwilling to reduce lending rates even when general liquidity improved and deposit rates began to fall. Between 1985 and 1988 the gross interest margin of the banks actually rose from 4.2 percent to 5.2 percent (table 7.4). The banks maintained high lending rates because they either were not collecting interest from their nonperforming loans or were forced to recover lost profits due to higher provisions for bad debts. Thus depositors and good borrowers were subsidizing the banks' losses from nonperforming loans. In the short term this approach benefited banks and the banking system, since the banks could recover to profitability sooner. But high real lending rates deterred new investment to aid the economic recovery effort, while low deposit rates encouraged disintermediation.

Table 7.4 Commercial bank loan margins, 1985–88
(annual percentages)

Indicator	1985		1986		1987		1988	
	Rate	Share	Rate	Share	Rate	Share	Rate	Share
Average lending rate	15.2	100.0	15.0	100.0	12.7	100.0	10.9	100.0
– costs of funds	11.0	72.4	10.1	67.3	7.6	59.8	5.7	52.3
= gross margin	4.2	27.6	4.9	32.7	5.1	40.2	5.2	47.7
– interest-in-suspense	1.4	9.2	2.1	14.0	2.3	18.1	2.5	22.9
= net margin	2.8	18.4	2.8	18.7	2.8	22.1	2.7	24.8
– overhead	3.5	23.0	3.2	21.4	3.2	25.2	3.2	29.4
– bad debt provisions	1.9	12.5	2.3	15.3	1.8	14.3	1.0	9.2
= net loan margin	–2.6	–17.1	–2.7	–18.0	–2.2	–17.4	–1.5	–13.8
+ nonloan income	2.1	13.8	2.2	14.7	2.7	21.3	2.8	25.7
= net yield	–0.5	–3.3	–0.5	–3.3	0.5	3.9	1.3	11.9

Source: Bank Negara Malaysia, various years.

To ensure that the benefits of lower deposit rates would pass through to the borrowers, Bank Negara persuaded the banks to reduce their operating costs and interest rate margins.

Institutional remedies

The central bank was only the lender of last resort to the banking system; it was prohibited by law from providing emergency liquidity to institutions not under its supervision. But there was a danger that the liquidity problems of failing unsupervised financial institutions would spread to the monetary sector, that is, to licensed banks and finance companies. The threat was exacerbated by the fact that sharp fluctuations in commodity, share, and property prices had subjected parts of the financial system to exceptional stresses that many institutions might not be able to absorb. In addition, the uneven quality of assets, management, capital cushion, and supervision within the financial system, including the formal sector, meant than an uncoordinated supervisory mechanism might not be able to cope with the impact of the recession. The system needed a legal framework that delineated supervisory powers and provided the administrative capacity to deal with future financial problems.

Deposit insurance. Bank Negara evaluated a scheme to cover small deposits that would keep small depositors at bay whenever news of instability surrounded a deposit-taking institution. A major disadvantage of the idea was that the burden of financing the deposit insurance fund would fall unevenly on the institutions, since the strong ones would be paying proportionately as much as the weak ones but drawing little or no cash support. In addition, any deposit insurance scheme runs the risk of encouraging moral hazard among bank managers who, knowing that their liabilities are protected, might take undue lending risks. In the end no deposit insurance scheme was established.

Prudential measures. In 1985–86 Bank Negara made a number of substantial changes designed to strengthen the structure of the banking system and the regulatory powers to prevent and control damage arising from the recession. These included key changes to the banking laws and regulations. A minimum capital adequacy requirement was introduced, effectively raising the average capital-asset ratio of Malaysian banks from 7.4 percent at the end of 1984 to 8.1 percent at the end of 1987. The holdings of

individuals, including family holding companies, in the equity of a financial institution were limited to 10 percent, while any company or cooperative was limited to a 20 percent ownership stake. Penalties were introduced to prevent abuses of authority in bank lending. Bank credit to single customers was restricted to 30 percent of shareholders' funds, and lending to the directors and staff of banks and finance companies was prohibited.

The central bank obtained powers to lend against the shares of, and purchase equity in, ailing financial institutions so that it could inject additional equity quickly in the event of insolvency or illiquidity. Bank Negara also introduced guidelines on suspension of interest on nonperforming loans and on provisions for bad and doubtful debts to ensure that the financial community followed sound, consistent, and prudent lending policies and to standardize the accounting treatment of income from those sources. Audit and examination committees were established to reinforce boards of directors' oversight of bank managements' handling of day-to-day operations. A central credit bureau was established to monitor and improve consolidated credit information on bank and finance company customers. Statistical reporting to the central bank was improved and computerized, including regular reporting on the size of nonperforming loans, exposures to share and property financing, loan margins, and bank productivity. In addition, on-site bank examinations were increased and the bank examination staff strengthened.

Legal changes. Regulations were promulgated in July 1986 to remedy legislative deficiencies that obstructed pursuit of illegal deposit-taking activities. These regulations also improved the central bank's ability to act quickly in an emergency. Bank Negara was empowered to investigate the affairs of any deposit-taker, including the power to enter and search any office or place of business, to interrogate on oath or affirmation, to detain people pending the completion of a search or interrogation, and to compel the production and retention of accounts, books, and documents. In addition, the law authorized the central bank to order property to be frozen and to restrict a person's departure from Malaysia, including impounding their passports. Bank Negara also gained the power to require institutions to cease taking new deposits, to refund existing deposits, and to assume control and carry on the business of the deposit-taker or appoint someone to do so. Furthermore, the law empowered the central bank to apply to the high court to appoint a receiver to manage the affairs and property of a deposit-taker or to petition the high court to wind up an illegal deposit-taker. To protect the public against abuse of these wide powers, the law established an advisory panel comprising representatives of the private sector and the Treasury, along with the attorney general and the chairman of the Association of Banks.

The government also changed the cooperative laws to restrict cooperatives to taking deposits for housing and eduction only—not savings or fixed deposits—from their members. The thirty-two deposit-taking cooperatives were placed under Bank Negara's supervision until all soft loans to acquiring institutions were repaid. To prevent lawsuits from creditors or depositors from jeopardizing the rescue effort, the high court appointed receivers from accounting firms to manage the cooperatives' assets. The high court also determined the priority of payment to unsecured creditors of such obligations as salaries and wages, legal fees, and essential services.

Rescue and restructuring

In light of prevailing economic circumstances and given the budgetary constraint imposed on government by high fiscal deficits, it was decided that Bank Negara should shoulder most of the burden of investigation, diagnosis, evaluation, and restructuring entailed in the broad rescue effort.

Banks. The central bank generally followed three steps in dealing with each problem bank. First, it required the ailing institution to recognize all losses and interest-in-suspense immediately, rather than stretching the losses out over time. Second, the bank's management was replaced. Bank Negara revamped the board of directors, appointed a reputable professional to serve as chief executive, and then allowed the new board to take necessary steps to stem losses and restore profitability. Third, shareholders were required to inject as much new capital as possible through rights issues, while the central bank filled any remaining gaps to meet the minimum capital adequacy requirements. In the case of especially weak institutions, the central bank tightened requirements for regular reviews, discussions, and follow-up inspections.

For three ailing banks, United Asia Bank, Perwina Habib Bank, and Sabah Bank, in which Bank Negara subsequently injected capital, inspections for fiscal 1985 revealed some common weaknesses. In all three cases bank management and shareholders had refused

to acknowledge the enormity of the problems facing the banks. Once Bank Negara took control in 1986, it appointed new directors and chief executives to undertake a thorough review. Rights issues yielded M$159 million in new equity from existing shareholders, against total losses in the three banks of M$1,203 million between 1985 and 1986 (table 7.5). The central bank took up the shortfall in rights by injecting M$672 million, and the balance was met through subordinated loans of M$401 million. Shares subscribed by Bank Negara are held in trust for disposal later under a buyback scheme that allows participating shareholders to repurchase their unsubscribed shares at par plus holding costs.

Deposit-taking cooperatives. Following the freeze on deposit-taking and investigations of the twenty-four ailing deposit-taking cooperatives in July-August 1986, pressure mounted for a quick rescue plan. The situation was highly charged because more than 522,000 depositors (in a country of 16.5 million people) and approximately M$1.5 billion in deposits were involved. To assess public opinion on the issue, the government appointed an action committee on cooperatives, chaired by Bank Negara, with representatives from the government and the private sector. Depositors believed that their deposits should be guaranteed in full by the government. They objected strongly to the conversion of their deposits into equity and demanded prompt legal action against the staff of the cooperatives responsible for mismanagement, fraud, and criminal breach of trust.[1]

The committee determined that the cooperatives' capital deficiency was at least M$680 million (table 7.6). It recommended that the government invite a number of strong banks or finance companies to assume the deposit liabilities and attendant assets of each deposit-taking institution whose net asset to deposit ratio was close to one.[2] To assist the rescue, the committee recommended that Bank Negara

Table 7.5 Indicators for three ailing commercial banks, 1984–87

(millions of ringgit)

Indicator	1984	1985	1986	1987[a]
Total deposits	4,309	4,568	3,945	3,513
Total loans	3,898	4,326	4,466	3,367
Total pretax losses	39	591	612	2
Change in capital[b]	38	−5	162	1,130
Capital adequacy ratio	4.3	3.0	2.8	5.2

a. Projected
b. Paid-up capital and subordinated loans.
Source: Bank Negara Malaysia, *Annual Report 1987.*

provide soft loans to meet the liquidity needs of the acquiring banks and finance companies. For cooperatives with large losses, the committee advised that depositors be offered a combination of cash and equity or convertible bonds.

The government white paper on the deposit-taking cooperatives adopted most of the committee's recommendations (Malaysia 1986a,b). The report revealed that the twenty-four ailing cooperatives had invested nearly half their total assets in connected lending or in subsidiaries and related companies and shares. One-fifth of total assets was tied up in land, property, and housing; another fifth was in loans to cooperative members. Only 9 percent was in cash and liquid assets at the time of the freeze, mainly because of panic deposit withdrawals. So that the public did not have to bear the full brunt of the large losses arising from bad management, depositors were to receive a share of the net asset backing of their cooperative proportionate to their deposits. To facilitate the reconstruction process, all rescue schemes involving debt-equity conversions for depositors would follow legal due process and be approved by the courts.

The final rescue package was carried out in three stages. Stage one involved the unfreezing of the deposits of eleven cooperatives with relatively small capital deficiencies. They had total deposits of M$191 million from 85,000 members, with net asset backing per ringgit of deposits of close to 1 ringgit. In January 1987 the eleven received soft loans from the central bank and reached agreement with their appointed banks or finance companies to take over their assets and liabilities. Depositors were to be repaid in full—but without interest—over periods of up to five years.

Stage two of the rescue plan involved the twelve cooperatives with moderate to heavy losses (average asset backing of 39 sen for every ringgit of deposits). The scheme provided for a 1:1 return to all depositors through a combined cash and equity arrangement. At least 50 percent would be in cash paid over a period up to December 1989, while the balance would be converted into equity in a licensed financial institution that would absorb all the assets and liabilities of the twelve cooperatives. Following passage of an amendment to the 1958 central banking law, Bank Negara purchased a small, ailing finance company, which it renamed Kewangan Usahasama Makmur Berhad (KUMB). KUMB acquired the net assets and deposit liabilities of the twelve institutions

Table 7.6 Losses of twenty-four failed deposit-taking cooperatives, 1986
(millions of ringgit)

Type of asset	Book value	Estimated losses	Losses as a share of book value (percent)
Fixed assets	150.5	4.4	2.9
Housing projects	185.5	30.6	16.5
Investment in shares	263.6	93.6	35.5
Loans	948.0	532.8	56.2
Other assets	214.3	21.7	10.1
Total	1,761.9	683.1	38.8

Source: Malaysia 1986b.

from their receivers. Depositors were to receive their equity in the form of ordinary M$1 shares of KUMB, which were to be floated publicly as soon as they became eligible for public listing, so that shareholders might reap capital gains.

Stage three involved the largest cooperative, Koperatif Serbaguna Malaysia (KSM), with deposits of M$549 million and 166,000 depositors. It had an asset backing of about 50 sen per ringgit of deposits. The government accepted a proposal by Magnum Corporation Berhad (MCB), a large publicly listed company, and its licensed finance company subsidiary, Magnum Finance Berhad, to take over the net assets and deposit liabilities of KSM, which had indirect interests in MCB. Depositors of KSM were to be repaid in full, half in cash (to be paid in stages between 1987 and 1989) and half in irredeemable, convertible, unsecured loan stock of MCB. The loan stock would be non–interest bearing for the first two years and would be convertible into ordinary MCB shares at a predetermined rate during 1989–91.

To enable the cooperative rescue scheme to work, the central bank provided the rescuing financial institutions with M$720 million in soft loans at 1 percent a year, plus M$280 million in commercial loans at 4 percent a year for a term of ten years. The rescue also incurred M$23.4 million in professional fees for the investigations and receivership.

Recovery

The prompt recapitalization of the three banks and announcement of the cooperative rescue package in 1987 and early 1988 reestablished public confidence in the financial system. A generalized panic was avoided at a time when the economy was in the trough of its deep recession. Commodity prices began to rise in the fourth quarter of 1986, leading to an immediate injection of liquidity into the banking system from growing export income. The economy rebounded strongly in 1987: GDP grew 5.3 percent in real terms, terms of trade improved 19.4 percent, the current account of the balance of payments showed a M$6.4 billion surplus, and gross external reserves rose to M$19.4 billion (7.4 months of retained imports).

In 1988 the economy continued to rebound vigorously. Although the federal budget remained in deficit despite cutbacks in development spending, the financing deficit was reduced sharply, to 5.6 percent of GNP, allowing the government to repay more than M$4 billion of its external debt. Real GDP grew at 8.8 percent and export proceeds rose 21.3 percent. As confidence revived, market capitalization in the Kuala Lumpur stock exchange rose by 45 percent to a peak M$101.9 million in August 1988, from its post-crash trough after October 1987. Similarly, property prices began to firm, with strong sales in low-cost housing in urban centers and revival in commercial property values from the low of M$180 a square foot in 1986 to M$279 in early 1989. The reflation of asset prices and enterprise cash flow improved bank profitability. Preliminary, unaudited data revealed pretax profits of M$794 million in 1988, compared with M$125 million in 1987. Bad debt provisions fell by 28.1 percent. Most of the recovery was in the writeback of provisions for nonperforming loans, amounting to M$828 million in 1988, or nearly double the amount the previous year. By 1989 the national external debt had fallen to M$42 billion, or 44 percent of GNP, compared with 76 percent in 1986. Clearly, the structural adjustment program was yielding results.

Enterprise restructuring

As the banking environment improved, the focus of loan rehabilitation switched from banks to enterprises. In 1988 the central bank established a M$500 million enterprise rehabilitation fund aimed at reducing the overhang of stalled projects and nonperforming loans. The fund, financed by Bank Negara and managed by a development bank, provides seed capital to recession-hit *bumiputera* (indigenous) enterprises that are found to be fundamentally viable. The projects are cofinanced with the existing lenders, who provide additional working capital for the turnaround enterprises. Specialist turnaround groups, composed of leaders in manu-

facturing, trade, agriculture, and property, evaluate the viability of eligible enterprises and recommend assistance under the fund.

Lessons

One key lesson of the Malaysian experience is that prompt, decisive action must be taken to address problem areas in ailing financial institutions. The extent of damage must be determined fairly and accurately and the problems of capital adequacy and competent management must be addressed. Failure to admit the size of the problems or delays in resolving them almost always compound the costs. The problems in Malaysia's ailing financial institutions generally were worse than they first appeared. Management was reluctant to recognize and report accurately to the regulatory authorities the extent of balance sheet and operating deficiencies.

Equity capital also proved to be a vital part of the rescue package. Nonperforming loans can be supported only by non–interest bearing capital. Lending high-interest loans to tide insolvent banks over a liquidity crisis merely pours good money after bad. Without adequate capital and an appropriate gearing ratio, even the strongest management would be hard-pressed to restore profitability.

Supervisory authorities and bank management must develop efficient and accurate reporting systems so that the true financial position, including risk exposure, is clear. Monitoring compliance with traditional balance sheet ratios is not enough. It is more important to monitor the profit and loss account frequently—monthly or even daily for certain operations—in order to pinpoint structural weaknesses. Devoting more resources to regular inspections and accurate monitoring is in the long run cheaper than rescue operations. Light supervision without lender-of-last resort facilities for the deposit-taking cooperatives resulted in large losses that were only partly attributable to the effects of economywide deflation in asset prices.

Financial supervision must evolve in line with competition, technology, internationalization, and the erosion of lines of business demarcation in banking. Supervisory authorities must monitor not only their traditional monetary institutions but also inter-relationships with capital markets, rural deposit institutions, development banks, and other financial intermediaries. The financial safety net may have to be strengthened and widened. Credit information needs to be pooled to provide an effective early warning system. Indeed, substantial economies of scale may be gained by coordinating and pooling supervisory resources.

Banking laws and regulations also need to change as technology evolves because the transmission of shocks accelerates through the payments mechanism, while the scope for insider trading and financial fraud and theft increases rapidly. Banking laws must give scope to greater competition in financial products while tightening prudential regulation against abuses of the system. At the same time laws relating to bankruptcy (market exit) need to be reformed to expedite and reduce the costs of financial restructuring. In 1989 a new Banking and Financial Institutions Bill addressing these issues was passed by Parliament. It included a provision authorizing the central bank to act quickly in future cases of financial distress in all sectors of the financial system. And with greater internationalization, regulatory supervision has to be coordinated not only across sectors but even across borders.

Although there remain pockets of unresolved problems, especially among the smaller finance companies, the Malaysian banking sector on the whole has regained health. To be sure, the rescue operations were costly: M$1.3 billion in equity and at least M$1.3 billion in assistance loans. Over time, with the sustained recovery in property values and turnaround operations, the equity component and a large part of the loans may well be recovered.

In the final analysis, after capital and proper control procedures are put in place, the key to sound and healthy financial institutions remains good management. Where large sums of money are involved, a code of ethics, improved internal controls and procedures, and penalties against breaches of the law are insufficient to deter insider trading, conflicts of interest, and lending to related parties. Fraud and abuse must be detected quickly and halted early so that better procedures and competent, professional, trustworthy management can be installed.

Finally, the success of bank restructuring owes much to Malaysia's macroeconomic adjustment. The beneficial effects of fiscal retrenchment and depreciation of the currency brought broadly based economic recovery, which assisted the bank restructuring process. Without a high level of national savings, recovery of underlying enterprise profitability, and

adequate foreign exchange reserves to cushion against systemic shocks, financial restructuring would have been much more protracted and difficult. The political will and financial discipline to address the twin deficits in the balance of payments and public sector were vital ingredients of the recovery program.

Notes

1. Twenty-two directors of eight deposit-taking cooperatives were charged in court. Four were found guilty and received jail sentences.

2. Among the options studied was a plan, referred to as the 25:25:50 solution, that involved the payment of up to 25 percent of deposits in cash immediately, a further 25 percent in two-year deposits at a maximum of 6 percent annual interest, and conversion of the balance into equity. This framework was rejected after it was leaked to the press. The option to place the twenty-four cooperatives into liquidation was rejected because forced selling would only increase the level of losses. Exchanging deposits into unit trust holdings (to facilitate depositor liquidity) was rejected because not all depositors would agree, and most of the cooperatives' assets would not qualify as trustee assets under existing law. Converting deposits into shares of a public company would have transferred losses to the public company, which then would have been unable to obtain a public listing under equity quotation guidelines. Merging several deposit-taking cooperatives into one apex cooperative bank would have transferred the losses to a single institution, and merging different managements and staff would have compounded the difficulties of rehabilitation. Full government guarantee of deposits implied a government cash injection of M$1.5 billion and losses of nearly M$700 million, unacceptable given prevailing fiscal and financial stringency.

References

Bank Negara Malaysia. 1987. "Press Statement on Purchase of Shares in Problem Banks." Kuala Lumpur.
———. 1988. "Press Statement by the Governor on Details of the Rescue Package of the Remaining Thirteen Deposit-Taking Cooperatives." Kuala Lumpur.
———. Various years. *Annual Report.* Kuala Lumpur.
Hussein, Tan Sri Dato' Jaffar. 1987. "The Management of the Banking System—Thoughts on Bank Regulation and Supervision." Address in conjunction with the Tenth Anniversary of IBBM. Bank Negara Malaysia, November, Kuala Lumpur.
International Monetary Fund (IMF). Various years. *International Financial Statistics.* Washington, D.C.
Malaysia. 1986a. "Investigation Report on Twenty-Four Deposit-Taking Cooperatives." Attachment to Command Paper 50.
———. 1986b. "Report on the Deposit-Taking Cooperatives." Command Paper 50. Kuala Lumpur.
Ministry of Finance. 1987. *25th Annual Report of the Director General of Insurance.* Kuala Lumpur.

Sheng, Andrew. 1987a. "Banking and Monetary Policies—A Framework for Economic Recovery." Bank Negara Malaysia, Kuala Lumpur.

———. 1987b. "Capital Adequacy and Banking." Bank Negara Malaysia, Kuala Lumpur.

———. 1988. "Regulation of the Banking System." Lecture presented to Bank Negara Malaysia staff, June, Kuala Lumpur.

World Bank. 1988. *Malaysia: Matching Risks and Rewards in a Mixed Economy.* World Bank, Asia Region, Country Operations Department, Washington, D.C.

Yusof, Zainal Aznam, and others. 1994. "Financial Reform in Malaysia." In Gerard Caprio, Izak Atiyas, and James Hanson, eds., *Financial Reform: Theory and Experience.* New York: Cambridge University Press.

CHAPTER 8

Ghana's Financial Restructuring, 1983–91

Andrew Sheng and Archibald A. Tannor

Financial sector restructuring in Ghana was part of a comprehensive economic recovery program introduced in 1983 to reverse years of economic decline. Poor economic management and prolonged drought had caused the real gross domestic product (GDP) to fall by an average of 0.5 percent a year between 1970 and 1982—30 percent overall in per capita terms—and export earnings to shrink by 50 percent. When economic growth declined 6.9 percent in real terms in 1982 and inflation accelerated to an annual rate of 123 percent the following year, the government realized that profound reforms were needed (table 8.1). The economic recovery plan introduced fundamental changes in macroeconomic policy, including liberalization of the exchange and trade system, improved fiscal and monetary discipline, and rehabilitation of the social and economic infrastructure. These changes were necessary to slow inflation, reinvigorate the real sector, and restore the solvency and efficiency of a banking system battered by years of severe financial repression and disintermediation.

A financial sector review begun in 1985 identified several financial sector issues as potentially serious obstacles to sustained economic recovery and price stability. Public sector credit accounted for 92 percent of total bank credit at the end of 1982. Negative deposit rates lowered the ratio of M2 to GDP (a measure of financial deepening) from 28 percent in 1975 to 12 percent in 1983 (table 8.2). Government intervention in the banking system resulted in an exceptionally high currency to deposit ratio of 77 percent by 1981 (Sowa 1989b). Savings in the banking system were clearly insufficient to finance the growing levels of domestic investment needed to sustain economic growth.

The financial sector restructuring begun in 1988 was one of the most comprehensive programs in Sub-Saharan Africa, with considerable assistance from the World Bank, the International Monetary Fund, and various donors. The program cost an estimated $300 million, or 6 percent of GDP (World Bank 1989). It involved not only significant institution-building in the financial sector, but also major changes in developing financial markets and indirect instruments of monetary control. To combat financial imbalances, banks were restructured through the innovative Nonperforming Assets Recovery Trust. Revaluation losses in the central bank also were carved out.

A second World Bank financial sector adjustment credit was approved in 1992, the start of the second phase of financial sector restructuring. The program's success ultimately will depend on continued improvements in external trade, economic performance, and external debt management, as well as sustained development aid and a revival of the private sector. Achievements in the structural adjustment program have been impressive: real growth has been sustained, fiscal discipline has been maintained, and inflation has been brought down to single digits. There also have been substantial improvements in the financial system, including enhanced supervisory and regulatory capacity and the development of a more market-oriented financial environment.

Structure of the Financial System

Ghana has both a formal and an informal financial system. The formal system consists of 3 main commercial banks, 7 secondary banks, a small cooperative bank, and 112 rural banks, all under the supervision of the Bank of Ghana. Some 300 credit unions, regulated by the Department of Cooperatives, round out the formal system. With one exception, all primary

Table 8.1 Macroeconomic indicators, 1970–91

(percent unless otherwise specified)

Year	Real growth in GDP	Current account/GDP	Terms of trade[a] (1980=100)	Inflation rate[b]	Government balance/GDP	Interest rates Lending	Interest rates Deposit	Exchange rate[c] (cedis/ U.S. dollar)
1970	9.7	–3.0	28.2	3.0	–2.2	—	—	1.0
1971	5.2	–6.0	17.4	9.5	–3.5	—	—	1.0
1972	–2.5	5.1	25.7	10.0	–5.7	—	—	1.3
1973	2.9	5.1	45.3	17.7	–5.3	—	—	1.1
1974	6.8	–5.9	54.3	18.1	–4.2	—	—	1.1
1975	–12.4	0.6	37.9	29.8	–7.6	—	—	1.1
1976	–3.5	–2.7	75.9	56.0	–11.3	—	—	1.1
1977	2.2	–2.5	161.4	116.4	–9.5	—	—	1.1
1978	8.5	–1.2	137.8	73.1	–9.0	19.0	11.5	1.7
1979	–2.5	3.0	146.7	54.4	–6.4	19.0	11.5	2.7
1980	0.5	0.7	100.0	50.1	–4.2	19.0	11.5	2.7
1981	–3.5	–9.9	70.3	116.5	–6.5	19.0	11.5	2.7
1982	–6.9	–2.7	53.2	22.3	–5.6	19.0	11.5	2.7
1983	–4.5	–4.3	75.7	122.9	–2.7	19.0	11.5	8.8
1984	8.6	–0.9	86.0	39.7	–1.8	21.1	15.0	35.9
1985	5.1	–2.9	74.3	10.3	–2.2	21.1	15.7	54.3
1986	5.2	–0.7	66.7	24.6	0.1	20.0	17.0	89.2
1987	4.7	–1.9	70.8	39.8	0.5	25.5	17.5	153.7
1988	6.3	–1.2	58.5	31.4	0.4	25.5	16.5	202.3
1989	5.1	–1.4	47.7	25.2	0.7	25.6	16.5	270.0
1990	3.3	–3.7	53.1	37.2	0.2	—	—	326.3
1991	5.3	–4.3	43.9	18.0	1.5	—	21.3	367.8

— Not available.
a. Ratio of the index of average export prices to the index of average import prices.
b. Consumer price index.
c. Average par rate.
Source: IMF, various years; World Bank data.

and secondary banks are wholly or partly state owned. The three main banks account for 57 percent of the total assets of the banking system. The largest, Ghana Commercial Bank, is state owned and accounts for just under half of total branches and one-third of total banking system assets. The other two, Barclays and Standard Chartered, have 40 percent and 25 percent state ownership, respectively. Of the secondary banks, three are government-owned development banks that shifted toward commercial banking activities in 1986. A money market is emerging around two discount houses, and the

Ghana stock exchange began trading the shares of twenty-five to thirty companies in 1990. Two merchant banks were established in the early 1990s. The insurance and social security sector is dominated by the Social Security and National Insurance Trust and about twenty small insurance companies.

The formal banking system is urban-based. The greater Accra area accounts for two-thirds of total bank deposits, and the Northern and Upper East and West regions account for about 10 percent each. Adding to this urban bias is the fact that commercial banks prefer short-term lending to the commercial

Table 8.2 Financial sector indicators, 1975 and 1980–83

(percent)

Indicator	1975	1980	1981	1982	1983
M2/GDP	27.6	20.0	17.2	18.5	11.9
Currency outside banks/GDP	9.2	8.0	8.2	7.8	5.5
Currency outside banks/M2	35.0	39.4	43.6	39.2	41.3
Currency/deposits	53.8	65.0	77.3	64.5	70.4
Deposit interest rate					
Three-month fixed	7.6	12.1	18.3	8.5	11.0
Savings deposits	7.5	12.0	18.0	8.0	11.5
Inflation rate	29.8	50.2	116.5	22.3	122.8

Note: Monetary figures are average monthly figures.
Source: World Bank 1989; IMF, various years.

and trade sectors, depriving the agriculture and manufacturing sectors of long-term financing.

The rural banking system was established in 1976 in an attempt to mobilize rural savings. The Bank of Ghana contributed to the initial capital of about 120 rural banks, as did some members of the rural communities. These institutions account for less than 3 percent of the total deposits of the banking system (nearly 7 percent of total savings). Rural banks operate the "Akuafo" check system for paying cocoa farmers. Although the rural banks serve farmers, their loan structure also is mostly short term, and they have accumulated a serious backlog of nonperforming assets since 1983.

There also are about 300 credit unions. Because they place their deposits in the formal banking system, they are an important link between the formal and informal systems. Credit unions are inherently conservative in their lending policies, and their transaction costs are low because most staff are voluntary. Nevertheless, credit unions also suffered a serious erosion of loan quality, resulting in a loan collection rate of only about 25 percent in 1987. The rural banks, credit unions, and group lending schemes through the Agricultural Development Bank and others provide credit to about 40 percent of small farmers.

The informal system includes a variety of financial arrangements: rural moneylenders, local money dealerships (*susu*), parallel foreign exchange markets, rotating savings and credit associations, privately organized groups that share a common bond, and trade credit among producers, wholesalers, and retailers. Informal credit markets expanded rapidly during the period of financial repression, when private sector borrowers were crowded out of the formal system and there were substantial differences between the official exchange rate and the black market rate.

Financial repression and disintermediation

Highly distorted interest rates over the past two decades created severe financial repression and disintermediation in the banking system. Except for 1985, when inflation was brought down to 10 percent, real deposit and lending rates were severely negative. The banking system was unable to mobilize deposits to any great extent because of a lack of public trust and the poor quality of customer services.

Suspicion of the financial system stems from the 1979 Banking and Financial Institutions (Request for Information) Decree, which opened private deposit accounts to government scrutiny. Other policies introduced in the 1970s and early 1980s also did not help. Demonetization of 50-cedi notes, for example, made over-the-counter bank transactions inconvenient—and time-consuming when cash was unavailable. To thwart black market activity, the government froze all deposit accounts in excess of 50,000 cedis in 1984 and investigated them for tax evasion, fraud, or corruption. These actions discouraged the use of bank deposits for long-term savings and encouraged greater use of currency and informal credit channels.

Because of the negative deposit rates, demand deposits accounted for more than 64 percent of total deposits in fiscal 1985. Time deposits, which had accounted for 14 percent of total deposits in the banking system in 1976, had fallen to well below 10 percent over the next decade. Such short-term deposit liabilities curtailed long-term lending.

The severe disintermediation was compounded by credit controls and allocation policies. The central bank imposed quarterly credit expansion guidelines consistent with its projections of economic growth and inflation. In addition, sector-specific credit restrictions were imposed on each bank according to its volume of outstanding loans and the priorities of the annual development plan. At least 20 percent of lending had to go to agriculture, and that sector also enjoyed preferential lending rates that encouraged demand for (but discouraged banks from supplying) agricultural loans. The lending quota for agriculture served as a ceiling on lending to other sectors. Banks kept surplus funds in liquid assets that far exceeded statutory reserve requirements. Despite government policies, however, commercial banks generally slowed their lending to agriculture, reduced their lending to mining, and increased their financing of manufacturing and trade (table 8.3). After 1986 most lending rates were unified and in late 1987 they were completely liberalized, but access to credit did not improve substantially. Lending rates moved very little and remained negative in real terms.

By the end of 1987 the banking system was suffering from several major sources of losses. First, high liquidity and reserve requirements ensured that all banks held substantial amounts of low–interest bearing assets. At the end of 1987 cash, demand deposits, and special deposits with the Bank of Ghana totaled 32 percent of bank assets. Lending to the public sector amounted to an additional 24 percent of total

Table 8.3 Loans and advances by sector, 1980–90
(millions of current cedis)

Year	Agriculture	Mining	Manufacturing	Construction	Other	Total
1980	412	61	483	282	1,055	2,293
1981	670	151	629	400	1,462	3,311
1982	1,102	243	635	511	1,211	3,702
1983	2,013	423	1,369	795	1,714	6,312
1984	3,779	498	3,288	1,274	3,157	11,996
1985	5,208	960	6,046	2,018	7,169	21,401
1986	7,476	1,437	10,880	3,899	14,963	38,656
1987	10,651	2,631	15,472	6,267	18,465	53,486
1988	10,351	1,254	20,964	7,230	25,950	65,748
1989	11,477	1,928	26,847	8,868	30,186	79,306
1990	12,645	1,074	27,099	11,012	27,570	79,401

Source: Aryeetey, Duggleby, and Hettige 1992.

gross assets. Second, banks had a net foreign exchange liability of 7.9 billion cedis ($39.7 million), exposing them to foreign exchange losses as the cedi depreciated. Third, loan losses continued to mount in the banks' credit portfolios as formerly protected enterprises adjusted to the liberalized trade regime. Finally, interest deregulation increased the banks' cost of funds without allowing them to pass on the full costs to their earnings base (because of the high level required of low-earning and liquid assets).

Regulation and supervision

Shortcomings in banking legislation and supervisory capacity also contributed to the buildup of bank losses. Since supervision previously had concentrated on compliance with credit allocations and ceilings—not on the quality of bank assets—the Bank of Ghana had insufficient capacity in bank supervision and on-site examination. The Banking Act of 1970 was grossly outdated, permitting high concentrations of portfolio risk, inadequate levels of capital and reserves, and overstatement of profits. There were no limits on unsecured lending. The lack of uniform accounting standards meant that interest accruals on nonperforming loans continued to be treated as income and that there was no effective method of assessing or classifying nonperforming loans. Consequently, transfers to reserves and provisioning for potential losses were insufficient. Since no minimum capital adequacy ratios were in place, lending risk and asset quality went unsupervised. Furthermore, development banks that engaged in commercial banking activities were not subject to provisioning standards. Finally, because the penalties for infractions of the banking law were not adjusted for inflation, they did little to deter abuses.

Financial Distress

Two features of the Ghanaian financial sector restructuring are common to centrally planned, highly indebted economies. First, because the financial system was mostly state owned and invested predominantly in the public sector, no sudden liquidity crisis or bank runs occurred. The main challenges were to restore public confidence in the banking system and to revive intermediation (deposit mobilization and credit allocation) in order to support general economic growth. The need for bank restructuring was not forced on the authorities by events, but was driven by the recognition that continuing losses in the banking system and inappropriate credit allocation were a drag on the economy. The time had come to deal decisively with the inherited damage to the enterprise and banking sectors.

Second, the burden of financing the fiscal deficit and the quasi-fiscal deficits arising from the depreciation of the cedi and revaluation of the external debt fell largely on the banking system. There was a danger that continued credit to loss-making public enterprises and monetization of the quasi-fiscal deficits would fuel inflationary pressures that, in turn, would retard efforts at structural adjustment and stabilization.

In 1987 international auditors were commissioned to assess nine of the eleven main banks. The audits revealed weak management, capital inadequacy and technical insolvency, high operational costs and overstated profits, weak accounting and management information systems, and low-quality loan portfolios with inadequate loan loss provisions (Tannor 1990). The nonperforming loans of the banking system reflected accumulated enterprise losses following years of high inflation, devaluation, and macroeconomic instability.

The incentives system was severely distorted. The industrialization drive that began in the mid-1960s was supported by protectionist policies that encouraged import substitution, raising value added in manufacturing to about 17 percent of GDP. Manufacturing capacity was relatively well developed and diverse compared with other West African countries. Still, domestic manufacturing, which accounted for 17 percent of employment and 20 percent of total bank loans in 1980, was highly inefficient because of the prolonged trade protection.

Also, economic prosperity in Ghana is closely linked to the performance of cocoa and gold. The world's third-largest exporter of cocoa, Ghana derived roughly two-thirds of its export earnings from that commodity alone as late as 1986. Between 1980 and 1982 cocoa prices fell by more than 50 percent. During the economic crisis of 1980–83 export proceeds fell 60 percent. The government responded to the foreign exchange shortage by imposing import restrictions on important factor inputs, which worsened the productive capacity of domestic industries. The depreciation of the cedi not only caused foreign exchange losses for firms that borrowed foreign exchange to finance their investments, but also increased their production and debt-servicing costs. These firms faced significant competition from cheaper imports when trade was liberalized. Output recovery also was inhibited by the collapse of the economic and social infrastructure. Inefficient but potentially viable enterprises—apparel, for example—were adversely affected by sudden trade liberalization, while dairy producers were severely damaged by imports of subsidized products from the European Community (Weissman 1990). By 1985 the average capacity utilization of Ghanaian industry was only 25 percent, recovering slowly to 40 percent by 1989.

A 1988 survey of distressed enterprises that had stopped servicing their bank loans found the most common problems to be:
- Foreign exchange losses.
- Limited access to new sources of capital (especially working capital).
- Poor management.
- High gearing.
- Failure of banks to appraise loans properly or monitor enterprise performance.

Distress affected enterprises across the board: the private sector accounted for a third of total nonperforming loans, state-owned enterprises for a quarter, and various joint ventures for the rest. The survey estimated that distressed enterprises might account for as much as one-quarter of domestic output. The need for financial sector restructuring was urgent, since the absence of efficient financial intermediation was impeding overall economic recovery.

Damage Control

Under the umbrella of the first World Bank financial sector adjustment credit, Ghana introduced a comprehensive financial sector adjustment program in 1988. The program focused on restructuring financially distressed banks, improving the regulatory framework, strengthening bank supervision, improving resource mobilization and credit allocation, and expanding mechanisms for rural finance. In 1992 a second financial sector adjustment credit aimed at correcting the structural imbalances that encouraged disintermediation, strengthening the Bank of Ghana (reducing its revaluation losses, revamping its organizational structure), and enhancing the effectiveness of nonbank financial institutions, such as insurance companies and capital markets, in mobilizing savings. In addition, the credit provided assistance for restructuring distressed but viable enterprises, continued the restructuring plans for banks, and provided training programs for bankers, accountants, and auditors to develop an indigenous cadre of financial professionals.

Improving resource mobilization and allocative efficiency

Several measures were designed to liberalize the financial sector and to deepen markets by creating an environment conducive to sound and efficient banking:
- Foreign exchange bureaus were introduced in April 1988 to continue the reform of the foreign exchange regime begun in 1986. This scheme legalized the thriving parallel market for foreign exchange by licensing individuals, banks, or firms to buy and sell foreign exchange. By early 1990 more than 180 such bureaus were in operation.
- The monetary authorities gradually moved away from credit ceilings and credit allocation policies toward the use of indirect instruments of monetary control (buying and selling government securities, charging reserve requirements). Even the mandatory minimum credit allocations for agriculture were eliminated in late 1990.
- To develop the money market, the first discount house was licensed in 1987 and a second in 1990. Both houses accept short-term deposits from

banks and hold at least 70 percent of their assets in treasury bills, bankers acceptances, commercial bills, and certificates of deposits. The second discount house was established to help develop a secondary market for commercial paper issued by public and private corporations.
* Two privately owned investment banks were established to develop investment banking, corporate advisory services, and the securities market.
* The Ghana stock exchange was reorganized to promote the growth of the capital market.

Other measures to liberalize and improve financial services included liberalizing interest rates in 1988 and giving banks the freedom to vary their hours of business. Controls over bank charges also were eliminated, laying the groundwork for rationalization of operations and a substantial reduction in transaction costs. The central bank also issued 500- and 1,000-cedi notes and monitored their impact on banking efficiency, with a view to introducing higher denominations if necessary. Also, a credit clearinghouse was established in 1991 as an affiliate of the Ghanaian Bankers Association to assist banks in assessing the debt leverage and concentration of prospective customers.

Regulation and supervision

A major component of the revamping of the financial sector was the strengthening of the regulatory and supervisory framework. Banks adopted new prudential reporting system and accounting standards, including auditing standards for external audits based on internationally accepted standards. In addition, an intensive training program was established for bank supervisors, and a computerized off-site surveillance system was installed to enable supervisors to monitor bank performance and detect problems. On-site inspection capabilities were strengthened with the assignment of two (external) examination specialists to the banking examination department and recruitment of new bank examiners. By 1990 banks accounting for about 70 percent of total deposits had been examined.

In August 1989 a new banking law replaced both the Banking Act of 1970 and the 1979 decree that had opened private deposit accounts to government scrutiny. The new law formed the basis of a comprehensive regulatory and supervisory reform aimed at improving transparency in banking operations and fostering competition and supervision in the formal banking system. It provided for the following improvements:

* New capital adequacy requirements were introduced for commercial and development banks. The capital adequacy ratio, which had been defined as a minimum of 5 percent of total deposits, was redefined as a minimum of 6 percent of the net risk-adjusted asset base (including off–balance sheet items).
* Risk exposures were regulated through credit limits on groups and individuals and through limits on loans and advances to bank directors and employees. Moreover, restrictions on direct exposure to all forms of real estate were established. Foreign exchange exposure limits were also formulated to safeguard the fledgling interbank foreign exchange market.
* New guidelines were imposed for classifying bad and doubtful loans and for treating accrued interest.
* Annual external audits and long-form audit reports were required of all banks. Year-end audits had revealed an increase in provisions for bad and doubtful loans from about 7 billion cedis at the end of 1987 to roughly 38 billion cedis at the end of 1988.
* The Bank of Ghana was granted powers to request information, impose fines for noncompliance with the law (including punishment for false and misleading reporting), levy liquid asset requirements, impose lending policies, and demand that banks take remedial actions.

A major drive in the reform program was institutional strengthening and training for commercial and central bankers. The program included skills training for banking personnel at all levels to encourage a more professional approach to bank management. A formal training college for bankers was established, and technical assistance was provided to the Ghana Institute of Bankers to develop standards and provide training comparable to that offered by bankers institutes abroad. In addition, training and professional development courses for accountants were offered through the Ghanaian Institute of Chartered Accountants.

Loss allocation

Although various reform alternatives, such as liquidation, merger or acquisition, and immediate privatization were considered, the phasing of banking sector reforms was dictated by pragmatism rather than by any particular model.[1] The immediate objectives included holding the line on further deterioration in the financial condition of distressed banks, turning struggling but viable banks around, and designing and implementing a feasible restructuring framework for banking institutions that would contribute to their future viability.

Who bore the brunt of the losses? One way to look at that question is by examining the changes in private sector liquid wealth, defined as money and quasi money less bank loans to the private sector (table 8.4). There was a sharp loss in the value of money and quasi money, equivalent to 22.6 percent of GDP in 1983, as a result of the depreciation in the official exchange rate. The parallel market had already depreciated significantly even before 1983. Thus banking system depositholders absorbed large losses in real terms, while the major beneficiary was the public sector. Some 90 percent of the credit from the banking system went to finance fiscal deficits and nonfinancial public enterprises.

Between 1984 and 1990 interest rate controls that resulted in negative real deposit rates depressed savings in the banking system. Little financial deepening occurred between 1983 and 1990 despite healthy real growth in the economy and improvement in the balance of payments. M3 as a share of GDP rose only from 11.3 percent of GDP in 1983 to 13.4 percent in 1990. Thus although depositors did not lose in nominal terms—the carve-out was borne by the budget—they had already taken a major loss in real terms in 1983. The cost to the budget for the carve-out, estimated at about 4 percent of GDP in 1989, was comparatively small relative to depositors' real losses. It was perhaps the shock of the large wealth loss that slowed the recovery in financial deepening in the banking system.

The restoration of the surplus in the budget generated sufficient resources to address the problems in the banking system. The banking system's net credit to the central government declined from a peak of 22.5 percent of GDP in 1987 to 8.4 percent in 1990. The improvement in the government's finances also facilitated the absorption of the revaluation losses in the books of the central bank, which amounted to as much as another 15 percent of GDP.

Managing the Restructuring Process

The bank restructuring program was guided by several principles:

- A bank's operations must be premised on sound banking principles.
- Every bank must have profit maximization as its objective, since meeting its social objectives and responsibilities as a corporate citizen depends on its solvency and profitability.
- Any public sector credit should be transparent and funded through the state budget.
- The board and management of each bank should be accountable and independent of outside interference, irrespective of bank ownership. Accordingly, the board and management must have the requisite experience, skills, and knowledge to fulfill these obligations.
- There should be effective regulation and supervision to foster safe and sound banking.
- Public confidence must be sustained through a responsive legal environment that guarantees transparency and due process and eliminates difficulties associated with the foreclosure of collateral. Banks should operate under the discipline of the market.

The implementation team for the restructuring program closely coordinated policy decisions among the Ministry of Finance, the central bank, and the banks concerned. The team had four components:

- An oversight committee to decide on policy issues on behalf of the government.
- A technical committee, which reported to the oversight committee, to monitor and execute the restructuring program.

Table 8.4 Change in private wealth, 1983–90
(percentage of GDP, in U.S. dollars)

Type of change	1983	1984	1985	1986	1987	1988	1989	1990
Money and quasi money	−22.6	−0.7	2.2	−0.2	−3.4	1.4	2.2	−0.1
Private sector credit	−2.3	0.3	0.9	0.5	−1.5	0.2	2.5	0.0
Net change	−20.3	−1.1	1.3	−0.7	−1.9	1.2	−0.2	−0.1
Net foreign assets of the banking system	−0.9	−2.2	−3.1	−1.2	−2.5	1.5	1.3	2.5
Memorandum items								
Claims on central government	15.9	14.6	14.6	16.6	22.5	15.7	9.9	8.4
Domestic credit	17.6	18.0	22.7	23.3	27.5	18.6	17.1	12.4

Source: IMF, various years.

- Consultants to develop the general framework of the restructuring program and bank-specific plans.
- Turnaround managers for each bank, supported by foreign experts or through twinning arrangements with international banks, to manage the institution-building and restructuring process.

Decisions on whether to liquidate, merge, or recapitalize and restructure problem banks (three development banks and six commercial banks) were made on the basis of external audits. A three-pronged approach involving managerial restructuring, organizational change, and one-time financial restructuring was devised for each of the banks. An initial estimate of 63.2 billion cedis ($222 million) was projected for recapitalizing the nine banks—providing provisioning, eliminating foreign exchange losses, and meeting new capital adequacy requirements.

Pending completion of the individual restructuring programs, urgent intermediate steps had to be taken to arrest the erosion of capital. Damage control measures introduced by the central bank in early 1989 covered prudential guidelines on lending operations, capital expenditures, operating costs, and other activities such as loan recoveries, treasury operations, and internal controls. Critically distressed institutions faced more stringent measures.

In January 1990 top management and boards of directors were reconstituted for banks that were being restructured. All restructured banks had independent management teams with autonomous decisionmaking powers, supplemented by full-time foreign experts. Twinning arrangements with international financial institutions were negotiated for some banks, whereas turnaround management teams were installed for others. Banks took steps to reduce staff, close branches, reduce operating costs, and improve efficiency.

Since the banks were predominantly state owned, it was decided that the state would absorb the losses. A carve-out, based broadly on the Spanish model (see chapter 5), was undertaken. Banks were categorized according to degree of distress or losses. Nonperforming loans and advances to the government and state-owned enterprises, including government guarantees, were first offset against government loans, and then remaining balances were converted into bonds. Nonperforming private sector loans were converted into bonds and transferred to the Nonperforming Asset Recovery Trust, based on each bank's degree of distress and other considerations. The state assumed ownership of the nonperforming assets after loans were exchanged for bonds, as well as responsibility for debt recovery.

Based on the audit results and consultant studies, all nonperforming loans to the government and to state-owned enterprises—amounting to 31.4 billion cedis at the end of 1989—were transferred to the Nonperforming Assets Recovery Trust. Under the Nonperforming Assets Recovery Law of 1989, all rights and obligations of nonperforming bank assets could be transferred to the trust, which was authorized to sue for recovery and administer proceeds from the debts. The trust was administered by a board consisting of representatives of the Ministry of Finance and the central bank, the chief administrator, an accountant and a lawyer from the private sector, and three other experts.

In the case of nonperforming public sector loans, which were replaced by interest-bearing bonds in 1990, the government retained responsibility for redeeming the loans at face value (principal plus interest) over time. Private sector nonperforming loans were replaced by long-term Bank of Ghana bonds in amounts equivalent to the face value of accumulated provisions or were offset against Bank of Ghana loans to the banks.

Another major step in the financial restructuring program was the government's assumption in 1990 of the revaluation losses of the Bank of Ghana, amounting to 274 billion cedis at the end of 1989 and equivalent to 19 percent of GDP. These losses were subsequently replaced by long-term government bonds at an adjustable yield. With this important measure the government recognized its quasi-fiscal deficits and freed the central bank to control liquidity and money supply without undue concern about the overhang of revaluation losses.

The results of the carve-out can be assessed fully only over time. Detailed profit and loss numbers are unavailable, but the impact on the balance sheet of the banks can be assessed. After adjustment and provisioning for all nonperforming loans according to international accounting standards, commercial banks (including the development banks) recorded a sharp decline in capital and reserves—from 13.4 billion cedis prior to adjustment to −2.5 billion cedis at the end of 1989. By the end of 1990 capital and reserves were restored to 48 billion cedis, or 25 percent of total assets, reflecting mostly the effect of capitalization and partly the benefits of relatively high spreads.

With a positive capital base, higher credit standards, and better management, the banks have enjoyed fairly good spreads of 7.0 to 7.5 percent of total assets since 1990. Although insufficient to cover the stock of inherited problem loans, the higher profitability is clearly an incentive for management to improve overall efficiency and lays the groundwork for possible privatization.

Rural finance

The rural sector also warranted special attention. Under a separate project with the World Bank, the government designed a program to improve intermediation in rural areas and to increase the flow of credit to small farmers. The project included a substantial line of credit to be administered by the banking system; institution-building, including restructuring two-thirds of rural banks; and strengthening the financial management capabilities of credit unions. Other efforts included improving the capacities of the Association of Rural Banks and the Credit Union Association to serve their members, strengthening rural credit appraisal, building stronger capacity within the Bank of Ghana for examination of rural banks, and establishing a unit for managing rural finance programs, rural finance policy research, and program monitoring.

In the roughly 10 percent of cases where liquidation was deemed necessary, restructuring of rural banks included a payout of the net claims of depositors (a one-time deposit guarantee by the Bank of Ghana as liquidator); shareholders received nothing. In most cases, however, rural banks with no prospects for recovery were merged with stronger units, and limits on shareholdings were changed from absolute amounts to percentages of total equity (5 percent for individuals, 10 percent for companies). The emphasis was on improving loan collection and provisioning for nonperforming debts, which were estimated at roughly 25 to 30 percent of the total. The government also established a recapitalization fund, to be replenished as restructuring progressed, with banks contributing at least 10 percent of the requirements.

Enterprise restructuring

Financial restructuring gave the banks the institutional and financial capacity to assist in restructuring their client enterprises. The Nonperforming Asset Recovery Trust, in addition, will attempt to restructure the assets of the banking system that it is responsible for recovering. The trust's role will be aided by the creation, envisaged in late 1991, of a new, mostly privately owned entity for providing venture capital and other financial, managerial, and technical services to viable public and private enterprises.

Public enterprises are being privatized, with twenty-five scheduled in 1991 alone. Those remaining in public ownership will be given greater autonomy in pricing, staffing, and procurement. Moreover, managers of the state-owned enterprises will be subject to performance-based incentive programs.

Conclusion

Ghana has achieved a remarkable recovery in economic and financial performance since 1983. Real growth has averaged about 5 percent a year. Inflation was brought down to 18 percent in 1991, compared with more than 100 percent a decade earlier. And there was a turnaround in the overall balance of payments despite weakening prices in cocoa and gold. External payment arrears were eliminated, and domestic trade and finance were significantly liberalized.

The country's achievements would have been impossible without significant stabilization policies in three areas: an exchange rate adjustment to achieve external balance, fiscal reforms that restored financial discipline and monetary stability, and institutional restructuring and building to develop a more market-oriented economy.

Substantial foreign aid, both financial resources and technical assistance, played a part. External grants amounted to 0.5 to 2.2 percent of GDP a year between 1985 and 1990. Annual net long-term official capital inflows averaged $175 million over the same period. By contrast, net private capital flows averaged only $14 million, although this figure rose to about $50 million in 1990. Clearly, the long-run sustainability of growth and price stability will hinge largely on the maintenance of fiscal and external balance, as well as on the reemergence of the private sector as the engine of growth.

The Ghanaian financial sector restructuring is almost a textbook example of how strong macroeconomic stabilization, coupled with financial sector reforms, can restore growth and price stability. Determination and political will were required to enact major reforms. The restoration of fiscal discipline was a key factor in assisting the financial sector restructuring. Major tax reforms, particularly the shifting of the tax base from the heavy tax on cocoa exports to taxes on domestic goods and services, restored the revenue-GDP ratio to about 15 percent, encouraged export production, and improved aggregate demand management. In addition, controls on expenditure, civil service employment, and subsidies, as well as a shift to infrastructure and social welfare investment, brought a remarkable turnaround in the fiscal position, from a deficit of 2.7 percent of GDP in 1983 to a small surplus in 1986. It was the restoration of the primary surplus that allowed the government to program repayments to the banking system, which released resources to correct the damages of the past and placed the banking system in a healthier, more sound position.

Ghanaian authorities were able to halt the disintermediation process in the banking system through a classic carve-out borne largely by the state. The carve-out became possible because of the improvement in the fiscal account. Depositors did not lose in nominal terms, but they already had borne significant real losses in earlier years because of financial repression and the inflation tax. Although the difficult tasks of institutional strengthening and improved supervision have begun, financial deepening in the banking system will require private sector confidence in the banking system. The potential for mobilizing additional domestic savings through the formal banking system is not insignificant, given the thriving informal sector.

A Ghanaian observer of the financial restructuring has summed up the lessons of the Ghanaian experience:

- The desire for a higher profile for the private sector in economic development signifies a disenchantment with the massively interventionist policies of the past. Building the private sector's role in the economy will require changes in philosophy and macroeconomic policies that guarantee consensus and entrench market discipline.
- If holding-action measures are not implemented in a timely and efficient manner, the crisis may get out of hand (Tannor 1990).

Note

1. This section is drawn substantially from Tannor 1990.

References

Aryeetey, Ernest, Tamara Duggleby, and Mala Hettige. 1992. "The Financial Sector in Ghana." World Bank, Central and West Africa Department, Washington, D.C.

IMF (International Monetary Fund). Various years. *International Financial Statistics*. Washington, D.C.

Sowa, Nii Kwaku. 1989a. "Financial Intermediation and Economic Development." In Emmanuel Hansen and Kwame Ninsin, eds., *The State and Development and Politics in Ghana*. London: CODESRIA.

———. 1989b. "Monetary Control in Ghana: 1957-1988." University of Ghana, Legon.

Tannor, Archibald A. 1990. "Financial Sector Restructuring: The Ghanaian Experience." Paper presented at the World Bank, Federal Reserve Board, and Bank of Ghana seminar for bank supervisors, February 5–18, Accra.

Weissman, Stephen R. 1990. "Structural Adjustment in Africa: Insights from the Experience of Ghana and Senegal." *World Development* 18(12): 1621–34.

World Bank. 1989. *World Development Report 1989: Financial Systems and Development*. New York: Oxford University Press.

CHAPTER 9

Yugoslavia: Financial Restructuring in a Transition Economy, 1983–90

Andrew Sheng

Yugoslavia presents an instructive case of the problems of transition from a socialist to a market economy.[1] A pioneer of transformation, Yugoslavia introduced worker self-management of enterprises in 1971, which broke enterprises up into what were called basic organizations of associated labor (Knight 1983). The lack of financial discipline on the part of these self-managed enterprises and their ownership of banks—conditions that mirrored the problems of connected lending in market-based economies—had implications that took more than a decade to unfold. In addition, constitutional changes in 1974 decentralized powers to individual republics, provinces, and local governments. But the financial and monetary consequences of local bodies' economic mismanagement fell on the central government, mostly the central bank (Bole and Gaspari 1991).

These structural weaknesses were exacerbated by an inward-looking investment strategy with high domestic protection, funded by high external borrowing in the second half of the 1970s. To these strains were added domestic price distortions and inadequate adjustment to the oil shocks. These factors helped create the conditions of economic and financial fragility that erupted into hyperinflation in 1989.

The Yugoslav case is particularly informative regarding the pivotal role of banks in maintaining financial discipline and facilitating the exit of loss-making enterprises. In socialist economies property rights and obligations were not clearly defined among the state, individuals, and economic entities. Such imprecision created the illusion of fiscal discipline in the form of apparent central government budget surpluses, when in reality the quasi-fiscal deficits of the state were extremely large. For example, the losses of self-managed enterprises (ultimately the burden of the state) averaged 6.6 percent of gross social product (GSP) during 1985–89, while the quasi-fiscal losses of the National Bank of Yugoslavia were as high as 8.7 percent of GSP as early as 1985 (Lahiri 1991).[2] In the Yugoslav case financial indiscipline, through losses in the enterprise sector, was ultimately reflected in the books of the banking system (including the national bank) and monetized and distributed throughout the economy by inflation.

The restoration of financial stability required not only a credible macroeconomic stabilization program, but also fundamental reforms in both the enterprise and financial sectors. Central to these reforms was the private ownership and management of economic and financial institutions. These efforts at reform—and the difficulties of loss allocation in a federal structure of autonomous republics—crumbled in the face of political and regional fragmentation.

Banking, Money, and Credit

The flawed structure of the Yugoslav financial system lay at the heart of the economic crisis of 1989. The banking system was little more than a conduit for funding enterprises and carrying out national credit plans. Under decentralized social ownership of the banking system, banks were seen as "service organizations" for enterprises rather than as autonomous, profit-making entities. Thus banks were owned by the enterprises that used their services (Knight 1983).

Banking structure

Yugoslavia had a loose federal banking system consisting of the National Bank of Yugoslavia and the national banks of the eight republics and autonomous regions. The system allocated credit from the center to regions, mainly through the national banks, in a manner intended to compensate for regional disparities in economic endowments and productivity. The national banks functioned like regional branches of the central bank, but with greater autonomy. Their refinancing of commercial bank credits to priority sectors was funded by the central bank. The central bank also offered discounting and emergency liquidity facilities, extended credits directly to the nonbank sector, and provided interest-free credits to commercial banks related to the transfer of foreign currency deposits.[3]

Until the 1989 Law on Banks and Other Financial Organizations the three types of banks were basic, associated, and internal. Basic and associated banks, together with national banks, accounted for more than 98 percent of the total assets of financial institutions (table 9.1). Nonbank financial institutions were small and comparatively insignificant financial actors.[4] About 145 basic banks formed the core of the commercial banking system. They were founded, owned, and directed almost exclusively by enterprises—mainly large ones—which also were their principal borrowers (although the actual borrowers were the basic organizations of associated labor that comprised the enterprises). Competition among banks was restricted since enterprises were allowed to keep only one bank account, which they held with their affiliated bank. Banks also were grossly undercapitalized, relying on retained earn-

Table 9.1 Assets of financial institutions
(share of total assets)

Year	National banks	Basic and associated banks	Other financial institutions	Total
1980	19.4	76.2	4.4	100.0
1981	19.9	76.0	4.1	100.0
1982	21.7	74.4	3.9	100.0
1983	24.2	72.5	3.2	100.0
1984	25.5	71.8	2.8	100.0
1985	26.4	71.0	2.5	100.0
1986	27.0	70.7	2.3	100.0
1987	22.7	76.0	1.3	100.0
1988	30.4	68.2	1.3	100.0
1989	29.1	70.2	0.6	100.0

Source: National Bank of Yugoslavia.

ings and contributions by the founders for capital and reserves.

The basic banks were overseen by nine banking groups, each of which included an associated bank to handle foreign exchange operations and large borrowing. Only one of the nine associated banks operated nationwide, and there was considerable variation among them in terms of their financial strength and their relationships with their basic bank. Associated banks could not issue checking or savings accounts, but their managerial strength, technological sophistication, large scale of operations, and specialized functions in foreign credit and exchange transactions allowed them to become the most powerful institutions after the bank reforms in 1989. Some 200 or so internal banks were organized within enterprises to conduct payments, lending, and credit transactions. They could accept deposits only from member enterprises (the basic organizations of associated labor) or workers within the group, but unlike basic and associated banks they were not subject to monetary regulation. As a result internal banks expanded their activities to become major suppliers of finance to enterprises.

Money and credit

The banking system was little more than a conduit for enterprise funding and federal and regional government policies. Monetary policy, bank credit management, accounting practices, and regulatory controls all failed to produce financial discipline.

In an effort to promote foreign exchange earnings and agriculture, monetary policies encouraged foreign exchange borrowing and monetization of losses through selective and interest-free credits to banks from the central bank. Central bank refinancing of credits to agriculture and exports at subsidized interest rates accounted for 42 percent of its total credit to banks at the end of 1982. Interest-free dinar credits to banks accounted for 48 percent. Banks lent to enterprises at highly subsidized rates while paying negative real rates on dinar deposits.

Bank credit management was severely handicapped by the close relationship with enterprises and weak accounting standards. Until 1986 banks borrowed foreign currency to finance dinar lending, thereby accumulating exchange risk. Most of the risk of devaluation on foreign currency deposit liabilities was transferred to the central bank under an insurance scheme introduced in 1978; after 1985 even interest rate risk was covered. The central bank also started assuming a significant portion of outstanding foreign currency debt, especially that owed by underdeveloped republics and regions. With the dinar devaluation in 1983 and subsequent downward adjustments, the net foreign exchange exposure of the banking system became a source of serious instability.

Since banks were not independent of enterprises, they placed few limits on credit to nonviable projects. Banks could not refuse rehabilitation loans to their founding member enterprises, nor could they liquidate loss-making borrowers. In addition, some enterprise losses were socialized. Losses were borne by other, profitable enterprises through joint reserve funds designed so that enterprises could help one another.

Poor accounting standards did not allow for sound credit evaluation. The Soviet-based system did not use accrual accounting and understated the losses of enterprise borrowers. Until 1987 interest on nonperforming loans often was capitalized (interest in arrears was added onto principal), so banks could not easily distinguish between good income and income on nonperforming loans. Outmoded accounting rules allowed enterprises to recognize foreign exchange losses only when the debts were paid; thus accounts grossly understated foreign exchange losses. Some foreign debt was incurred by banks on behalf of their member enterprises. Between 1981 and 1984 some one-quarter to one-third of banks' total long-term loans were in arrears.

The supervisory framework also was inadequate. The central bank and the national banks supervised all basic and associated banks, focusing mainly on compliance with monetary, credit, and foreign exchange rules. The Social Accounting Service, an autonomous institution with branches nationwide, audited banks, enterprises, and sociolegal entities—but it did so using auditing and accounting standards that did not accurately measure the solvency of banks according to international standards.

As a result of these weaknesses the banking system incurred increasingly large net foreign exchange liabilities, reaching 32 percent of GSP in 1985 (table 9.2). The national banks' stock of foreign exchange liabilities accounted for 70 percent of their total liabilities in 1987, or 24 percent of GSP. With the continuing depreciation of the dinar, foreign exchange losses amounted to more than 60 percent

Table 9.2 Net foreign exchange liabilities of the banking system, 1973–89

(share of gross social product)

Year	Banking system	National banks	Deposit money banks
1973	1.4	–4.2	–2.8
1975	–2.5	--	–2.5
1980	–16.5	–4.3	–12.2
1985	–31.6	–12.3	–19.2
1989	–26.4	12.7	–39.1

Source: National Bank of Yugoslavia.

of total assets, more than 70 percent of which was estimated to have resulted from the foreign exchange insurance scheme. The rest arose from the foreign exchange borrowings of the central bank and from transfers to the central bank of foreign exchange losses of selected enterprises.

The large foreign exchange exposure of the banking system stemmed partly from banks' external borrowing on behalf of their enterprise borrowers, but also from the rising level of foreign currency deposits. Yugoslavia initially benefited from the large foreign currency remittances of nationals working abroad, which were deposited in the banking system. But these deposits later became a channel of capital flight as dinar depositholders attempted to escape negative real deposit rates and fears of devaluation by switching to foreign currency accounts. Between 1984 and 1986 total deposits as a share of GSP fell from 78 percent to 64 percent (table 9.3). The share of dinar deposits continued to fall until 1988, when dinar deposits became less than half of the money supply, resulting in the near dollarization of the economy. The rising disintermediation was reversed only in 1989 as a result of the extremely high real interest rates paid during the period of hyperinflation.

Table 9.3 Disintermediation in the banking system, 1984–89

(share of gross social product)

Year	Dinar deposits	Foreign currency deposits	Total deposits	Foreign currency deposits as a share of total deposits
1984	49.1	28.5	77.6	36.7
1985	44.4	27.1	71.5	37.9
1986	40.5	23.3	63.8	36.6
1987	33.6	31.8	65.4	48.6
1988	32.7	39.6	72.3	54.8
1989	49.3	68.4	117.6	58.1

Source: National Bank of Yugoslavia.

Economic Instability in the 1980s

Yugoslavia's break in the 1950s from the Soviet model of centralized planning gave Yugoslav authorities an opportunity to experiment with economic and political decentralization and with worker control and management of production. Planning was devolved to republics, communes, and enterprises, and the market was used as a guide for resource allocation. By 1981, 61 percent of the work force was in the socialized sector, which accounted for 85 percent of gross domestic product (GDP). In the agriculture sector, however, private ownership prevailed, accounting for 71 percent of production and 92 percent of the jobs.

Financial institutions, owned by their borrowers, the regionally based enterprises, concentrated risks geographically and sectorally. Macroeconomic policy was designed to support enterprise growth without adequate checks on leverage, efficiency, and viability. Monetary policy, for example, supported enterprises through highly negative real lending rates. In addition, experiments with price reform—through state fixing of prices or interenterprise agreements under a social compact—further distorted resource allocation.

This structure of production was unsustainable in the long run because it tended to distort resource allocation, but it did produce impressive results initially. Between 1970 and 1979 real GDP growth averaged 6 percent a year (table 9.4), and investment exceeded 30 percent of GDP. Enterprises expanded in the favorable environment of the 1970s, when world trade was growing and foreign exchange resources were readily available. But external resources were cut off when the international debt crisis erupted in 1982, and the economy had to deal simultaneously with its large external debt and the inefficient enterprise structure. It was at this point that the flaws of regionalism and self-managed enterprises began to surface. Growth took place in highly segmented domestic markets that reflected regional investment decisions that were duplicative, restrictive on interregional mobility of capital and labor, and missed out on economies of scale.

Four related factors contributed to the economic crisis that emerged in the 1980s: an overvalued exchange rate, poor trade performance, low productivity growth, and overreliance on external and subsidized domestic financing. Between the fourth quarters of 1972 and 1979 the dinar appreciated more

Table 9.4. Macroeconomic indicators, 1970–91

(percent unless otherwise specified)

Year	Real growth in GDP	Current account/GDP	Terms of trade (1980=100) [a]	Inflation rate [b]	Government balance/GNP	Nominal deposit interest rate	Nominal lending interest rate	Exchange rate (dinars/ U.S. dollar) [c]
1970	5.6	—	—	9.2	1.4	—	—	0.0013
1971	8.1	—	0.0	16.0	0.5	—	—	0.0017
1972	4.3	—	15.0	15.8	−0.4	—	—	0.0017
1973	4.9	—	−13.0	19.6	−0.8	—	—	0.0016
1974	8.6	—	−16.9	21.9	−1.3	—	—	0.0017
1975	3.6	—	0.1	23.5	−1.2	—	—	0.0018
1976	3.9	0.5	−2.7	11.2	−2.6	—	—	0.0018
1977	8.0	−2.9	−6.6	14.7	−1.1	3.4	—	0.0018
1978	6.9	−2.3	4.0	14.1	−0.5	4.7	11.5	0.0019
1979	7.0	−5.4	0.0	20.7	−0.3	4.9	11.5	0.0019
1980	2.3	−3.8	−2.9	30.9	−1.1	5.9	11.5	0.0029
1981	1.4	−1.6	2.0	39.8	−0.1	7.4	12.0	0.0042
1982	0.5	−0.9	7.8	31.5	0.1	12.0	16.3	0.0062
1983	−1.0	−0.8	2.7	40.2	0.0	12.0	34.0	0.0126
1984	2.0	1.5	−1.7	54.7	0.0	30.8	44.5	0.0212
1985	0.5	2.1	0.0	72.3	−0.1	60.5	71.5	0.0313
1986	3.6	2.1	12.6	89.8	0.0	55.7	82.0	0.0457
1987	−1.0	1.9	−7.2	120.8	0.0	79.3	111.3	0.1244
1988	−2.0	4.2	13.8	194.1	0.1	279.2	455.2	0.5211
1989	−0.6	3.1	6.0	1,294.9	0.3	5,644.8	4,353.8	11.8160
1990	−7.6	−2.1	—	583.1	0.3	5,644.8	4,353.8	10.6574
1991	—	−1.2	—	121.0	0.3	—	—	—

— Not available.
a. Ratio of the index of average export prices to the index of average import prices.
b. Consumer price index.
c. New dinars, end of year.
Source: IMF, various years; National Bank of Yugoslavia; World Bank data.

than 15 percent in real terms against the currencies of the country's ten major trading partners, mainly because the authorities pegged the dinar against the dollar even though domestic inflation was higher than international rates (Edwards and Ng 1985). Partly as a result of the overvaluation, as well as the worsening terms of trade, the deficit in the current account increased to $3.7 billion in 1979. In the domestic sector labor productivity consistently fell behind real personal incomes because self-managed enterprises paid high nominal wages and encouraged overemployment and because of the poor quality of investment projects in the 1970s.

The authorities accommodated domestic growth by granting liberal access to external borrowing and making loans at negative real interest rates. Total external debt rose from about $2.0 billion in 1970 to $15.2 billion in 1979. To encourage remittances from workers abroad, the authorities permitted foreign exchange–denominated deposits, which rose from 16 percent of broad money in 1975 to 22 percent in 1979. These deposits were channeled by the banks to the central bank (which absorbed the foreign exchange risk) in exchange for dinars for onlending to enterprises. Funds were easy to access because enterprises also received favorable rediscount facilities—especially for exports, equipment, and agriculture—from the central bank through their commercial banks at 6 percent a year, while inflation averaged 17 percent a year during the 1970s. Normal lending rates also averaged only 8 to 12 percent a year.

Three shocks hit the Yugoslav economy in the early 1980s: the sharp increase in oil prices, the international recession, and the international debt crisis. These developments raised the costs of debt servicing and reduced the availability of foreign funds. External resources dried up, with net external borrowing falling from $3.3 billion in 1980 to $30 million in 1983. Since enterprises were committed to large investments, the decline in exports and high debt servicing costs created large losses, estimated at 1.4 percent of gross material product in 1981. But because enterprises were managed by workers, there was little incentive to liquidate loss-makers and retrench excess workers to improve efficiency. Such losses were covered through interenterprise and bank borrowings and pooled reserves at the commune and republican levels.

A series of economic stabilization efforts throughout the 1980s aimed initially at weathering the storm but subsequently focused on long-term structural adjustment. The economic stabilization program adopted by the Federal Assembly in 1983 attempted to address four institutional factors that had distorted resource allocation: inefficient investment, wage and price distortions, the arbitrary foreign exchange allocation mechanism, and lack of financial discipline within banks and enterprises. Efforts to get these reforms entrenched continued through the rest of the 1980s.

The road to hyperinflation has been well documented elsewhere. Bole and Gaspari (1991) identify three critical periods. Between 1982 and 1984 the authorities tried to suppress demand and achieve external balance by pushing exports, using devaluation, export subsidies, and import and price controls. The authorities also tried to suppress inflation with direct price controls, but differences in pricing policies across republics and provinces resulted in price anomalies, and the criteria for setting prices were too vague to be applied successfully. Nevertheless, price controls were alternately relaxed and reimposed until 1988, and the anticipation of their reimposition caused firms to raise prices more than they would otherwise have done. Each time controls were reimposed the level of inflation jumped, reaching 50 percent a year in 1984.

During the second period, 1985–86, a relaxation of policies allowed real wages to rise, stimulating demand and growth. Still, inflation accelerated to 90 percent a year by the end of 1986. By the third period, starting in 1987, indexation and changes in accounting techniques had embedded inflation in business practices and household expectations. Inconsistencies in macroeconomic policies—with substantial changes in interest rates, exchange rates, and wage policies—did nothing to slow inflation. By 1989 the combination of the 23 percent devaluation in June 1988, the lifting of wage and price controls, the Tanzi effect fiscal gap resulting from the shrinking value of import taxes (caused by the lag between taxation and collection in a high-inflation environment), and an accommodating monetary policy culminated in hyperinflation.

Enterprise losses

Enterprise losses, banking system losses, and policy mistakes all contributed to the sequence of events that finally ended in hyperinflation. The inefficient structure of enterprises was the root cause of losses in the economy. In a market economy losses cannot continue unless they are financed. In a socialized economy, with no clear definitions of ownership and obligations, all losses ultimately become a burden on the state. The built-in instability of the socialist system lay in its flawed accounting and incentives system, whereby the state taxed enterprises regardless of their profitability, the banks continued to lend regardless of solvency or inefficiency, and the losses of the budget, banks, and enterprises continued to build up in the banking system as a monetary overhang. These quasi-fiscal losses were hidden because the central government maintained what appeared to be a balanced fiscal account.

Incentives within the socialized management system were highly distorted. Worker management and the regional orientation of enterprises politicized decisionmaking. Low productivity reflected not only the poor quality of investment decisions, but also the selection of energy-intensive, inward-oriented, and import-intensive industries with long payback periods. Because foreign exchange risks were borne by the central bank, undervaluation of the cost of capital was endemic to the system. Moreover, the high rate of enterprise taxation discouraged the use of retained earnings to finance investment.

Enterprise accounting did not address problems of solvency or efficiency. Taxes were imposed on enterprises before wages were paid, so enterprises paid taxes even if they incurred losses (Rocha 1991). Enterprise losses rose from 3 percent of GSP in 1985 to 15 percent in 1989, and yet wage payments rose from 10 percent of income to 14 percent over the same period (table 9.5). Similarly, taxes on enterprises remained at 7 to 9 percent of GSP despite enterprise losses. The losses were funded by the banking system, which was compelled by the connected ownership structure to provide funds.

An example of distorted incentives was the rationing of foreign exchange by the central bank during the early 1980s. Export proceeds were divided into two pools: one for the central bank and the government to service external debt, and the other for enterprises to purchase imports and service enterprise debt. With foreign exchange at a premium and relatively easy access to domestic financing, firms engaged in exports—even at a loss—in order to have access to foreign exchange.

Banking system losses

The 50 percent devaluation in 1983 did not correct distortions in internal resource allocation, but it did result in a current account surplus between 1984 and 1988 and a net repayment of $3–$4 billion in outstanding external debt. On the other hand, growth slowed to 0.7 percent a year between 1981 and 1985, and the inflation rate accelerated to 80 percent a year by the end of 1985.

The devaluation had an adverse impact on enterprises and banks. Eighty percent of external debt was owed by enterprises, and half of that was guaranteed by associated banks. By 1985 external liabilities were so great that the central bank assumed $4–$5 billion of the external liabilities of enterprises and banks, mostly in the underdeveloped regions. More than 80 percent of the central bank's revenues were used to finance interest payments on foreign debt. The bank also assumed liability for the foreign currency deposits of the commercial banks, which were owed mostly to Yugoslav citizens (and were not part of the external debt).

The central bank's purchase of foreign exchange to service foreign debt, payment of interest on foreign currency deposits, and continued lending to banks to refinance loss-making enterprises were highly expansionary in terms of money supply. Whereas foreign borrowing had been used to finance excess demand during the 1970s with little inflationary consequence, excess demand during the 1980s

Table 9.5 Enterprise losses and expenditures, 1985–90

(percent)

Item	1985	1986	1987	1988	1989	1990
Losses as a share of total revenue	0.8	0.9	3.9	5.8	4.6	2.3
Wages as a share of total revenue	10.3	12.4	12.7	11.7	14.0	16.5
Materials as a share of total revenue	77.1	74.4	73.9	72.5	57.6	74.0
Taxes as a share of total revenue	1.6	2.4	2.5	2.3	3.6	2.4
Interest payments	5.6	6.2	9.2	14.0	23.8	4.0
Losses as a share of gross social product	2.8	3.0	6.6	5.7	15.0	—
Taxes as a share of gross social product	7.2	8.7	8.2	7.2	7.4	—
Taxes as a share of public sector revenue	22.2	25.9	24.4	22.2	24.0	18.0

— Not available.
Source: Lahiri 1991.

was accommodated by expansionary monetary policies. This approach resulted in a vicious circle of inflation and currency depreciation (figure 9.1). Had the uncovered capital losses of the central bank resulting from its large foreign exchange liabilities been borne by the enterprises and the budget instead, both would have been forced to cut spending to maintain solvency—bringing aggregate demand back to equilibrium with aggregate supply at a lower rate of inflation.

Gaspari (1989) was the first to point out the enormity of the central bank's uncovered capital losses resulting from its large net foreign exchange liabilities. Capital losses rose from 3.3 percent of GSP in 1981 to 11.8 percent in 1986. Mates (1991), in calculating the entire public sector deficit, includes the quasi-fiscal deficit of the central bank accumulated in various forms: subsidized loans, losses assumed by the central bank, and claims on banks which were written off. These quasi-fiscal deficits amounted to 5 percent of gross material product between 1980 and 1989, some 3.0 to 3.5 percent of it financed by seigniorage.

Although data on central bank losses have never been published, the item "other assets" in the central bank's balance sheet contains both revaluation and other accumulated losses. Other assets grew from 36 percent of total central bank assets in 1982 to 69 percent by 1987, before declining somewhat as net foreign liabilities fell (table 9.6). As a share of GSP, other assets grew by an average of 6 percent a year between

Table 9.6 Change in balance sheet item "other assets" as a proxy for central bank losses, 1982–90
(percent)

Year	Other assets		Change	Currency as a share of social product
	Share of total central bank assets	Share of gross social product		
1982	35.5	15.4	n.a.	6.7
1983	49.1	26.9	11.5	6.2
1984	54.7	31.6	4.7	5.2
1985	60.9	33.6	2.0	4.9
1986	61.6	30.6	−3.0	5.3
1987	68.9	41.0	4.4	4.4
1988	65.0	46.3	5.3	3.9
1989	53.1	58.3	12.0	5.6
1990	49.9	—	—	—

n.a. Not applicable.
— Not available.
Source: National Bank of Yugoslavia; author calculations.

1982 and 1989—about the level of average quasi-fiscal losses calculated by Mates.

Under these circumstances control over monetary supply was lost because foreign exchange transactions enlarged the money supply autonomously (Gaspari 1989). Central banking authorities relied on direct credit controls, rather than open market operations, to restrain credit growth. But defects in the design of credit ceilings actually accommodated increases in domestic spending because they did not take into account the revaluation of foreign currency deposits, whose dinar value increased with every exchange rate devaluation. Furthermore, commercial banks were

Figure 9.1 The effects of expansionary policy

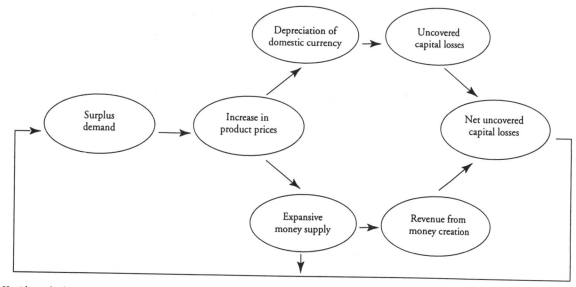

Source: Kessides and others 1989.

able to circumvent the ceilings, which in any case did not apply to selected credits or to overdrafts. Even though bank lending halved in real terms during the 1980s, disintermediation provided parallel sources of financing for enterprises through interenterprise credit. Moreover, household consumption increased because foreign currency deposits grew in dinar terms with every devaluation, creating the illusion of wealth. These factors, together with continued negative interest rates, undermined stabilization even though monetary policy officially was restrictive.

Hyperinflation develops

Monetary policy was loosened in 1985–86 to avert widespread enterprise bankruptcies. During this period of "programmed inflation," money was pumped into the economy to push growth and improve the export sector. Real wages were allowed to increase by an average of 8 percent a year in these two years, after a decline of 9 percent a year in the previous two years. Although inflation continued to rise, economic performance improved as international interest rates and oil prices fell. Moreover, the dinar was allowed to appreciate in real terms in 1986–87, which helped the inflation-adjusted public sector deficit and slowed the rise in inflation. The increase in domestic demand from higher real wages and government spending stimulated real growth of 3.6 percent in 1986, the highest since 1979. Largely for political reasons, wage indexation was introduced in 1987.

The revival of domestic demand in this second phase was not sustainable. Domestic inflation continued to accelerate, and the trade and payments positions worsened. Although in 1987 export performance improved and imports declined substantially, confidence in the dinar was shaken, resulting in a net outflow of short-term capital of nearly $3 billion.[5] In the absence of structural reforms in the enterprise sector, and with negative real interest rates continuing until 1988, inflation accelerated to 120 percent in 1987 and real incomes fell again in 1987 and 1988.

In May 1988 the government renewed its efforts to restrain domestic demand and inflation. The new program, an attempt to introduce comprehensive discipline, aimed to contain inflation with progressive reductions in money and wage growth targets and with indexation of time deposits to reduce the subsidy on bank credits to enterprises (Coricelli and Rocha 1991). The foreign exchange allocation system

was liberalized, the dinar was devalued by almost 20 percent (even though Yugoslavia was running a current account surplus), and steps were taken to liberalize domestic prices and foreign trade regimes.

The program, however, was inconsistent and ineffective. Because the program did not address the quasi-fiscal deficits in the central bank and enterprises, fiscal adjustments were not rigorous enough to compensate for such losses. Money and credit growth targets were poorly defined and permitted excessive expansion, even though real interest rates became positive and interenterprise lending to loss-making enterprises was reduced. Rising interest costs caused enterprises to default on their bank loans. Money growth targets were abandoned as the costs of financing hidden losses rose.

Several factors appear to have been critical to the development of hyperinflation in 1989. Because of wage indexation the large real devaluation in 1988 quickly fed back into inflation with higher wages. And enterprises quickly factored into their prices the higher costs of imported inputs. In bringing interest rates to positive real levels, banks significantly raised the costs of production, with the interest component of enterprise costs rising from 9 percent of revenue in 1987 to 14 percent in 1988 and to nearly one-quarter in 1989 (see table 9.5). As before, the increase in losses was accommodated by bank credit policy, which kept credit flowing to loss-makers.

In addition, with positive real deposit rates and the benefits of devaluation stimulating capital inflow—on top of an increase in the surplus of the current account—the central bank's foreign exchange reserves increased by $1.6 billion in 1988 and another $1.8 billion in 1989, thus injecting further liquidity into the system and accommodating the rising prices. Worse, the reduction in import tax collections in June 1989 aggravated the budget deficit and generated an enormous Tanzi effect, which also required budgetary funding. Prices rose by more than 240 percent in 1988, and exploded to 1,200 percent in 1989.

Crisis in the Banking System

Inflation had a highly distortionary effect on the banking system. Disintermediation was evident— narrow money (M1) fell from 24 percent of GSP in 1980 to 6 percent in 1989, and foreign currency deposits came to account for more than half of total deposits (see table 9.3). Highly negative real deposit and lending rates eroded financial deepening. Between 1980 and 1986 money and quasi money fell from 79 percent of GSP to 58 percent. There was also a corresponding decline in domestic credit, from 102 percent of GSP in 1980 to 56 percent in 1986, as borrowers benefited from the erosion of their real debt. Enterprises responded to attempts to restrict bank credit by increasing their reliance on credit from other enterprises, in the form of supplier or trade credits and the accumulation of interenterprise arrears. The volume of interenterprise credit increased from 26 percent of total credit in 1980 to 39 percent in 1987 as a result of the dramatic rise (150 percent) in enterprise arrears.

As the currency depreciated and inflation rose, capital flight from dinars and dinar deposits became evident as domestic savers switched to foreign currency deposits. These deposits rose to more than a quarter of banking system liabilities in 1989, compared with less than 15 percent in 1980, inflating the net foreign liabilities of the banking system. Thus the banks were vulnerable to large losses whenever the dinar was devalued.

The impact on banks of enterprise losses, foreign exchange exposure, and inefficient bank operations could be detected—despite poor accounting standards—from the steady erosion of the capital base of basic and associated banks (table 9.7). A large share of foreign exchange liabilities was transferred to the national banks, but some was retained on the books of basic and associated banks. The continued depreciation of the dinar affected these banks' financial position. With loan portfolios concentrated on a limited number of borrowers—usually affiliated enterprises—some banks began to incur losses several times the value of their capital.

Table 9.7 Real interest rates of basic and associated banks

(percent)

Year	Discount rate	Deposit rate	Lending rate	Capital-asset ratio
1980	−19.0	−19.1	−14.8	2.8
1981	−24.2	−23.2	−19.9	2.5
1982	−13.3	−14.8	−11.6	2.3
1983	−7.3	−20.1	−4.4	1.8
1984	−5.0	−15.5	−6.6	1.5
1985	−6.5	−6.8	−0.4	1.4
1986	−17.8	−18.0	−4.1	1.6
1987	4.6	−18.8	−4.3	1.0
1988	60.5	28.9	88.0	1.2
1989	518.5	328.8	252.0	8.1

Source: IMF, various years.

Starting in 1987 banks had to deduct current foreign exchange losses from their current income. This move improved transparency but reduced bank profits. Provisioning for accumulated losses on doubtful loans started in 1987 but did not reflect fully the degree of risk, leaving open the question of future drains on current income. Even after 1987, when some enterprise debt was transferred to the central bank, nearly 46 percent of bank loans (27 percent of assets) were still in foreign currency. In addition, contingent liabilities (guarantees) represented more than half of banks' total assets, and a large portion of these were foreign guarantees.

Banks attempted to recover their losses through high interest rate spreads, which averaged 34 percent in real terms in 1987. A 1987 World Bank study found that commercial banks would have had to charge a spread of 78 percent over deposit rates of 73 percent to recover the costs of (low-interest) public sector loans, low yields on reserves and liquidity requirements, the costs of provisioning for nonperforming loans, and foreign exchange losses. As spreads reached 70 to 80 percent in 1988 and 1989, and nominal lending rates hit more than 150 percent, the burden of nonperforming loans and losses in the banking system began to fall on good borrowers.

These real rates on captive borrowers placed an additional strain on debtors, encouraged distress borrowing, promoted disintermediation, and deterred new investment. In addition, to stem the losses of the central bank, after October 1988 commercial banks could no longer transfer foreign exchange deposits to the central bank. Thus commercial banks became fully responsible for the exchange risk on new deposits, though they were still prohibited from lending in foreign currency (although they could continue to sell the currency to obtain funds for dinar lending). Dinar lending rates, therefore, had to reflect the depreciation risks. When hyperinflation reached 1,200 percent in 1989, real lending rates rose as high as 252 percent.

Such high real interest rates distorted resource allocation as much as negative real rates had. Insolvent enterprises had no qualms about borrowing, since they had no intention of repaying. Worse, they used interenterprise credit, so their insolvency threatened even healthy enterprises. The liquidity crunch passed the burden of high real interest rates to viable enterprises, which were decapitalized, fueling further distress borrowing.

At the heart of the banking problems lay the fundamental need to restructure inefficient and unprofitable enterprises. Weak accounting frameworks, linked bank and enterprise ownership, distorted wage and price levels, inappropriate taxation, and bad investments had resulted in a scale of enterprise losses that was difficult, if not impossible, to measure accurately. By the end of 1989 enterprise losses were estimated at $10.4 billion (about 15 percent of GSP), more than three-quarters of it in industrial sectors (especially mining and energy). Tight monetary policy in early 1990 led to 350 enterprise failures by mid-May, affecting 210,000 workers. About 7,000 enterprises were unable to pay back bank loans in the first half of the year, and 1.5 million workers were not paid in March and April so that enterprises could meet their other financial obligations.

Precise estimates of banking system losses are not possible when domestic prices are severely distorted. Estimates for 1988 suggest that 35 to 40 percent of banking assets were nonperforming (Kos and Cvikl 1991). Some $8–$10 billion was affected (social product was $55–60 billion, bank capital $3.0–$3.5 billion). A preliminary estimate for 1991 lifted the total to $12–15 billion (external audits were not completed satisfactorily because of the political upheaval in 1991).

Stabilization and Restructuring

In December 1989 the Markovic administration announced a comprehensive stabilization program to combat hyperinflation. The central government was limited in its financial control, however, because the federal budget accounted for only 15 to 20 percent of public expenditure and the center had little control over spending by the republics and provinces—especially at the enterprise level. Nevertheless, the burden of fiscal restraint fell on the federal government when the central bank's quasi-fiscal operations were incorporated in the state budget. Stabilization involved tight monetary and fiscal policies, a fixed nominal exchange rate pegged to the deutsche mark, a six-month wage freeze, and a comprehensive program of price and trade liberalization. Also included was a package of measures related to ownership, long-term economic development, and bank and enterprise restructuring (Gaspari 1990). The currency was recalibrated at a rate of 1 new dinar to 10,000 old dinars.

These measures initially met with great success. Inflation fell to zero by June 1990, and foreign exchange reserves increased to about $9 billion. The financial sector, however, began to suffer from classic problems of deflation in the post-hyperinflation phase of recovery. In early 1990 annual real lending rates were still high, at roughly 45 percent, while deposit rates were 15 percent. Tight monetary policies actually facilitated the disintermediation of funds to the interenterprise credit market and increased distress borrowing because of systemic losses. Enterprise losses climbed, and with them nonperforming bank loans. The number of illiquid enterprises soared from less than 1,000 at the end of 1989 to more than 3,900 by October 1990, involving 1.6 million workers. During the same period the number of bankruptcy proceedings increased from 200 to just under 1,000.

The real sector was not helped by rapidly rising domestic prices relative to international prices. With the pegged nominal exchange rate these inflation disparities caused the dinar to appreciate by more than 122 percent in real terms, pushing the current account deficit to $850 million. Enterprises lost export markets. In the fourth quarter of 1990 the economy was hit by the higher oil prices caused by the Gulf war, as well as by lost export contracts and worker remittances. Industrial output shrank 10 percent and inflation rose to nearly 600 percent in 1990 as real wages kept rising and monetary policy was relaxed at the regional level.

Financial sector restructuring

Despite the considerable political and macroeconomic difficulties, significant efforts were made to address the weaknesses of the banking system. A new central bank law in 1989 (the Law on Banks and Other Financial Organizations) strengthened the bank's powers to restructure the banking system and develop open market operations. Rediscounts on selective credits were phased out, and any remaining subsidies were to be funded from fiscal revenues. The burden of foreign currency losses was transferred from the central bank to the federal government. The federal government no longer had any automatic access to central bank credit. Short-term credits from the central bank could be made only at the request of the Federal Executive Council.

The 1989 banking law gave the central bank the authority to introduce regulations on capital requirements and exposure limits. The 145 basic and 9 associated banks were to be restructured and consolidated into universal banks licensed by the central bank. To introduce profit-making as the key operating principle, the law provided for banks to be transformed into joint-stock companies, which would make them independent business entities. Ownership was opened to individuals and foreigners. The law also removed many structural impediments to competition, including the limitation of one bank account per enterprise. All banks meeting minimum financial criteria would be relicensed by the central bank. By February 1991, 102 commercial banks had obtained licenses. In addition, a 1989 accounting law (later amended) moved the Yugoslav system closer to internationally accepted standards and increased the transparency and meaningfulness of information.

The 1989 banking law established the principle that banks undergoing restructuring should write off losses against capital and suspend bank management immediately. A Bank Rehabilitation Agency was created to restructure banks by arranging mergers or takeovers, purchasing assets, investing or recapitalizing, and attempting to privatize them. Bank restructuring was intended to unlink restructured banks from their former problem debtors and bring fundamental change to bank ownership by replacing enterprises as owners. The commercial and investment functions of banks were to be separated from other activities by assigning them to capitalized subsidiaries (Gaspari 1991).

For a key group of strategic banks, holding more than half the assets of the banking system, the program called for a combination of across-the-board help and partial recapitalization. For a middle group of insolvent but salvageable banks the program would reduce insolvency. A third group of solvent banks was expected to benefit quickly from the reforms. In addition, case-by-case restructuring would deal with individual banks according to their degree of distress. Prior to implementation of the across-the-board measures, it was estimated that group A banks had a negative net worth of 98.7 billion dinars and group B banks of 1.6 billion dinars. Group C banks had a positive net worth of 2.3 billion dinars.

Across-the-board measures consisted of both asset and income rehabilitation operations. Asset rehabilitation included writing off $962 million in foreign debt by transferring it to the federal budget and repaying $4.2 billion in valuation losses on the principal of certain foreign obligations. Under the repayment effort, the federal government was to provide a specified portion of the dinar value of the annual repayment by banks. Other measures involved refinancing $400 million of selective credits and rescheduling some of the $300 million in credits from the Soviet Union, thereby allowing some loans to be reclassified into categories with lower loan loss provisions. To improve banks' income position, interest rates on required reserves were raised to 26 percent and 16 billion dinars in bad assets were eligible for replacement by renewable six-month central bank bills at 26 percent a year on "conditional" terms. The banks were not allowed to cash in on these bills to generate more bad credits.

For banks that were to be closed case-by-case measures included revoking licenses, voluntary realization or liquidation of assets and liabilities, assumption of good assets and legitimate liabilities by another bank, and, when all else failed, bankruptcy proceedings. For banks that were to be rehabilitated rather than closed, measures involving the Bank Rehabilitation Agency included writing off capital and assuming assets, purchasing bad loans, building up capital, and replacing management.

Financing for the initial across-the-board asset and income rehabilitation was estimated at 18.5 billion dinars ($1.4 billion). About two-thirds of it was to come directly from the (federal) budget, 2.3 billion dinars from the central bank, and the rest from the rehabilitation agency. After this initial effort, it was estimated that an additional $6.2 billion (at current dinar exchange rates) would be needed for case-by-case restructuring and another $1.4 billion over five years to meet the commitments of the initial across-the-board measures. It was argued that these outlays would:

- Arrest the erosion of the financial position of banks.
- Prevent relationships between banks and their major borrowers from multiplying.
- Lay the foundations for a transformation in the ownership of banks, ultimately leading to self-sufficiency.

The restructuring of illiquid banks began in May 1990, but progress was impeded by questions about the accuracy of comprehensive audits and the size of losses. Measures that would force bankruptcy on inefficient enterprises were still absent, and the political commitment to financial discipline weakened under severe political strain (*Transition* 1991). Since efficient labor and capital markets were not yet in place, bankruptcies increased unemployment and depleted the resources of the social safety net, placing an insupportable burden on fiscal policy. Restructuring was disrupted by the advent of civil war and the declaration of independence by Croatia and Slovenia in 1991.

Who bore the losses?

The prolonged crisis in the 1980s meant that losses were spread over almost a decade, but were not widely eliminated from the system. The distortionary effects of hyperinflation and devaluation make it difficult to establish who bore the losses in dinar terms. An examination of the banking system's balance sheets between 1980 and 1989, deflated in dollar terms, reveals that the dollar value of credit to enterprises declined by $40.5 billion during the 1980s—indicating that enterprises received enormous wealth transfers to pay for their inefficiencies. The dollar value of money and quasi money fell by $25.7 billion over the same period, indicating that households bore the brunt of the wealth transfer, particularly in the form of negative real deposit rates and devaluation.

"Other assets" of the central bank (a proxy for central bank losses) increased by $9.8 billion over the same period. Losses actually totaled $15 billion as of the end of 1987, but an improvement in the central bank's net foreign liability position in 1988–89 substantially reduced its losses. Thus enterprise losses over the decade were borne roughly two-thirds by households, one-quarter by the central bank, and the balance by bank capital. These losses were enormous by any standard.

Conclusion

All transition economies face the complex task of finding a way to distribute real sector losses that are embedded in the banking system without contributing to large-scale macroeconomic instability (Sheng 1990). In the Yugoslav case the difficulties were enormous, made worse by an inherently unstable enterprise and banking structure, as well as by great regional economic disparities.

The worker self-management experiment in Yugoslavia created fundamentally unstable and inefficient enterprise and bank structures. Easy access to domestic and foreign resources encouraged the system to grow in the 1970s. But regionalism and inappropriate economic policies created an inefficient structure unable to adjust to a competitive international environment when external resources were cut off in the 1980s.

In the early 1980s Yugoslav authorities were able to maintain external balance through devaluation and spending cuts at the federal level, but they were unable to maintain internal balance. By transferring the foreign exchange burden to the central bank without correcting the structural flaws, the authorities failed to reduce excess demand and enforce financial discipline at the regional, enterprise, and household levels. A central bank burdened with net foreign exchange liabilities could not maintain national financial discipline even if it were empowered to do so. Instead, the banking system facilitated (rather than checked) credit creation, and households believed that depreciations increased their wealth in foreign currency deposits.

The inflation tax initially transferred resources from dinar depositholders to creditors, thus alleviating the pain of fiscal adjustment. But financial discipline required the quasi-fiscal deficits of uncovered capital losses of the central bank—roughly 5 percent of GSP—to be absorbed in the budget. Although it would have been difficult politically to raise taxes to pay for these and other enterprise losses, delaying these fundamental corrections allowed the losses to be monetized. Thus instability in the banking system reinforced fundamental flaws in the real sector, creating the vicious circle of stagflation that ultimately degenerated into hyperinflation, helped along by the indexation of wages and built-in expectations of inflation. Since loss allocation had regional implications, these economic mistakes only compounded regional and political tensions.

The Yugoslav experience contains important lessons for other countries engaged in enterprise and financial sector reforms. It demonstrates the importance of the following conditions for successful reforms:

- Property rights and obligations must be clearly defined, particularly among individuals, enterprises, banks, and the state.
- Legal and accounting frameworks must be clear and transparent to enforce financial discipline. In addition, a hard budget constraint must be imposed at all levels.
- Structural adjustment must be accompanied by fiscal and monetary policies that foster competition, growth, and financial discipline. Attention should focus on policies that promote structural improvements in competition and stability, as

well as those that reduce repression and remove price distortions.

- The institutional framework should develop both institutions and human skills, with proper incentives for efficiency, stability, and equity. Particular attention must be given to relations between the central bank and the banking system, especially the central bank's monetary and supervisory responsibilities.

- The right reforms need to be introduced at the right time, including the sequencing of real sector reforms with financial sector changes. For example, early liberalization of the capital account (through the introduction of foreign currency deposits) became a source of instability when authorities tried to correct domestic structural distortions.

- Structural adjustments of the magnitude envisaged cannot be achieved without high losses in employment and real income. Allocation of losses within and among regions, institutions, and groups stretches the limit of political will and consensus, without which economic reform cannot proceed.

Notes

1. Until 1991 the Socialist Federal Republic of Yugoslavia comprised six republics and two autonomous republics, with a total population of 23.7 million people in 1989. In 1991 the republics of Croatia and Slovenia declared independence.

2. Gross social product, which is 7 to 8 percent less than gross domestic product (GDP), is equivalent to gross material product (total value added in the production of goods) plus the services regarded as productive inputs.

3. Such credits were the dinar counterpart of individuals' foreign currency deposits with the banks, which were redeposited with the central bank. This scheme was discontinued in 1988.

4. These comprised an export bank that was funded by the basic and associated banks, various savings banks that offered loans to households and whose investments were restricted to bank deposits, and investment loan funds, which financed projects in less-developed regions. Insurance companies, with negligible total assets, offered life, general, and casualty coverage but could invest only in bank deposits.

5. This sizable outflow led to debt rescheduling in 1987.

References

Bicanic, Ivan. 1989. "Systemic Aspects of the Social Crisis in Yugoslavia." In Stanislaw Gomulka, Yong-Chool Ha, and Cae-One Kim, eds., *Economic Reforms in the Socialist World.* Armonk, N.Y.: M.E. Sharpe..

Bole, Velimir, and Mitja Gaspari. 1991. "The Yugoslav Path to High Inflation." In Michael Bruno, Stanley Fischer, Elhanan Helpman, Nissan Liviatan, and Leora (Rubin) Meridor, eds., *Lessons of Economic Stabilization and Its Aftermath.* Cambridge, Mass.: MIT Press.

Coricelli, Fabrizio, and Roberto de Rezende Rocha. 1991. "Stabilization Programs in Eastern Europe: A Comparative Analysis of the Polish and Yugoslav Programs of 1990." Policy Research Working Paper 732. World Bank, Washington, D.C.

Edwards, Sebastian, and Francis Ng. 1985. "Trends in Real Exchange Rate Behavior in Selected Developing Countries." CPD Discussion Paper 16. World Bank, Washington, D.C.

Estrin, Saul, and Lina Takla. 1991. "Reform in Yugoslavia: The Retreat from Self-Management." Paper presented at a conference by the World Bank, London School of Economics, and Portuguese Catholic University, January 31, Washington, D.C.

Gaspari, Mitja. 1989. "Balance of Payments Adjustment and Financial Crisis in Yugoslavia." Economic Development Institute and European University Institute seminar series on financial reform in socialist economies. EDI, World Bank, Washington, D.C.

———. 1990. "Recent Developments in Yugoslavia." Paper presented at a symposium on central banking issues in emerging market-oriented economies. Sponsored by the Federal Reserve Bank of Kansas City, August 23–25, Jackson Hole, Wyoming.

———. 1991. "Bank Restructuring in Yugoslavia." Paper presented at the seminar for senior bank supervisors sponsored by the World Bank and the U.S. Federal Reserve, October 28–November 15, Washington, D.C.

IMF (International Monetary Fund). Various years. *International Financial Statistics.* Washington, D.C.

Kessides, Christine, Timothy King, Mario Nuti, and Catherine Sokil, eds. 1989. *Financial Reform in Socialist Economies.* Economic Development Institute Seminar Series. Washington, D.C.: World Bank.

Klaus, Vaclav. 1991. "A Perspective on Economic Transition in Czechoslovakia and Eastern Europe." In Stanley Fischer, Dennis de Tray, and Shekhar Shah, eds., *Proceedings of the World Bank Annual Conference on Development Economics 1990.* Washington, D.C.: World Bank.

Knight, Peter T. 1983. "Economic Reform in Socialist Countries: The Experiences of China, Hungary, Romania, and Yugoslavia." World Bank Staff Working Paper 579, Management and Development Series 6. Washington, D.C.

Kos, Miroslav, and Milan Cvikl. 1991. "Banking Supervisory Activities in Yugoslavia." National Bank of Slovenia, Ljubljana.

Lahiri, Ashok Kumar. 1991. "Yugoslav Inflation and Money." International Monetary Fund, European Department, Washington, D.C.

Mates, Neven. 1991. "Inflation in Yugoslavia: A Specific Form of Public Deficit Caused by the Parafiscal Operations of the Central Bank." Institute of Economics, Zagreb.

National Bank of Yugoslavia. Various issues. *Quarterly Bulletin.* Sarajevo.

———. Various issues. *Statistical Survey.* Sarajevo.

Rocha, Roberto De Rezende. 1991. "Inflation and Stabilization in Yugoslavia." Policy Research Working Paper 752. World Bank, Washington, D.C.

Saldanha, Fernando, "Self-Management: Theory and Yugoslav Practice." World Bank, Financial Operations Department, Washington, D.C.

Sheng, Andrew. 1990. "Bank Restructuring in Transitional Socialist Economies: From Enterprise Restructuring to Bank Restructuring." Economic Development Institute senior policy seminar on financial reform in transitional socialist economies, September 10–12, Paris.

Transition: The Newsletter About Reforming Economies. 1991. World Bank, Vol. 2, No. 1.

CHAPTER 10

Financial Liberalization and Reform, Crisis, and Recovery in the Chilean Economy, 1974–87

Andrew Sheng

Chile is one of the most open, dynamic, and stable economies in Latin America today. But to get there, Chile had to follow a long path of political and economic reform, crisis, and recovery (Bianchi 1992). Financial liberalization was part of that process, and the techniques of bank restructuring that Chile adopted have important implications for developing countries.

The Chilean case must be viewed against the backdrop of the remarkable institutional reforms and policy changes implemented over the past twenty-five years. The Allende administration (1970–73) nationalized the entire financial system, as well as the mining, transport, and communications sectors. The Pinochet military regime that seized power in 1973 adopted an aggressive program of liberalization and privatization. It was during this regime (1973–81) that the conditions for widespread financial instability developed (Harberger 1985). Those conditions erupted into economic crisis in 1981–83, exacerbated by enterprise failures, a sharp decline in Chile's terms of trade, a withdrawal of international sources of credit, and sharply rising interest rates, capped by a massive currency devaluation. These problems were resolved only after the public sector resumed extensive supervision of and intervention in the financial system.

During the second half of the 1980s a pragmatic policy approach led the way to recovery through an outward-oriented, export-led growth strategy, reinforced by prudent monetary and fiscal policies aimed at maintaining low inflation and a healthy balance of payments. Recovery was aided by an emphasis on private sector–led growth, through the encouragement of competition and foreign direct investment.

What Went Wrong?

There is broad agreement on what went wrong in Chile (Velasco 1991). Financial, monetary, and economic policies supported rapid expansion and excessive risk-taking by domestic and foreign financial institutions, which made large loans to undercapitalized and highly indebted enterprises. Neither a macroeconomic nor a microeconomic explanation of the crisis is wholly satisfactory. Viewed from a long-term perspective, Chile's experience illustrates how doctrinaire swings in policies, on top of external shocks and fragile domestic economic conditions, can exacerbate the consequences of financial boom and bust.

The Chilean case, particularly in 1980–81, exhibits many of the characteristics associated with the business-cycle theory of escalating enterprise indebtedness leading to speculation and eventually crisis (Minsky 1988; Kindleberger 1978). It also suggests that governments, enterprises, and financial markets have long learning curves (Valdés-Prieto 1992). Policymakers must learn that imperfect markets do not react like textbook markets. Long-repressed financial markets are so informationally and institutionally imperfect that they cannot immediately adapt to the market-pricing mechanism for credit (de la Cuadra and Valdés-Prieto 1989). Similarly, enterprises must learn that speculative bubbles do burst and that excessive indebtedness cannot be sustained forever.

A number of factors converged to cause the crisis. Although some were more important than others, each played a part in the economic downturn.

Real sector factors

High commodity concentration. The economy was highly vulnerable to fluctuations in international demand for a single commodity, copper, which accounted for 83 percent of total exports in 1973. Chile's boom and bust cycle, especially in the early years, was closely related to the international price of copper.

International developments. Like many other developing countries, Chile was severely affected by the international recession of 1981–82 (table 10.1). When the OECD countries decided to tackle inflation by using tight demand management, international interest rates were driven sharply upward. The subsequent international liquidity squeeze was compounded by the debt crisis ignited by Mexico in 1982, when international banks withdrew credit to many highly indebted countries, especially those in Latin America.

Trade reform. An aggressive trade liberalization program initiated in 1975 brought the average nominal tariff from 105 percent at the end of 1973 to a uniform rate of 10 percent by 1979 (Cortés-Douglas 1990). This rapid liberalization created large losses for the previously protected import-substituting enterprises and sparked an import boom for consumer durables, financed by the first-time availability of consumer credit under financial liberalization (Schmidt-Hebbel 1988).

An overvalued exchange rate, coupled with excessive wage rigidity. The use of the exchange rate as a stabilization tool led to a large overvaluation, which increased demand for nontradables and reduced the competitiveness of domestic industries, especially among exporters and previously protected import-competing firms (Galvez and Tybout 1985). Between the second quarter of 1979 and the end of 1981 the real exchange rate appreciated by 45 percent. In addition, wage indexation, introduced by the 1979 labor law, increased enterprise losses at a time when Chile was suffering sharp falls in export prices and sharp increases in international interest rates (Edwards 1985). In August 1981, with inflation near zero and export prices down because of the international recession, wages were increased by 14 percent as required by law, worsening international competitiveness and the financial position of enterprises.

Table 10.1 Macroeconomic indicators, 1970–90
(percent unless otherwise specified)

Year	Real growth in GDP	Current account/ GDP	Terms of trade[a] (1980=100)	Inflation rate[b]	Government balance/GDP	Nominal interest rate		Exchange rate (pesos/U.S. dollar)
						Lending	Deposit	
1970	2.1	−1.1	238.3	32.5	−3.0	—	—	—
1971	8.9	−1.9	189.9	20.0	−8.0	—	—	—
1972	−1.2	−3.9	174.3	74.8	−13.0	—	—	—
1973	−5.6	−2.7	211.4	361.5	−7.0	—	—	—
1974	1.0	−2.6	153.0	504.7	−5.0	—	—	0.8
1975	−12.9	−6.8	108.1	374.7	0.1	—	—	4.9
1976	3.5	1.5	108.7	211.8	1.4	—	—	13.1
1977	9.9	−4.1	100.7	91.9	−1.0	163.1	93.8	21.5
1978	8.2	−7.1	95.2	40.1	−0.2	86.1	62.8	31.7
1979	8.3	−5.7	109.9	33.4	4.8	62.1	45.1	37.2
1980	7.8	−7.1	100.0	35.1	5.4	47.1	37.4	39.0
1981	5.5	−14.5	86.4	19.7	2.6	52.0	40.8	39.0
1982	−14.1	−9.5	79.7	9.9	−0.1	63.9	47.9	50.9
1983	−0.7	−5.6	85.8	27.3	−2.6	42.8	27.9	78.8
1984	6.3	−11.0	80.8	19.9	−2.9	38.3	23.3	98.7
1985	2.4	−8.3	79.3	30.7	−2.3	41.3	32.2	161.1
1986	5.7	−6.8	72.8	19.5	−1.0	29.7	20.1	193.0
1987	5.7	−4.3	77.9	19.9	0.5	38.3	26.6	219.5
1988	7.4	−0.8	94.2	14.7	−0.2	21.2	15.1	245.0
1989	9.9	−3.0	97.9	17.0	1.5	35.9	27.7	267.2
1990	2.2	−2.8	82.3	26.0	0.8	48.8	40.3	304.9

— Not available
a. Ratio of the index of average export prices to the index of average import prices.
b. Consumer price index.
Source: IMF, various years.

Premature opening of the capital account, which allowed excessive foreign borrowing by the private sector. This point is controversial. Larrain Garces (1988) argues that foreign banks were inexperienced in recycling funds from the oil-exporting countries and lent large amounts to countries like Chile without adequately assessing their debt servicing capacity. In addition, Chilean firms were not experienced with overseas borrowing and accumulated excessive external debt. Valdés-Prieto (1992), on the other hand, argues that it was the implicit foreign exchange guarantee originating in the pegged exchange rate policy that was the major policy error.

Rapid denationalization, which resulted in substantial concentration of industrial wealth. Beginning in 1974, banks and enterprises were sold to the private sector on credit, with 10 to 40 percent down and the balance at ten-year (two-year for banks) indexed loans at 10 percent real interest rates. Groups (*grupos,* or economic conglomerates) bought banks on credit and then borrowed from the banks to buy privatized firms. By 1979 the groups controlled more than half of the largest private corporations (Cortés-Douglas 1990). Harberger (1985) and Larrain Garces (1988) point out that many state-owned enterprises were insolvent when they were sold to highly geared private owners and so had no defenses against the crisis when it broke.

Speculation in shares and property. Between 1977 and 1981 gross domestic product (GDP) grew by an average of 7.9 percent a year in real terms, while the inflation rate fell steadily. The real index of stock prices, however, increased by 323 percent between 1977 and 1980 (Edwards 1985). With the onset of the crisis, market capitalization fell by 38 percent in peso terms from its peak in 1980 to its trough in 1983. In dollar terms market capitalization declined over the same period from $9.4 billion to $2.6 billion and continued its drop to $2.0 billion in 1985. The conglomerates, in particular, benefited from low financial costs and high returns on share transactions during the share boom (Galvez and Tybout 1985). Between 1979 and 1981 misguided optimism, first about future income and later in anticipation of a devaluation, spurred accumulation in construction and imported capital goods (Corbo 1985). The compression in share and property values reduced the net wealth of enterprises, extinguished collateral values, and resulted in large bank losses to overgeared borrowers.

Financial sector factors

Financial liberalization without adequate supervision. Financial liberalization was wide-ranging and included bank privatization, licensing of new domestic and foreign banks, desegmentation of financial services, progressive reduction of banks' reserve requirements, creation of index-linked financial instruments, gradual freeing of capital flows, and elimination of interest rate ceilings, credit allocation controls, and barriers to entry. In 1974 nineteen domestic banks—representing all the domestic banks except Banco del Estado—were privatized. "Free banking" (with little government supervision) reigned, with new foreign entrants spurring heated competition. The freeing of interest rates in 1975 promoted the development of finance companies (*financieras*), under little supervisory control and in direct competition with banks. Between 1974 and 1981 the number of financial intermediaries nearly tripled to twenty-three domestically owned banks, eighteen foreign banks, and thirteen finance companies.

Rapid expansion in financial intermediation. Liberalization was extremely successful at expanding financial intermediation, with total financial assets rising from 20 percent of gross national product (GNP) in 1975 to 48 percent in 1982 (Velasco 1991). Domestic savings did not expand, however, but averaged only 12 percent of GDP in the high-growth 1977–81 period, compared with gross domestic investments of 19 percent of GDP. Foreign savings rose from 4 percent of GDP in 1977 to 15 percent in 1981, serving as the unsustainable cause of growth in financial assets.

High concentration in the banking system. The five largest banks controlled more than half the credit market. The banks controlled by the two largest groups (Banco de Chile and Banco de Santiago) accounted for 42 percent of credit and 59 percent of nonperforming loans. The five banks requiring official intervention in 1983 (Bancos de Chile, de Santiago, Concepcion, Internacional, and Colocodora) accounted for 45 percent of total credit and 66 percent of nonperforming loans (Hinds 1987).

Excessively high real interest rates. Real interest rates on loans averaged 77 percent a year during 1975–82 (table 10.2). Since such rates were clearly unsustainable, there is considerable evidence that distress borrowing was going on (Galvez and Tybout 1985).

Excessive external debt. As the economy boomed during the second half of the 1970s, it relied more

Table 10.2 Real peso interest rates, 1975–83

(percent)

Year	Loan rate	Deposit rate
1975	164.9	68.7
1976	176.4	125.1
1977	92.9	58.9
1978	55.0	38.6
1979	23.1	10.9
1980	15.7	8.5
1981	42.4	32.2
1982	42.4	29.7
1983	15.9	3.9
1975–82[a]	76.6	46.3

Note: Rates correspond to short-term (30–90 day) bank transactions.
a. Average.
Source: Velasco 1991.

and more on external financing. In 1981 the current account deficit rose to 14.5 percent of GDP, financing two-thirds of gross domestic investment. External debt in 1981 climbed by 35 percent—to nearly $15 billion—and reached 70 percent of GDP in 1982 (table 10.3). By 1982, 73 percent of net foreign debt had been incurred by the private sector.

Moral hazard. Private sector liabilities, expressed as domestic deposit liabilities of the banking system plus the external debt of private enterprises, were assumed by the government once the crisis began to unfold. The free-banking policy, which assumed that bank failure and external debt were private contracts that could be resolved privately, was abandoned. The Chilean government ended up assuming all private foreign debt and implicitly guaranteeing all deposits in the banking system. Thus a private sector debt crisis was transformed into a national debt crisis.

Inappropriate responses

Thus by the end of the 1970s economic policy had swung from wholesale nationalization of the banking system to pursuit of unfettered financial liberaliza-

Table 10.3 Capital inflows and external debt, 1977–82

(millions of U.S. dollars)

		External debt	
Year	Capital inflow	Total	As a share of GDP (percent)
1977	568	4,862	36.3
1978	1,946	6,407	41.7
1979	2,248	8,201	39.6
1980	3,160	10,746	39.1
1981	4,469	14,483	44.0
1982	1,304	16,953	70.3

Source: Velasco 1991.

tion. The policy debate encompassed the full range of options from free banking to protection through financial repression, with support as well for the prudential regulation approach (Cortés-Douglas 1990). Most observers agree that there was inadequate banking system supervision in the period leading to the crisis and that this contributed to the magnitude of the problem.

During the early stages of financial liberalization, for instance, when the free-banking approach prevailed, the Superintendency of Banks focused more on whether banks were in compliance with quantitative standards than on whether they were acting prudently. Only in 1980–81 did the superintendency establish a system for risk-based loan classification, provisioning rules, and exposure limits. Not until 1981–82 did it crack down on excessive lending by banks to related companies and approve a more precise definition of loan limits to single enterprises. The superintendency also obtained powers to regulate the investments, lending, credit rollovers, and collateral requirements of banks classified as unstable or poorly managed. But these initiatives came too late to avert financial disaster.

The government compounded the error of inadequate regulation and lax enforcement by encouraging the perception of government readiness to intervene and underwrite deposits in failing financial institutions. In 1977 regulators took over control of Banco Osorno, the first bank failure since 1926. The central bank supported deposits, and the government announced a limited but explicit guarantee scheme for small deposits in banks, supervised finance companies, and supervised savings and credit cooperatives. The government also covered the deposit losses that had occurred at two major finance companies, although it offered no cover for deposits in failed informal institutions. In 1977 the government also intervened and protected the deposits in several cooperatives, bailing out all creditors.

These structural subsidies had another unintended effect when the exchange rate policy shifted to fixed nominal rates to combat inflation (de la Cuadra and Valdés-Prieto 1989). The deposit guarantee scheme protected not only the nominal value of deposits but also their external value in real terms. At a time (1981) when Chilean bank regulators were unable to impose stringent loan loss provisioning on banks, the government, through its fixed exchange rate policy, was assuming vast contingent liabilities on the foreign exchange exposure of banks. "Above the line" government deficits appeared to be eliminated through orthodox fiscal restraint, with budget surpluses averaging 4.2 percent of GDP between 1979 and 1981. In reality, however, the government's quasi-fiscal deficit was growing rapidly as the government absorbed large contingent liabilities through implicit or explicit deposit and foreign exchange guarantees.

The Crisis

The six-year boom ended abruptly in 1981 as copper prices fell sharply in the wake of the international recession. Employment shrank by 22 percent between mid-1981 and the end of 1982. The trade deficit reached 17 percent of GDP following the rapid appreciation of the peso. In the first half of 1982 capital inflows fell to just more than a third of their volume in the second half of 1981. Sustained appreciation of the peso led to serious problems for industries in the tradable goods sectors, increasing the demand for credit and pushing up interest rates. Indeed, between 1978 and 1981 the volume of peso and foreign currency loans (excluding overdue ones) increased from 162 billion to 800 billion pesos equivalent. A large share of domestic currency debt was short-term maturities, increasing the liquidity squeeze on enterprises.

Share prices peaked in the first quarter of 1981 and began a sharp decline. Real lending rates climbed from 7 percent in the third quarter of 1980 to 44 percent in the first quarter of 1981. With continued access to foreign funds, banks borrowed $3.1 billion as construction activity increased 16 percent (following a 26 percent rise in 1980) and high real wages kept domestic consumption rates high.

Signs of problem loans began to emerge as early as 1980. Auditors for Banco Espanol qualified their report for 1979 by stating that 37 percent of loans could not be evaluated because of lack of information on the debtors' ability to pay—even though the loans had been rolled over repeatedly. Anticipating government intervention, the owners sold Banco Espanol to another business group in early 1981. The government-authorized sale did not require the new owners to inject new capital in the bank.

During the second half of 1981 an important company in good standing with international banks went bankrupt. Three banks, four finance companies, and a development bank, together accounting for 6 to 7 percent of loans in the financial system,

failed in November 1981, and the government intervened in their operations. Banco Espanol was among those taken over, only months after the change in ownership. Significantly, these failures occurred before the economic crisis and devaluation of 1982, but were followed by intervention in two more banks and a finance company in 1982.

The magnitude of the impending problem was not perceived early enough. In-mid 1982, at the time of the maxi-devaluation of the peso, the new loan classification procedure introduced by the Superintendency of Banks in 1980 showed that only 6 percent of loans were at risk. Provisions amounted to only 1.7 percent of loans, but the level of capital and reserves suggested that at end-1981 the banking system still had substantial positive net worth (de la Cuadra and Valdés-Prieto 1989).

As the recession worsened during 1981–82, borrowing from banks increased sharply to meet domestic liquidity needs. Financial system loans to the private sector increased to 62 percent of GDP in 1981, compared with 51 percent in 1980, and jumped to 76 percent by late 1982. International interest rates also rose sharply during 1978–81, affecting the debt servicing of floating-rate debt. Net external debt rose 66 percent in 1981 and nearly 24 percent in 1982. Delinquent loans increased from 2.3 percent of total loans at the end of 1981 to 6.3 percent by May 1982. The business conglomerates increasingly shifted the collateral for their bank loans from their indebted limited liability corporations and societies to entities beyond the reach of their banks. Lack of consolidated accounting concealed the extent of interest rate and foreign exchange exposure of highly leveraged conglomerates. Small and medium-size firms also fell deeply into debt in 1981.

Capital flight accelerated in the last two months of 1981, and international credit (particularly to domestic banks) dried up in the first quarter of 1982. The central bank lost $1.4 billion in reserves in 1982 as a whole. Following a June 1982 18 percent devaluation of the peso, the exchange rate floated for a while, and then moved to a crawling peg. The peso sank steadily, and by June 1983 it had fallen by 99 percent. Exchange controls were reintroduced, tariffs were raised to a uniform 20 percent, and in early 1983 the peso was declared inconvertible (Edwards 1985). At this point the position of Chilean companies was so precarious that authorities acted swiftly to introduce a preferential exchange rate for dollar debtors.

The crisis worsened in 1983. As share prices fell, ten mutual funds collapsed in January, their net book value shrinking from a peak of 27 billion pesos ($693 million) at the end of 1980 to 4.3 billion pesos ($56 million) in February 1983. Their collapse resulted in bankruptcies and large losses to the related insurance companies, including the three largest, which had invested up to half their assets in these funds. In January 1983 the Superintendency of Banks intervened in eight banks, while the central bank had to provide 87.5 billion pesos ($1.1 billion) to support bank liquidity. By the end of 1983 the banking system was revealed to be severely insolvent (table 10.4). It faced losses of 70 billion pesos and had more than doubled the volume of delinquent loans it was carrying—even after massive sales to the central bank.

Crisis Resolution

By early 1983 the need for wholesale government intervention and support of the banking system was widely recognized. The government intervened in seven banks and one finance company (accounting for 41 percent of total deposits), immediately liquidating three of them. Two of the commercial banks, later returned to the private sector, were Chile's largest and the flagships of two of the largest conglomerates. Whereas earlier rescues had come with a 100 percent guarantee of all deposits and interest, this time the government guaranteed only 70 percent of deposits to domestic creditors (Larrain Garces 1988). The government did fully compensate foreign creditors' claims, however, to preserve Chile's international financial standing.

This second round of interventions followed on efforts in 1981–82 to tighten and enforce prudential regulations, reflecting a belated but important turnaround in official policy. In addition, the government developed an extensive program for subsidized repro-

gramming of enterprise debt that enabled both enterprises and the financial system to survive the crisis.

The restructuring effort lasted about five years—from 1982 to 1987—and spanned the period of economic recession and recovery. Legal and institutional changes were made to the regulatory and supervisory infrastructure. The thrust of the effort, however, was the socialization of bank losses from bad enterprise debt through the central bank, financed partly with cash but mostly through official debt instruments of the central bank.

Diagnosis and supervision

In 1976 the Superintendency of Banks had only ten inspectors to supervise the country's fourteen banks and twenty-six finance companies. Subsequent regulatory changes improved bank accounting, mandated bank auditing, and levied penalties against fraudulent accounts. In 1980–81 authorities introduced long-overdue regulations to improve diagnosis and supervision of the system. The central bank also sent forty staff members to bolster the superintendency's inspection capacity. A number of other supervisory and regulatory changes were introduced during the crisis.

Risk classification and provisioning. In 1980 the superintendency set up a risk classification system for loans. Banks were required to classify loans according to risk level (A to D) for their 30 largest borrowers. This requirement eventually was extended to the 400 largest borrowers, covering about 75 percent of total portfolios. Previously, credit rollovers—particularly among loans to related companies—tended to hide the extent of nonperforming loans. Provisioning was improved in 1981 by requiring general provisions amounting to 0.75 percent of total loans, in addition to specific provisions against bad loans.

Early warning system. Banks were classified as low-, medium-, or high-risk based on capital adequacy, asset quality, management quality, earnings, and liquidity (the CAMEL system).

Diversification of loans. In 1981 the superintendency introduced measures forcing banks to shed loans from related persons and companies in order to reduce concentration. The concentration limit was set at 100 percent of bank capital and reserves. Banks, however, evaded these limits by channeling funds through newly created overseas subsidiaries.

Regulatory forbearance. Because of the severity of the crisis, the authorities had to exercise some regula-

Table 10.4 Delinquent loans and bank capital, 1982–83, selected months
(billions of pesos)

Month, year	Delinquent loans	Loans sold to central bank	Capital and reserves	Loan loss provisions	Net worth
December 1982	41.1	41.6	105.0	34.7	57.0
January 1983	47.7	37.5	102.9	35.7	53.0
June 1983	126.9	36.9	104.3	55.4	−4.1
December 1983	92.2	109.7	127.7	61.9	−12.2

Source: de la Caudra and Valdés-Prieto 1989.

tory leniency. They extended from thirty to ninety days the threshold for declaring delinquent loans nonperforming and stretched the time that banks had to make provisions for these loans from three to five years. The authorities also allowed banks more flexibility in crediting interest accruals, meeting capital adequacy standards, disposing of physical assets acquired from debtors, and accounting for the effect of devaluation on foreign currency liabilities.

Banks, which had accumulated inordinately large stocks of physical assets as part of their debt recovery efforts, were given three years to dispose of these collateral assets. The law also allowed three years for profits or losses from these disposals to be recognized in the accounts. To minimize the impact of rapid asset disposals on prices and bank profitability, the superintendency allowed the banks five years to record the losses incurred from collateral asset sales.

The superintendency also allowed the banks to phase in (between 1982 and 1983) the negative effects of the currency devaluation on their foreign exchange liabilities. Moreover, the capital adequacy requirement was eased by allowing 25 percent of loan loss provisions to be included in the capital base. And starting in 1983, cumulative losses at year-end could be written off against capital and reserves within five years.

Damage control

The four main types of damage control assisted borrowers, alleviated foreign exchange pressures, helped depositors, and aided financial institutions.

Borrowers. Two major rescheduling exercises covering an estimated 25 percent of the financial system's loans were undertaken in 1983 and 1984. In 1983 a mandatory 30 percent of the debts of viable borrowers in "productive" sectors (which excluded consumer, mortgage, foreign, trade-related, and certain other loans, as well as loans to investment companies) were rescheduled. Debts were rescheduled for a term of ten years at 7 percent real interest, with a grace period of five years on principal and one year on interest. Debtors in foreign currency obtained the same terms, but the interest rate was computed on the rescheduled debt in foreign currency. Mortgage and consumer loans were also refinanced and rescheduled by the central bank. Rescheduling covered unpaid installments since 1981 and a declining share of installments due during 1983–87. The rescheduled amounts were denominated a special unit of account (*Unidad de Fomento*, or UFs) indexed to inflation and had to be repaid at an 8 percent real interest rate.

The 1984 rescheduling lowered interest rates and expanded the amounts eligible for rescheduling, including more favorable terms for small borrowers. Real interest rates on the rescheduled portion were lowered to 5 percent for the first two years, 6 percent for years three through five, and 7 percent for the sixth year. Debt could be rescheduled for no less than five years, and up to ten years for large borrowers and fifteen years for small borrowers. Across-the-board restructuring was curtailed after 1984, and banks were encouraged to swap debt for equity. In addition, incentives such as tax concessions and loan loss deferrals encouraged flexibility and facilitated loan restructuring for small debtors. Mortgage refinancing was also expanded, and the real interest rate was lowered to 6 percent for large debtors (4 percent for small debtors). The central bank also provided special lines of credit at below-market interest rates for working capital needs, payroll financing, hiring incentives, construction and public works, and reforestation.

Foreign exchange. To cushion the impact of the devaluation on distressed firms and banks with net foreign exchange liabilities, the central bank in 1982 established a preferential exchange rate scheme for debt servicing on certain dollar-denominated debt. Until mid-1985 preferential rates were indexed to inflation, so that real devaluations increased the spread between preferential and market rates and thus the size of the central bank subsidy. The subsidy was paid in the form of central bank notes with a maturity of six years. This subsidy was gradually phased out. In 1984 the central bank assumed a one-time loss when it allowed borrowers who were rescheduling their loans to convert dollar liabilities into pesos at a favorable rate.

The bank also provided swap facilities to domestic debtors owing foreign liabilities. After an interruption in foreign loan servicing and repayments in 1983, banks continued to collect on dollar loans. Since there was little domestic demand for dollar loans, banks deposited their dollars with the central bank under repurchase agreements. The central bank paid a premium over international market rates on these accounts, and in mid-1985 it converted the liabilities into a special account. Peso devaluation increased the domestic currency value of the dollar deposits, creating a central bank loss; however, the devaluation adjustments were not paid in cash, but accrued. Banks could draw from the currency accounts only for external debt servicing, but they could draw on central bank credit lines denominated in the inflation-adjusted UFs at predetermined interest rates. At the end of 1986 the amount of special accounts was equivalent to 22 percent of financial system loans. The premium on the special accounts was eliminated in 1987.

Depositors. To prevent a systemwide run on banks following its January 1983 intervention in the banking system, the state issued an explicit guarantee of all domestic deposits. This explicit guarantee was lower than the implicit 100 percent protection that had prevailed before. Domestic depositor losses from the three financial institutions that were liquidated averaged 30 percent. The guarantee was extended until April 1985, when the deposit insurance scheme was overhauled.

Ailing banks. The most innovative feature of the Chilean restructuring was the part-flow, part carve-out solution used for the banks. To ease liquidity during the crisis (the flow solution), the central bank provided emergency lines of credit to banks and subsidies on rescheduling of loans and other credit programs. To facilitate the rescheduling, the central bank sold six-year notes to the commercial banks at a 12 percent real rate and bought ten-year commercial bank notes at a 5 percent real rate (with five years' grace on principal and one years' grace on interest payments). This provided banks with a 7 percent annual risk-free spread.

Recapitalizing banks

The carve-out efforts by the central bank involved direct purchases of substandard loans. In June 1982, immediately following devaluation, the central bank purchased the worst loans (up to 100 percent of capital and reserves) of the banks in which it had intervened, using ten-year zero-coupon notes (*letras*). This gave banks a ten-year period in which to write off loans and avoided costly losses that would have eroded bank capital. This scheme was replaced in early 1984 by one that allowed the central bank to purchase loans up to 150 percent of capital and reserves. The banks used the cash to pay off their outstanding central bank credits and to purchase interest-bearing central bank promissory notes (*pagares*). This method stanched the monetary effect of the central bank's cash infusions into the banking system.

Banks could sell additional substandard loans (up to 100 percent of capital and reserves) in exchange for zero-coupon central bank notes under a ten-year loan repurchase agreement (at their initial value) or for cash under a ten-year repurchase agreement at 5 percent (real) interest. Shareholders had to commit to repurchasing all loans sold to the central bank. In other words, the loans that were carved out by the central bank became future liabilities of past shareholders rather than of the general taxpaying public. In 1985 loan sales were opened to all banks (not just those in which the government had intervened), but as of August 1985 banks under intervention accounted for 75 percent of the $2.36 billion of central bank loan purchases.

In early 1985 the Superintendency of Banks was given the authority to require banks subject to intervention to increase their equity. New shares were offered first to existing shareholders, and then to third parties at favorable discounts under extended easy payment terms, with tax incentives. Bank creditors could capitalize the amounts owed by converting them into equity. Finally, the state development bank, Corfo, could take on a bank's outstanding central bank emergency credits and convert them to equity shares. Corfo's stake could not exceed 49 percent of bank equity, and it had to sell its shares within five years or transfer them free of charge to shareholders who had initially subscribed to new capital. The treasury would reimburse part of any loss the central bank might eventually assume from these transactions. These sales popularized share ownership of banks and attracted more capital than was anticipated. All the banks under intervention were returned to the private sector, although Colocadora lost its autonomy when it was merged with Banco de Santiago.

Who bore the losses?

Looking back, it is apparent that the exceptional economic performance of 1979–81 was unsustainable, consumption-led, and financed principally through foreign currency borrowing. These factors ensured a particularly hard landing when Chile's terms of trade worsened.

Chilean banks expanded their loan portfolios by about 500 percent during 1977–81, while the ratio of bank loans to GDP increased from 15 percent to 55 percent. Credit expansion was driven by unsustainably high interest rates. The interest rate issue is important. The excessively high interest rates meant that enterprises could not sustain debt servicing payments. Annual real rates of 40 percent implied that

Table 10.5 Potential gains from fully leveraged stock market speculation, 1976–82

Year	Stock market price index (1980=100)	Investment fully financed at the nominal peso loan rate[a]	Gain or loss
1976	3.7	3.7	0.0
1977	12.5	9.7	2.0
1978	26.9	18.1	8.8
1979	52.3	29.4	23.9
1980	100.0	43.2	56.8
1981	75.5	65.7	9.8
1982	68.3	107.7	–39.4

a. See table 10.1 for nominal lending rates.
Source: World Bank and IMF data.

lenders intended to recover their principal within two-and-a-half years, suggesting that banks would require borrowers to have an even shorter time horizon for capital payback.

There may be some validity to the view that the sharp policy swing from nationalization to liberalization and privatization under highly leveraged conditions for the privatized banks and enterprises was ill-timed, given Chile's circumstances. Light supervision, pegged exchange rates, and implicit deposit guarantees during 1974–80 allowed excessive risk-taking and external borrowing—moral hazard behavior at its worst. And as many other countries have found, overvaluation of the exchange rate encourages resources to move into nontradables. A fully leveraged purchase of shares on the Santiago stock market in 1976 would have made substantial profits until 1980 and would not have shown heavy losses until 1982 (table 10.5). A Kindleberger-Minsky bubble was clearly at work.

As bad loans accumulated, banks sought high spreads to compensate for lost income and to support dividend payments. The authorities realized too late that the state would have to bear the burden of private sector speculation: the government was responsible not only for its own domestic debt but also for guaranteeing all external debt and the banking system's deposit base. Thus the state paid high real interest rates and the burden of state obligations was eventually passed back into the economy through higher taxes, devaluation, inflation, and unemployment.

The first indication of financial imbalance occurred in 1977, when lending to the private sector began to exceed total money and quasi-money; the banking system became overextended and started borrowing abroad. But net private wealth—that is, the value of stocks, money, and quasi-money, less loans from the banking system—continued to rise from 1978 and peaked in 1980 at $5.7 billion (table 10.6). Net foreign liabilities did not materially change during that period, but gross foreign liabilities rose to $5 billion—the same amount as foreign assets—at the end of 1980.

In 1981, with the decline in copper and share prices and the emergence of banking problems, stock market capitalization dropped by $2.4 billion, reducing net private liquid wealth (table 10.7). M3 continued to grow, however, and domestic borrowing increased by $4.9 billion and net foreign debt by $2.5 billion. The net loss to the system was $4.6 billion, or 14 percent of GDP. The devaluation in 1982 caused further losses in wealth as the value of domestic money declined by $2.7 billion and capital fled

Table 10.6 A balance sheet approach to private sector wealth, 1978–90

(billions of U.S. dollars)

Type of wealth	1978	1979	1980	1981	1982	1983	1984	1985	1986	1987	1988	1989	1990
Market capitalization[a]	4.8	6.6	9.4	7.0	4.4	2.6	2.1	2.0	4.1	5.3	6.8	9.6	13.6
Money and quasi-money	3.0	4.6	7.9	10.6	7.9	8.0	6.9	5.8	6.5	7.5	9.2	10.1	10.9
Private sector credit	3.8	6.3	11.6	16.5	13.8	12.8	11.1	9.8	10.3	10.8	12.6	12.2	12.6
Net private liquid wealth (market capitalization + money and quasi-money – private credit)	4.1	4.9	5.7	1.1	–1.5	–2.2	–2.1	–2.0	0.3	2.0	3.4	7.5	11.9
Foreign assets	1.8	3.3	5.0	5.0	3.5	3.6	3.8	3.2	3.5	3.6	4.3	4.4	7.4
Foreign liabilities	1.8	2.9	5.0	7.5	8.2	9.4	11.4	10.9	11.7	11.3	9.5	6.8	6.6
Net foreign liabilities (foreign assets – foreign liabilities)	0.0	0.4	0.0	–2.5	–4.7	–5.8	–7.6	–7.7	–8.2	–7.7	–5.2	–2.4	0.8

Note: The balance sheet is priced in U.S. dollars to remove the distorting effects of domestic inflation and devaluation. In an open economy with full capital mobility, a private investor evaluates changes in wealth against an international numeraire, such as the U.S. dollar.
a. Capitalization of the stock market is used as a proxy for real asset growth since other data are not available.
Source: Calculated from IMF, various years.

Table 10.7 Change in private liquid wealth, 1981–84

(billions of U.S. dollars)

Type of change	1981	1982	1983	1984
Stock market capitalization	−2.4	−2.6	−1.8	−0.5
M3	2.7	−2.7	0.1	−1.1
Credit	4.9	−2.7	−1.0	−1.4
Private liquid wealth[a] (stock market capitalization + M3 − credit)	−4.6 (−14.1)	−2.6 (−10.7)	−0.7 (−3.5)	−0.1 (−0.5)
Financed in part by net foreign liabilities[b]	−2.5	−2.2	−1.1	−1.8

a. Numbers in parentheses are shares of GDP (percent).
b. A minus sign denotes an increase in net foreign liabilities.
Source: Calculated from table 10.6.

the country (net foreign liabilities rose by $2.2 billion). The loss amounted to 10.7 percent of GDP. The devaluation reduced the real value of domestic debt (in dollar terms), to the loss of domestic depositholders, whose deposits were guaranteed only in nominal, domestic currency terms. Accordingly, there was a massive redistribution of wealth between borrowers and depositors.

The carve-out effectively transferred the losses of the private sector (particularly foreign exchange liabilities) and the banking system to the central bank. Although the government's fiscal deficits remained small (1.0 percent of GDP in 1982, rising to 3.0 percent in 1984 but declining to 2.4 percent in 1985), the quasi-fiscal deficits in the central bank's books were large. In 1981 total central bank claims on the central government, private sector, and banks totaled only 12 percent of GDP. By 1985 the total was 124

percent of GDP, more than three times the domestic money supply (table 10.8). The central bank also had assumed external liabilities equivalent to 38 percent of GDP and had a net foreign liability position equivalent to 18 percent of GDP. By the end of 1986 the central bank had accumulated a portfolio of bad and doubtful loans amounting to 640 billion pesos—equivalent to 31 percent of total loans, 185 percent of capital and reserves of the entire banking system, or 20 percent of GDP. Two large banks, Bancos de Chile and de Santiago, accounted for 62 percent of that total.

The carve-out postponed the full monetary impact of the banking crisis, but the process of increasing credit to the banking system undermined economic and monetary stability. The size of the intervention eroded public confidence in the financial system and undermined the stability of the exchange rate while raising inflationary expectations. The central bank's credit expansion complicated macroeconomic stabilization efforts by boosting the quasi-fiscal deficit. The bank had to walk a fine line between stabilizing inflation and the exchange rate while providing sufficient credit to prop up weak banks and let the enterprise restructuring process work itself out. The cost was a ballooning of central bank obligations. The stock of outstanding central bank bonds and short-term securities rose from $277 million in 1982 to $3.8 billion in 1988, accounting for 62 percent of total outstanding bonds in Chile.

However painful it was, the carve-out had a number of positive effects. It bought sufficient time for the real economy to turn around, and by the end of

Table 10.8 Monetary aggregates, 1976–90

(percentage of GDP)

Item	1976	1977	1978	1979	1980	1981
Claims on central government	29.1	31.3	19.6	16.2	10.2	4.7
Central bank	28.2	30.5	18.9	15.1	10.1	4.6
Banks	0.8	0.8	0.7	1.1	0.1	0.1
Claims on private sector	15.6	20.0	26.5	31.9	42.1	50.5
Central bank	6.1	0.7	7.1	6.9	5.1	4.7
Banks	9.5	19.3	19.4	25.1	37.0	45.8
Central bank claims on banks	2.5	2.1	3.7	2.7	2.4	3.1
Foreign liabilities	12.5	15.5	12.4	14.9	18.0	22.9
Central bank	8.5	10.2	6.6	6.4	4.3	2.6
Banks	4.0	5.2	5.8	8.5	13.7	20.4
Capital accounts	15.2	14.7	16.0	19.9	19.6	17.1
Central bank	6.9	7.7	10.5	14.2	13.3	10.9
Banks	8.3	7.0	5.5	5.8	6.2	6.2
Money and quasi-money	20.1	16.0	21.3	23.3	28.6	32.3
Currency	3.5	3.2	3.4	3.2	3.3	3.5

Source: IMF, various years.

1986 bank restructuring was virtually complete. By financing the purchase of bad loans primarily with debt instruments rather than with cash, the central bank deferred the monetary impact while maintaining the viability of the financial system. Restrictions imposed on bank shares also blunted the monetary effects of the loan purchases by channeling banks' future profit streams to repurchases rather than to dividend payments. In this way the central bank avoided the wholesale bailout of shareholders in restructured and assisted banks.

Rebuilding profitability

Although the 1982 devaluation had a massive impact on private wealth, it was the return to international competitiveness that generated the resources for recovery. The trade balance went from a deficit of $2.7 billion in 1981 to a surplus of $1.0 billion in 1983. Tight monetary and fiscal policies, greater openness to trade and foreign investment, and greater attention to enterprise and bank restructuring paid off. Between 1985 and 1989 Chile cut its external debt by $8 billion by permitting citizens to use foreign exchange resources to retire debt, by allowing foreign creditors to swap debt for equity, and by repurchasing debt in the international secondary market.

Furthermore, economic recovery after 1985 greatly improved the aggregate corporate balance sheet, which permitted a reduction in long-term indebtedness. As real growth revived in 1985, the quality of banks' assets improved. Past-due loans dropped from 8 percent of total assets in 1983 to 2 percent in 1988.

Rescheduled credits as a share of total outstanding credits fell from 22 percent in 1985 to 11 percent in 1988. As domestic confidence improved, the stock market revived and private liquid wealth expanded from –13 percent of GDP (in U.S. dollar terms) in 1985 to 43 percent in 1990.

As the authorities encouraged higher levels of equity capital, capital-asset ratios in the banking system rose from 5.4 percent in 1985 to 7.0 percent in 1986, and equity went from 9 percent of assets in 1985 to 11 percent in 1988. Bank profitability improved considerably as real returns on capital rose from –5.1 percent in 1985 to 8.4 percent in 1988.

The crisis and its resolution left Chile's banking structure largely unchanged, although foreign banks made some gains in market share at the expense of domestic institutions. Competition came not only from foreign banks, but also from the securities markets and from securitized products. The number of domestic banks and finance companies decreased from twenty-five in 1983 to nineteen in 1988, while the number of foreign banks rose from nineteen to twenty-two. Private domestic banks' market share fell from 68 percent of the banking system assets in 1983 to 61 percent in 1988. The Banco del Estado, the one state-owned commercial bank that emerged from the crisis unscathed, accounted for 18 percent of total system assets at the end of 1988, roughly the same share as in 1983.

As the crisis ebbed and a new banking law was enacted in late 1986, bank supervision reverted to an orthodox stance. The new law promoted self-regulation through stiffer requirements for market

1982	1983	1984	1985	1986	1987	1988	1989	1990
8.9	15.2	27.9	51.3	52.6	49.1	40.7	32.7	33.2
4.3	10.4	22.1	43.9	46.8	45.2	40.2	32.4	33.0
4.6	4.8	5.8	7.4	5.8	3.9	0.4	0.3	0.3
81.7	71.9	75.4	70.1	65.0	62.2	57.6	53.4	50.2
14.2	14.7	14.7	13.9	12.7	11.2	9.5	1.3	1.3
67.4	57.3	60.7	56.2	52.3	51.0	48.2	52.1	49.0
12.3	38.5	46.3	65.8	58.1	49.0	33.7	27.7	25.6
48.8	52.8	75.5	77.9	74.3	64.6	43.5	30.0	26.3
5.8	17.6	30.3	38.4	35.7	35.8	24.2	16.1	13.9
43.0	35.2	45.2	39.5	38.6	28.8	19.3	13.9	12.4
30.1	32.5	14.1	35.9	34.6	58.2	22.2	23.0	23.7
22.1	26.5	9.1	8.7	8.1	34.2	7.0	7.1	7.4
8.0	6.0	4.9	27.2	26.5	24.0	15.2	15.9	16.3
46.6	45.0	47.1	41.2	40.9	43.1	42.1	44.1	43.6
3.5	3.3	3.4	3.1	3.3	3.3	3.4	3.3	3.4

information. The Superintendency of Banks was required to publish information about the nature and quality of bank assets three times a year so that depositors, investors, and supervisors would be better informed about financial institutions. The law also attempted to eliminate the practice of related lending and defined more precisely the concept of "client." It tightened capital adequacy standards and compliance sanctions, reinforced the leveraging ratios applied to banks, and set out a mechanism for bank rescues by other banks. Banks were also required to dispose of acquired assets quickly or to write them off fully, and loans to related companies were to be reduced to no more than 5 percent of the total portfolio by the end of 1990.

Finally, the scope of state deposit guarantees was scaled down to protect mainly small depositors. Demand deposits continue to carry a 100 percent guarantee in full, but only 90 percent of time deposits per depositor are protected up to UF 120. State insurance on larger deposits was phased out. Consequently, while the state guarantee on time deposits covers only 7 percent of total system balances, it protects 80 percent of savings deposits and covers two-thirds of all depositors.

Lessons

The Chilean case shows the immense difficulties of shifting from a highly nationalized and repressed economy into a fully open, liberalized, and privatized system. Highly leveraged and decapitalized banks and enterprises do not necessarily seek long-run, productive investments. They are more likely to engage in short-run, high-risk activities in order to recapitalize themselves. The presumption that the market would correct structural deficiencies through high real interest rates proved wrong so long as the state provided a guarantee on bank deposits and private sector external borrowing. Large bank spreads between deposit and loan rates weakened the enterprise sector and discouraged household savings without improving the long-run profitability of banks.

The Chilean case has important lessons for the post–centrally planned economies. Because of hyperinflation, radical economic stabilization measures were needed at the same time as the market was being liberalized. For example, rapid privatization transferred loss-making public enterprises to the private sector. Simultaneous bank privatizations led to the concentration of both enterprises and financial

institutions in a few highly leveraged groups. But prolonged overvaluation of the domestic currency to stabilize inflation perpetuated market distortions, fueling the shift toward nontradables—which was financed by external borrowing with the opening of the capital account. Domestic and international indebtedness rose to undesirably high levels, made possible by a favorable external environment and the inexperience of international banks in recycling surplus petrodollars to developing countries and that of domestic firms in assessing the true costs of foreign borrowing under an overvalued exchange rate.

Another key policy error lay in the presumption that private external borrowing is ultimately a state obligation. External borrowing financed enterprise indebtedness and consumption-led growth while temporarily keeping the exchange rate artificially high. Facing pressure from international creditors, the government assumed the external debt obligations and, in addition, bailed out distressed enterprises through a preferential exchange rate subsidy administered through the central bank.

The Chilean economy was already in a fragile state when the terms of trade deteriorated rapidly in 1981. A sharp jump in international interest rates and the abrupt withdrawal of international credit ensured a downward spiral of asset prices. Could better regulatory and supervisory vigilance have averted the financial crisis? Chile's experience provides useful lessons on the dangers of financial liberalization without strong supervision and enforcement to avoid such market abuses as related lending, risk concentration, and capital flight.

Free banking with few controls on capital mobility reduced the capacity to tax entrepreneurs and wealthholders, while state guarantees on domestic deposits and external borrowing worsened moral hazard and free-rider problems. Large concentrations of wealth were built up and used for speculative purposes. When losses occurred capital fled the country through the open capital account, so much of this wealth evaded taxation. Thus the losses were borne by the central bank.

The Chilean case also demonstrates the importance of national risk management. Policymakers should focus on preventing excessive risk-taking and the accumulation of large financial imbalances, whether in domestic currency or in foreign exchange, in both state and private sectors. Because of a doctrinaire belief that a free market would correct itself, the authorities ignored the dangers that capital flight could destabilize the economy by eroding public confidence in the banking system—at a time when the state had to absorb all losses and had limited resources to deal with the losses.

Thus macroeconomic stabilization and financial liberalization policies have to take into account the structural deficiencies in real and financial markets. The institutional framework for regulation and supervision must be in place to allow the restructuring of enterprises, labor, and financial markets without disrupting monetary stability. Bank restructuring was ultimately a success in Chile, but it came at considerable cost following the successful opening of the Chilean economy to international competition and massive changes in tax, pension, and labor structures.

References

Bianchi, Andrés. 1992. "Chile: Economic Policies and Ideology During the Transition to Democracy." In Pedro Aspe, Andrés Bianchi, and Domingo Cavallo, eds., *Sea Changes in Latin America*. Washington, D.C.: Group of Thirty.

Corbo, Vittorio. 1985. "Reforms and Macroeconomic Adjustments in Chile during 1974–84." *World Development* 13(8): 893–916.

Cortés-Douglas, Hernán. 1990. "Financial Reform in Chile: Lessons in Regulation and Deregulation." Paper presented at the seminar on financial sector liberalization and regulation, "Changing the Rules of the Game." Sponsored by the World Bank's Economic Development Institute, Washington, D.C.

de la Cuadra, Sergio, and Salvador Valdés-Prieto. 1989. "Myths and Facts about Instability in Financial Liberalization in Chile: 1974–83." Universidad Catolica de Chile, Institute of Economics, Santiago.

Edwards, Sebastian. 1985. "Stabilization with Liberalization: An Evaluation of Ten Years of Chile's Experiment with Free-Market Policies, 1973–83." *Economic Development and Cultural Change* 32 (January): 223–54.

Galvez, Julio, and James Tybout. 1985. "Microeconomic Adjustments in Chile during 1977–81: The Importance of Being a *Grupo.*" *World Development* 13(8): 969–94.

Harberger, Arnold C. 1985. "Observations on the Chilean Economy, 1973–83." *Economic Development and Cultural Change* 33(3): 451–62.

Hinds, Manuel. 1987. "Financial Crises in Developing Countries." World Bank, Country Economics Department, Washington, D.C.

IMF (International Monetary Fund). Various years. *International Financial Statistics.* Washington, D.C.

Kindleberger, Charles P. 1978. *Manias, Panics, and Crashes: A History of Financial Crises.* New York: Basic Books.

Larrain Garces, Mauricio. 1988. "Treatment of Banks in Difficulties: The Case of Chile." Background paper prepared for *World Development Report 1989.* World Bank, Washington, D.C.

Minsky, Human P. 1982. "The Potential for Financial Crises." Department of Economics Working Paper 46. Washington University, St. Louis, Missouri.

Schmidt-Hebbel, Klaus. 1988. "Consumo e Inversión en Chile (1974–82): Una Interpretación real del Boom." In Felipe Morandé and Klaus Schmidt-Hebbel, eds., *Del Auge a la Crisis de 1982.* Santiago: ILADES.

Valdés-Prieto, Salvador. 1992. "Financial Liberalization and the Capital Account: Chile, 1974–84." Paper presented at the conference on the impact of financial reform sponsored by the World Bank, April, Washington, D.C.

Velasco, Andres. 1991. "Liberalization, Crisis, Intervention: The Chilean Financial System, 1975–85." In Vasudevan Sundararajan and Tomas Balino, eds., *Banking Crises: Cases and Issues.* Washington, D.C.: International Monetary Fund.

CHAPTER 11

Argentina's Financial Crises and Restructuring in the 1980s

Luis A. Giorgio and Silvia B. Sagari

Argentina began and ended the 1980s in financial crises. Financial sector restructuring proceeded continuously, with the central bank intervening in, liquidating, or forcibly merging about 10 percent of the financial system's institutions each year between 1981 and 1988. One hundred sixty-eight formal financial institutions closed. Deposits in the financial system became highly volatile, and financial institutions' assets were frozen. Restructuring and the financial instability that it reflected fueled the internal disequilibrium that characterized the decade. This in turn contributed to the demonetization and disintermediation that traditionally accompanies high-inflation environments.

This vicious circle was caused primarily by the government's inability to bring spending in line with current revenues and its attempts to finance this gap by printing money and issuing more debt. This led to a growing debt service burden and, ultimately, to a quasi-fiscal debt in the central bank (Rodriquez 1991). The debt had to be financed at higher and higher interest rates given the continual erosion of demand for money or debt instruments denominated in local currency. The rising cost of borrowing increased public sector borrowing needs and undermined exchange rate stability, which led in turn to higher interest rates. The tight monetary policy of the 1980s ultimately backfired, since high interest rates eventually fed back into inflation. Caught in a debt-distress trap, the system exploded into hyperinflation, which approached an annual rate of 5,000 percent in 1989. In early 1990—through the forced conversion of commercial bank time deposits into ten-year, dollar-denominated treasury "external bonds" that traded at a deep discount (Beckerman

1992)—the government repudiated a large portion of its private sector debt, decapitalizing many banks in the process.

The economic and financial deterioration of the 1980s had transformed the financial sector, so the crisis of 1989, although related to the 1980–82 crisis, was qualitatively different. In 1982, 80 percent of financial sector assets involved credit to the nonfinancial sector; thus the condition of the financial sector was inextricably linked to that of the nonfinancial sector. The 1989 crisis, by contrast, was precipitated by unsound and poorly managed public finances, coupled with the closing of international credit markets to highly indebted countries. This closure eliminated one of the few noninflationary instruments that the Argentine government had to finance its deficits in the short term (Cavallo and Peña 1983).

Over the decade the banking system was used to finance the central bank, which onlent primarily to state-owned and other public banks at preferential rates. This process substituted for direct central bank financing of the treasury, made the banking system a captive of public finance, and displaced private, market-based banking activity. Banks basically stopped lending to the nonfinancial sector and instead transferred resources to the central bank. By the end of 1988 the central bank held 65 percent of the deposits of the financial system.

Macroeconomic Background and Financial Sector Framework

Extensive government intervention in the mobilization and allocation of resources during the 1970s helped turn Argentina into a high-inflation, slow-growth economy (table 11.1; Rodriquez 1991). During the 1980s real gross domestic product (GDP) fell by an average of 0.9 percent a year. Savings as a share of GDP dropped because of the sharp fall in public savings. Capital formation also steadily declined, from 25 percent of GDP in 1980 to 9 percent in 1989 (Beckerman 1992).

The foundations of financial sector instability

Since 1961 the government had been running a primary deficit (Rodriquez 1991). Until 1976 the budgetary shortfall was financed by printing money. In 1976 debt began to play a role in financing the fiscal deficit, greatly facilitated by access to foreign borrowing in the late 1970s. Borrowing eased the inflationary impact of deficit financing, but when external financing was cut off in 1982 it inaugurated a funding crisis that eventually led to hyperinflation (Beckerman 1992).

Starting in 1982 government revenues increased and spending grew more slowly than GDP. Despite this relative decline in the primary deficit, the cost of financing it remained high, unleashing a public finance crisis that had been building for more than a decade. The stock of debt continued to mount. Savers, anticipating devaluation and accustomed to endemic

inflation, demanded higher and higher remuneration for holding financial assets denominated in local currency. Since dollarization increased pressure on the exchange rate, the government continually had to raise interest rates. High real interest rates hurt the profitability—and ultimately the solvency—of enterprise borrowers, which in turn undermined the stability of banks. External credit also increased the overall indebtedness of the productive sectors of the economy.

In 1978 the government adopted an economic program that used the exchange rate as the anchor for domestic prices. Preannounced daily devaluations were intended to reduce the gap (more than 1 percent a month) between domestic and international interest rates by minimizing the exchange risk implicit in the high domestic rates. Domestic inflation meant that international interest rates were negative, causing a massive inflow of foreign capital in 1979. Large enterprises increased their gearing ratios and suffered an erosion of liquidity; those with access to external borrowing increased foreign debt as a share of total assets. Other firms, however, did not switch to foreign currency borrowing because of the general lack of confidence in the appreciating peso exchange rate—fueling the boom in domestic lending.

Inflation slowed sharply toward the end of 1979, but uncertainty about the economic program under-

Table 11.1 Macroeconomic indicators, 1970–90
(percent unless otherwise specified)

Year	Real growth in GDP	Current account/GNP	Terms of trade[a] (1980=100)	Inflation rate[b]	Exchange rate (local currency/U.S. dollar)
1970	5.18	−0.71	138.4	13.6	n.a.
1971	4.47	−1.57	141.1	34.7	n.a.
1972	1.19	−0.89	126.8	58.5	n.a.
1973	3.58	1.82	166.8	61.3	n.a.
1974	5.74	0.22	134.4	23.5	n.a.
1975	−0.66	−3.36	121.4	182.9	0.000003
1976	0.00	1.73	119.6	444.0	0.00001
1977	6.32	2.72	109.9	176.0	0.00004
1978	−3.52	4.37	104.3	175.5	0.00007
1979	6.75	−1.01	107.0	159.5	0.0001
1980	0.62	−8.50	100.0	100.8	0.0001
1981	−9.80	−8.43	97.9	104.5	0.0004
1982	−6.66	−4.52	90.2	164.8	0.002
1983	2.18	−4.10	96.2	343.8	0.01
1984	2.63	−3.45	96.9	626.7	0.06
1985	−3.28	−1.57	89.7	672.2	0.60
1986	7.28	−3.84	85.3	90.1	0.94
1987	2.15	−5.54	81.7	131.3	2.14
1988	−2.83	−1.78	86.2	387.7	8.75
1989	−8.00	−2.40	89.6	4923.6	423.0
1990	3.48	1.80	91.5	1343.9	4876.0

n.a. Not applicable.
a. Ratio of the index of average export prices to the index of average import prices.
b. Consumer price index.
Source: National Institute of Statistics and Census; Central Bank of Argentina.

pinned the 31 percent real interest rate reached by the beginning of 1980. As early as 1979 the real sector of the economy had started to experience problems from the incompatibility between real interest rates and the profit rates of companies that were highly indebted in domestic currency.

The nominal anchor exchange rate policy resulted in a steep real appreciation of the peso, which distorted relative prices by encouraging import substitution and production of nontradables. The import boom and export slump caused a current account deficit at the end of 1979, exacerbated by the effect of the increasing external debt service burden on the invisibles account. The onset of an international recession in 1981 affected the terms of trade of internationally traded goods as well. High real interest rates, competition from imported goods, and an increase in real wages lowered profits and increased the incidence of insolvency for a wide range of enterprises (Baliño 1987). Expectations of devaluation merely increased the pressure on the financial system.

There were two large devaluations in the first half of 1981. After the second one the exchange market was split into a commercial market—for which the rate was set by the central bank—and a free-floating financial market. The government also introduced an exchange insurance scheme to encourage the rollover of longer-term loans (more than eighteen months) and compensated borrowers for the effects of the June 1981 devaluation on loans rolled over for at least one year. These initiatives were augmented later in the year by a swap facility for six-month operations. By the end of 1981 the foreign exchange market was reliberalized and most of these short-term stabilization techniques were eliminated. In addition, the exchange market was unified and the

peso was allowed to float. Controls were briefly reapplied when the Falkland Islands conflict with Great Britain began in April 1982, but were lifted again toward the end of 1982. Appreciation of the real effective exchange rate had been halted, and decline had begun.

Nevertheless, the erratic nature of exchange rate policies contributed to a general lack of confidence in stabilization efforts. Devaluation brought increased foreign exchange to the central bank, with an attendant impact on the money supply. The banking system bore the brunt of ensuing efforts at monetary control, while the increasing need for public sector borrowing crowded out the private sector. Devaluation also increased the debt service burden of both the public and private sectors. Enterprises had such problems servicing their debt that the central bank assumed the private sector's external debt. Domestic saving was declining, boosting internal financing costs. And though government expenditures were cut in the early 1980s, tax revenues began to decline, so no real progress was being made in economic restructuring.

Financial sector growth and instability

Financial institutions expanded rapidly throughout this period of uncertainty and mounting real sector problems (table 11.2). Despite demonetization and disintermediation, the number of banks increased because of the demand for more intensive intermediation brought about by the general internal disequilibrium. By the end of 1989 real money was worth about one-third its value at the end of 1979. At the same time, the average term of deposits fell from 310 to 10 days and the velocity of circulation of sight deposits doubled as the public acted defensively

Table 11.2 Financial sector branches and staffing, 1979–89

Year	Government-owned banks		Private banks		Total banks		Nonbank financial institutions	
	Branches	Personnel (thousands)	Branches	Personnel (thousands)	Branches	Personnel (thousands)	Branches	Personnel (thousands)
1979	1,813	79	2,032	63	3,845	142	261	10
1980	1,840	80	1,999	66	3,839	146	280	11
1981	1,876	79	2,046	63	3,922	142	277	11
1982	1,877	78	2,215	63	4,092	141	272	9
1983	1,892	79	2,481	66	4,373	145	268	7
1984	1,914	81	2,645	68	4,559	149	231	6
1985	1,935	81	2,568	64	4,503	145	193	4
1986	1,953	80	2,540	61	4,493	141	164	4
1987	1,969	80	2,411	58	4,380	138	138	3
1988	1,990	82	2,458	61	4,448	143	92	3
1989	2,003	82	2,480	65	4,483	147	44	2

Note: Excludes the central bank.
Source: Central Bank of Argentina.

against high inflation. Though the operational efficiency of many banks declined steadily and bank closures escalated, the number of bank branches rose by 638 between 1979 and 1989.

With the nationalization of deposits in 1973, the central bank became the only depositholder until 1977. During that time financial entities played the role of deposit collectors, for which they received a commission; depositors collected interest from the central bank. Banks could lend capital, reserves, and rediscount funds, but the deposits were in effect subject to a 100 percent reserve requirement. The financial system contracted as depositors looked for alternatives to bank deposits, which they found in the form of indexed government bonds.

In 1977 changes were introduced to the laws affecting financial institutions, especially with respect to solvency and liquidity, monetary and credit policy, and entry and bank branching. Deposit insurance also was introduced, initially covering 100 percent of peso-denominated deposits.[1] Deposit insurance and the freeing of deposit interest rates aided the remonetization of the economy and boosted activity in the formerly repressed financial system.

Selective credit practices were lifted under the new system, leaving most credit and investment decisions with the financial intermediaries. Banks, however, were required to pay into a central bank "monetary regulation account" based on the loan capacity generated by their sight deposits. The central bank used this account to compensate the banks for the reserves they were required to hold against time deposits. Although the reserve requirements were imposed to counter the expansionary monetary effects of the other changes in policy, these arrangements later contributed to the central bank's quasi-fiscal deficit.

Foreign and domestic borrowing accounted for 65 percent of total government financing over the 1977–81 period. But from 1982 to mid-1985 the central bank was the sole financier, through expansion of the monetary base, thus thwarting the effect of anti-inflationary initiatives. By 1983 the fiscal deficit had increased to 16 percent of GDP. Moreover, the devaluations in 1982, and ensuing assumption of private external debt by the central bank, led to a reversal of public policy regarding the banking sector. Deposit interest rates once again became subject to controls, while lending rates were depressed by a compulsory rescheduling of private loans at negative rates. At this point the central bank

also stopped collecting its charge rate on banks, although the regulation account continued to pay interest on reserves. Although the central bank had prevented a complete decapitalization, the banking system was once again highly repressed and suffered extensive disintermediation.

The Austral Plan

The Austral Plan, introduced in mid-1985, affected the structure of the financial system through the end of the 1980s. The plan included a wage and price freeze; devaluation, followed by a fixed exchange rate; creation of a new currency, the austral, to replace the peso; and fiscal reforms, including a commitment by the central bank not to print money to finance treasury deficits (Beckerman 1992). The central bank began using the financial system as the main supplier of funds, and in so doing (temporarily) lowered the inflation rate from 672 percent in 1985 to 90 percent in 1986. Eventually, though, the plan also became a source of hyperinflation because the central bank assumed several fiscal and quasi-fiscal activities:

- Servicing of the nationalized public and private external debt, for which it purchased surplus current account funds.
- Financing of real sector operations through loans to the banking sector, mainly government-owned institutions.
- Redemption of maturing government securities.

Thus the path to hyperinflation was open. Improving the stability of the banking system was impossible without radical fiscal reform, which was not forthcoming.

In June 1985 the financial system began supplying financing through the reserve requirements and forced investments imposed by the central bank. Forced investments took the form of so-called inaccessible deposits. Unlike reserve requirements, these deposits could not be drawn down even if a bank's deposits declined, and the interest earned on them could not be withdrawn but had to be capitalized into the deposit balance. They had the advantage, therefore, of not adding to high-powered money. And unlike the previous system of reserve requirements, the inaccessible deposits did not lead to disintermediation of funds from the formal sector.[2]

The system once again became tightly repressed, not unlike it was before the liberalization of the mid-1970s. It was also inherently unstable. Whereas in June 1982 reserves had amounted to only 3 percent

Table 11.3 Consolidated financial system balance sheet

(percent)

Balance sheet item	June 1982	December 1982	December 1985	July 1988	December 1988
Assets					
Total reserves	3	14	12	19	25
Loans and other credits	78	73	71	60	46
Fixed assets	7	6	8	9	7
Other assets	12	7	9	12	22
Total	100	100	100	100	100
Liabilities					
Deposits	39	17	33	32	33
Rediscounts	5	16	9	12	13
Other liabilities	47	60	46	39	36
Capital and reserves	9	7	12	17	18
Total	100	100	100	100	100

Note: Excludes institutions in liquidation and the central bank.
Source: Central Bank of Argentina.

of assets, by December 1988 reserves held by the central bank accounted for about a quarter of the assets of the consolidated financial system (table 11.3). The nature of credit risk also changed as loans and other credit fell from 78 percent of assets in June 1982 to 46 percent in December 1988. Loans to the nonfinancial private sector fell by half in real terms during this period.

The stock of the financial system's liabilities with the central bank also increased: rediscounts alone rose from 5 percent of total liabilities in June 1982 to 13 percent in December 1988. Rediscounts were earmarked to both economic activities and financial intermediaries. In fact, 80 percent of rediscounts were channeled to public sector banks, which increased their share of loans from 35 percent at the end of 1979 to 61 percent by the third quarter of 1989.

Not surprisingly, the quality of banks' loan portfolios deteriorated, with the system's share of nonperforming assets increasing from 11 percent at the end of 1982 to 27 percent by December 1988. The position of private banks improved slightly, with nonperforming loans falling from 11 percent to 8 percent, while the nonperforming portion of public banks' portfolios rose from 11 to 37 percent.

The Banking Crisis of 1980–82

The Argentine banking crisis of the early 1980s was different from the crisis of 1989–90 and—in that it was caused primarily by the private sector's inability to service its financial commitments—similar to the crises of other Latin American countries at the time. The rapid drop in inflation in late 1979 and 1980 pushed real interest rates to more than 31 percent a year. This worsened the impact of the recession caused by competition from imports, which itself was caused by real effective exchange rate appreciation. The extent of nonperforming loans and the number of bankrupt firms had a direct impact on the profitability and solvency of financial institutions. Loan portfolios were deteriorating in quality just as financial institutions were experiencing a steep increase in liabilities, resulting in severe capital losses to banks and other financial institutions. The first indication of a crisis came in March 1980 with the bankruptcy of one of the largest private banks in Argentina, Banco de Intercambio Regional (BIR).

The seeds of crisis

To finance the progressively heavier loan portfolio, institutions such as BIR initiated aggressive campaigns to attract depositors by offering increasingly higher interest rates (Arnaudo and Conejero 1985). The supervisory and institutional framework at the time encouraged this practice in a number of ways. First, deposit insurance covered 100 percent of local currency deposits, making depositors risk-neutral investors for whom the solvency of their financial intermediary was irrelevant (Fernandez and Rodriquez 1983). Moreover, there was a perception that public banks—whether national, provincial, or municipal—were implicitly insured despite the fact that most did not take part in the central bank deposit insurance scheme.

Second, although the regulatory regime was designed to promote discipline, soundness, and safety in the financial system, monitoring and enforcement could not keep pace with the rapid increase in the number of financial institutions. Furthermore, supervisors tended to focus on compliance with the rules rather than on qualitative assessment of assets (Baliño 1987).

Restructuring

Between the end of 1979 and 1981 twenty-five private domestic banks and thirty-four nonbank institutions went bankrupt. Even financial institutions that survived the crisis had extremely poor-quality portfolios. At least half the aggregate portfolios of all financial institutions were nonperforming. The crisis, which started with the collapse of the BIR, was resolved by liquidating financial entities, reimbursing all depositors, and transferring resources from the depositors to the debtors of the system. This was done mainly through central bank operations (see below). As a result of these efforts the nonfinancial private sector was no longer the main debtor of the financial system by the end of 1982.

During 1980 alone the central bank provided liquidating institutions with loans equal to 5 percent of GDP (or 12 percent of the total deposits of the financial system). The bank also took over administration of all institutional assets. The repayment of deposits was financed by expanding the monetary base. The balancing entry on the asset side of the central bank balance sheet was "credit to financial institutions in liquidation," but the only assets these institutions had to repay with were their buildings and their loan portfolios, which were of extremely poor quality and low market value.

These early steps did not stem the tide of banking failures, however. By December 1982 eighty-three institutions had been closed down. Central bank loans to the institutions undergoing liquidation equaled 3 percent of GDP that year.

During 1981–82 the government assumed private foreign debt liabilities. Part of the foreign debt was exchanged for pesos, converted at a below-market exchange rate The balance was to be paid over time (in pesos) at an interest rate that after 1984 fell below market. The foreign debt of public enterprises also was transferred to the treasury. The debt service costs on this exposure were to be financed through money creation by the central bank, combined with increased reliance on the financial system to absorb part of the additional liquidity—thereby crowding out productive investment.

The monetary and financial reform package introduced in July 1982 was the first systematic attempt to address the solvency crisis. The plan focused on alleviating the indebtedness of private enterprises in order to forestall further banking failures. Debts were liquified through refinancing at negative real interest rates with terms extended beyond five years. By this time, however, the average term for deposits was only about forty days—a highly unstable situation for banks. To stabilize the banks' position and to dampen upward pressure on interest rates, loans were refinanced by the central bank at the same rates and terms as were extended to the private borrowers. The subsidies implicit in this restructuring

reached $3.2 billion, equivalent to about 7 percent of GDP (table 11.4).

Part of the subsidy ultimately was borne by holders of regulated-rate deposits. Since regulated rates were negative in real terms, depositors were taxed implicitly. Moreover, the government restricted the amounts and terms of deposits yielding market (unregulated) interest rates, effectively creating a niche market for regulated-rate deposits. Although there was a 100 percent reserve requirement on regulated deposits, the central bank paid interest to banks on the reserves at the same rate that banks paid to depositors. The implicit tax paid by depositors was equivalent to $2.3 billion. The $0.9 billion difference between this amount and the total subsidy was absorbed by the central bank through the spread between the inflation rate and the interest rate on the refinancing of restructured corporate loans.

Institutions that remained in operation also refinanced their nonperforming loans through the central bank, so they were not disadvantaged by the restructuring operations. Still, the structural changes under way by the end of 1982 did have a profound impact on them. The real value of monetary aggregates had shrunk by half compared with three years earlier. At the same time, investors began switching to dollar-denominated assets and substantially shortened their investment horizons for local currency investments.

Financial entities ultimately refinanced nearly all the credit granted by the central bank to the nonfinancial private sector. This had a temporary salutary effect on commercial banks, causing the share of nonperforming loans in the financial system to drop sharply to 11 percent of the total portfolio at the end of 1982. But the process was a fundamentally inflationary remedy. Both the dollarization of the financial system and the increase in money velocity made it difficult to control the growth of the monetary base and to counter the upward pressure on interest rates, two dilemmas that persisted throughout the decade.

The Road to the 1989 Crisis

The apparent stabilization of the financial system was short-lived. In June 1985 the Austral Plan introduced a direct assault on inflation—but without providing a strong commitment to fiscal reform. Declining money demand undermined efforts to restrain monetary growth in 1986 and early 1987, adding to inflationary pressure. Moreover, public spending increased

Table 11.4 The transfer of resources between debtors and creditors of the regulated financial system, July–December 1982

Month	Credit to the private sector (millions of australes)	Real lending interest rate (percent)	Implicit subsidy to debtors[a] (millions of australes)	(billions of dollars)	Interest-bearing deposits of the public (millions of australes)	Real deposit interest rate[b] (percent)	Implicit tax on savers (millions of australes)	(billions of dollars)	Net result[a] (millions of australes)	(millions of dollars)
July	34.2	17.1	5.9	1.0	20.9	−18.3	3.8	0.7	2.1	346
August	37.1	8.7	3.2	0.7	21.5	−9.8	2.1	0.4	1.1	231
September	38.6	9.4	3.6	0.8	22.3	−10.8	2.4	0.5	1.2	254
October	40.4	1.7	0.7	0.1	24.0	−3.3	0.8	0.1	−0.1	−18
November	47.3	4.4	2.1	0.3	26.4	−6.1	1.6	0.3	0.5	76
December	47.8	4.9	2.4	0.3	29.6	−6.7	2.0	0.3	0.4	56
Total	—	—	—	3.2	—	—	—	2.3	—	945

a. At the free market exchange rate.
b. Weighted average rate, with weights given by the amount of each type of deposit. Computed using the general wholesale price index.
Source: Central Bank of Argentina and authors' calculations.

prior to elections in September 1987. The growth in money supply was directly related to public financing of external debt service, rediscount facilities, and amortization of the domestic public debt. Monetary expansion was absorbed largely through reserve requirements and forced investments, but because these controls were imposed on the financial sector there were quantity and price impacts on borrowed funds. Funds to support productive activity diminished, and interest rates rose. In addition, a fundamental redistribution of income between creditors and debtors was under way.

Whenever the Ministry of Economics lacked the funds to service its foreign debt, for example, the central bank expanded the monetary base to buy foreign exchange from the export sector. At the same time, it increased its indebtedness to the financial system in order to absorb part of the additional liquidity it was creating. Between the third quarter of 1985 and the end of 1988 interest payments to service overseas debt totaled $13.5 billion.

Similarly, the central bank financed domestic real sector operations by using rediscounts (table 11.5). From 1985 to 1986–87 the real outstanding value of these instruments increased 80 percent, resulting in an increase in the money supply. When interest rates were freed in October 1987, the indebtedness of the central bank to the banks rose along with interest rates because it continued to pay interest from the regulation account even though the account accrued no income. Money creation could be sterilized only by issuing more interest-bearing debt to commercial banks—debt that would have to be serviced and ultimately redeemed.

The monetary base was also expanding as a result of government redemption of its outstanding securities. As the internal public debt of the treasury increased, economic agents demanded higher real interest rates (up to 40 percent a year) and shorter debt maturities. When the securities fell due, some were redeemed with funds borrowed by the treasury from the central bank, and some were refinanced with new bonds. The bond debt increased in real terms as the government borrowed to service its existing debt in a grand Ponzi scheme.

The authorities tried to absorb the immediate impact of the expanding monetary base through reserve requirements and forced investments imposed on the financial system. This process repressed the banking sector and redistributed funds from the private to the public banks. As a result, between December 1985 and December 1988 the central bank debt to the financial system in terms of remunerated reserve requirements increased by 59 percent in real terms. By the end of 1988 nearly two-thirds of total deposits were held in the form of reserve requirements at the central bank, compared with only one-third at the end of 1983. This led to further deterioration in bank portfolios, which was

Table 11.5 Balances of total rediscount line
(millions of australes)

Year	Current prices	Constant 1985 prices
1985	4.6	4.6
1986	13.1	7.8
1987	38.4	8.2
1988	214.4	6.7

Source: Central Bank of Argentina.

compounded by the unregulated activities of banks in the interfirm market.

Interfirm market

The noninstitutional, interfirm market developed with a highly interconnected infrastructure. Operations, which consisted mainly of the absorption and placement of short-term local currency funds, typically were collateralized with government securities. Market participants avoided reserve requirements and regulations on related lending, portfolio concentration, and minimum capital. This less-rigid framework gave intermediaries a higher credit capacity per unit of borrowed funds, allowing them to charge lower lending rates and to pay investors higher deposit rates—and making them more profitable than their formal sector counterparts. For borrowers, the interfirm market represented easy access to credit unconstrained by central bank regulations.

Formal and informal channels of credit were still linked, however. Some of the financial institutions that participated in the interfirm market dedicated themselves to it entirely, allocating all managers, staff, branches, and so on. The high level of risk in interfirm operations led to solvency crises in some institutions when massive withdrawals of interfirm deposits could not be met by the resources from counterpart loans. In these circumstances intermediaries would use the funds from the institutional market, book imaginary loans, and pay off the interfirm deposits. In this manner the solvency problems of the informal system spilled over to the formal system, at which point the central bank's deposit insurance system rescued depositors. Thus the monetary base expanded, leading to additional reserve requirements.

A new system discouraging interfirm market operations was adopted in October 1986 to break this vicious circle. Marginal reserve requirements were sharply lowered and were no longer remunerated. In addition, the stock of remunerated reserve requirements held at the central bank was immobilized and consolidated into a deposit account that yielded an interest rate equivalent to the market average. As a result the average reserve requirement was significantly higher than the marginal one. In the context of demonetization, the immobilized deposits translated into an effective increase in reserve requirements. This system of high average and lower marginal reserve requirements increased

the volume of funds channeled through the formal institutions. About $1 billion equivalent—15 percent of the interest-bearing deposits in local currency at the time—were brought from the interfirm market. The main disadvantage of the new system was its inflexibility in terms of deposit withdrawals, which proved a serious problem in the first half of 1989 when hyperinflation led to a generalized run on deposits.

Structural change

Between 1982 and the end of 1988 banks decreased their lending to the private sector from 362 billion australes (at constant December 1988 values) to 118 billion australes. Funds instead were increasingly going to the central bank in the form of reserve requirements. By the end of 1988 the central bank had a quarter of the total assets of the consolidated financial system, essentially in the form of these reserve requirements. These assets, however, were effectively frozen. The stock of total liabilities of the financial system held by the central bank—much of which had been channeled to the public sector through public banks—also rose sharply. This meant that a large portion of liabilities was tied to local, municipal, and state public finance, raising the potential for substantial losses.

As a consequence of the higher real cost of the scarce credit available to the private sector, banks' loan portfolios again started to deteriorate. This time, however, it was not the health of the aggregate financial system that was at stake, but the viability of specific, poorly managed financial intermediaries—among them, public institutions. Portfolios began to deteriorate during the six months following the introduction of the Austral Plan. In May 1985, 23 percent of the total portfolio was nonperforming, but by December that figure had risen to 30 percent, largely because real interest rates were averaging 5 percent a month. By the end of 1988 the nonperforming part of the aggregate portfolio had fallen slightly to 27 percent, but the position of government-owned banks had worsened (table 11.6). And rather than make provisions against these exposures, the banks accrued the outstanding interest, even where part of the principal was known to be lost. Realized losses were covered by the national government through capitalizations, financed through monetary emissions by the central bank. Such techniques merely obscured the extent of bank losses.

Table 11.6 Nonperforming assets in the banking system, December 1982–December 1988
(percent)

Type of bank	December 1982	May 1985	December 1985	July 1988	September 1988	December 1988
Government-owned	10.8	33.0	39.4	29.6	35.0	36.7
Private	10.9	9.5	11.4	8.3	8.6	7.9
Total	10.9	23.2	30.3	21.4	25.7	27.1

Source: Central Bank of Argentina.

Banking operations

Private and government-owned banks differed substantially in terms of operating efficiency. The government-owned banks concentrated on financial intermediation. They absorbed 41 percent of the deposits of the system and granted 63 percent of loans, but by the end of 1988 they also were receiving 76 percent of the total rediscount lines of the central bank. Their easy access to credit made government-owned banks less diversified than their private counterparts, which went into new lines of business such as capital market operations, corporate finance, and investment banking.

In addition, private banks had an average of twenty-three employees per branch, compared with forty in public banks. Private banks also invested in computers, which allowed them to achieve far greater operating efficiencies than public banks. Moreover, they participated in the formation of computer service companies, which provided fee-based services to smaller financial institutions.

Public banks eventually lost the advantage of implicit deposit insurance when some public provincial banks were forced to close. And emerging private mega-banks fostered a "too big to fail" impression among depositors—which gave the banks the protection of implicit deposit insurance, eroding the privileged position of government-owned banks.

The 1989 Crisis

By December 1988, 206 financial institutions were under central bank liquidation. Of these, 84 institutions had been transferred to the central bank before December 1982. The debts of these 206 institutions, in terms of loans granted by the central bank for repayment of deposits, reached $7.8 billion. In real terms this was nineteen times the debt balance in December 1982. The central bank made provisions covering 93 percent of the value of these credits.

The situation in late 1988 was vastly different from that in 1982 because the private sector had become a net creditor to the public sector. Public liabilities totaled $7.5 billion—$5.8 billion in reserve requirements held in the central bank, $1.7 billion in national treasury bonds. These liabilities severely restrained economic policy because they were short term and yielded high positive real interest rates (averaging 30 percent a year). In addition, there was little propensity in the economy to hold narrow or broad money. The central bank could thus service its debt only by creating money that no one wanted to hold or by creating interest-bearing debt that could only be sold at exorbitant interest rates.

The authorities had hoped to lift restraints on the banks by reducing reserve and inaccessible deposit requirements. Instead, as inflation rose, they had to increase these burdens. An inflow of foreign exchange, caused by a favorable trade balance in grain exports to the United States, added to inflationary pressures. Rising inflation put further pressure on the free market exchange rate, widening the difference with the official rate.

The Primavera Plan

It was under these circumstances that the authorities introduced the anti-inflationary Primavera Plan in July 1988. The essence of the plan was a devaluation, followed by a multiple exchange rate system designed to fill the central bank's coffers. The plan was supported by external aid, appropriation of a portion of the surplus generated by the higher value of exports, maintenance of high interest rates to make it more attractive to invest domestically than externally, and revaluation of the real exchange rate through a system of selling foreign exchange at the parallel market rate and purchasing it at an official rate, which was expected to earn revenue for the central bank. Monetary policy would be aimed at whatever interest rates were necessary to maintain a free market exchange rate spread of 20 to 25 percent above the official rate. There were also wage agreements, substantial price increases, and further measures to decrease fiscal imbalances. These measures included cuts in public employment and investment and a 50 percent reduction in the financial assistance offered by the central bank to Banco Hipotecario, the national housing bank and a major recipient of rediscounts. In addition, measures were taken to liberalize imports.

Although this program was similar to earlier efforts, the economic team behind the Primavera Plan had far less public credibility, partly because interest rates had risen to very high real levels. There was also doubt about the viability of wage agreements and the response to public offerings of foreign exchange, since demand might outstrip supply. Nevertheless, during the first two months of the plan inflation dropped into single digits and the foreign exchange spread between official and market rates was maintained at 20 to 23 percent. The program's continued success depended entirely on exchange rate expectations. There was no reduction in the fiscal deficit.

The decrease in the exchange rate spread was achieved by means of a real interest rate that was highly positive in terms of dollars. During the plan the accumulated deposit interest rate reached 78 percent, while the exchange rate devaluation of the free dollar was only 24 percent. This stability was fragile from a macroeconomic viewpoint, given that the interest rates were supported by the central bank (through the remunerated reserve requirements on interest-bearing deposits). Private sector demand for credit was practically nil. The exchange rate spread ultimately was maintained through the quasi-fiscal deficit of the central bank.

The Primavera Plan ended when expectations about the exchange rate changed in January 1989 and the public increased its demand for dollars offered for sale by the central bank. Faced with the possibility of losing a significant amount of international reserves, the central bank stopped selling foreign exchange, forcing those who had foreign debts to finance them through exchange purchases in the free market. The exchange rate spread widened, disabling the only brake on the increase in internal prices. In February the government introduced another devaluation and hyperinflation began.

Crisis in the financial system

The economic crisis was evident from a number of economic indicators. Demonetization reached a historic peak—in June 1989 M1 was just 1.6 percent of gross national product (GNP). The M6 aggregate, including all types of deposits and government securities, fell from $13.2 billion equivalent in September 1988 to $3.9 billion (valued at the free exchange rate) in June 1989. Private credit was unavailable and, therefore, its cost was infinite. In June 1989 tax collections were only half those of a year earlier in real terms. GDP fell an estimated 13 percent in the second quarter of the year, and the purchasing power of salaries decreased 30 percent between March and June. Consumer prices increased 1,877 percent between February and July, while the free exchange rate increased 3,723 percent. By the end of June international reserves were not sufficient to cover short-term debts.

Hyperinflation substantially altered the operations of the financial system. Commercial banks suffered heavy deposit withdrawals as investors rushed to dollar-denominated assets. During the first half of 1989 there were eight banking holidays and twelve exchange holidays, and limits were frequently set on the withdrawal of sight and time deposits. The volume of deposits decreased in real terms and there was an increase in deposit withdrawals. To avoid restrictions on withdrawals, people opened multiple accounts, boosting the ratio of bank accounts to bank personnel 10 percent between December 1988 and July 1989. As bank illiquidity worsened, the central bank released reserves and inaccessible deposits, provided rediscounts, and ultimately permitted widespread reserve shortfalls and informal overdrafts by commercial banks. In April the central bank raised the interest it paid on reserves to the commercial banks. Further changes in the exchange rate failed to staunch the hyperinflationary spiral because of the increase in base money the central bank was providing to banks to forestall closure.

The financial system's consolidated balance sheet continued to reflect the real decrease in the volume of financial intermediation and the increasing indebtedness of the public sector (including the central bank) to the banks. Despite this, however, banks' net worth rose because of the indexation of their fixed assets— the central bank's accounting norms require revaluation of fixed assets in line with inflation—and the profits accrued by the banks during this period. Even in the hyperinflationary environment of the first half of 1989, in fact, the accrued profitability of the financial system was positive, and higher than during the previous July when the inflation rate had been stable, albeit high. This performance was attributable to two factors: the distinctions made among deposit interest rates according to deposit size (smaller deposits received a lower interest rate) and an increase in central bank remuneration on forced investments.

Still, the financial system was hardly viable because the government—which was effectively bankrupt— once again started to use it as a financier. In July 1989 the Menem administration implemented the BB Plan, whose sharp devaluation (more than 110 percent) was intended to improve the fiscal account by encouraging exporters to surrender foreign exchange.[3] There were massive increases in public prices and price freeze agreements with major private enterprises. These moves were intended to restore public confidence so that the government could borrow from the financial system at reduced interest rates as part of its structural adjustment program.

But until the primary surplus rose sufficiently to cover interest on the domestic debt, stability depended on monetary policy. The central bank decided not to resort to inaccessible deposits, but to sell its own bills ("certificates of participation") to financial institutions in open markets in order to control liquidity (Beckerman 1992). The initial (monthly) 5 percent rate offered on the certificates was too low to deter time-deposit withdrawals, which put additional pressure on the exchange rate. So the central bank raised the rate to 15 percent. Because of the volume of outstanding public debt, however, the cost of borrowing at this rate was more than the central bank could support. The rates dropped to 4 percent between July and October, however, as commercial banks voluntarily absorbed these new instruments—about $3 billion worth—without opening the spread between the official and parallel exchange rate.

But the BB Plan went the way of the Primavera Plan as the private sector defected. The interest rate on the certificates was too low to maintain the target exchange rate, so the central bank again raised the rate to deter deposit withdrawals from commercial banks. The government was caught in its own debt trap: it raised rates on certificates of participation to competitive levels to staunch further flight to the dollar, but it could not service its debt at competitive rates without borrowing more to do so. Depositors recognized the futility of this effort, and commercial banks were thrust into panic because liquidation of certificates of participation to meet deposit withdrawals would only depress the value of their assets.

Emergency measures adopted in November 1989 accomplished nothing. By December interest rates had again reached 15 percent a month. The authorities admitted defeat as they devalued the official rate from 655 australes to 1,010 australes to the dollar. The team that had designed and implemented the BB Plan resigned, and a new economic team took office.

At this point complete dollarization of the economy seemed plausible. To avert this possibility the government announced dramatic measures on January 1, 1990 to halt the hyperinflation that had plagued the economy during the 1980s. The Bonex Plan forced the conversion of commercial banks' time deposits into cash (up to $500 equivalent) and external bonds (Bonex) with a maturity of ten years, a two-year grace period, and an interest rate slightly above LIBOR. Treasury and central bank obligations to the banks also were converted, thereby eliminating the impact of this large domestic debt on public sector borrowing requirements. The Bonex Plan also included a unilateral writedown of public debt to the private sector since Bonex bonds would trade at a discount that would widen as the outstanding debt stock increased. The effort to restore central bank solvency by eliminating the bank's quasi-fiscal deficit meant unprofitability and widespread insolvency for commercial banks. Moreover, it further eroded confidence in the Argentine financial system and killed demand for local currency or public securities. At the time, however, there were few other options, and implicitly declaring public bankruptcy may well have been the best of a bad lot.

Conclusion of the Crisis

The 1989 crisis was the final unwinding of an unstable financial situation that began in the late 1970s with financial sector liberalization. The basic cause of the crisis in the early 1980s was the rapid expansion of private financial institutions at a time of liberalized interest rates and extensive external borrowing, coupled with large fiscal deficits and overvalued exchange rates. But the cutoff of international resources during the 1982 debt crisis raised domestic real interest rates and forced successive devaluations that fueled inflation and increased disintermediation. The solution to the private sector debt distress of the early 1980s— assumption by the central bank of private external debt—placed the bank in a perilous net foreign liability position, thus reducing its capacity to manage monetary policy.

During the second half of the 1980s, as public deficits again ballooned, nonfinancial public borrowing requirements reached unsustainable levels, climbing from 2.5 percent of GDP to 15.9 percent. The central bank tried to stem disintermediation from the banking system by paying higher and higher real interest rates, which generated large quasi-fiscal losses on its books. By 1989 the central bank's quasi-fiscal balance was estimated at 6 percent of GDP, with total central bank interest-bearing liabilities reaching 37 percent of GDP in the first quarter of 1989.

The 1989 financial crisis therefore was fundamentally a case of public sector debt distress. The private sector was not a major player in the crisis because it could not compete for resources at the high real interest rates paid by the public sector. The public sector losses had to be passed on to other sectors. It was no longer possible to pass the losses to the external sector because external debt was already in arrears. Repudiation of the external debt was ruled out. Attempts to generate a primary surplus sufficient to pay for the combined public (including central bank) interest burden also failed. The only alternative was to repudiate internal debt.

The January 1990 conversion of austral-denominated time deposits and public sector debt into $3.5 billion in dollar-denominated Bonex (at an accounting exchange rate of 1,800 australes per dollar) reduced central bank debt and—since interest rates on australes were considerably higher than rates on Bonex securities—debt servicing interest rates. To the extent that commercial banks reduced their time deposits and remunerated reserves with the central bank, the central bank eliminated its interest-bearing liabilities and hence its capacity to generate further quasi-fiscal deficits. The conversion was a stock adjustment that passed the losses on to depositholders.

Since Bonex traded at a discount of almost two-thirds, the conversion created large losses for holders of time deposits. The immediate impact was a reduction in M3 of roughly 8.5 percent of GDP. The debt conversion did not stop inflation, however. Partly because of policy uncertainties, deposits for tax and wage payments, and exemptions for senior citizens and on deposit conversions for withdrawals of up to 500,000 australes, more than half the deposits at the end of 1989 were still available to depositors. After another short burst of inflation in March 1990, when inflation reached 96 percent a month, inflation began to subside as the fiscal position and the balance of payments showed improvement in the first half of 1990.

The losses borne by the private sector during the 1980s are shown in table 11.7, using financial sector

Table 11.7 Financial system assets and liabilities, December 1981–June 1990

Item	December 1981	June 1989	June 1990
Public sector credit	40.3	292.3	99.3
Private sector credit	119.9	91.3	43.6
Private sector liabilities	100.0	84.3	25.0

Note: Private sector liabilities in December 1981 are used as the base.
Source: Central Bank of Argentina

liabilities to the private sector as a base. Credit to the public sector rose by more than seven times, while private claims on the financial sector declined 15.7 percent in real terms between December 1981 and June 1989. After inflation and debt conversion public real debt dropped by two-thirds. Private debtors gained by more than half, while private depositors and currencyholders lost 70 percent of the real value of their claims on the financial sector.

In effect, the Argentine economy had to deal with systemic debt distress. It had to stop financing public deficits by borrowing from the financial sector—which was the primary cause of inflation—and deal with the suspension of debt with external creditors. The Argentine case was the most severe instance of financial distress (other than that of Yugoslavia), and its solution the most extreme.

Lessons

The Argentine crisis in the early 1980s demonstrates the dangers of financial liberalization without adequate attention to supervision in an environment lacking fiscal discipline. An overvalued exchange rate, high domestic interest rates, and external borrowing added to the private enterprise distress that resulted in deterioration of the portfolio of the financial system. This pattern was common to a number of other countries in the early 1980s, notably Chile and Colombia.

The assumption of private sector distress by the public sector, without first restoring fiscal discipline, led to a vicious circle of deteriorating public finance that gradually spiraled into public sector debt distress. Even the rescuer of the financial system, the central bank, was caught in the debt trap—and thus became part of the problem.

The Argentine case also demonstrates the need for careful monitoring of all quasi-fiscal deficits, whether in public enterprises, state banks, or the central bank. Failing to address these deficits ultimately escalates the costs of rescuing the financial system through an implicit or explicit deposit insurance scheme. If the state's capacity to finance the total fiscal deficit is limited, and the primary surplus is insufficient to pay the interest burden of the public sector, then public sector debt distress is a mathematical inevitability.

Postscript

Although the January 1990 debt conversion did not solve the crisis, it created the political and economic conditions that allowed the government to put in place a package of policy changes that enabled recovery and improved general stability. During 1990–91 the government initiated a major effort in fiscal reform by widening and making uniform the value-added tax and improving tax collection. In addition, the bureaucracy was reduced and privatization was accelerated. Through debt negotiations, the external stock of debt was reduced by $7 billion, partly through debt-equity swaps in the privatization process. Major efforts were also made in trade and tariff reform and deregulation. In the financial sector efforts were made to restructure and downsize the major public banks, including significant staff reductions. The April 1991 Law of Convertibility guaranteed convertibility of the peso at a rate of one peso to one dollar, thus making the central bank a de facto currency board.

Notes

1. In 1979 the deposit insurance scheme was changed to require monthly contributions from member banks, assessed at a fixed percentage rate on their average liabilities subject to reserve requirements. Banks were not compelled to join the scheme, which in any event was not fully funded. Depositors were protected up to 100 percent of the first 1 million pesos, and 90 percent of deposits above that. Foreign currency deposits were not covered.

2. The previous system had provided an incentive to disintermediation because the yield on remunerated reserves was less than could be earned on alternative lending operations. Financial groups thus allowed their commercial banks' deposits to decrease and invested their funds in the interfirm financial market (Beckerman 1992).

3. The plan was called "BB" because President Menem drew his economic team from the executive ranks of the Argentine corporation Bunge y Born (Beckerman 1992).

References

Arnaudo, Aldo, and Rafael Conejero. 1985. "Anatomia de las Quiebras Bancarias de 1980." *Desarrollo Economicó* 24 (January/March): 605–16.

Baliño, Tomas. 1987. "The Argentine Banking Crisis of 1980." IMF Working Paper. International Monetary Fund, Central Banking Department, Washington, D.C.

Beckerman, Paul. 1992. "Public Sector Debt Distress in Argentina, 1988–89." Policy Research Working Paper 902. World Bank, Washington, D.C.

Cavallo, Domingo, and Angel Peña. 1983. "Deficit Fiscal Endeudamiento del Gobierno y Tasa de Inflación: Argentina 1940–1982." *Estudios* 26 (April/June): 39–78.

Fernandez, R., and C. A. Rodriquez. 1982. "Inflación y Estabilidad." Ediciones Macchi.

———. 1983. "Las Crisis Financieras Argentina: 1980–1982." *Jornadas de Economia Monetaria y Sector Externo*, Banco Central de la Republica Argentina, Buenos Aires.

Gaba, Ernesto 1981. "La Reforma Financiera Argentina: Lecciones de una Experiencia." *Ensayos Economicos* 19 (September): 1–52.

Piekarz, Julio. 1987. "El Deficit Cuasi Fiscal del Banco Central." Banco Central de la Republica Argentina, Buenos Aires.

Rivas, E. 1984. "Costos Bancarios, Produccion Multiple y Rendimientos a Escala." Serie de Estudios Tecnicos 61. CEMYB, Banco Central de la Republica Argentina, Buenos Aires.

Rodriquez, C. A. 1991. "The Macroeconomics of the Public Sector Deficit: The Case of Argentina." Policy Research Working Paper 632. World Bank, Washington, D.C.

CHAPTER 12

Post-Liberalization Bank Restructuring

Andrew Sheng

Financial markets are derivatives of the real economy. Restructuring banks in the post-liberalization world ignore this at their peril.

Most developing countries have emerged from the devastation of the 1980s, a decade of high debt and low growth. In the past several years increasing numbers of developing countries have introduced market-oriented reforms, producing great strides in trade reform, financial liberalization, and the development of capital markets. Still, the transition to market remains a major challenge for most of the post–centrally planned economies.

The banking problems of the 1980s were almost forgotten by 1993, when banks earned record profits. Low interest rates and renewed faith in the global recovery fed bubbles in both bond markets and emerging-market share prices. Privatization, financial innovation, and investment by industrial country pension and mutual funds led to enormous capital flows to the developing countries, especially in Asia and Latin America. Around the world, bank profits rose as margins increased, lending recovered, and proprietary trading offered new sources of income—especially in foreign exchange, money market instruments, and derivatives.

The momentum began to slow in 1994 as interest rates in the United States started rising. Problems with derivatives surfaced with well-publicized losses, most notably those of Metallgesellshaft, Proctor & Gamble, and Orange County. The Mexican currency devaluation in December revived the specter of sovereign risk, forcing the U.S. government and multilateral agencies to piece together a $50 billion rescue package to stem a potential default that would have had systemic impacts on other highly indebted countries. In January 1995 the knock-on effects of capital withdrawal from emerging markets caused a ripple of speculation—successfully beaten back—against a number of East and Southeast Asian currencies. In February the U.K.'s Barings Bank was brought down by losses of more than $1 billion through speculation of more than $26 billion in the Nikkei stock index and Japanese government bond futures. The turmoil in the currency markets continued in March with a sharp slide in the U.S. dollar and devaluation of the Spanish peseta and Portuguese escudo. Banking problems resurfaced in Mexico, while French banks began to show large losses from the managerial autonomy given to the state-owned banks over the past five years.

As funds fled in search of security, banks in emerging markets again witnessed liquidity and potential solvency problems. In defending their currencies against speculative attacks, policymakers discovered that their vulnerable spots were not fiscal deficits, but potential quasi-fiscal deficits in their banking systems, whose fragility was exposed in the newly liberalized, global financial environment.

Thus—despite considerable progress in the 1990s—banking fragility has not gone away, and the debates over bank restructuring remain. Should governments devote considerable resources to bailing out failed banks? Why can't the market take care of itself? Should state resources be used to bail out failing enterprises, the sources of the bad loans for the banking sector? What is the correct sequencing of interventions? Has financial liberalization impaired the ability of bank supervisors to manage the financial institutions of the 1990s? Are the lessons of the

1980s relevant to bank distress in the 1990s? This chapter reviews the lessons of bank restructuring covered in the introduction and considers alternative approaches to the issues developed there.

Bank Restructuring in the Post-Liberalization World

Bank restructuring should not be confused with bank crises. Crises are events; restructuring is a process. The variety and origins of crises change, and the techniques of reform and resolution must adjust accordingly. But the basic processes of bank restructuring identified in this volume—diagnosis, damage control, loss allocation, and rebuilding—remain as valid in the 1990s as they were in the 1980s.

The new world

With the emergence of financial globalization and innovation, aided by improved telecommunications and technology, developing country financial markets have changed rapidly to keep up with U.S. and European bankers—with what Kaufman (1994) refers to as the "Americanization of financial markets." These changes occurred partly under the wave of deregulation that swept the globe in the 1980s, led by London's 1986 "Big Bang" financial liberalization, and partly in response to the need to synchronize financial market reforms with real market changes. Even the most conservative financial authorities in developing economies realized that there were limits to financial repression of traditional banking markets as a means of financing growth and industrialization.

The progressive dismantling of exchange controls and the increasing inflow of portfolio and foreign direct investment pose new challenges for developing country central bankers used to controlling their markets. The most marked change has been the increasing strength of nonbanks relative to banks, powered mostly by capital markets. Short-sighted banking specialists often fail to recognize the challenge posed by these markets. For example, in five Asian economies—Hong Kong, Malaysia, the Philippines, Singapore, and Thailand—market capitalization in the equity market is already larger than the total domestic currency assets of the banking system. A Malaysian stockbroking firm can earn more profits in one year than many of the five largest banks. Nonbank financial intermediaries in the Republic of Korea have more deposits and assets than

the (highly regulated) banks. The rapid emergence of such extensive holdings in newly open financial systems complicates the supervision and regulation of emerging markets and their relationship with the banking system.

Are the principles of oversight of capital markets different from those of the banking system? Banking systems and capital markets are both complementary and competitive channels of resource allocation in a market economy. Developing country policymakers have always concentrated on supervising the banking sector, because that has been the primary channel of resource allocation, savings, and credit—which explains many governments' desire to own and strictly regulate banks. The emergence of capital markets, both equity markets and money and debt markets, has changed that landscape and challenged these conventional perspectives.

Domestic and global markets today thrive on the arbitrage of information, skills, taxes, regulations, and even differential transaction costs. There are a number of reasons for the phenomenal growth of capital markets—and the corresponding move away from more traditional banking—and most relate to increasing levels of regulatory and tax arbitrage:

- Developing country governments have imposed extensive regulations on the degree of financial innovation in the banking system, partly for fear of exposing it to higher risks, but also for fear of losing control over the monetary base.
- In almost all countries with rapid capital market growth, there has been no capital gains tax on securities transactions, whereas interest on bank deposits is taxable, particularly for corporations.
- Because of securitization and financial innovation, the cost of intermediation through capital markets is significantly lower than through bank credit. U.S. experience suggests that spreads on funds obtained through the debt market are only 50 basis points, compared with nearly 200 basis points for bank loans. Indeed, the remarkable growth of derivative markets can be attributed to the ability to hedge risks at very low transaction costs.
- As more developing countries discover the benefits of privatizing through capital markets, banking risks actually drop because the overall gearing of borrowers declines with higher capital bases raised through equity markets. And national risk management improves with efficient capital markets.

• Resource allocation is more efficient through capital markets because capital markets enable enterprises to swap assets and liabilities through equity and debt, rather than through bank financing.

But while private sector banking systems and securities markets have moved fast, the regulatory and supervisory systems in many developing countries have not caught up in terms of resources and understanding, particularly regarding the complexity and volatility of markets. As a result many policymakers have found themselves with less freedom and fewer instruments to deal with the crises arising from market flows.

Derivatives and systemic risks

A significant development in the 1990s (led by the United States and the European Union) has been the merging of banking and financial markets. Such consolidation of different product markets into large financial groups is meant to improve economies of scale in product delivery and reduce risks through diversification. Steps have been taken in the United States to remove the Glass-Steagall restrictions on bank participation in securities markets. In the European Union insurance companies have begun to merge with banks, banks have taken over securities houses, and building societies have upgraded themselves to banks. In Malaysia and Mexico emerging securities houses have generated so much capital that they have absorbed banks within their groups. With the rapid growth of emerging markets and derivative instruments, money center banks in the United States have transformed themselves into investment houses, while securities houses have become conglomerate investment banks with subsidiary banks, credit card companies, derivatives traders, and asset managers. The eight money center banks now account for more than 85 percent of the total volume of derivatives activities by U.S. banks (Moody Investors Service 1994).

The melding of financial institutions makes the separation of banking from financial markets increasingly difficult. As banks engage in securities business and securities businesses engage in banking, cross-border transactions increase in size and volatility. Bank supervisors now find themselves needing to talk not only to domestic financial market regulators—such as the insurance commissioner or securities exchange commission—but also to the regulators' foreign counterparts.

The speed and complexity of markets makes the post-liberalization world dazzling to bankers and policymakers. Markets have become more liquid and volatile as a result of liberalization and innovation. Technology has made banking services faster, cheaper, and more convenient. In Hong Kong, for example, funds can be transferred into twelve different foreign currency accounts by telephone. Deregulation—particularly the lifting of capital controls—has removed barriers to inflows and outflows. Portfolio choices are no longer restricted to domestic currency assets. Financial innovation, particularly in derivatives, has created low-cost services and products that can be tailored to an investor's needs. Banks and securities houses thrive on selling such products.

Investors, for their part, can now quickly shift funds into a variety of products to protect their total return. The result is that any perception that investors will suffer a deterioration in total return, for whatever reason, may trigger large portfolio shifts. Because news travels fast—regardless of whether it is true—investors can protect their investments using a variety of hedging instruments, particularly forwards, futures, and options, so long as a counterparty is willing to bet the other way. Programmed trading would allow computer-generated trading to take advantage of minor variations in prices through "anomaly trading" or to activate selling programs once prices touch certain trigger levels. With global markets linked by Reuters, Telerate, and Bloomberg news services, and trading on a virtual twenty-four-hour basis, any bad news can generate a tidal wave of fund flows.

So can the market take care of itself, since there will always be another investor willing to bet the other way? Unfortunately, the answer is no since the world still operates on imperfect information. When bad news prompts capital flight, the only counterparty willing to absorb the other side of the hedge may be the authorities, seeking to establish stability in the markets. If the authorities are unwilling or unable to intervene, then prices may freefall, creating a major price shift that could devastate the economy. Thus there is sympathy for a Mexican manufacturer who was profitable and efficient a year ago, but who today faces considerable difficulties because currency depreciation has pushed import prices up 80 percent. Of course, there is always the response that free markets imply that the manufacturer should have anticipated the price adjustment.

One policy response to market volatility is to "throw some sand into the wheels," that is, make fund flows less volatile by reimposing or threatening to reimpose capital controls. Variations of this approach have been used by Chile and by Malaysia in early 1994 when massive capital inflows threatened to negate domestic monetary policy objectives.

Another policy response for those who fear the "dark side" of high-speed, high-power financial markets is to ban or impose restrictions on such instruments as derivatives. The Barings Bank disaster and other well-publicized losses by corporations that experimented with derivatives have created an aversion to these exotic products. But derivatives, like all financial tools, have their advantages and disadvantages, depending on how they are used. The Group of Thirty and the Bank for International Settlements agree that there should be greater transparency in the disclosure of derivatives products and transactions, that issuers and users should have adequate risk management systems, and that regulators should closely examine the legal issues of netting and collateral and the greater use of clearinghouse arrangements for over-the-counter products.

The derivatives market evolved in response to the need to hedge and to manage risks better. Derivatives can improve the liquidity of markets and reduce transaction costs in portfolio management. But because of the leverage factor, users of derivatives can suffer large losses from market volatility and defaults of counterparties. Advocates of the derivative market often forget that while individual institutions can reduce risks through derivatives, the system as a whole is a zero-sum game. Systemic risk is not reduced simply because one part of the financial system is active in derivatives hedging activity—the risks spread to other parts of the financial or nonfinancial system. Indeed, reducing risks in one part of the economy may even increase risks in other parts.

Advocates also tend to forget that bank loans are derivatives of corporate earnings. Banking has been highly regulated because banking is a highly leveraged business and consumer deposits need to be sheltered from losses. The dangers of the modern derivative business stem more from the fact that sellers of derivatives are offering highly leveraged (low margin) products and assuming large credit risks in the meantime. Since derivatives are mostly accounted "below the line" and are off–balance sheet, the sellers of derivatives are not required to provide the same amount of capital as providers of loans. Together with the low transactions costs associated with derivatives, this accounts for the rapid growth in gross outstanding derivatives—reaching as much as $7 trillion by the end of 1991, as much as the total cross-border assets of Bank of International Settlements reporting banks.

Some analysts argue that regulators should not be concerned with the gross values of derivatives, but only with the net replacement cost of derivatives trading. Net replacement costs could be quite low when the volatility of markets is low. But in unusual markets, such as the wild swings in currency markets during the exchange rate mechanism crisis of the European monetary system in 1992, underlying markets can dry up and bid-ask spreads can widen considerably, resulting in many derivatives models not being able to price their derivatives correctly and placing their buyers and sellers in a high-risk environment. The failure of Barings Bank indicates that bankers must be concerned not only with their net exposure, but also with their gross exposure. The current lack of transparency in derivatives trading means that many regulators are not aware of the true size of the risks being assumed by their banking systems. This blind spot, caused by financial innovation and liberalization, may be the biggest problem for regulators in the post-liberalization era.

Why do banks fail if the market can take care of itself?

Banks fail because of bad policies, poor banking practices, and weak institutional frameworks. In a globalized financial market the management of banks and financial systems must be placed in not only a sectoral, but also a national and international context. The Barings failure involved a British bank speculating on Japanese index futures in the Singapore International Monetary Exchange. Since Barings was a major international asset manager, the failure affected investors and depositors all over the world; its rescue involved a Dutch banking conglomerate. Mexico's problems threatened Latin American and emerging markets as OECD investors sought to reduce their exposure to emerging markets as a whole. Policymakers therefore must consider their exposure to international risks when designing structural adjustments to their economies and banking systems.

Current problems also have roots in the misguided policies of the 1980s. This volume has attempted to show how such policy mistakes, including poorly designed financial liberalization programs and inadequate supervision, led to banking crises. In the rush to liberalize as a correction to central planning and excessive regulation, many policymakers and their advisers lost themselves in the herd instinct, assuming that markets will always correct themselves. There was universal underestimation of the volatility of markets in a global world.

Market analysts used to say "the trend is your friend." For policymakers the trend can also be the end. The herd instinct can cause market prices to vary tremendously, mainly because of information asymmetry. Markets do not have the information or the confidence in the economy or banking system that policymakers have. In addition, financial liberalization programs have placed limits on the instruments, such as capital controls, that policymakers have to deal with such swings. Central banks, even in the OECD countries, are not as capable as market players of resisting market trends through intervention. The classic advice, that policymakers in a market economy must make sure that the fundamentals are sound, is more valid than ever. But in the real world most countries do not get all their fundamentals right at the same time.

The sharp swings of the 1990s suggest that policymakers and bankers alike must pay attention to risk management at the institutional, sectoral, and national levels. Simple rules, such as never using short-term resources to finance long-term investments, apply equally to banks and economies. The reliance on short-term portfolio flows to finance current account deficits exposed many countries to financial instability when capital flows changed direction.

When national balance sheets were rewritten in the 1980s in response to financial liberalization and other reforms, many policymakers underestimated the risks posed by the global economy. Volatile capital flows, made possible by the removal of capital controls, can reward good reforms, but they can also punish policy mistakes rapidly and severely. Policymakers have little time to correct such weaknesses because once the market perceives that there are policy errors, capital flight puts pressure on the exchange rate, which in turn puts pressure on asset prices such as stock and property prices and ultimately domestic inflation. Policymakers who seek to ensure overall price stability in order to foster growth suddenly find that speculation could destabilize all their reform efforts.

Lessons for Post-Liberalization Bank Restructuring

This section reviews the relevance of the lessons of the 1980s to bank restructuring in the 1990s.

Lesson 1 *Financial stability rests on the government's ability to maintain a stable currency*

The speed of market reactions in the post-liberalization world does not allow policymakers to reflect on their policy mistakes. A stable financial system rests on monetary stability, without which good business decisions cannot be made. But in the post-liberalization world monetary stability needs to be redefined. A simplistic view of monetary stability is that the government maintains fiscal discipline by running a budgetary surplus. But since banks can create money through their credit operations (and by absorbing counterparty risks in derivative trades), there is also a need to maintain banking discipline. Some observers have suggested that policy credibility can be maintained through a currency board system. But a currency board system cannot generate foreign exchange on its own, while a banking system can generate domestic currency through its credit operations. Consequently, so long as domestic banks are willing to absorb credit risks by lending (either by acting as the counterparty to a derivative trade involving domestic currency or through direct loans in domestic currency), the foreign exchange reserve-domestic currency ratio can always be diluted to erode the credibility of the external value of the currency.

For example, speculation against a country's currency will always succeed if domestic banks are willing to lend domestic currency to the speculators. When foreign investors have better credit ratings than domestic clients, banks may be tempted to lend to fuel speculative attacks against their own domestic currency. Such behavior implies that policymakers, including bank regulators, must take bank supervision issues into account in the management of their monetary policy.

There is an inherent conflict between monetary policy and bank supervision policy. At a time when the central bank is concerned with maintaining a stable currency, there may be a need to rescue banks, which creates a quasi-fiscal burden. Monetary creation through lending to rescue banks negates the ability of tight monetary policy to combat inflation or capital flight.

Removing exchange controls also removes a major tool of policymakers, leading to conflicting targets of maintaining either the internal value of currency (domestic prices) or the external value (exchange rate). As the basic Mundell (1967) model shows, in a world of free capital flows the central bank must choose between stabilizing the exchange rate or stabilizing the interest rate—it cannot do both. Central banks can still exploit certain inefficiencies in the market to influence both rates, but only in the short term.

As market information improves and investors become more sophisticated, disintermediation from the banking system occurs quickly once wealthholders foresee future asset losses because of bad policies, ineffective management, or weak institutional frameworks. Restoring financial discipline in the economy begins with restoring fiscal and monetary discipline.

Lesson 2 Banks fail because of losses in the real sector, compounded by poor risk management and fraud

Because money is a derivative of real value in an economy, tampering with the value of money risks tampering with the entire financial structure. At the same time, the value of bank money is a derivative of the performance of the real economy. Problems or losses in the real sector ultimately surface in the banking system. Thus bank restructuring cannot be achieved without reform or restructuring of the real sector.

Real sector losses show up in the banks through the failure of counterparties to honor their contracts, such as credit losses. Thus bank restructuring requires that bank regulators understand the ability of both banks and their clients to manage their risks. For example, the large capital inflows of the past several years led some policymakers to allow domestic enterprises, as well as the government, to borrow short-term flows to finance long-term investment. The borrowers incurred excessive maturity mismatches, as well as foreign exchange mismatches, since the borrowers may not have access to foreign exchange earnings. Such poor risk management occurred because borrowers had no experience with risks of this sort, never having operated in a liberalized environment. Taking advantage of their newfound freedoms, and fearful that capital controls would be reimposed, enterprises engaged in extensive external borrowing. When the prospect of devaluation developed, the fear of suffering devaluation losses on loans prompted both lenders and borrowers to engage in hedging activities, thus

precipitating a currency crisis that eventually caused large losses in the real economy. In a number of countries bank losses were compounded by an overconcentration of assets geographically, sectorally, or in terms of ownership, which encouraged connected lending and credit abuses. At both the microeconomic and macroeconomic levels, bank managers and policymakers have not managed their risks very well.

At the macroeconomic level, diversifying national export income and attracting foreign investment help reduce risks, but certain economies and banking systems have limited space in which to adjust. If an economy is landlocked or has inherited a highly concentrated industrial or agricultural base, its ability to adjust is necessarily limited. Such rigidities are not in themselves defects—it depends on whether policies are devised to compensate for the economy's rigidities. The ability to think about national risk management is important. Are there risks in the economy that policymakers should take account of? Countries participating in the global market may have to maintain significantly higher foreign exchange reserves given the volatility of capital flows.

Lesson 3 Liberalization programs often fail to take into account the wealth effects of relative price changes, and inadequate supervision creates further losses

This is perhaps the major lesson of financial sector liberalization in the Southern Cone (Argentina, Chile, Uruguay) economies in the 1980s, but some of the problems of the 1990s show that the lesson has not been fully learned. The overly rapid trade liberalization of the 1980s created trade shocks for previously protected enterprises in many countries, leading to large bank losses. Where these enterprises belonged to business groups that also owned banks—and bank supervision was inadequate—these banks often financed distress borrowing at unrealistically high real interest rates.

In the 1990s the failure to adequately address bank supervision resulted in weak banks that were unprepared to compete in global markets. Credit risks were not evaluated properly, and banks had high levels of bad loans remaining on their books and inadequate capital relative to such risks. If policymakers raised interest rates to protect the domestic currency from capital flight, banks simply raised interest rates and transmitted the losses to enterprise borrowers. The failure of borrowers threatens to become a systemic issue, infecting the banks and requiring public rescue. A credible bank restructuring program requires strong bank supervision and enforcement, together with laws that encourage debt discipline and avoid bank owner-borrower conflicts.

Lesson 4 *Bank losses ultimately become quasi-fiscal deficits*

Widespread bank failures simply cannot occur in most countries. Allowing banks to fail during a period of capital outflows encourages domestic and foreign capital flight. And most policymakers understand that widespread bank failures suggest that the government is unable to maintain overall stability. The result is that even with limited deposit insurance schemes in place, many policymakers have not dared to pass large bank losses on to depositors.

This pattern implies that bank losses are ultimately the burden of the state. Thus the state has to ensure that it maintains fiscal and banking discipline. Running a small primary surplus is not sufficient if the budget is threatened by the large fiscal cost of recapitalizing the banking system. A deposit insurance scheme is only a temporary means of calming depositors during a crisis. What is required is to address the fundamental problems in the banking system and to put in place sound, preventive bank supervision.

Lesson 5 *Failure recognition is important because a banking crisis is a solvency problem, not a liquidity issue*

Bankers and policymakers tend to attribute fundamental problems to a temporary liquidity (flow) problem rather than to a crisis of solvency (stock). Providing liquidity only buys time for restructuring to occur. Capital outflows or disintermediation from the banking system are symptoms of bank failure, not causes. The basic cause of bank and enterprise losses is overleveraging with inadequate capital relative to the risks undertaken. Failure recognition requires that a proper diagnosis be made of the causes of bank losses, including the use of marked-to-market accounting. Because of the lack of transparency in bank and enterprise accounting in many developing countries, losses often are significantly larger than anticipated or earlier reported. Insolvent banks can easily hide their losses with bad accounting (evergreening of bad loans). The failure to deal with hidden losses can create perverse incentives in the banking system, leading to bad resource allocation and adding to macroeconomic instability.

Lesson 6 *Stopping the flow of future losses is critical*

Damage control involves changing incentives within the real and financial sectors. Consider the example of the excessive leveraging of buyers of privatized banks, who are then more concerned with paying off their debts than with maximizing profits. There is a danger that such owners will engage in risk-taking behavior and the financing of capital flows in order to pay off their foreign currency obligations. Where incentives are distorted and cause losses, ownership or management should change. Changing management is essential at the bank level. Failure to address the incentives structure invites a recurrence of banking problems in the future.

Lesson 7 *The method of loss allocation determines the success of the restructuring program.*

Someone must pay for bank losses. In a world of free capital flows this burden tends to fall on those who are unable to escape it. Loss distribution is a political matter that must be addressed by individual societies. Countries differ, calling for case-by-case restructuring. Since losses are allocated across society, either to depositors through an inflation tax or to taxpayers through future taxes, bank supervisors must obtain public support. Successful loss allocation—while preserving macroeconomic stability—depends on whether the budget is able to generate a primary surplus to service its debts (including debts incurred by the carve-out) without excessive monetary creation. In the global market foreigners will not be part of the burden-sharing exercise, except perhaps the multilateral agencies. But if policy credibility can be secured, foreign capital flows, particularly foreign direct investment, can help generate the growth to pay for the losses.

Lesson 8 *Success depends on sufficient real sector resources to pay off losses, adequate financial sector reforms to intermediate resources efficiently and safely, and the budget's ability to tax "winners" and wind down "losers" without disturbing monetary stability*

Without growth, there are not enough resources to pay for bank losses. Without the right incentives and social stability, there is no growth. Recession, unemployment, and banking crises all threaten social stability. Thus policymakers have to establish policy credibility—in the form of public confidence—in order to create the preconditions for eradicating bank losses. Because financial markets are derivatives of the real economy, bank losses are rooted in real sector financial imbalances—inextricably linking bank restructuring to fiscal and enterprise sector reforms. In the post–centrally planned economies this phenomena is known as the troika problem. Recapitalizing banks without addressing the underlying enterprise losses, inefficiencies, or fiscal problems risks repeating banking problems in the future.

Lesson 9 Rebuilding a safe and profitable banking system requires good policies, reliable management, and a strong institutional framework

A key question in the new world of financial innovation is whether bank management and policymakers are capable of supervision in such a volatile market environment. Restructuring banks requires strong policy diagnosis, effective damage control, and efficient loss allocation in order to rebuild safe, sustainable, and profitable banks. This requires strong ministries of finance, central banks, and bank supervisors, as well as a salvageable banking system.

Building strong government and market institutions will necessarily take time. Thus overzealous privatization without first introducing appropriate regulation and national risk management measures may result in costly financial crises. Resources will have to be found to strengthen the supervisory process, as well as to develop risk management skills in the financial community.

Getting the incentives structure right is critical to rebuilding stable and sustainable markets and institutions. Incentives should not induce moral hazard behavior. Neither should they inspire overregulation. Balancing the risks and rewards of the marketplace requires considerable reregulation efforts. For example, the current global financial system clearly is not a level playing field. Investment banks, mutual funds, and hedge funds are not required to maintain the same regulatory regimes and capital adequacy levels as banks. Derivatives do not attract the same capital requirements as credit instruments. Increasing the transparency of instruments, institutions, and regulations would help to level the playing field. Banking systems must be restructured to fit into a more market-oriented and volatile world.

Moving toward this goal will require credible policy measures that encourage stability, competition, and growth. Equitable and clear contract and bank-ing laws and court processes must be put into place. Banking laws and regulations should be enforced. Accounting frameworks should encourage the measurement and disclosure of economic performance using international accepted accounting standards. The payments and operating systems within the financial sector must work efficiently and robustly.

Lesson 10 Time and timing are of the essence

Banking crises may seem to develop overnight, but the structural problems of bank weaknesses generally are longstanding, hidden by a lack of transparency. The sooner problems are recognized and dealt with, the lower the costs to the economy and the banking system. In the 1980s—when economies were closed and markets were less efficient—policymakers and bankers had more time to adjust to changes in world markets because of information asymmetry and market rigidities. But there is little time for protracted decisionmaking in the current world of open capital accounts and high-tech financial markets. The failure to act quickly and decisively causes the swiftly moving market to punish the policy error. At the microeconomic level, the failure of the Barings Bank suggests that market volatilities could be significantly riskier than was anticipated in what appeared to be low-risk hedging strategies. Nevertheless, the more you delay, the more you pay.

Conclusion

While the instruments and circumstances are different, the basic principles of bank restructuring have not changed much since the 1980s. The important issue of market and policy fundamentals remains the same. Those who ignore the fundamentals will likely have less time to deal with their shortcomings.

Supervisory frameworks must be expanded to encompass both banks and capital markets. Furthermore, the emergence of a global financial network means that there are large gaps in global supervision. The uneven playing fields of global financial markets are fenced by domestic regulations that the market is rapidly finding ways to circumvent. Domestic banking problems now have global dimensions, and international cooperation is required to solve them.

The basic objective of oversight of capital markets is no different from that for banking systems: efficient and sound resource allocation. Secondary objectives include protecting small savers, minimizing fraud, and protecting the channels of macroeconomic policy management. The same instruments are used to regulate market access, price, quantity, and product innovation. The same regulatory principles apply: the supervision of solvency, through evaluation of capital adequacy and creditworthiness; liquidity, through proper treasury and risk management; earnings, through costs of intermediation and efficiency; and quality of management, the human element. Although significant progress has been made in recent years through the efforts of the Basle Committee on Banking Supervision and the International Organization of Securities Commissions, much remains to be done to promote international cooperation in supervision.

Global markets would be much more transparent, efficient, and better managed for risk if multinational corporations were less focused on their headquarters and domestic regulators were less concerned with protecting national capital markets. Local markets selling local financial products to all consumers, including some foreigners, is not what constitutes a global market. Global markets mean that the entire range of international financial products will be available for transaction locally. This has profound implications for the national and international regulatory framework.

The challenges of supervision and bank restructuring in a globally liberalized financial setting include:

- Strengthening sectoral and national risk management, particularly by avoiding risk mismatches that could be exploited by speculative arbitrage. This requires paying considerable attention to getting the fundamentals right.
- Creating a more level playing field between banks and other financial institutions.

- Improving access to domestic capital markets, not only for smaller and newer domestic companies but also for foreign (including regional) companies to widen the range of financial products and investment opportunities for better risk management.
- Adapting the legal framework to enable bank and capital market supervisors to cooperate and coordinate better both domestically and internationally.
- Strengthening the financial infrastructure, such as the integrity and robustness of securities settlement, clearing, and payments systems.
- Deepening over-the-counter and exchange markets for new financial products, including futures, options, and other derivatives, and creating a level playing field for these tools in the regulatory framework.
- Promoting international cooperation in the closer integration of regional and international markets, to allow domestic markets to trade financial products on a global basis.

Given the rapid changes in the global economy and the market's ability to find ways around national barriers, bank restructuring will continue as economies and financial systems adjust to these new realities.

References

Kaufman, Henry. 1994. "Structural Changes in the Financial Markets: Economic and Policy Significance." *Federal Reserve Bank of Kansas City Economic Review* 79(2): 5–15.

Moody Investors Service. 1994. "Derivatives Activity of U.S. Commercial Banks." New York.

Mundell, Robert A. 1967. *International Economics.* New York: Macmillan.

Sheng, Andrew, and Yoon Je-Cho. 1993. "Risk Management and Stable Financial Structures." Policy Research Working Paper 1109. World Bank, Washington, D.C.